Understanding Business Strategy

CONCEPTS PLUS • 3E

R. Duane Ireland
Texas A&M University

Robert E. Hoskisson
Rice University

Michael A. Hitt
Texas A&M University

SOUTH-WESTERN
CENGAGE Learning

Australia • Brazil • Japan • Korea • Mexico • Singapore • Spain • United Kingdom • United States

SOUTH-WESTERN
CENGAGE Learning

**Understanding Business Strategy:
Concepts Plus, 3e**
Ireland, Hoskisson, and Hitt

Vice President of Editorial, Business:
Jack W. Calhoun

Publisher: Melissa Acuna

Sr. Acquisitions Editor: Michele Rhoades

Executive Director, Development: John
Abner

Sr. Editorial Assistant: Ruth Belanger

Marketing Manager: Jonathon Monahan

Marketing Coordinator: Julia Tucker

Sr. Content Project Manager: Tim Bailey

Media Editor: Rob Ellington

Frontlist Buyer, Manufacturing: Arethea
Thomas

Sr. Marketing Communications Manager:
Jim Overly

Production Service: MPS Limited

Sr. Art Director: Tippy McIntosh

Internal and Cover Design: Craig Ramsdell,
Ramsdell Design

Rights Acquisitions Specialist: John Hill

Permissions Research: PreMediaGlobal

Cover Images: ©Trout55, ©Liv Friis-Larsen,
©Chromatika Multimedia, ©Jacob
Wackerhausen, ©Neustockimages,
©Nikada: iStock; ©Richard Newstead,
Lifesize, ©Jupiterimages, Brand X Pictures:
Getty Images

For product information and technology assistance, contact us at
Cengage Learning Customer & Sales Support, 1-800-354-9706

For permission to use material from this text or product,
submit all requests online at **www.cengage.com/permissions**
Further permissions questions can be emailed to
permissionrequest@cengage.com

ExamView® is a registered trademark of eInstruction Corp. Windows is
a registered trademark of the Microsoft Corporation used herein under
license. Macintosh and Power Macintosh are registered trademarks of
Apple Computer, Inc. used herein under license.

Cengage Learning WebTutor™ is a trademark of Cengage Learning.

Library of Congress Control Number: 2011923217

ISBN-13: 978-0-538-47681-2

ISBN-10: 0-538-47681-8

South-Western Cengage Learning
5191 Natorp Boulevard
Mason, OH 45040
USA

Cengage Learning products are represented in Canada by
Nelson Education, Ltd.

For your course and learning solutions, visit **www.cengage.com**

Purchase any of our products at your local college store or at our
preferred online store **www.cengagebrain.com**

Printed in China
2 3 4 5 6 7 15 14 13 12

BRIEF CONTENTS

© Nikada, iStock

CONTENTS

**Case abstracts and full cases are available online at
www.cengagebrain.com**

To our son Scott: Your commitment to running
and the goals you are reaching in light of that
commitment are inspirational. "Everybody's
got a hunger, a hunger they can't resist." Your
desire to "reach" and "develop" through
running is a path through which I am learning
a great deal about pursuit, perseverance,
acceptance, and understanding. I am deeply
proud of you, Scott.

R. Duane Ireland

To all my children, Robyn (Luke), Dale
(Allison), Becky (Stephen), Angela, Joseph and
Matthew, thank you for your love and support
and patience over the years. You are all terrific
human beings.

Bob (Dad)

To my grandchildren, Mason, Michelle, Ashlyn
and Aubrey. You are all very special to me.
I love you.

PaPa

PREFACE

In the Preface to the first edition of this book, we noted that "firms are important to all of us." This remains the case as we introduce the third edition of our text to you. To explain why this is so, take a few minutes to think about the importance of firms to a variety of people. As customers, we buy products (goods and services) from firms producing them; as employees, we work for them; as suppliers, we sell raw materials to them; and, firms often are a vital part of the communities in which we live. Thus, for many reasons, all of us benefit when firms perform well. Indeed, when firms are successful, they are (1) producing, selling, and servicing products that as customers we want to buy, (2) providing employees with well-paying jobs, and (3) contributing in various ways to the communities in which they are located. But what influences a firm's performance? Why do some perform exceptionally well while others fail to perform adequately and some even end up in bankruptcy?

Both the experiences of companies competing in all types of industries across the world's different regions and countries and the insights associated with academic studies suggest that the strategic management process (the focus of this book) strongly influences firm performance. Stated simply, firms with leaders and personnel who understand how to effectively use the strategic management process tend to succeed. In contrast, firms without leaders and personnel who understand the strategic management process and how to use it depend more on luck and tend to fail.

Our purpose in writing the third edition of this successful text is to provide you with a succinct and action-oriented explanation of how to manage a firm strategically. To do this, we present ten concise chapters to you for the purpose of explaining a number of important concepts. As you can see from examining the following list of features, this book is very reader-friendly.

Let's examine some examples of how this book is accessible to you.

- The writing style is lively, engaging, and application-oriented. You'll find examples in each chapter of how firms that you likely know actually use strategic management concepts and tools. These examples bring the strategic management process to life and highlight its relevance to real firms around the globe. For example, in Chapter 1, we discuss how Lego Group (based in Billund, Denmark) recently renewed its emphasis on its core competence of designing creative collections of models that require imaginative assembly by customers to improve the firm's performance. We describe the "green" policies Walmart is using so the firm can have a more positive impact on the physical environment in which it operates. Virtually all of these examples (such as the ones about Lego and Walmart) are new to this edition of our text and the others have been substantially updated.
- Each chapter is organized around "Knowledge Objectives." Appearing at the beginning of the individual chapters, these objectives clarify what you can expect to learn as a result of studying the materials in the chapters.
- Key terms are placed in the margins for easy mastery of terminology that is important to understanding the strategic management process.
- We open each chapter with a feature called "Focusing on Strategy." Each Focusing on Strategy illustrates how a particular company uses the part of the strategic management process that is explained in the chapter. These features bring strategic management issues to life by showing their application in actual firms. Almost all of the Focusing on Strategy features are new to this edition; the remaining ones have been totally updated.
- In each chapter, we also include a feature ("Understanding Strategy: Learning from Success") to explain how one or more actual firms have benefited by successfully using a particular part of the strategic management process. We include a related feature in each chapter ("Understanding Strategy: Learning from Failure") to explain how one or more firms suffered poor performance because of their failure to effectively use one or more parts of the strategic management process. Virtually all of the Understanding Strategy features are new to this edition.

© Neustockimages, iStock

- Current references (from business publications such as *The Wall Street Journal, BusinessWeek*, and *Fortune* and from academic publications) appear at the end of each chapter. The references we use demonstrate the currency of the firm-specific examples appearing in each chapter as well as our commitment to use results from recent academic research to provide you with the latest thinking about strategic management. Additionally, our presentation of the strategic management process is grounded in proven business practices as well as "classic" research from the academic literature.
- The **"Strategy Toolbox"** end-of-chapter feature, expertly prepared by Paul N. Friga of University of North Carolina–Chapel Hill, presents you with a tool or technique firms actually use with the strategic management process. In addition to learning how firms use strategic management, you will be able to use these helpful tools to help analyze cases.
- At the end of each chapter, we present a **"Mini-Case"** that deals with an actual firm and explains, in some detail, how that firm uses one or more parts of the strategic management process. Each **Mini-Case** is more comprehensive than the **Focusing on Strategy** and **Understanding Strategy** features. To help you learn more about the firm discussed in the case and to enhance your strategic management skills, each case closes with a set of discussion questions. These questions are designed to help you think about the issues in the case and enhance your learning of the chapter's concepts. Each **Mini-Case** has been thoroughly updated or is new in this edition.
- Two **"Experiential Exercises"** are included in the end-of-chapter content. We are grateful to Charles M. Byles (Virginia Commonwealth University) for preparing these exercises. Each cognitive or experiential exercise involves you, as an active learner, in a way that will help you develop a better understanding of the chapter's topics. Typically, you are provided with some discussion questions that facilitate efforts to apply the learning gained from each exercise.
- To increase the book's visual appeal, a full four-color format is used to enhance the presentation of the concepts presented in the book's ten chapters. This format enables us to include interesting color photographs to further illustrate each chapter's content.

What's New to this Edition?

We are pleased to highlight materials and items that are "new to this edition" of our text. In an overall sense though, we held fast to the objective of substantially updating all aspects of the book's contents to verify that we are presenting a totally up-to-date introduction to the strategic management process to you. Next, we present a list of specific items that are new to this version of *Understanding Business Strategy*:

- A new **CengageNOW Case Library** containing new and updated cases that you can assign to your students. We present cases to you about familiar companies (including TomTom, Best Buy, NetFlix, eBay, and Apple) as well as cases about smaller firms and those in service industries. A selection of the cases contain auto-gradable objective questions that assess student comprehension of the case's key facts and issues and better prepare them to engage in classroom discussion.
- Most of the **Focusing on Strategy** segments that appear at the beginning of each chapter are new to this edition; all others have been totally updated to reflect a firm's current situation.
- Virtually all of the **Mini-Cases** that close each chapter are new (the others have been totally updated).
- Almost all of the **Learning from Success** and **Learning from Failure** boxed features are new to this edition. Through these features, you'll learn about very recent instances of success or failure as firms use the strategic management process as a means of enhancing their performance.
- **New examples** of business firms' strategies and operations appear throughout all of the chapters. These examples, which describe the actions of companies located throughout the world, deal with firms competing in different industries and different countries and regions. Virtually all of these company-specific examples are new to this edition.
- **Updated research findings** are integrated throughout the chapters to present and highlight the latest insights about the strategic management process. The currency of the cutting-edge research results that are the foundation for many of the discussions in the text make it possible for you to be confident that you have access to very recent insights about strategic management.

Acknowledgments

We are especially grateful to those who prepared assignment content: Paul N. Friga, University of Carolina—Chapel Hill, who wrote the "Strategy Toolbox" materials; Charles M. Byles, Virginia Commonwealth University, who developed the "Experiential Exercises"; Gail Christian, Arizona State University, for her updating and preparation of many of the cases, and Paul Mallette, Colorado State University, who developed the case questions included within the CengageNOW Case Library.

The feedback and guidance provided by our reviewers for this text were especially helpful. We are grateful for their insights about how to present you with an interesting, accessible, and complete explanation of strategic management.

Todd M. Alessandri
Northeastern University

Sonny Ariss
University of Toledo

Kunal Banerji
Eastern Michigan University

Janice A. Black
California State University—Bakersfield

Keith Brigham
Texas Tech University

Carol A. Decker
Tennessee Wesleyan College

Rocki-Lee DeWitt
University of Vermont

Scott Droege
Western Kentucky University

Bahman (Paul) Ebrahimi
University of Denver

Tamela D. Ferguson
University of Louisiana at Lafayette

Cameron M. Ford
University of Central Florida

Debora J. Gilliard
Metropolitan State College—Denver

Steven Hamilton
University of Alaska, S.E.

Peter Hom
Arizona State University

Deloris James
University of Maryland—University College

Franz W. Kellermanns
University of Tennessee

Raihan Khan
SUNY Oswego

Leslie A. Korb
Georgian Court University

Joseph W. Leonard
Miami University

Joseph T. Mahoney
University of Illinois at Urbana-Champaign

Paul Mallette
Colorado State University

Brian L. Maruffi
Yeshiva University

George D. Mason
Providence College

Dennis Mathern
University of Findlay

Brett P. Matherne
Loyola University New Orleans

Donald Neubaum
Oregon State University

Frank Novakowski
Davenport University

Daewoo Park
Xavier University

Clifton D. Petty
Drury University

Laura H. Poppo
University of Kansas

Jude Rathburn
University of Wisconsin, Milwaukee

Janice J. Reily
Mount Mercy University

Mitrabarun Sarkar
Temple University

Khaled Sartawi
Fort Valley State University

Deepak Sethi
Old Dominion University

Amit J. Shah
Frostburg State University

Katsuhiko Shimizu
Keio University

Thomas D. Sigerstad
Frostburg State University

f. i. smith
Missouri Western State University

William L. Smith
Emporia State University

Jeffrey E. Stambaugh
Midwestern State University

Linda Thacker
El Centro College

Laszlo Tihanyi
Texas A&M University

Klaus Uhlenbruck
University of Montana

Floyd G. Willoughby
Oakland University

Joette Wisnieski
Indiana University of Pennsylvania

Our focus group participants helped us a great deal in understanding instructors' and students' needs in teaching and learning about strategic management in an action-oriented manner. We are grateful for the excellent observations the following scholar-teachers provided.

Donald Baack
Ball State University

Rick Crandall
Appalachian State University

Fred Doran
University of Mississippi

Chuck Englehart
Salem International University

Steven Hamilton
University of Alaska, S.E.

Ed Murphy
Embry Riddle University

Tyge Payne
Texas Tech University

Bill Ritchie
Florida Gulf Coast University

Michelle Slagle
University of South Alabama

Eva Smith
Spartanburg Technical College

We also want to express our sincere appreciation for the excellent support we've received from our editorial and production team at South-Western, Cengage Learning. In particular, we want to very sincerely thank Michele Rhoades, senior acquisitions editor, our editor and product champion; John Abner, director of content development; Tim Bailey, senior content project manager; and Jon Monahan, our marketing manager. We are truly grateful for their dedication, professionalism, and commitment to work closely with us to prepare a high-quality book and an excellent and comprehensive package of support materials. It has been a great team effort.

Supplements

Instructor's Resource DVD (1–111–82138-0)

Place resources at your fingertips with this efficient Instructor's Resource DVD, including Instructor's Resource Manual, Test Bank, ExamView Testing software, Microsoft PowerPoint®, and Case Notes. Easily access the 50Lessons video collection featuring world business leaders.

Instructor's Case Notes (1–111–82220-4)

The Case Notes provide details about all of the cases available in the CengageNOW Case Library. These Case Notes include directed assignments, financial analysis, and thorough discussion and exposition of issues in the case. Select cases will also have assessment rubrics tied to AACSB outcomes standards that can be used for grading each case. The Case Notes provide consistent and thorough support for instructors, following the method espoused by the author team for preparing an effective case analysis. The Case Notes are available as a print supplement or electronically on the Instructor's Resource DVD and Companion Web Site.

Test Bank

This thorough Test Bank contains more than 1,000 questions, including multiple-choice, true/false, and essay questions for every chapter. Answers are cross-referenced to pages within the text making it easy to pinpoint related material. The AACSB assurance of learning standards reflected in each Test Bank question have been identified to allow for the assessment of student achievement as it relates to these key measures. The Test Bank is available on the Instructor's Resource DVD or Companion Web Site.

ExamView®

The ExamView test creation software, which is an easy-to-use Windows-based program, contains all of the questions in the printed Test Bank. Instructors can add or edit questions, instructions, and answers, and select questions by previewing them on the screen, selecting them randomly, or selecting them by number. Instructors can also create and administer quizzes online, whether over the Internet, a local area network (LAN), or a wide area network (WAN). ExamView is included on the Instructor's Resource DVD.

Instructor's Resource Manual

One of the most exciting, useful instructor's aids available, this Manual offers comprehensive chapter over-views and outlines, instructor's notes, and answers to end-of-chapter questions. The Manual is available on the Instructor's Resource DVD or Companion Web Site.

PowerPoint Slide Presentations

Bring your lectures to life with this comprehensive set of PowerPoint slides that highlight figures from the text, reinforce all main concepts and terms, and assist with classroom discussion questions. Encourage active learn-ing in each chapter with these slides, available on the Instructor's Resource DVD or Companion Web Site.

50 Lessons Video Collection

Bring the latest challenges of today's business leaders throughout the world into your course with new videos by 50 Lessons. Available on the Instructor's Resource DVD, these short, powerful videos offers a compre-hensive, compelling resource of management and leadership lessons as leaders share their business acumen and outline principles guiding their business decisions and careers.

CourseMate (1-111-75027-0)

Engaging, trackable, and affordable, the new Understanding Business Strategy CourseMate Web Site offers a dynamic way to bring course concepts to life with interactive learning, study, and exam preparation tools that support this printed edition of the text. Watch student comprehension soar with all-new flash cards, engaging games, streaming videos, and more in this textbook-specific Web site. A complete e-book provides you with the choice of an entirely online learning experience. Understanding Business Strategy CourseMate goes beyond the book to deliver what you need!

CengageNOW (1-111-94615-9)

This robust, online course management system gives you more control in less time and delivers better student outcomes—NOW. CengageNOW™ includes teaching and learning resources organized around lecturing, creating assignments, case work, grading, quizzing, and tracking student progress and performance. Flexible assignments, automatic grading and a gradebook option provide more control while saving you valuable time. A Personalized Study diagnostic tool empowers students to master concepts, prepare for exams, and become more involved in class.

WebTutor for Blackboard (1-111-77787-X)
WebTutor for WebCT (1-111-77789-6)

Jumpstart your course with customizable, rich, text-specific content within this Course Management System! Access a wealth of interactive resources in addition to those on the Companion Web Site to supplement the classroom experience and further prepare students for professional success. This resource is ideal as an inte-grated solution for your distance learning or web-enhanced course.

Text Companion Web Site

Access important teaching resources on this Companion Web Site. For your convenience, you can download electronic versions of the instructor supplements at the password-protected section of the site, including the Instructor's Resource Manual, Test Bank, PowerPoint® presentations, and Case Notes. To access these addi-tional course materials and companion resources, please visit www.cengagebrain.com. At the CengageBrain.com home page, search for the ISBN of your title (from the back cover of your book) using the search box at the top of the page. This will take you to the product page where free companion resources can be found.

R. Duane Ireland

R. Duane Ireland is a Distinguished Professor of Management and holds the Conn Chair in New Ventures Leadership in the Mays Business School, Texas A&M University. He teaches courses at all levels (undergraduate, master's, doctoral, and executive). He has won multiple awards for his teaching and research. His research, which focuses on managing resources, innovation, corporate entrepreneurship, strategic entrepreneurship, and entrepreneurship in informal economies, has been published in a number of journals including *Academy of Management Journal, Academy of Management Review, Academy of Management Executive, Administrative Science Quarterly, Strategic Management Journal, Organization Science, Journal of Management, Entrepreneurship Theory and Practice*, and *Journal of Business Venturing*, among others. His published books include *Competing for Advantage,* second edition (2008), *Strategic Management: Competitiveness and Globalization*, ninth edition (2011), and *Entrepreneurship: Successfully Creating New Ventures*, third edition (2010). He recently completed a term as editor of the *Academy of Management Journal*. Previously, he served as an associate editor for the *Academy of Management Executive* and as a consulting editor for *Entrepreneurship Theory and Practice*. He received awards for the best article published in *Academy of Management Executive* (1999) and *Academy of Management Journal* (2000). In 2001, his article published in *Academy of Management Executive* won the Best Journal Article in Corporate Entrepreneurship Award from the U.S. Association for Small Business & Entrepreneurship (USASBE). He is a Fellow of the Academy of Management, a Fellow of the Strategic Management Society, and a Research Fellow in the Global Entrepreneurship Consortium. He received the 1999 Award for Outstanding Intellectual Contributions to Competitiveness Research from the American Society for Competitiveness, the USASBE Scholar in Corporate Entrepreneurship Award (2004), and the 2004 Falcone Distinguished Entrepreneur Scholar Award from Syracuse University. He is the current Vice-President-Elect and Program Chair-Elect for the Academy of Management.

Robert E. Hoskisson

Robert E. Hoskisson is the George R. Brown Chair of Strategic Management at the Jones School of Business at Rice University. His research topics focus on corporate strategy and governance and he teaches courses in corporate and international strategic management, among others. Professor Hoskisson has served on several editorial boards for such publications as the *Strategic Management Journal* (current Associate Editor), *Academy of Management Journal* (Consulting Editor), *Journal of International Business Studies* (Consulting Editor), and

Journal of Management (Associate Editor). His research has appeared in over 100 publications including the *Strategic Management Journal, Academy of Management Journal, Academy of Management Review, Organization Science, Journal of Management, Academy of Management Executive, Journal of World Business, California Management Review,* and *Long Range Planning,* among others. He has coauthored over 20 books including *Strategic Management: Globalization and Competitiveness* (9th Edition) and *Competing for Advantage* (2nd Edition). He has also coauthored *Downscoping: How to Tame the Diversified Firm.* He was recently ranked among the top 25 scholars in business and economics by the *Times Higher Education* for the number of published articles with more than 50 citations. He has served on the Board of Directors and is currently the president-elect and a Fellow of the Strategic Management Society. He has served on the Board of Governors and is also a Fellow of the Academy of Management and is a charter member of the Academy Journal's Hall of Fame.

Michael A. Hitt

Michael Hitt is a Distinguished Professor of Management at Texas A&M University and holds the Joe B. Foster Chair in Business Leadership. He received his Ph.D. from the University of Colorado. Dr. Hitt has coauthored or coedited 26 books and authored or coauthored many journal articles. A recent article in the *Journal of Management* listed him as one of the ten most cited authors in management over a 25-year period. Additionally, the *Times Higher Education* in 2010 listed him among the top scholars in economics, finance and management based on the number articles with a high citation rate on the Web of Science. He has served on the editorial review boards of multiple journals and is a former editor of the *Academy of Management Journal* and former co-editor of the *Strategic Entrepreneurship Journal.* He received the 1996 Award for Outstanding Academic Contributions to Competitiveness and the 1999 Award for Outstanding Intellectual Contributions to Competitiveness Research from the American Society for Competitiveness. He is a Fellow in the Academy of Management and in the Strategic Management Society, a Research Fellow in the Global Entrepreneurship Consortium and received an honorary doctorate from the Universidad Carlos III de Madrid. He is a former President of the Academy of Management, a former President of the Strategic Management Society, and a member of the Academy of Management Journal's Hall of Fame. He received awards for the best article published in the *Academy of Management Executive* (1999), *Academy of Management Journal* (2000), and the *Journal of Management* (2006). In 2004, Dr. Hitt was awarded the Best Paper Prize by the Strategic Management Society. In 2001, he received the Irwin Outstanding Educator Award and the Distinguished Service Award from the Academy of Management. In 2006, he received the Falcone Distinguished Entrepreneurship Scholar Award from Syracuse University.

PART 1
Vision

CHAPTER 1
The Foundations of Strategic Management

KNOWLEDGE OBJECTIVES
Reading and studying this chapter should enable you to:

1. Define strategic management.

2. Discuss why firms use the industrial organization (I/O) model to analyze their external environment.

3. Discuss why firms use the resource-based view of the firm (RBV) model to analyze their internal organization.

4. Define stakeholders and understand their importance.

5. Explain the work of strategic leaders.

Are You a Left-Handed Guitar Player? If So, We Have a Product Just for You!

> He's found a great niche, since about one out of ten people is left handed. That's one of the best niche businesses I've ever heard of.
>
> *(Irwin Miller, Counselor with SCORE, a group offering advice to small business owners)*

Some feel that need is the foundation for innovation and, hopefully, a firm's competitive success. This may be the case for Jim Duncan, cofounder and current owner of Southpaw Guitars.

Located in Houston, Texas, Southpaw Guitars has been in business for 30-plus years, now selling only acoustic and electric guitars that are made specifically for left-handed players. Duncan came to this business "naturally" given that he is a left-handed guitar player who at the age of ten and for many subsequent years had trouble finding a guitar that met his needs. To describe his products, Duncan notes that compared to a guitar for a right-handed player, "everything is backwards—the bracing, strings, and bridge." Thus, the products sold in Duncan's business are intended to serve a need (for a specialized guitar) for a particular type of customer (a left-handed guitar player). The fact that Southpaw Guitars' sales are increasing annually indicates that the store is satisfying its customers' needs.

© Simon Stanmore/Photographer's Choice/Getty Images

The firm Duncan leads today differs from the one he cofounded in 1980. At first, the store sold only a few left-handed guitars, largely because of uncertainty regarding the size of the "lefty" market. By the mid-1990s and though, sales of left-handed guitars exceeded those of guitars for right-handed players. Supporting the increasing sales of guitars for lefties was Duncan's accumulation of a mailing list of over 8,000 left-handed guitar enthusiasts. The importance of this mailing list is declining somewhat, though, as Southpaw Guitars now relies on the Internet to sell products on a worldwide basis through its Web site (http://www.southpawguitars.com). The firm stocks a wide variety of guitars with over 900 instruments physically in the store at all times.

Southpaw Guitars is successful largely because it has chosen a particular strategy and has developed competitive advantages as the foundation for successfully implementing that strategy. Specifically, Southpaw Guitars uses a focused-differentiation strategy. (We define strategy and competitive advantage in this chapter and fully discuss the focused differentiation strategy in Chapter 5. In essence, the focused differentiation strategy means that this firm is satisfying the needs of a particular target group—left-handed guitar players in this instance—particularly well.) The firm's competitive advantages are excellent service before and after the sale and an extremely wide selection of guitars from many different manufacturers. In terms of service, potential customers are told on the firm's Web site that they should ask to talk to Jim Duncan or Larry Bararata (store manager) when calling if they have limited time to select a product. With respect to the second competitive advantage, consider what an observer of the firm's operations says: "The key to Southpaw Guitars' success is having a deep selection." Duncan echoes this view, saying that while there are other left-handed guitar stores online, none offer the broad and deep product selection that is available from his firm. Southpaw Guitars is proud of the fact that it serves professional musicians as well as "weekend players" throughout the world and that its customers are very loyal as shown by their repeat purchases. So, if you are left handed and want a guitar that is made for you, Southpaw Guitars may have the product you are seeking!

Sources: D. Kaplan, 2010, "Where lefties rule," *Houston Chronicle Online*, http://www.chron.com, July 7; 2010, "Welcome," Southpawguitars.com, http://www.southpawguitars.com; 2010, "About us," Southpawguitars.com.

Do you sometimes wonder why some firms are more adaptive and successful than others? Why, for example, was Southpaw Guitars able to successfully alter its original strategy of serving the needs of all types of guitar players to focusing on selling guitars for only left-handed players? Why was Circuit City unable to successfully compete against competitors such as Best Buy, and why did it ultimately file for bankruptcy as a result? Why is a pilot-training school like Helicopter Services of Houston, Texas, successful at a time when Silver State Helicopters of Las Vegas, Nevada, filed for bankruptcy? (*Hint*: Some believe that the success of Helicopter Services is a function of the firm's ability to control its costs while providing highly personalized attention to every customer.)[1]

Although the reasons for Southpaw Guitars, Best Buy, and Helicopter Services' success as well as the successes of many other firms sometime seem mysterious, they really aren't. As with these three companies, firms use the strategic management process as the foundation for being successful. The purpose of this book is to explain each part of the strategic management process—*vision, analysis,* and *strategy*. We think you will enjoy learning about the process and know that you will benefit from doing so.

What is Strategic Management?

Strategic management is the ongoing process companies use to form a *vision, analyze* their external environment and their internal organization, and select one or more *strategies* to use to create value for customers and other stakeholders, especially shareholders. Let's define the parts of the strategic management process so we can see the differences among them. In this chapter, we will merely introduce you to the parts of this important process. You'll learn more about each part in the book's remaining chapters. We'll also define a number of terms in this chapter that are used throughout the book.

We first consider a firm's vision. As the following statement indicates, Jack Welch, former General Electric (GE) CEO, strongly believes that a vision is important for a firm and that strategic leaders (to whom we introduce you in this chapter and fully describe in Chapter 2) are responsible for forming it: "Good business leaders create a vision, articulate the vision, passionately own the vision, and relentlessly drive it to completion."[2]

The **vision** contains at least two components—a mission that describes the firm's DNA and the "picture" of the firm as it hopes to exist in a future time period.[3] DNA includes the core information and characteristics necessary for the firm to function. The vision is intended to inspire the firm's employees and its other stakeholders to realize or "picture" the future aspirations of what the firm can become and to help establish a framework for ethical behavior. For example, the vision for Intoweb Design is "to become the best Web Developers in South Africa."[4] General Motors' vision is "to be the world leader in transportation products and related services."[5] Google's vision is "to organize the world's information and make it universally accessible and useful." The vision statements for these companies should inspire employees and hopefully result in actions and outcomes that will satisfy each firm's stakeholders (we'll talk more about stakeholders later in this chapter).

An effective vision informs the selection of the firm's strategy. A **strategy** is an action plan designed to move an organization toward achievement of its vision. The firm's mission, which flows from the vision, is focused on the markets the firm serves and the products (either goods or services) it provides. Thus, the

strategic management

the ongoing process companies use to form a *vision, analyze* their external environment and their internal organization, and select one or more *strategies* to use to create value for customers and other stakeholders, especially shareholders

vision

contains at least two components—a mission that describes the firm's DNA and the "picture" of the firm as it hopes to exist in a future time period

strategy

an action plan designed to move an organization toward achievement of its vision

mission defines the firm's core intent and the business or businesses in which it intends to compete. Amazon.com's mission is "to build a place where people can come to find and discover anything they might want to buy online." Social networking site Twitter's mission is to provide a "service for friends, family, and co-workers to communicate and stay connected through the exchange of quick, frequent answers to one simple question: What are you doing?" Each of these mission statements indicates the firm's core intent and the business or businesses in which it will compete.

The **external environment** is a set of conditions outside the firm that affect the firm's performance. Changes in population trends and income levels, competition between firms, and economic changes are examples of the many conditions in a firm's external environment that can affect its performance. Consider, for example, that a fragile retailing sector in the United States in recent years is causing firms such as J. Crew Group, Gap, and Limited Brands to expand into markets outside their domestic market in pursuit of additional business.[6]

The **internal organization** is the set of conditions (such as strengths, resources, capabilities, and so forth) inside the firm that affect the choice and use of strategies. **Strengths** are resources and capabilities that allow the firm to complete important tasks. For example, "...meeting individual consumer electronics needs with end-to-end solutions, which involves greater employee involvement and increased services" is one of the strengths on which Best Buy relies to implement its strategy.[7] **Resources** are the tangible and intangible assets held by the firm. A strong balance sheet is one of Coca-Cola's tangible assets, while the knowledge held by its employees is one of Google's intangible assets. **Capabilities** result when the firm integrates several different resources in a way that allows it to effectively and efficiently complete a task or a series of related tasks.[8] 3M integrates the knowledge of its scientists (an intangible asset) with other resources, including its sophisticated scientific equipment (a tangible asset), to create its innovation capability. **Core competencies** are capabilities the firm emphasizes and performs especially well while pursuing its vision. Returning to its historical focus on product design as a capability is a core competence that is contributing to LEGO's competitive resurgence. The firm struggled in the early to mid-2000s as a result of trying to extend its brand by venturing into new products such as the Galidor line. All about action figures, this line of products was indistinguishable from competitors' offerings and worse, did not "...require building skills or much in the way of imagination, the hallmark of the more traditional LEGO construction toys."[9] Recognizing these problems, LEGO's leaders renewed the firm's emphasis on its core competence of designing creative collections of models requiring imaginative assembly by customers.

Core competencies that differ from those held by competitors are called **distinctive competencies**. Design is a distinctive competence for LEGO as is innovation for Gillette. The Sensor razor is an example of a product Gillette developed by using its distinctive competence of innovation. Introduced in 1990, the Sensor gave way to Gillette's newer innovation (the MACH3) in 1998. Incremental innovations to this product over time led to the MACH3 Turbo and MACH3 Power.[10] When a firm's core competencies or its distinctive competencies allow it to create value for customers exceeding the value competitors create for them, the firm has a **competitive advantage**. Product design at LEGO and innovation at Gillette are competitive advantages, respectively, for these firms. Today, personal computer manufacturer Lenovo Group claims that it relies on its distinctive competence in research and development to form innovation as a competitive advantage. According to company documents, "Lenovo owns the greater track

mission

defines the firm's core intent and the business or businesses in which it intends to compete

external environment

a set of conditions outside the firm that affect the firm's performance

internal organization

the set of conditions (such as strengths, resources, capabilities, and so forth) inside the firm that affect the choice and use of strategies

strengths

resources and capabilities that allow the firm to complete important tasks

resources

the tangible and intangible assets held by the firm

capabilities

result when the firm integrates several different resources in a way that allows it to effectively and efficiently complete a task or a series of related tasks

core competencies

capabilities the firm emphasizes and performs especially well while pursuing its vision

distinctive competencies

core competencies that differ from those held by competitors

competitive advantage

exists when a firm's core competencies or its distinctive competencies allow it to create value for customers exceeding the value competitors create for them

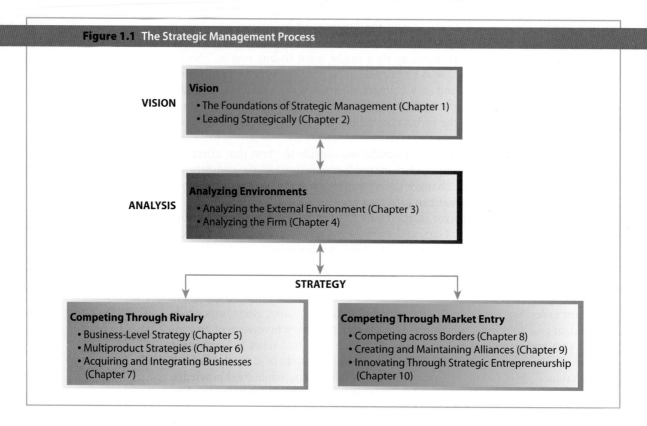

Figure 1.1 The Strategic Management Process

record for innovation in the PC industry and remains committed to innovation in its products and technology; innovation drives our business and adds value for customers."[11]

Figure 1.1 presents the strategic management process while the key characteristics of strategic management are listed in Table 1.1. We continue our introduction of the parts of the strategic management process in the next few sections.

The Three Parts of the Strategic Management Process

As suggested in Figure 1.1, strategic leaders are responsible for forming a firm's vision (we describe this responsibility in greater detail in Chapter 2). As noted

Table 1.1 Key Characteristics of Strategic Management

Strategic management is:

- Performance oriented
- Ongoing in nature
- Dynamic rather than static
- Oriented to the present and the future
- Concerned with conditions both outside and inside the firm
- Concerned with performing well and satisfying stakeholders

Table 1.2 Vision and Mission Statements

VISION STATEMENTS

McDonald's

To give each customer, every time, an experience that sets new standards in value, service, friendliness, and quality.

NASDAQ

To build the world's first truly global securities market ... A worldwide market of markets built on a worldwide network of networks ... linking pools of liquidity and connecting investors from all over the world ... assuring the best possible price for securities at the lowest possible cost.

Petsmart

To be the premier organization in nurturing and enriching the bond between people and animals.

Wachovia

Wachovia's vision is to be the best, most trusted and admired financial services company.

MISSION STATEMENTS

Bristol-Myers Squibb

Our mission is to extend and enhance human life by providing the highest-quality pharmaceuticals and health care products.

GlaxoSmithKline

GSK's mission is to improve the quality of human life by enabling people to do more, feel better and live longer.

Merck

The mission of Merck is to provide society with superior products and services by developing innovations and solutions that improve the quality of life and satisfy customer needs, and to provide employees with meaningful work and advancement opportunities, and investors with a superior rate of return.

Wipro

The mission is to be a full-service, global outsourcing company.

earlier, an effective mission provides direction to the firm, while an effective vision inspires stakeholders to ethical actions as the firm moves toward its intended future. We present different firms' vision statements and mission statements in Table 1.2. Which of the vision statements shown in Table 1.2 inspire you? Which mission statement does the best job of telling you about the direction a firm is taking? Would you make changes to any of the vision or mission statements shown in the table? If so, why and what would those changes be?

Figure 1.1 also suggests that firms must *analyze* their external environment and their internal organization before strategies can be chosen and *implemented*. Here's an example of how this process is taking place today at Starbucks, a company with a vision "to inspire and nurture the human spirit—one person, one cup and one neighborhood at a time."[12]

Starbucks CEO Howard Schulz recently announced that his firm intends to establish thousands of units in China over time. Currently, the firm has fewer than 400 units in China where it sells products that are adapted to local tastes and customs.[13] In the process of opening many more units, China would eclipse Japan as Starbucks largest market outside of North America. Additionally, Schulz wants his firm to eventually open storefronts in Vietnam and India. Schulz says the reason for expanding into these countries is that "Asia clearly represents the most significant growth opportunity on a go-forward basis."[14] Thus, in looking

© Tim Graham/Getty Images

Extension of the Starbucks brand across China is a strategy CEO Howard Schulz has clearly identified based on analysis of the external environment, though its implementation will no doubt challenge the company.

at its external environment, Starbucks identified what it believes are major opportunities to expand internationally, particularly in Asia.

Implementing this international growth strategy will challenge Starbucks. The firm will need to continue wisely using its resources and capabilities as the foundation for customizing its products to meet local tastes while trying to convince customers to pay up to three times the cost of competitors' offerings for Starbucks' drinks. Developing marketing campaigns to reach consumers with these messages is another difficult task. But Schulz is undeterred when it comes to meeting these strategy-implementation-related challenges, saying, "We are still at the embryonic stage of what Asia will be for the company."[15] Additionally, Schulz believes in his employees' abilities to find and purchase the highest-quality Arabica coffee beans and to process those beans in ways that create a superior product that customers want to purchase.[16]

Earlier in this chapter, we mentioned that a strategy is an action plan designed to move an organization toward achievement of its vision. Strategy is about finding ways for the firm to be different from its competitors. The most effective companies avoid using "me-too" strategies—strategies that are the same as those of their competitors. A firm's strategy should allow it to deliver a unique mix of value to customers.[17]

As shown in Figure 1.1, firms use business-level strategies, multiproduct strategies, and merger and acquisition strategies to directly compete with rivals. With product names such as Mastiff and Pitbull, Big Dog Motorcycles uses the focused differentiation business-level strategy to build premium, heavyweight motorcycles that are targeted for customers with needs for these unique products. (In addition to the focused differentiation strategy, we discuss four other business-level strategies in Chapter 5.) Big Dog competes directly against Harley-Davidson with its business-level strategy. In this chapter's *Focusing on Strategy,* we described how Southpaw Guitars relies on service and a broad and deep inventory to successfully implement its focused differentiation strategy. Procter & Gamble uses a related diversification multiproduct strategy (discussed in Chapter 6) in battles with global competitors such as Unilever, Kimberly Clark, and Johnson & Johnson. We won't provide examples here of companies using the other strategy, mergers and acquisitions, which is a means of competing directly with competitors, or of the three strategies (see Figure 1.1) firms use to compete against competitors by entering additional markets. We will, however, provide examples of how firms use these strategies in the relevant chapters (Chapters 7 through 10).

Once chosen, strategies must be put to use. **Strategy implementation** is the set of actions firms take to use a strategy after it has been selected. Advertising itself as "America's Largest Pet Pharmacy," 1-800-PetsMed.com offers the largest selection of prescription and nonprescription pet medications to consumers at competitive prices. Using the Internet and telemarketing to sell products to customers is a critical part of how the firm implements its cost leadership strategy (see Chapter 5).[18] Starbucks uses its distribution skills and ability to customize products to implement its international strategy in regions (e.g., Asia) and countries (e.g., China) outside North America.

In *Understanding Strategy: Learning from Success*, we describe Walmart's success as a grocer. (You will learn more about Walmart and other actions the

strategy implementation

the set of actions firms take to use a strategy after it has been selected firm is taking to successfully implement its cost leadership strategy in Chapter 5's *Focusing on Strategy*.) The world's largest public corporation by revenue, Walmart uses its famous and widely recognized inventory management and distribution distinctive competencies to drive its continuing success. Because Walmart's inventory management and distribution distinctive competencies allow it to create value for customers that exceeds the value Walmart's competitors create for customers, they are competitive advantages for the firm.

After reading *Understanding Strategy* about Walmart as a grocer, are you able to conclude that the company is effectively using the strategic management process? What future do you envision for Walmart as a grocer? Can you anticipate Walmart taking its grocery store concepts to still additional countries? How intense do you think the competitive battles will become between Walmart and Tesco in the United States (Walmart's home market) and in the United Kingdom (Tesco's home market)? What about CompUSA? Read *Understanding Strategy: Learning from Failure* to learn about this company's path to liquidation. What is your assessment of CompUSA's use of the strategic management process? What might you have done differently if you were leading CompUSA? In your opinion, before it was liquidated, did CompUSA ever find a unique way to pursue a unique opportunity in its external environment and to form a competitive advantage as the foundation for pursuing a unique opportunity?

As the CompUSA example shows, organizational success (certainly success over time) is not guaranteed for any firm. Indeed, success is strongly influenced by how well a firm uses the strategic management process. In your opinion, was this process used successfully and consistently at CompUSA before the firm was liquidated?

We've now introduced you to the strategic management process, provided examples of vision statements and mission statements, and described in some detail how Walmart is successfully using it. We also examined CompUSA as an example of a situation in which more effective use of the strategic management process might have had a positive effect on the firm's performance, certainly in the years before the firm was liquidated.

We'll use the remainder of this chapter to tell you a bit more about how firms analyze their external environment and their internal organization. Decision makers use the information gathered from these two analyses to select one or more strategies (see Figure 1.1). Before closing the chapter with a brief discussion of the contents of the book's remaining chapters, we'll introduce you to stakeholders and strategic leaders. In essence, stakeholders are the individuals and groups that firms try to satisfy when using the strategic management process, while strategic leaders are responsible for making certain their firms effectively use this process.

The Industrial Organization Model

Firms use the industrial organization (I/O) model to analyze their external environment. Using this model as the foundation for identifying opportunities and threats is indeed an important part of the strategic management process. We introduce you to this model here and provide you with a fuller discussion of it and its use in Chapter 3.

Opportunities are conditions in the firm's external environment that may help the firm reach its vision. **Threats** are conditions in the firm's external environment that may prevent the firm from reaching its vision. Performance often declines in

opportunities

conditions in the firm's external environment that may help the firm reach its vision

threats

conditions in the firm's external environment that may prevent the firm from reaching its vision

Walmart's Grocery Business: Can the Momentum and Success Be Maintained?

With a goal of "saving people money to help them live better," Walmart generates more sales revenue annually than any firm in the world. To generate this revenue, the firm sells everything from electronics and groceries to medication at "everyday low prices." However, grocery sales are becoming even more prominent for Walmart as indicated by the fact that for the first time, groceries accounted for over one-half (51 percent) of the firm's U.S sales revenue in 2009. Perhaps not surprisingly, Walmart is now the largest grocer in the United States by sales revenue.

With the first dedicated grocery store established in Bentonville, Arkansas, in 1998, Walmart "the grocer" is relatively new. Called Neighborhood Markets, these grocery stores average 42,000 square feet and offer a variety of products, including pharmaceuticals, health and beauty aids, and photo-developing services in addition to groceries. At the beginning of 2010, Walmart had opened over 150 Neighborhood Markets in the United States and established these units in 14 other countries as well. Using its inventory management and distribution competitive advantages, Walmart implements the cost leadership strategy in its grocery stores as it does in its other units

Beyond its large domestic competitors in the grocery business, Walmart is also facing new entrants into the U.S. market such as Great Britain's Tesco PLC, which has launched more than 150 of its neighborhood-oriented Fresh & Easy Markets.

such as Walmart Supercenters and Sam's Clubs. Walmart is recognized for aggressive pricing of its grocery items, an approach that helps the firm implement its cost leadership strategy.

Increasingly, Walmart is converting many of its existing stores into supercenters. Averaging 100,000 square feet, grocery items are prominently featured in these new supercenters. A key reason for this is that groceries are a powerful draw for customers who, once in a supercenter, are encouraged through advertising and store layout to shop for other inventory items such as electronics and household furnishings. Thus, Walmart is selling groceries through two distribution channels—"regular" stores (e.g., supercenters) and dedicated grocery storefronts.

In addition to competition from U.S. competitors, such as grocers Kroger and Safeway, and from discounters, such as Target, Tesco PLC is engaging Walmart in the grocery business in multiple markets, but certainly in the United States and the United Kingdom. A British-based international grocery and general merchandise retail chain, Tesco

is the world's third-largest retailer (behind Walmart and France's Carrefour). Just a few years ago, Tesco opened its first U.S. grocery stores in Los Angeles. Called Fresh & Easy Neighborhood Markets, these units are about half the size of Walmart's Neighborhood Markets. By mid-2010, Tesco had established over 150 of these units in the United States. Impressed by Tesco's success with its U.S. operations, 2010 was a year in which Walmart "…launched an ambitious program to boost its presence in the United Kingdom." With an emphasis on low prices, Walmart is establishing small supermarkets that are similar to Tesco's Express stores as a means of improving its ability to compete against Tesco in U.K. urban areas.

While competing against domestic and global competitors, Walmart constantly tries to create additional types of value for customers. A commitment to become a preeminent retailer of environmentally friendly, organic grocer items and household products suggests a set of actions the firm hopes will create value for customers interested in preserving the world's physical environment. In the United States, for example, Walmart's Heritage Agriculture program encourages "…farms within a day's drive of one of its warehouses to grow crops that now take days to arrive in trucks from states like Florida and California." Additionally, in the summer of 2010, Seventh Generation (the leading brand of nontoxic and environmentally friendly household products in the United States) formed a strategic partnership with Walmart to distribute its products through Walmart's storefronts and its rapidly growing Web presence (http://www.walmart.com). Overall, customers' initial reactions to the quality of Walmart's organic food items and to its increasing emphasis on selling environmentally friendly household products were positive.

Sources: M. Duff, 2010, "Walmart vs. Tesco: Why the odds favor the British retailer," *bnet*, http://www.industry.bnet.com, May 4; C. Farnell, 2010, "The world's top retailers," *Food and Drink Digital*, http://www.foodanddrinkdigital.com, April 6; C. Kummer, 2010, "The great grocery smack down," *The Atlantic Online*, http://www.theatlantic.com, March; A. Sage, 2010, "Walmart to slash grocery prices," *Reuters Online*, http://www.reuters.com, March 19; K. Tally, 2010, "Walmart's grocery sales expand," *The Wall Street Journal Online*, http://www.wsj.com, March 31; 2010, "Seventh Generation and Walmart announce strategic partnership to offer environmentally friendly, sustainable products at more than 1,500 stores," *The Wall Street Journal Online*, July 26; 2010, "Walmart Stores Inc.," *Standard & Poor's Stock Report*, http://www.standardandpoors.com, July 17.

© Jonathan Alcorn/Bloomberg/Getty Images

© Greg Epperson, iStock

UNDERSTANDING STRATEGY
LEARNING FROM FAILURE

"CompUSA is Closing its Stores," the Headlines Read. What Happened?

With the name Soft Warehouse, the firm that came to be known as CompUSA was founded in 1984 as a seller of software. The firm then expanded its operations in order to sell consumer electronics products and personal computers. In 1991, when the firm went public, its name was changed to CompUSA.

During the 1990s, CompUSA struggled to find its identity and to select a strategy to successfully implement. Was it primarily a seller of software or of products using software applications and consumer electronics products? Continuing declines in the prices of personal computers as well as competition from direct seller Dell damaged the company as did intense competition from big box retailers Best Buy and Circuit City and from Walmart as

Facing increasing direct-to-consumer competition from Dell and the lower prices of larger competitors like Best Buy and Walmart, CompUSA failed to implement a strategy that would have lead to competitive advantage within the evolving marketplace.

well. Because of their size, these three competitors were able to offer greater selection and lower prices on consumer electronics products (e.g., televisions) carried by CompUSA.

Throughout its turbulent history though, some saw value in CompUSA. In 1999, for example, Mexican telephone and retailing magnate Carlos Slim took a stake in the firm and then acquired other companies to increase its size. Slim later spent roughly $800 million to take the firm private. Over time, Slim's total investment in CompUSA was close to $2 billion.

Although "the chain went through several CEOs and tried different turnaround strategies such as a move (in 2007) to focus on core customers such as gadget lovers and small business owners," nothing really worked. As a result, Slim decided in late 2007 to close the firm's remaining stores (severely underperforming units had been previously closed). CompUSA was then sold to retail-store liquidator Gordon Brothers Group.

But all may not be lost! Saying, "We believe the value of the CompUSA brand remains very high," Systemax CEO Richard Leeds announced about a month after Gordon Brothers took control of CompUSA's assets that his firm was purchasing CompUSA's brand, trademarks, and e-commerce business. A few years later, the "Reborn" CompUSA was using what it called Retail 2.0 in its stores as part of its strategy to appeal to customers. (The firm also had established a Web site presence.) In essence, the Retail 2.0 concept was one through which products (e.g., a widescreen TV on display) became a "...computer monitor with its own keyboard for easy surfing" by a customer examining a particular product. This capability allows customers to "surf the net" while in the store to compare the CompUSA price for a product with competitors' prices and to learn more about the product by visiting various sites to gain access to information. But is Retail 2.0 enough to make CompUSA competitive? Is it a competitive advantage for CompUSA? This may not be the case. In considering possible results from using Retail 2.0, one analyst wondered "...what 'pop' in sales the technology has given the chain and whether it justified the cost." So, questions still remain about the firm's ability to use the strategic management process in a way that ensures its long-term success.

Sources: B. Schlachter, 2010, "Reborn CompUSA banks on a new customer experience," *Dallas Star-Telegram Online*, http://www.star-telegram.com, April 7; 2010, "About us," CompUSA Home Page, http://www.compusa.com, July 22; J. Cheng, 2008, "Back from the dead: CompUSA assets snapped up by TigerDirect," *Answers from Laptop Experts*, http://www.arstechnica.com, January 7; 2008, "Systemax agrees to purchase CompUSA assets," *IT Business Edge*, http://www.itbusinessedge.com, January 28.

firms that do not carefully study the threats and opportunities in their external environment. Firms use the components of their internal organization (resources, capabilities, and so forth) to pursue environmental opportunities and to overcome environmental threats.

Let's consider two examples of firms now pursuing opportunities in their respective external environments. Recently, Target opened its first store in East Harlem, New York. Seeing this as an opportunity to "...push into urban markets to fuel its growth," this Target store is selling merchandise that is tailored to the neighborhood. Spanish-language greeting cards, multicultural dolls, and religious candles are examples of these tailored products.[19] Seeing an opportunity that is created by constraints on global energy sources and an interest among a growing number of firms to produce environmentally sustainable products, "Daimler AG and Chinese battery maker BYD Co. (are establishing) a new brand of electric cars for the Chinese market..."[20] In the long term, these partnering companies seek to develop a Chinese brand of electric cars with characteristics that will appeal to customers throughout the world.

Interesting too is the fact that what may be a threat for one firm can simultaneously be an opportunity for another. Consider the effects of the recent economic conditions on book purchasing patterns. Booksellers with large storefronts such as Borders are struggling; but, "The tough economic times are a boon to the used book business,"[21] says an analyst. A key reason for this is that the prices for used books are much cheaper, making them more affordable in the eyes of customers trying to control expenses during difficult economic times. Thus, for Borders, tough economic times as well as increasing competition from online booksellers such as Amazon.com and the growing popularity of electronic books are threats. (The fact that for the first time Amazon.com sold more e-books than hardback books during the three months of May, June, and July 2010 indicates that electronic books are a threat to storefronts such as Borders and perhaps to used-book sellers as well.)[22]

Conditions in the global airline industry also illustrate how opportunities and threats surface in a firm's external environment. Economic conditions, a part of the firm's external environment, influence travel decisions. During difficult economic times, for example, people might choose not to travel at all or to use other, typically less expensive travel modes (e.g., car or commercial bus) instead of traveling by air. As an important raw material to an airline's operations, the cost of fuel can also have a dramatic effect on an airline company's profitability. Not surprisingly, given the amount of fuel airplanes require (Boeing's mid-size 737 requires about 100 pounds of fuel per minute on average, for example), experience shows that increasing fuel costs tend to negatively affect an airline's profitability while decreasing fuel costs tend to have the opposite effect.

To deal with some of the threats in their external environment, several carriers see using a merger strategy as an opportunity. A merger strategy, which we describe in detail in Chapter 7, is one in which firms agree to combine their operations on a relatively equal basis as the foundation for forming a single company. By combining operations, two airline companies could hopefully make their service more attractive to customers by increasing the number of flight options available to them and could reduce their costs (for fuel, for example) by buying in larger quantities. Combining firms' fleets, airport facilities, frequent-flyer programs, and workforces are additional examples of benefits airlines might gain through a merger.

Given potential advantages such as those described above and seeing pursuing these advantages as an opportunity, Continental Airlines and United Airlines announced their intended merger in 2010. Valued at $3.2 billion, this merger would create the world's largest airline. Commenting about the anticipated benefits of the merger, Continental's CEO said that "combining these two companies is the best way to position ourselves...to thrive in the constantly changing and competitive airline industry."[23] By mid-2010, antitrust regulators from the

Figure 1.2 Using the Industrial Organization (I/O) Model to Analyze the External Environment

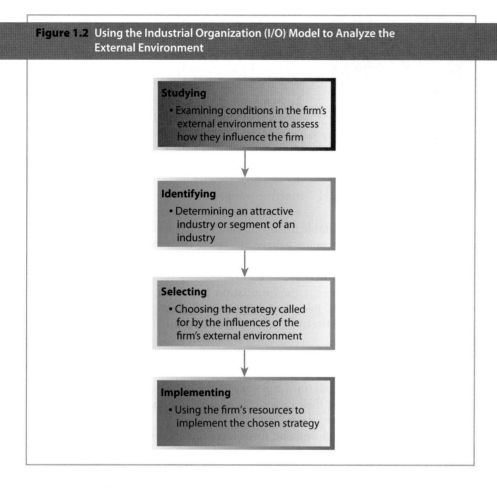

European Commission approved the merger. With anticipated approval from the U.S. Justice Department, the companies hoped to complete the merger by the end of 2011.[24]

In Figure 1.2, we diagram how firms use the I/O model to analyze their external environment. The information gained from this analysis is used to help strategic leaders choose one or more strategies as is the information gained by using the resource-based model to study the firm's internal organization.

The Resource-Based View of the Firm Model

While the I/O model focuses on the firm's external environment, the resource-based view (RBV) model describes what firms do to analyze their internal organization. The purpose of analyzing the internal organization is to identify the firm's resources, capabilities, core competencies, and distinctive competencies, all of which are the source or foundation of the firm's competitive advantages. Thus, the I/O and RBV models complement each other; one (the I/O model) deals with conditions outside the firm, and the other (the RBV model) deals with conditions inside the firm. We introduce you to the RBV model here and offer a fuller description of it in Chapter 4.

The RBV model suggests that effective management of the firm's operations creates resources and capabilities that are unique to that firm. Therefore, the bundle

© THOMAS COEX/AFP/Getty Images

Louis Vuitton successfully translates its competitive advantages in product design and manufacturing into value for a select group of customer who associate the brand with "buying into a dream."

of productive resources across firms can vary quite substantially.[25] Louis Vuitton's resources and capabilities, for example, differ from those of competitors Prada, Gucci, Hermes, and Coach. With resources and capabilities that differ from its competitors, each of these firms has a chance to develop distinctive competencies and competitive advantages that can be used to create value for a group of customers. Let's describe how Louis Vuitton uses its unique resources and capabilities to develop core competencies and perhaps distinctive competencies that in turn allow the firm to create value for a group of customers.

The world's most profitable luxury brand, Vuitton has design skills and manufacturing efficiencies that some believe are better than those of its competitors. These distinctive competencies contribute to Louis Vuitton's ability to generate higher operating margins. Because of this superiority relative to its competitors, its distinctive competencies are the foundation for Vuitton's competitive advantages in product design and manufacturing; in turn, these competitive advantages are critical to the firm's effective use of its focused differentiation strategy (see Chapter 5).

Although expensive, the firm's products do create value for a group of customers. One customer sees this value as "buying into a dream." In this particular customer's words, "You buy into the dream of Louis Vuitton. We're part of a sect, and the more they put their prices up, the more we come back. They pull the wool over our eyes, but we love it."[26]

Unlike the external environment, firms have direct control over conditions in their internal organization. Each firm's strategic leaders make choices about the resources and capabilities the firm wants to control and about how they'll be nurtured and used. The ability to control the firm's resources, capabilities, and core competencies and to develop them in ways that differ from those of the competitors increases the number of strategic options. Thus, from the RBV perspective, the uniqueness of the firm's resources, capabilities, core competencies, distinctive competencies, and competitive advantages influences the choice of one or more strategies.

Figure 1.3 diagrams how firms use the RBV model to analyze their internal organization. Notice how the firm's resources, capabilities, and core competencies influence the choice of a strategy.

Next, we discuss stakeholders—the individuals and groups the firm seeks to satisfy by using the strategy or strategies it has selected.

Stakeholders

stakeholders

individuals and groups who have an interest in a firm's performance and the ability to influence its actions

Stakeholders are individuals and groups who have an interest in a firm's performance and the ability to influence its actions.[27] In essence, stakeholders influence firms by deciding the degree to which they will support the firm's strategy. Shareholders, customers, and suppliers are stakeholders, as are a firm's employees and the communities in which it conducts business. Shareholders, for example, exercise their influence by deciding whether they will keep their shares in the firm or sell them. Employees decide whether they will remain with their employer or work for another firm, perhaps even a competitor. Not surprisingly, firms use the

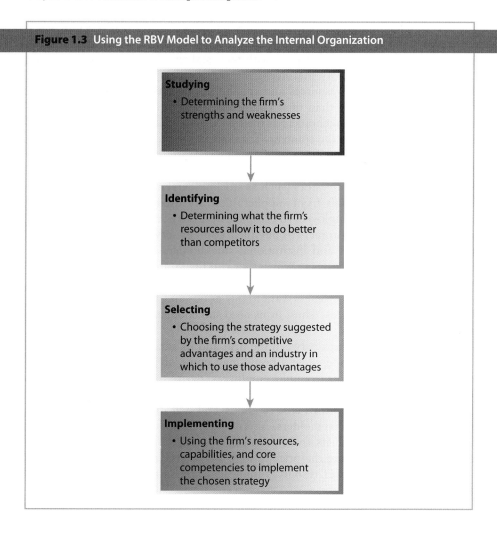

Figure 1.3 Using the RBV Model to Analyze the Internal Organization

strategic management process to select and implement strategies that create value for stakeholders.[28]

As shown in Figure 1.4, firms have three major stakeholder groups: owners (shareholders), external stakeholders, and internal stakeholders. Each stakeholder wants the firm in which it has an interest to satisfy its needs. Generally speaking, stakeholders continue to support firms that satisfy their needs. However, in general, stakeholders withdraw their support from firms failing to meet their needs.

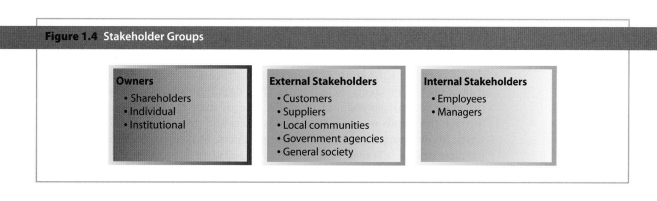

Figure 1.4 Stakeholder Groups

Stakeholders' interest in performance coupled with their ability to influence the firm through their decisions to support the firm or not, suggests that companies have important *relationships* with their stakeholders. These relationships must be managed in a way that keeps the stakeholders committed to the firm. Firms able to use their resources and capabilities to manage relationships with their stakeholders better than their competitors may gain a competitive advantage.[29] These firms see stakeholders as their partners and keep them well informed about and involved with the company's actions.[30]

Firms and stakeholders have relationships because they need each other. To launch a company and operate it on a continuing basis, firms need capital (that is, money) provided by investors (such as stockholders) and financial institutions (such as banks), materials from suppliers that are used to produce a good or provide a service, and employees to complete necessary tasks. In addition and importantly, firms need customers to buy their good or service. Similarly, investors (individual stockholders and institutional stockholders such as pension funds) need to find viable businesses in which they can invest and earn a return on their capital. Employees need to work for organizations for income and at least some personal satisfaction. Customers want to buy goods and services from companies that will satisfy their needs. Thus, firms need stakeholders, but stakeholders also need firms.

Managing relationships between the firm and its stakeholders is difficult because satisfying one stakeholder's needs may come at the expense of another stakeholder. Consider, for example, employees' desire to be paid more for their work. If wages are increased without an identical increase in productivity to offset the higher costs, the firm's cost of goods sold will increase, reducing the return on investment for shareholders. Alternatively, think of customers wanting to buy higher-quality products from a firm at ever-decreasing prices. The net result of the firm's lowering the price of its good or service without reducing the cost to produce it is fewer resources for wages and salaries and for returns to shareholders.

Although other examples could be offered, the main point here is that firms must manage their relationships with stakeholders in ways that will keep all stakeholders at least minimally satisfied. In other words, the firm wants to retain quality suppliers, loyal customers, and satisfied employees while providing returns to shareholders that cause them to retain their investment in the firm. As these comments show, managing relationships among various stakeholders is a challenging yet important task for the firm's strategic leaders.

Strategic Leaders

Strategic leaders are the individuals practicing strategic leadership. (We fully discuss strategic leadership in the next chapter.) Effective strategic leaders are ones who make it possible for the strategic management process to be successfully used in their firm.[31] As CEO of Apple, for example, Steve Jobs must make certain that his firm uses the strategic management process so it can continue benefiting from a host of products including the iPod digital music player, the iPhone, and the more recently introduced iPad. Because of their capabilities to be enriched through thousands of applications, consumers and programmers alike are enthusiastic about being involved with these products. In fact, part of Apple's strategy for these products is to develop an array of software applications that creates the most value for customers.[32]

strategic leaders

the individuals practicing strategic leadership

A firm's board of directors holds the CEO and top management team responsible for ensuring that an effective strategic management process is developed and properly used throughout the organization. When doing their work, top-level managers concentrate on the big picture to envision their firm's future and the strategies necessary to achieve that vision.[33]

Increasingly, CEOs and members of the firm's top-management team are being drawn from a global talent pool. Currently, the "head of the Altria Group was born in Egypt, PepsiCo's is from India, the Liberty Mutual Group's is a native of Ireland, and Alcoa's was born in Morocco."[34] At Acer, the world's second-largest personal-computer manufacturer by shipments after Hewlett-Packard,[35] the top-management team "...includes a French executive who oversees mobile phones, an Italian marketing chief, a German running China, an Austrian leading the U.S., and an American managing Brazil."[36] Diversity at the helm of companies, such as is the case for the companies mentioned here, makes it more likely that an all-important global perspective will be adopted throughout the firm when using the strategic management process.

In small firms, the CEO may be the sole owner and may not report to a board of directors. In this instance, of course, that person is responsible for both designing and using the strategic management process. Decisions that strategic leaders make when using the strategic management process include determining what resources are acquired, what prices are paid for those resources, and how to manage those resources so a firm will be able to pursue opportunities in its external environment while reducing or eliminating the effects of threats.[37] Through the firm's vision statement, strategic leaders try to stimulate their employees' creativity to develop new products, new processes to produce the firm's products, and the administrative routines necessary to successfully implement the firm's strategies.[38]

The CEO and top management team are also responsible for shaping and nurturing the firm's culture. **Organizational culture** is the set of values and beliefs that are shared throughout the firm. *Values* reflect what is important, while *beliefs* speak to how things should be done. In 3M's organizational culture, respect for the contribution of each employee and continuous innovation are important values.[39] The most effective organizational culture lets people know that they are appreciated and that they are expected to contribute to efforts being taken to reach the firm's vision.[40]

Intangible in nature, culture can't be touched or seen, but its presence is felt throughout every organization. Think of companies where you've worked, university classes you've attended, or other groups to which you've belonged. Consider the values and beliefs held by each of those groups. How did it feel to be a member of those groups? The groups you are thinking about are different in terms of their values and beliefs, aren't they? The same can be said of business organizations.

© Tony Avelar/Bloomberg/Getty Images

The inner-connectedness of CEO Steve Jobs' strategic vision and the value of the Apple brand itself has led some to question whether the company could maintain its competitive edge without him.

organizational culture

the set of values and beliefs that are shared throughout the firm

Increasingly, responsibility for effectively using the strategic management process is becoming more decentralized in companies. The logic behind this is to have the people who are "closest to the action" making decisions and taking actions.[41] Thus, the strategic management process is often shared among many people in an organization.[42] As a result, each of us should be prepared to take on leadership roles regardless of our position in an organization. Additionally, frequent communication among all involved with the process helps ensure that changes are made when and where they are needed.

However, we should understand that even though many different people may be involved, the final responsibility for effective use of the strategic management process rests with the firm's top-level strategic leaders (i.e., the CEO and the top management team). In addition, it is important to note that the best strategic leaders as well as all others throughout the firm act ethically.

Ethics are concerned with the standards for deciding what is good or bad, right or wrong[43] as defined by most members of a particular society.[44] In an organizational context, ethics reveal a value system that has been widely adopted by the firm's employees[45] and that other stakeholders recognize as an important driver of decisions and actions. Firms can record their ethics in documents such as a code of conduct. On a daily basis, however, ethics can be inferred by observing the actions of the firm's stakeholders, especially its employees.[46] Even a brief review of events in the business world shows that an organization's ethics are of interest to the general society as well as to other stakeholders whose interests can be negatively affected when a firm acts unethically. Thus, as explored further in Chapter 2, ethical practices are a vital part of effective strategic leadership and strategic management.

How the Book is Organized

The book has three major parts corresponding to the three parts of the strategic management process. Two chapters form Part 1 of this book. We introduced you to the strategic management process in Chapter 1. Using a strategic perspective, we follow this with a description of strategic leadership in Chapter 2. Strategic leadership is being effectively practiced when everyone in a firm is aware of its vision and the important role each person plays in pursuing it. We also describe the most important actions strategic leaders take to guide their organizations. Being an effective strategic leader (especially an effective CEO) is challenging. And the fact that CEO turnover remains high suggests that stakeholders have high-performance expectations of the person serving as the firm's CEO.[47]

In Part 2, which also has two chapters, we focus on two analyses firms use to gather and evaluate the information needed to choose strategies for pursuing the firm's vision. Chapter 3 focuses on the external environment. A firm analyzes the external environment to identify factors outside the company that can affect the strategic actions the firm is taking to achieve its vision. Firms can influence but not directly control conditions in their external environment. The focus of Chapter 4 is inside the firm. Here, the purpose is to understand how the firm's unique resources, capabilities, core competencies, and distinctive competencies can be used to create value for customers. Using resources, capabilities, core competencies and any distinctive core competencies the firm may possess in ways that create value means that the firm has one or more competitive advantages.

Part 3 examines different types of strategies. The strategies the firm chooses are a product of the vision and the conditions in the firm's external environment and its internal organization. The insights gained from the topics presented in the book's first four chapters strongly guide the selection of strategies. In Chapters 5, 6, and 7, our concern is with different strategies (business-level, multiproduct, and mergers and acquisitions, respectively) that firms use to successfully compete in different markets. Each chapter also provides guidelines for implementing different strategies. We follow these discussions with explanations in Chapters 8, 9, and 10 of strategies (international, cooperative alliances, and new ventures) that firms use to enter new markets.

SUMMARY

Our primary purpose with this chapter is to introduce the strategic management process and to discuss how firms use this important organizational tool to create value and continuously improve their performance for stakeholders as a result of doing so. To reach this purpose, we examined the following topics:

- **Strategic management** is the ongoing process firms use to form a vision, analyze their external environment and internal organization, and select one or more strategies to create value for customers and satisfy stakeholders. Strategic management is concerned with both formulation (selection of one or more strategies) and implementation (actions taken to ensure that the chosen strategies are used as intended).
- Firms use the industrial organization model (the I/O model) to examine their **external environment** in order to identify opportunities and threats in that environment. Firms use the resource-based view of the firm model (the RBV model) to analyze their **internal organization** in order to identify their resources, capabilities, core competencies, distinctive competencies, and competitive advantages. A firm must use both models to have the knowledge it needs to choose strategies that will enable it to achieve its vision.

- **Stakeholders** are individuals and groups who have an interest in how the firm performs and who can influence the firm's actions. Firms and their stakeholders are dependent on each other. Firms must operate in ways that satisfy the needs of each stakeholder (such as shareholders, customers, suppliers, and employees). Firms failing to satisfy stakeholders' needs will likely lose their support. Owners, external stakeholders, and internal stakeholders are the three primary stakeholder groups with which firms are involved. But stakeholders need firms as well. Consider, for example, that investors (as owners of the firm) want to invest in profitable firms, employees want to work for acceptable wages and have opportunities to advance their careers, and customers want to buy products that create value for them.
- **Strategic leaders** practice strategic leadership when they make certain that their firm is effectively using the strategic management process. Increasingly, effective strategic management results when many people are involved with the strategic management process and when strategic leaders demand that everyone in the firm act responsibly and ethically in all that they do.

KEY TERMS

Capabilities, 5
Competitive advantage, 5
Core competencies, 5
Distinctive competencies, 5
External environment, 5
Internal organization, 5

Mission, 5
Opportunities, 9
Organizational culture, 17
Resources, 5
Stakeholders, 14
Strategic leaders, 16

Strategic management, 4
Strategy, 4
Strategy implementation, 8
Strengths, 5
Threats, 9
Vision, 4

DISCUSSION QUESTIONS

1. What is strategic management? Describe strategic management's importance to today's organizations.
2. What is the industrial organization (I/O) model? Why do firms use it to analyze their external environment?
3. What is the resource-based view (RBV) of the firm model? Why do firms use this model to examine their internal organization?
4. Who are stakeholders? Why are stakeholders important to firms? What does it mean to say that the firm has relationships with its stakeholders?
5. What is the nature of the strategic leader's work?

STRATEGY TOOLBOX

Introduction

A major problem facing strategic leaders is maintaining focus within a firm given the dynamic and complex nature of today's competitive environment. Effective strategic leaders use the strategic management process (which we define in this chapter) to increase the probability that their firm will properly conduct an external analysis and an internal analysis—two core activities that are the foundation for selecting the company's strategy.

© Jan Paul Schrage, iStock

Strategic Management Steps

External Analysis
- Examine the trends in the Macro Environment (including customers)
- Profile the Industry (including competitors)
- **Outcomes:**
  - Document and prioritize "Threats"
  - Document and prioritize "Opportunities"

Internal Analysis
- Inventory the company's resources
- Assess the company's capabilities
- **Outcomes:**
  - Document and link "Strengths" and "Weaknesses" to opportunities
  - Identify "Core Competencies"
  - Identify current and potential "Distinctive Competencies"

Strategy
- Establish the "Mission"
- Communicate the "Vision"
- Roll out the "Strategies"
- **Outcomes:**
  - Successful implementation
  - Decision-making alignment
  - Motivated employees

Earth Fare: "Providing the Best Tasting Local, Natural, and Organic Foods Available"

Desiring to inspire the healthy person in each of us and discouraged by the amount of processed foods being sold through traditional grocery stores, Roger Derrough established Dinner for the Earth in 1975. Supporting the decision to open his business was Derrough's belief that a sufficient number of people in a particular geographic location shared his food-related dissatisfactions and related interests to purchase healthier foods and that, as such, he was taking advantage of an opportunity that he identified in the external environment.

Located in Asheville, North Carolina, the initial storefront for Derrough's natural foods' business was only 1,200 square feet. In 1993, the firm's name was changed to Earth Fare to reflect its intention of pushing both natural and organic foods "…to the forefront of the American culinary experience."

Desiring to generate loyalty among its customers and committed to forming a community with them, this business grows slowly by design. It was 1995 before the firm opened its second store (in Charleston, South Carolina). Still interested in using its resources and capabilities to pursue orderly rather than rapid growth, Earth Fare operated only 19 stores in mid-2010. With an average size of roughly 24,000 square feet and with its largest store being only 28,000 square feet, Earth Fare's stores are not large; still, the company is one of the largest natural and organic food retailers in the United States.

Earth Fare is interested in changing the way people think about and then purchase food. The company believes that in combination, what it stocks in inventory and how it operates makes healthy eating convenient, affordable, fun and delicious. Let's learn more about what Earth Fare carries in its inventory and how it operates.

With respect to inventory, Earth Fare does not stock any items with "…high fructose corn syrup, trans fats, artificial colors, synthetic growth hormones (in the meat and milk), preservatives, antibiotics, synthetic growth hormones, bleached or bromated flours and irradiated spices, and unnatural sweeteners." But, unlike some smaller local competitors in the markets they serve, Earth Fare uses

its resources and capabilities to form and operate a full-service grocery store. In this sense, Earth Fare offers just about all products one finds in a traditional supermarket. The difference is that each Earth Fare product is all natural. Close interaction with local farmers to buy their locally grown organic products is a way Earth Fare seeks to differentiate itself from competitors.

Although successful, Earth Fare does face competitors such as Whole Foods, a firm that is similarly committed to offering only natural and organic products. (You will learn more about Whole Foods in Chapter 5's *Understanding Strategy: Learning from Success*.) And, there is Walmart which, as we noted earlier in this chapter, is using its Heritage America program to support its commitment to offer organic food items. How does Earth Fare measure against these competitors? Seemingly quite well at this stage. In describing why he prefers Earth Fare to Whole Foods, one customer said that "they [Earth Fare] make a greater effort to carry local and organic produce and meats, their prices are generally lower, and many of the products are better." A large number of natural and organic food shoppers reaching the same conclusion would indeed be very positive for Earth Fare. In terms of Walmart, one has to wonder if the giant food retailer can develop the type of "sense of community" among customers shopping for natural and organic foods that exits among Earth Fare shoppers. Thus, it seems that Earth Fare may be favorably positioned relative to these two competitors.

Sources: T. Adams, 2010, "Earth Fare opens today," *Ledger-enquirer.com*, http://www.ledger-enquirer.com, June 23; D. Auerbach, 2010, "Earth Fare challenging Whole Foods," *Independent Weekly Online*, http://www.indyweek.com, June 10; 2010, "About our company," Earth Fare Home Page, http://www.earthfare.com, July 28; 2010, "Earth Fare Inc.," *Hoovers Company Profiles*, http://www.hoovers.com, July 23; 2010, "Earth Fare: The healthy supermarket," *careerbuilder.com*, http://www.careerbuilder.com, July 23; 2010, "Earth Fare aims to eliminate childhood obesity with launch of Itty Bitty Bites," *PR Newswire*, http://www.prnewswire.com, March 17.

Questions

1. Using materials available to you, including Earth Fare's Web site (http://www.earthfare.com) and the Internet, learn as much as you can about Earth Fare's organizational culture. (Remember that organizational culture is the set of values and believes that are shared throughout the

firm.) Describe Earth Fare's culture with as much detail as you can. Do you think Earth Fare's culture may be a source of competitive advantage? If so, why and how?

2. Using Earth Fare's Web site and the Internet, learn as much as you can about the firm's future plans. Do you find evidence that Earth Fare will continue growing by opening additional units? If so, where might those units be established and why? If you determine that the firm may continue growing, what challenges do you believe Earth Fare might face as a result?

3. The industrial organization (I/O) model and the resource-based view of the firm model are introduced in this chapter. Find evidence in the case showing that Earth Fare is influenced by its external environment. Additionally, find evidence in the case suggesting, if not proving, that the firm may have distinctive competencies that serve as a competitive advantage. If you find them, what are the firm's distinctive competencies?

EXPERIENTIAL EXERCISES

Exercise One: The Culture, Vision, and Strategy Linkage

A firm's vision and mission statements should be aligned with its organizational culture. Together, these statements give employees direction in any situation by providing them with values and purpose that set key priorities and orient action.

In Small Groups

In a small group, determine what your group thinks is the culture for each of the following companies. Then link that culture to your view of the firm's vision and mission as you understand it. How does your concept of the firm's culture, vision, and mission fit with what you understand about its strategy, which is the basis for its success?

- Target
- Mary Kay Cosmetics
- UPS
- Starbucks

Whole Class

Groups should then compare their answers to the question that was answered in small groups. The purpose of this activity is to highlight differences as well as similarities in the small groups' answers. Finally, go to each firm's Web site and find its vision and mission statements (both statements may not be available to you for each firm). How well do the statements align with the culture and strategy you identified?

Exercise Two: Gathering and Assessing External and Internal Information

The industrial organization, or I/O, model discussed in the chapter focuses on the firm's external environment and helps identify opportunities and threats. In contrast, the resource-based view focuses on the internal organization and helps firms identify strengths and weaknesses. Your instructor will assign one of the following firms to you. For that firm, find one aspect of the external environment that has been an opportunity or threat and one aspect of the internal organization that has been a strength or a weakness. Use sources such as *Bloomberg BusinessWeek, Fast Company, Forbes, Fortune, The Wall Street Journal,* and others suggested by your instructor.

- Amazon
- Boeing
- Nike
- US Airways
- Walmart

ENDNOTES

1. S. Bretting, 2008, "Helicopter school fills a niche need," *The Houston Chronicle Online,* http://www.chron.com, February 15.
2. 2010, Mission Expert, http://www.missionexpert.com, July 10.
3. S. Kantabutra & G. C. Avery, 2010, "The power of vision: Statements that resonate," *Journal of Business Strategy,* 31(1): 37–45.
4. 2010, Intoweb, http://www.intoweb.co.za, July 2.
5. 2010, General Motors vision statement, http://www.samples-help.org, July 2.
6. E. Holmes, 2010, "U.S. apparel retailers map an expansion to the North," *The Wall Street Journal Online,* http://www.wsj.com, March 29.
7. 2010, Best Buy Co. Inc., *Standard & Poor's Industry Report,* http://www.standardandpoors.com, July 17.
8. S. E. A. Dixon, K. E. Meyer, & M. Day, 2010, "Stages of organizational transformation in transition economies: A dynamic capabilities approach," *Journal of Management Studies,* 47: 416–436; D. J. Teece, 2007, "Explicating dynamic capabilities: The nature and microfoundations of (sustainable) enterprise performance," *Strategic Management Journal,* 28: 1319–1350.
9. J. Greene, 2010, "How LEGO revived its brand," *BloombergBusinessweek Online,* http://www.businessweek.com, July 23.
10. R. B. Tucker, 2008, "Innovation: Core competence for the 21st century," *The Innovation Resource,* http://www.innovationresource.com, February 15.
11. 2010, "Our company," Lenovo Home Page, http://www.lenovo.com, July 20.
12. 2010, Starbucks Coffee Company, http://www.starbucks.com, July 9.
13. D. Bardsley, 2010, "Starbucks brews up a new line for China," *The National,* http://www.thenational.com, March 11; A. Lomax, 2010, "Starbucks eyes China," *The Motley Fool,* http://www.fool,com, April 15.
14. M. Sanchanta, 2010, "Starbucks plans major China expansion," *The Wall Street Journal Online,* http://www.wsj.com, April 13.
15. Ibid.
16. 2010, "Whole bean coffee," *Starbucks Home Page,* http://www.starbucks.com, July 22.
17. D. G. Sirmon, M. A. Hitt, R. D. Ireland, & B. A. Gilbert, 2011, "Managing resources to create competitive advantage: Breadth, life cycle, and depth effects," *Journal of Management,* in press.
18. 2010, 1-800-PetsMed.com, http://www.petsmed.com, July 8.
19. A. D'Innocenzio, 2010, "Target takes Manhattan with East Harlem store," *The Houston Chronicle Online,* http://www.chron.com, July 23.
20. N. Shirouzu, 2010, "Daimler, BYD plan electric car for China," *The Wall Street Journal Online,* http://www.wsj.com, April 24.
21. S. Rodriguez & V. Vaughan, 2010, "It's a tale of two market segments," *The Houston Chronicle Online,* http://www.chron.com, July 23.
22. G. A. Fowler & J. A. Trachtenberg, 2010, "Amazon says e-book sales outpace hardcovers," *The Wall Street Journal Online,* http://www.wsj.com, July 20.
23. A. Smith, 2010, "United and Continental to merge," *CNNMoney.com,* http://www.money.cnn.com, May 3.
24. S. Carey, 2010, "UAL-Continental merger moves ahead," *The Wall Street Journal Online,* http://www.wsj.com, July 28.
25. J. G. Combs, D. J. Ketchen, Jr., R. D. Ireland, & J. W. Webb, 2010, "The role of resource flexibility in leveraging strategic resources," *Journal of Management Studies,* in press; E. T. Penrose, 1959, *The Theory of the Growth of the Firm,* New York: Wiley.
26. C. Matlack, R. Tiplady, D. Brady, R. Berner, & H. Tashiro, 2004, "The Vuitton machine," *BusinessWeek,* March 22: 98–102.
27. R. Garvare & P. Johansson, 2010, "Management for sustainability—A stakeholder theory," *Total Quality Management & Business Excellence,* 21: 737–744; K. Basu and G. Palazzo, 2008, "Corporate social responsibility: A process model of sensemaking," *Academy of Management Review,* 33: 122–136.
28. F. J. Greene, A. Burke, & S. Fraser, 2010, "The multiple effects of business planning on new venture performance," *Journal of Management Studies,* 47: 391–415; W. C. Kim & R. Mauborgne, 2009, "How strategy shapes structure," *Harvard Business Review,* 87(9): 72–80.
29. A. P. Cowan & J. J. Marcel, 2011, "Damaged goods: The board's decision to dismiss reputationally compromised directors," *Academy of Management Journal,* in press; A. King, 2007, "Cooperation between corporations and environmental groups: A transaction cost perspective," *Academy of Management Review,* 32: 889–900.
30. G. Hamel, "Moon shots for management," 2009, *Harvard Business Review,* 87(2). 91–98; J. L. Campbell, 2007, "Why would corporations behave in socially responsible ways? An institutional theory of corporate social responsibility," *Academy of Management Review,* 32: 946–967.
31. A. Ignatius, "We had to own the mistakes: An interview with Howard Schultz," *Harvard Business Review Online,* http://www.hbr.org, July 12; P. F. Drucker, 2004, "What makes an effective executive," *Harvard Business Review,* 82(6): 58–63.
32. J. Hudson, 2010, "The iPad's quid pro quo marketing strategy," *The Atlantic Wire Online,* http://www.theatlanticwire.com, April 2; N. Wingfield, 2008, "Apple is transparent in bid to broaden iPhone's reach," *The Wall Street Journal Online,* http://www.wsj.com, March 1.
33. C. Meyer & J. Kirby, 2010, "The big idea: Leadership in the age of transparency," *Harvard Business Review Online,* http://www.hbr.org, April.
34. L. Story, 2007, "Seeking leaders, U.S. companies think globally," *The New York Times Online,* http://www.nytimes.com, December 12.
35. T. I. Tsai, 2010, "Acer predicts world no. 1 status," *The Wall Street Journal Online,* http://www.wsj.com, June 18.
36. B. Einhorn & T. Culpan, 2010, "Acer: Past Dell, and chasing HP," *BloombergBusinessWeek Online,* http://www.businessweek.com, February 24.
37. J. E. Coombs, D. L. Deeds, & R. D. Ireland, 2009, "Placing the choice between exploration and exploitation in context: A study of geography and new product development," *Strategic Entrepreneurship Journal,* 3: 261–279; D. G. Sirmon, M. A. Hitt, & R. D. Ireland, 2007, "Managing resources in dynamic environments to create value: Looking inside the black box," *Academy of Management Review,* 32: 273–292.
38. F. Yuan & R. W. Woodman, 2010, "Innovative behavior in the workplace: The role of performance and image outcome expectations," *Academy of Management Journal,* 53: 323–342.
39. 2010, "About 3M", 3M, http://www.3m.com, July 23.
40. J. O' Toole & W. Bennis, 2009, "What's needed next: A culture of candor," *Harvard Business Review Online,* http://www.hbr.org, June.
41. R. Makadok & R. Coff, 2009, "Both market and hierarchy: An incentive-system theory of hybrid governance forms," *Academy of Management Review,* 34: 297–319; A. T. Hall, M. G. Bowen, G. R. Ferris, M. T. Royle, & D. E. Fitzgibbons, 2007, "The accountability lens: A new way to view management issues," *Business Horizons,* 50: 405–413.
42. L. Hrebiniak, 2008, "Making strategy work: Overcoming the obstacles to effective execution," *Ivey Business Journal Online,* http://www.iveybusinessjournal.com, March/April.
43. R. Trudel & J. Cotte, 2009, "Does it pay to be good?" *MIT Sloan Management Review,* 50(2): 61–68; B. W. Heineman, Jr., 2007, "Avoiding integrity land mines," *Harvard Business Review,* 85(4): 100–108.
44. E. R. Pedersen, 2010, "Modelling CSR: How managers understand the responsibilities of business towards society," *Journal of Business Ethics,* 91(2): 155–166.
45. K. G. Jin & R. G. Drozdenko, 2010, "Relationships among perceived organizational core values, corporate social responsibility, ethics, and organizational performance outcomes: An empirical study of information technology professionals," *Journal of Business Ethics,* 92: 341–359; D. Pastoriza, M. A. Arino, & J. E. Ricart, 2008, "Ethical managerial behavior as an antecedent of organizational social capital," *Journal of Business Ethics,* 78: 329–341.
46. M. J. Neubert, D. S. Carlson, K. M. Kacmar, J. A. Roberts, & L. B. Chonko, 2009, "The virtuous influence of ethical leadership behavior: Evidence from the field," *Journal of Business Ethics,* 90: 157–170; M. A. Hitt & J. D. Collins, 2007, "Business ethics, strategic decision making, and firm performance," *Business Horizons,* 50: 353–357; M. A. Hitt, R. D. Ireland, & G. W. Rowe, 2005, "Strategic leadership: Strategy, resources, ethics and succession," in J. Doh & S. Stumpf (eds.), *Handbook on Responsible Leadership and Governance in Global Business,* New York: Edward Elgar Publishers.
47. 2010, "CEO turnover rate," *The Economist Online,* http://www.economist.com, May 20.

CHAPTER 2
Leading Strategically

© Robert Daly, OJO Images/Getty Images

KNOWLEDGE OBJECTIVES

Reading and studying this chapter should enable you to:

1. Define and explain strategic leadership.

2. Explain how vision and mission create value.

3. Define the meaning of a top management team and the value of having a heterogeneous top management team.

4. Explain the importance of managerial succession.

5. Define human capital and social capital and describe their value to the firm.

6. Describe an entrepreneurial culture and its contribution to a firm.

7. Explain the importance of managerial integrity and ethical behavior.

8. Discuss why firms should have a control system that balances the use of strategic controls and financial controls.

Changes in Corporate Governance Have Reformed the Role of the CEO in Strategic Leadership

The role of the chief executive officer (CEO), especially in the United States, has been changing due to increased scrutiny by boards of directors and corporate governance trends in general. One of the most visible changes has been the separation of the CEO role from that of the chairperson of the board of directors. Historically, many CEOs resisted sharing power by insisting on holding both roles simultaneously. One analyst noted: "Ten years ago, 80 percent of S&P 500 company CEOs were also the chairmen of their boards. Since then, the percentage of boards that combine the chairman and CEO roles has steadily declined, to 74 percent in 2004, and 63 percent in 2009." Furthermore, the chairperson being independent of the board has created a situation in which "the age of the imperial CEO" is declining. Where the roles are separate, boards often have separate planning meetings in which board members might examine important strategy or executive succession issues. Additionally, in many boards, members are more likely to engage investors in concerns around executive pay and takeover defenses. Much of the unease regarding corporate governance has been due to the enactment of the Sarbanes-Oxley Act of 2002, which was a response to the accounting scandals of Enron and WorldCom in 2001.

© AP Photo/Carlos Osorio, File

However, because of the separation of the board chairperson and CEO roles, questions arise as to how these roles should be carried out in regard to important strategic issues. The basic question is, "Who has the power to formulate strategy?" Interestingly, U.S. executives have been looking to Great Britain, which forced major public companies to divorce the two roles in 1992 during a period of corporate governance reform. As such, the board chairperson in large British companies usually comes from outside company ranks. Increasingly, the boards of U.S. firms have likewise been naming former CEOs with no affiliation to the focal company to fill the chairperson role.

Critics, however, have warned that this new breed of chairpersons may be tempted to get involved in management issues that are reserved for the actual CEO, creating confusion for shareholders as to who is actually in charge. Under the new board reforms, the board will have an outside director who is not part of the firm's employment structure historically. Accordingly, 96 percent of the boards of Standard & Poor's 500 companies had a lead or presiding director by 2008. Although this person is not necessarily the board chair, he/she can hold independent meetings without executives from the board and can consult with other outsider directors regarding issues that pertain to strategy and management succession without political influence from the current CEO. As such, these new changes and other changes associated with the Sarbanes-Oxley Act of 2002 mean more power sharing in important issues related to strategy of the overall firm.

Examples of companies that have recently divided the two roles and have hired a strong external chairperson of the board are Walt Disney Company, Ford, and Marsh & McLennan among many others. Some of these companies sought to reassure stockholders, after a scandal or bad corporate report, that they would pursue better corporate governance procedures. These changes in corporate governance have led to a decrease in the CEO's power and an increase in power sharing among board members and the CEO in regard to overall strategic responsibilities and direction of the company. Thus, the CEO is not only accountable to shareholders, but also more accountable to a chairperson or a lead outside director who can consult with an increasing number of independent outside directors on boards regarding important strategic issues.

Power sharing has also occurred because firms have more diffuse supply chains as well as numerous and often complex strategic alliances or joint ventures with numerous partner firms. As such, strategic leaders find that they must manage with more employee involvement as well as more involvement from the managers of these complex partnering arrangements. In essence, this situation requires less top-down strategic leadership and more power sharing and joint decision making with middle managers, strategic partners, and supplier and customer firms in regard to important strategic decisions.

In summary, strategic leadership is more diffuse because of corporate governance as well as other strategic partnering arrangements that are necessary to manage a large firm both domestically and globally. Consequently, strategy becomes more of a dynamic process that involves continual evaluation rather than a set solution to establish long-term sustainable competitive advantage. Thus, strategy has become a process of continual creation and re-creation rather than a stable set of characteristics that differentiate the company from its competitors.

Sources: J. H. Daum, 2010, Spencer Stuart board index: How boards are changing, *Bloomberg BusinessWeek*, http://www.businessweek.com, March 16; R. Duchin, J. Matsusaka, and O. Ozbas, 2010, When are outside directors effective?, *Journal of Financial Economics*, 96: 196–214; M. McDonald and J. Westphal, 2010, A little help here? Board control, CEO identification with the corporate elite and strategic help provided to CEOs at other firms, *Academy of Management Journal*, 53: 343–370; R. Walkling, 2010, CEO-centric firms: Risks and remedies, *Directors and Boards*, 34(2): 17–18; I. Filatotchev and B. Boyd, 2009, Taking stock of corporate governance research while looking to the future, *Corporate Governance: An International Review*, 17(3): 257–265; R. Iyengar and E. Zampelli, 2009, Self-selection, endogeneity, and the relationship between CEO duality and firm performance, *Strategic Management Journal*, 30: 1092–1112; K. Kim, H. Al-Shammari, B. Kim, and S. Lee, 2009, CEO duality leadership and corporate diversification behavior, *Journal of Business Research*, 62: 1172–1180; J. J. Penber, 2009, What lead directors do, *MIT Sloan Management Review*, 50(4): 15–17; J. S. Lublin, 2008, When chairman and CEO roles get a divorce, *The Wall Street Journal*, January 14, B1; C. A. Montgomery, 2008, Putting leadership back into strategy, *Harvard Business Review*, 86(1): 54–60.

Strategic leadership involves developing a vision for the firm, designing strategic actions to achieve this vision, and empowering others to carry out those strategic actions. As defined in Chapter 1, *strategic leaders* are the individuals practicing strategic leadership. Strategic leaders hold upper-level organizational positions. As *Focusing on Strategy* indicated, today's strategic leaders are involving people throughout the firm as well as other governance participants (board of director members and other stakeholders [suppliers and customers]) in strategic management. Thus, any person in the firm (and outside) responsible for designing strategic actions and ensuring that they are carried out in ways that move the firm toward achievement of the vision is essentially playing the role of a strategic leader.

It goes without saying that strategic leadership is important, but this is actually confirmed by a substantial amount of research.[1] In this chapter, we examine important strategic leadership actions: establishing the firm's vision and mission, developing a management team and planning for succession, managing the resource portfolio, building and supporting an entrepreneurial culture, promoting integrity and ethical behavior, and using effective organizational controls. These strategic leadership actions are displayed in Figure 2.1. To illustrate the overall strategic leadership process, we examine the leadership of CEO John Chambers at Cisco, a global Internet manufacturing, software, and service company. Chambers has moved Cisco from a $1.2 billion Internet equipment manufacturer focused on routers and switches to a $36.1 billion diversified networking company, focused

strategic leadership

developing a vision for the firm, designing strategic actions to achieve this vision, and empowering others to carry out those strategic actions

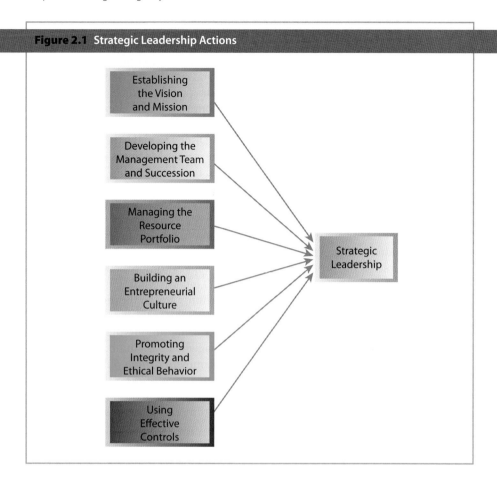

Figure 2.1 Strategic Leadership Actions

- Establishing the Vision and Mission
- Developing the Management Team and Succession
- Managing the Resource Portfolio
- Building an Entrepreneurial Culture
- Promoting Integrity and Ethical Behavior
- Using Effective Controls

→ Strategic Leadership

not only on manufacturing but also on software that runs the Internet at all levels. In the early stages of Cisco's history, Chambers' leadership style was oriented to "command and control" and was very centralized. However, this management structure was changed to deal with both globalization and diversification across different businesses, as Chambers and Cisco executed growth through mergers and acquisitions, alliances, and direct entry. Today Cisco runs seamlessly through councils and operating committees. The management structure is not dependent upon one person. As the Internet moved from focusing on e-mail and file transfer to playing video and instant video and collaboration, new business models were required. Cisco has a leadership structure that allows it to manage the variety of cultures that will be needed across its businesses, not only in developed economies but also in emerging ones such as China, India, and Brazil, as well as across its diverse hardware and software businesses.[2] We begin with a discussion of how vision and mission are used to direct the firm's future.

Establishing the Vision and Mission

Most strategic plans are designed for a three- to five-year time period, but a vision is usually targeted for a longer time, generally 10 to 20 years. As explained in Chapter 1, the *vision* contains at least two components—a statement describing the firm's DNA and the "picture" of the firm as it hopes to exist in a future time period. The second part of the vision is *mission,* which defines the firm's core intent and the business or businesses in which it intends to operate. The mission flows from the vision and compared to the vision is more concrete in nature.

Visions can differ greatly across firms depending on the strategic leaders' intentions. For example, Steve Jobs, CEO of Apple, continues to develop visions of new products and markets. He developed not only Apple, but also Pixar—an extremely successful animation company that teamed with Disney to make the movie *Finding Nemo.* He created the Mac revolution with the Apple Macintosh computer; reshaped the music industry with Apple's iPod and the iTunes online music venture; and more recently introduced the iPhone, Apple TV, and now the iPad. These new products are part of Jobs's vision to dramatically change the computer, music, cell phone, and media industries. However, his vision has recently been extended to include all of the application firms that develop media and software for these networked products. Interestingly, because these software and media applications work on multiple Apple product platforms, an application producer "can write a single version of their app and reach roughly 100 million Apple customers."[3] This capability helps dramatically increase the opportunity for application producers.

Other firms have simpler visions even though they still may be difficult to achieve. For example, some firms may envision being among the most admired firms for their performance and effective management. A number of organizations now rank firms on a regular basis. For example, *Fortune* publishes a list of the world's most admired companies based on an annual survey; the top 20 firms for 2008, 2009, and 2010 are shown in Table 2.1. Although *Fortune*'s ranking includes only U.S. firms, the ranks change over time as some firms' strategies fall out of favor or strategic leaders make errors of strategic judgment. For example, Dell has been having a hard time relative to competitors such as Hewlett-Packard (HP). Similarly, Walmart's reputation has declined as it finds itself on the negative side of much media attention. On the other hand, Apple's reputation has ascended and remained strong, most likely due to strong strategic leadership.

An effective strategic leader not only can develop a vision of the future, but also can inspire stakeholders to commit to achieving it. It is especially important for the leader to gain the support of the company's shareholders and employees. If the shareholders do not support the vision, they may pressure the board of directors to change it or find new strategic leaders. Similarly, employee commitment to the vision is needed because they must help implement the strategy designed to achieve the vision. Consider the case of Volkswagen. In 2007, CEO Martin Winterkorn of Volkswagen Group unfurled a new vision. He pronounced boldly that Volkswagen would strive to be the number one automobile maker within a decade in worldwide unit sales, profits, quality, and image. As such, Volkswagen would have to overtake Toyota and not just be Europe's largest automaker. Volkswagen Group's 42 percent acquisition of Porsche AG and the eventual merging of the two companies in 2011 is the most recent move toward realizing this aspect of its vision. The one piece remaining to realize this vision is a significant North American strategy. It has made a $1 billion investment in an assembly plant in Chattanooga, Tennessee, and has set a goal of selling one million vehicles in the United States by 2018, which is more than triple the number that it sold in 2008. It will be interesting to see if the vision statement of Volkswagen can be realized by 2018.[4] As we mentioned earlier, and as exemplified by Volkswagen, strategic leaders often use their team of managers as well as others in the firm to help make major decisions, especially to define and implement a vision for the firm. This team also helps formulate the firm's strategy. Next, we examine the teams of managers that strategic leaders use in the decision process.

Table 2.1 *Fortune's* Most Admired Companies Ranking

2010	2009	2008
1. Apple	1. Apple	1. Apple
2. Google	2. Berkshire Hathaway	2. Berkshire Hathaway
3. Berkshire Hathaway	3. Toyota	3. General Electric
4. Johnson & Johnson	4. Google	4. Google
5. Amazon.com	5. Johnson & Johnson	5. Toyota
6. Procter & Gamble	6. Procter & Gamble	6. Starbucks
7. Toyota	7. FedEx	7. FedEx
8. Goldman Sachs Group	8. Southwest Airlines	8. Procter & Gamble
9. Walmart Stores	9. General Electric	9. Johnson & Johnson
10. Coca-Cola	10. Microsoft	10. Goldman Sachs Group
11. Microsoft	11. Walmart Stores	11. Target
12. Southwest Airlines	12. Coca-Cola	12. Southwest Airlines
13. FedEx	13. Walt Disney	13. American Express
14. McDonald's	14. Wells Fargo	14. BMW
15. IBM	15. Goldman Sachs Group	14. Costco Wholesale
16. General Electric	16. McDonald's	16. Microsoft
17. 3M	17. IBM	17. United Parcel Service
18. J. P. Morgan Chase	18. 3M	18. Cisco Systems
19. Walt Disney	19. Target	19. 3M
20. Cisco Systems	20. J. P. Morgan Chase	20. Nordstrom

Sources: A. Bernasek, 2010, The world's most admired companies, *Fortune*, March 22, 121; G. Colvin, 2009, The world's most admired companies, *Fortune*, March 16, 75; A. Fisher, 2008, America's most admired companies, *Fortune*, March 17, 65.

Developing the Top Management Team and Succession

Top Management Team

Because of the complexity of their roles, most strategic leaders form teams to help them complete their work. A **top management team** is the group of managers charged with the responsibility of developing and implementing the firm's strategies. Generally, the top management team is composed of officers of the company with the title of vice president and higher.[5]

Typically, when people select individuals for a team to work with, they prefer to choose people who think like them and are more likely to agree with them. Although such a team can facilitate making fast decisions (because members of the team more easily agree), these teams are more prone to making mistakes. A team of people with similar backgrounds (a *homogeneous team*) may achieve a quick consensus about issues but may lack sufficient knowledge and information needed to make an effective decision. Additionally, because they "think alike," they may overlook important issues and make errors in judgment. Therefore, to be most effective, strategic leaders need a management team composed of members who see and think differently. The team members may have different types of education (such as engineering, chemistry, and business) or varying amounts and types of experience (working in different functional areas, companies, or industries). We refer to this type of group as a *heterogeneous team*. A heterogeneous

top management team

the group of managers charged with the responsibility of developing and implementing the firm's strategies team is likely to take more time to make decisions but also likely to make better decisions. However, such teams may hinder strategic expansion if they have problems relating socially to one another.[6]

Historically, Nissan included only Japanese employees in its management teams. However, in 2000, it was nearly bankrupt at the time Carlos Ghosn took over as CEO. Ghosn was born in Brazil, raised in Lebanon, and attended school in Paris, France. As such, he had a broad understanding of global issues and was able to help Nissan recover dramatically. He also was promoted to be the CEO of Renault, which has a joint venture with Nissan. Part of Ghosn's success at Nissan was due to the diversity of the management team that he brought in to help revive the company. Although Nissan subsequently stumbled, it has had recent successes with the subcompact Versa. Also, the fully-electric Leaf came out ahead of schedule in December 2010. He recently has developed a partnership with Daimler (the conglomerate that owns Mercedes Benz) "to pool costs on small cars, engines, commercial vehicles and electric cars."[7] Even though he is seen as a "visionary" for the industry, he won't succeed as a one-person team. So he needs to continue to develop his top management team.

Management Succession

In addition to forming the management team, strategic leaders must develop people who can succeed them. In fact, having people with skills to take over a job when needed is important to a firm's success. Some companies use sophisticated leadership screening systems to select people with the skills needed to perform well as a strategic leader.[8] The people selected then normally participate in an intensive management development program to further hone their leadership skills. The "ten-step talent management" development program at General Electric (GE) is considered one of the most effective programs for developing strategic leaders. Because of the quality of its programs, GE "is famous for developing leaders who are dedicated to turning imaginative ideas into leading products and services."[9]

Obviously, a change in CEO is a critical succession event in firms. The effects of CEO succession can be different based on whether the new CEO is from inside or outside the firm. The majority of CEO successions are from the inside, with a person groomed for the position by the former CEO or the board of directors. Often chief operating officers (COOs) are chosen to succeed the CEO, especially in firms where operations (say, versus marketing) are crucial.[10] "Hiring from the inside" motivates employees because they believe that they have opportunities to receive promotions and more challenging jobs if they perform well. A recent inside CEO succession was announced at Procter & Gamble (P&G). The transition from A. G. Lafley to Robert McDonald as CEO of P&G was a smooth one because the company had implemented a long-term system of evaluation and planning for the internal transition to the position. P&G has a long-term plan for all executives, not just for the CEO position.[11] However, when Ken Lewis stepped down as CEO of Bank of America, declaring it was "time to begin a transition to the next generation of leadership,"[12] there were several problems. First, there was no direct candidate for succession identified, although Lewis as the CEO should have been seeking to execute such a transition and prepare for it in a transparent manner. Most new CEOs selected for the job in an inside succession are unlikely to change in any drastic way the strategies designed under the leadership of the former CEO.[13] However, when the firm is performing poorly, it is more common to select an outside successor.

When new CEOs are chosen from outside the organization, the board often does so with the desire to change the firm's strategies. A change in strategies may be desired because the firm is performing poorly or because opportunities and threats in the competitive landscape require adjustments to avoid poor performance in the future.[14] For example, Lou Gerstner helped to provide significant change at IBM when he was recruited from a consumer goods firm to become the CEO. Gerstner transformed IBM into a successful performer again with a major change in its strategy.[15] Under Gerstner, IBM moved from a strategy based on selling separate pieces of hardware to a strategy calling for the firm to emphasize its service solutions and consulting services. Interestingly, however, recent research has found that although outsiders may facilitate change over time, after three years inside successors outperform outside CEO successors.[16] So, CEO succession needs to be accomplished with great care.

With a long-term system in place to effectively manage the succession of top executives, the replacement of P&G CEO A. G. Lafley with Robert McDonald was executed without any significant disruptive effects on the organization.

At times, it is more difficult to determine whether a succession is from the inside or the outside. For example, in 2008, John Donahoe was selected to be the new CEO of eBay to replace Meg Whitman who planned to retire. Donahoe was recruited in 2005 to become the president of eBay's main auction business unit. He was a managing partner of Bain Consulting Company and thus came to eBay as an outsider. However, he is considered an insider given that he has been managing the core auction business for several years. Thus, it is hard to tell at times whether a successor is an insider or an outsider.[17] Interestingly, research shows that companies perform significantly better when they appoint insiders to the job of CEO. However, this research also suggests that many companies do not have succession plans; as such, when it comes time to find a new CEO, many firms turn to outsiders.

Of course as already noted, both insiders and outsiders have strengths and weaknesses depending on the conditions of the firm. Nonetheless, by utilizing a strong succession plan and developing a strong set of training programs for managers, firms can develop internal candidates who have a strong outside perspective. These executives in training can spend much of their time away from the main operations of the organization, that is, away from headquarters and working with new businesses that are different from the dominant business. They can be appointed CEOs of these business units and thus have the opportunity to manage the whole business. They can also be mentored to preserve their outside perspective and learn how to turn their new ideas into successful businesses that are protected from the dominant culture in the organization. Ultimately, they can be CEOs who have an understanding of the inside approach to management, but also have the ability to transform the dominant organization in new ways should this be required.[18]

As discussed next, managing the firm's resource portfolio is another critical component of strategic leadership.

Managing the Resource Portfolio

Resources are the basis of a firm's competitive advantages and strategies (see Chapter 4). Even though we often think of tangible resources such as buildings, manufacturing plants, offices, machinery, and computers as being important,

UNDERSTANDING STRATEGY
LEARNING FROM FAILURE

Trying to Make Yahoo! Competitive Again

Yahoo!, a Web portal focused on Internet search, content, and e-mail, has experienced significant declines in its stock price relative to competitors like Google. Yahoo!, under Jerry Yang, the founder and former CEO, sought a merger with Microsoft to compete against Google in 2008. This turned into a failed takeover attempt by Microsoft, which left Yahoo! in a vulnerable position. When Carol Bartz took over as CEO in 2009, Microsoft was no longer interested in an acquisition. However, Bartz worked out a partnership with Microsoft after arriving at Yahoo!. The partnership was aimed at challenging Google by combining Microsoft's Bing search engine with Yahoo!'s Web site portal. The Microsoft deal has allowed Yahoo! to potentially increase operating margins (due to reduced costs) while focusing on services other than search.

Can the integration of Microsoft's Bing search engine into its Web site and a strategy focused on acquiring new content keep Yahoo! competitive against the likes of Google and Facebook?

Bartz has focused the company's resources on making acquisitions in content. The company found that it did not have the resources to compete with Google in search, as mentioned above, and has combined with Microsoft's Bing (a search engine) to manage and defend its advertising revenues in this area. However, Yahoo!'s positioning in the content area has several problems. First, there are other competitors focusing on this sector including AOL and a number of powerful Web sites such as *The Wall Street Journal, The New York Times, USA Today,* and many cable companies such as MSNBC and CNN. Second, Bartz's competitive background is not in content. Formerly, she was the CEO of Autodesk, a producer of sophisticated design and engineering software such as AutoCAD. Third, large Internet sites such as Google and Yahoo! are no longer as strong as they once were, as many people are moving their center of focus to other Internet tools, especially social network sites such as Facebook and Twitter. Accordingly, much ad revenue

is moving to these sites from Web portals such as Google and Yahoo!. Consequently, the role of Web portals is shrinking as users move to these social network sites.

Although Yahoo! has substantial financial capital (cash on hand), investors are looking at how Yahoo! is using its resources in a competitive way and buying and selling their shares according to the strategic issues and how the strategic leaders are using those resources given the challenges the firm faces. Bartz was able to cut expenses by getting rid of some businesses and becoming more focused. Furthermore, the Yahoo! homepage has many new entry points of services, which they were building up through sites such as Yahoo! Finance and the Flickr Photo Site. They also have been allowing users more access to other company sites such as Facebook and Twitter from their main Web portal page. To counter this, Bartz is using the resources of the firm by focusing on improved positioning and is building its Web page counts. Although Yahoo! still has a significant presence on the Internet through the number of people who come to its Web site, Bartz was "dealt a bad hand of cards" and the company is facing a stiff challenge in maintaining competitiveness with its rivals. It remains to be seen whether her strategic changes will be enough to allow Yahoo! to remain competitive.

Sources: *BusinessWeek*, 2010, Yahoo! CEO Carol Bartz rates her first year a B-, http://www.businessweek.com, January 8; J. Menn, 2010, Yahoo faces battle to keep up with its sleeker rivals, *Financial Times*, January 25, 16; J. Menn and N. Tait, 2010, Microsoft alliance with Yahoo is approved, *Financial Times*, February 19, 13; M. Peers, 2010, For Yahoo, a chase to the bottom, *The Wall Street Journal*, May 27, C12; J. E. Vascellaro, 2010, Corporate news: Yahoo earnings rebound but sales slip, *The Wall Street Journal*, January 27, B2; S. Sanberg, C. Bartz, and J. Jackson, 2009, My work/life philosophy, *Fortune*, September 28, 115.

© Justin Sullivan/Getty Images

© kimeveruss, iStock

intangible resources may be more important. Indeed, recent estimates suggest that as much as 75 percent of a firm's value may be contained in its intangible resources.[19] Intangible resources include human capital, social capital, and organizational capital (such as the organizational culture). Additionally, financial capital is a critically important resource. These aspects of managing resources are illustrated in the *Learning from Failure* example on Yahoo!.

Intellectual property can be an especially valuable intangible resource in high-technology companies. For example, TiVo, a company that popularized digital video recorders (DVRs), lost much of its value when more generic DVRs were produced and undercut its success. However, because TiVo was a first mover in this market of 20 million users, the Patent and Trademark Office recognizes TiVo's patent on "time-warp" technology, which allows users to record one program while watching another. Because TiVo sees itself as a technology company, it has been creating partnerships and licenses with firms such as NBC Universal and cable companies such as Comcast and Cox that pay a premium to download TiVo's software on their generic DVRs. Previously, where others had been copying its technology, TiVo filed lawsuits in order to protect its intellectual property. For instance it filed a suit against EchoStar Communications, a satellite television producer, and has pending suits against Verizon and AT&T, cable producers with their own DVRs.[20] TiVo continues to move from a focus on hardware to an increased emphasis on software and processing advertising data as part of its strategy to facilitate advertising media expenditures through DVR systems. Additionally, it is seeking to help the television industry move to a media-on-demand strategy that will allow content delivery directly to people's television sets and to their PCs. However, TiVo is struggling with its business model as many firms are seeking to include variations of its technology in their products. Also local network router producers such as Cisco's Linksys are considering making DVR capabilities part of their local household networks as equipment computing power increases.[21]

A firm's intellectual property—such as Tivo's—is developed by its human capital. **Human capital** includes the knowledge and skills of those working for the firm. Employees' knowledge and skills are critical for all organizations. According to Ed Breen, CEO of Tyco International, "Companies compete with their brains as well as their brawn. Organizations today must not only outgun and outhustle competitors, they must also outthink them. Companies win with ideas."[22] To outthink competitors, a firm must depend on the knowledge of its workforce (managers and nonmanagerial employees) and continuously invest in developing their knowledge and skills. Such organizations are focused on learning. Knowledge can be acquired in training programs or through experience on the job. Learning from failure is a quality that leaders will experience repeatedly. The difference between some people and others is that some "fail better than others." In other words, it is not whether you fail but how you fail and what you learn from it that really matters.[23] It is the strategic leader's responsibility to help the firm learn faster and persevere better than others when mistakes are made.

Effective strategic leaders base their strategies on the organization's human capital.[24] Research suggests that creative CEO leadership also helps to develop social and human capital, which fosters the firm's internal knowledge development. The focus on operational leadership leads to exploitation, and existing growth paths may be less helpful in producing new product and market domains for the firm. They do so because the human capital in the organization must have the skills and motivation needed to implement chosen strategies. As such, leaders must help develop skills throughout the firm's workforce, motivate employees to use their skills when working to implement strategies, and reward them for doing so.[25]

human capital

includes the knowledge and skills of those working for the firm

Another important resource is social capital. **Social capital** includes all internal and external relationships that help the firm provide value to customers and ultimately to its other stakeholders. *Internal social capital* refers to the relationships among people working inside the firm. These relationships help each organizational unit effectively complete its work while contributing to the overall value of the firm's human capital. W. L. Gore & Associates illustrates well-developed internal social capital by emphasizing nonhierarchical leadership and teamwork effectiveness. They have an advanced collaborative leadership system where the associates are not constrained by the chain of command and where teamwork is continually evolving between leaders and followers. "Gore's lattice organizational structure allows them to interact directly with other associates that they need to in order to best accomplish the work."[26]

External social capital refers to relationships between those working within a firm and others (individuals and organizations) outside the firm. Such relationships are essential because they provide access to needed resources. Few firms have all of the resources they need. Furthermore, most firms cannot do everything well. It may be better to outsource some activities to partner companies who can perform those activities exceptionally well, thereby increasing the quality of the focal firm's ability to produce products. External social capital can also help firms enter new markets. New companies may seek the financial support and expertise of venture capitalists, whereas more established companies often develop alliances with reliable suppliers or joint ventures with highly competent partners. In a sense, strategic leaders serve as key points of effective linkages for their firm in a network of relationships with other organizations. Some relationships involve strong ties where trust exists between the parties and reciprocity is expected, whereas other relationships represent weaker ties that serve more informational roles and allow strategic leaders to stay on top of the latest developments—even outside their industry—that may affect their firm (such as technology developments). So both strong and weak ties are important in strategic leaders' networks.[27]

The most effective exchange of social capital occurs when partners trust each other (strong ties). Effective strategic leaders have well-developed relational skills that help them establish trusting relationships with others inside and outside the organization. Andrea Jung, CEO of Avon Products, suggests that compassion is one of the key characteristics of effective leaders. As such, she believes that leaders should treat people fairly, with dignity and respect. In so doing, leaders are leading with their heart as well as their head.[28] One analyst suggests that leaders of today, such as Jung, need "the essential qualities of what we now call a Cross-Enterprise Leader—a leader adept at building, fostering, and influencing a complex web of relationships across all levels—from employees, partners, and suppliers to customers, citizens, and even competitors."[29]

Other resources such as financial capital are also important. In fact, firms with strong human capital and social capital are more likely to build a good base of financial capital.[30] Some also believe that an organization's culture can be a valuable resource. We discuss that topic next.

Building an Entrepreneurial Culture

Strategic leaders are concerned about the organization's culture because it can have major effects on employees' actions. An organizational culture is based on the core values of an organization that are largely espoused by its leaders. When these values support opportunities to innovate, an entrepreneurial culture may

social capital

includes all internal and external relationships that help the firm provide value to customers and ultimately to its other stakeholders

General Mills Creates Wealth with a Focus on Healthier Products

In 2007, Kendall Powell replaced Steve Sanger as the CEO at General Mills. Powell has had a 28-year career at General Mills. As such, his promotion is seen as an inside succession since his appointment is part of the company's long-time succession plan.

Under Powell's leadership, not only has General Mills had many product line extensions and innovative food products, but it has done so in an efficient way. A key component of General Mills' success lies in its "holistic margin management" implemented largely by CEO Powell. It is an initiative that cuts costs not only via the traditional supply-chain route, but focuses on permeating "every aspect of the company, from marketing to payroll administration." Interestingly, at General Mills this is not just a cost-cutting approach, but Powell has noted that it has been the key that has "enabled us to invest in brands. We have been able to do more marketing initiatives on the Internet so we can reach more consumers. And we've had very strong investment in R&D, which resulted in a string of really good products." For example, examine Nature Valley Granola Bars. "Somebody figures out how to seal these bars with no waste on either end. Then we can put the bar in a slightly smaller box. Now we can fit more cases on a pallet in a truck, and all of a sudden there are these very significant logistics savings."

Probably one of the biggest changes has been its success in pursuing healthier product lines. Susan Crockett, who runs the company's Bell Institute of Health and Nutrition, an internal group of scientists who study and conduct health research, has been pushing the company to pursue healthier products. In this effort, the division heads, as well as Powell, have found that they had to compensate managers for meeting more healthy product goals. The consumer trend in the food industry is toward healthier packaged food products. Also, Kellogg's, Kraft Foods, Campbell Soup Company, and Sara Lee have all been pushed by regulators and consumer advocates to increase nutrition in their products.

Many food companies such as General Mills are focusing on producing low-salt food lines. For instance, General Mills produces Progresso brand soups. This line has a long-term salt reduction strategy that has been developed in incremental steps so that the consumer will be more aware of the reduction strategy over time. Sodium levels in Honey Nut

Cheerios have been cut by 16 percent, while they've been reduced by 36 percent in Chex Snack Mix. Additionally, the company has focused not only on salt, but also on cutting fat and sugar while adding vitamins, whole grain, and fiber. Under its Fiber One brand, General Mills recently introduced the 90 Calorie Chewy Bar that contains five grams of fiber and 2.5 grams of fat. The Institute of Medicine recommends that Americans over the age of four eat at least 25g of fat each day. The Fiber One 90 Calorie Chewy Bar allows a person to achieve 20 percent of the recommended daily fiber requirement in one snack.

With a holistic focus on margin management, General Mills has found new ways to cut costs while at the same time investing more in the R&D necessary to introduce new products targeting increasingly health-conscious shoppers and launching its major brands in emerging markets across the globe.

They also focused on marketing their innovations through advertising to multicultural groups, for example, to Hispanics on networks such as Univision and Telemundo. Similar advertisements have been put on the Web for multicultural consumers who are the fastest-growing consumer group. Additionally, they have entered emerging economies successfully. For instance, in China they started their Häagen-Dazs ice cream business in the coastal cities and are now pressing inland to larger cities that are starting to develop a strong middle class. They are also doing well in China with Bugles and Fruit Roll-Ups snacks under the Trix brand.

Although it experienced some failures with its innovative approach, 34 percent of its products now meet its new standards for healthier products. Overall, the company reformulated more than 200 products and introduced at least 100 new ones. Even more important, significant firm sales growth and profits have come from these new lines.

Sources: A. Cordeiro and N. Becker, 2010, Corporate News: General Mills' earnings climb 15%, *The Wall Street Journal*, March 25, B4; *Entertainment News Weekly*, 2010, General Mills: Cheerios partners with Martina McBride and Cal Ripken, June 18, 63; M. Goodman, 2010, Snack Attack, *Brand Week*, April 26, 16; M. Hughlett, 2010, General Mills leads by its slim margins: CEO Ken Powell talks about the food giant's success with savings through 'holistic margin management,' and where he sees growth opportunities, *McClatchy-Tribune Business News*, http://www.mctdirect.com, March 30; M. Hughlett, 2010, General Mills to cut salt levels in many foods, *McClatchy-Tribune Business News*, http://www.mctdirect.com, April 14; T. Rivas, 2010, Waking up to General Mills, *Barron's*, April 26, 24–25; B. White-Sax, 2010, Manufacturers milk cereal sales with nutritional boosts, *Drug Store News*, March 1, 51.

© BOB FILA/KRT/Newscom

© Greg Epperson, iStock

develop. An **entrepreneurial culture** encourages employees to identify and exploit new opportunities. It encourages creativity and risk taking but also tolerates failure. Championing innovation is rewarded in this type of culture.[31] Building an entrepreneurial culture is of particular importance to strategic leaders.

Because of the pressure to be innovative yet profitable, many leaders try to focus their firm's innovation to increase the chances of success. For example, as explained in *Understanding Strategy: Learning from Success*, General Mills recently focused on innovative activities designed to provide foods that are healthier and products that meet government agency health standards.[32] As this example illustrates, such an approach has improved its new product growth rates and profitability.

Innovation is important in high-technology industries such as computers and in creative industries such as music and film animation. Steve Jobs is an appropriate strategic leader for Apple with his emphasis on creativity and innovation. However, 3M operates in several different industries with lower technology, such as adhesives (i.e., Scotch tape), traffic signs, and sandpaper. Yet the firm has been a pioneer, being the first to introduce products in its markets such as the Post-it note. Therefore, an entrepreneurial culture is important in both firms.

The preceding discussions suggest the importance of innovation and strategic leadership. Even though the type and focus of innovation may vary, it is important in nearly all industries. As a result, building an entrepreneurial culture is a vital task for strategic leaders. Strategic leaders also must demonstrate ethical behavior. Next, we discuss the importance of integrity and ethical behavior for strategic leaders.

Promoting Integrity and Ethical Behavior

Strategic leaders not only develop standards for behavior among employees, but also serve as role models in meeting and exceeding those standards. Even though quality of performance is an important criterion, showing integrity and behaving ethically are also essential. So strategic leaders should determine the boundaries of acceptable behavior; establish the tone for organizational actions; and ensure that ethical behaviors are expected, praised, and rewarded. Lack of integrity and unethical behavior can be serious and extremely costly for a firm and for the person lacking integrity and behaving unethically. In fact, recent research shows that firms that do not uphold ethical standards have less productivity.[33] Of course, extraordinary unethical behavior can even lead to a firm's demise; Enron and Arthur Andersen are well-known examples.

Recently, cases in which strategic leaders acted opportunistically in managing their firms have been a major concern. In the recent financial crises spawning the recession, managers have been blamed for acting opportunistically, meaning that managers are making decisions that are in their own best interests rather than in the investors'.

Because of opportunistic behavior in a number of companies, significant emphasis has been placed on how firms govern themselves (*corporate governance*). Corporate governance begins with the board of directors, whose members are responsible for overseeing managerial activities and approving (or disapproving) managerial decisions and actions. As illustrated in the opening *Focusing on Strategy*, the outcry from shareholders and the public in general has placed pressure on board members to be more diligent in examining managerial behavior. Legislation (such as Sarbanes-Oxley) passed in the United States requires greater managerial responsibility for the firm's activities and outcomes. Institutional

entrepreneurial culture

encourages employees to identify and exploit new opportunities owners in particular have pressured boards to enact better governance practices. For example, they generally want more independent outsiders than inside officers on the board. They believe that independent outside board members will be more objective and are less likely to agree with the CEO if he/she takes actions that appear not to be in the firm's best interests. In this way, managers' opportunistic actions can be curtailed.[34]

One form of potential opportunism, **related-party transactions,** involves paying a person who has a relationship with the firm extra money for reasons other than his or her normal activities on the firm's behalf. For example, Apple CEO Steve Jobs was reimbursed $1.2 million for costs he incurred while using his personal jet on company business. Two directors for Ford Motor Company, William Clay Ford and Edsel Ford, receive hundreds of thousands of dollars in consulting fees in addition to their compensation for serving as directors. Many of these transactions are legitimate, but some can be for questionable purposes as well. The Securities and Exchange Commission has started to carefully scrutinize related-party deals because of the opportunity for unethical behavior. Related-party deals were curtailed in the United States by Sarbanes-Oxley. Interestingly, research has found that the market devalues firms that use related-party transactions relative to those who are less likely to do so.[35]

Often worse than opportunistic actions by managers are fraudulent and other unlawful activities in which managers and companies' representatives engage. As an example, Bernard Madoff misappropriated $65 billion of investors' funds in a "Ponzi scheme" where he would take in investors' funds fraudulently and redeem some to attract other investors while keeping most of the money for personal use. He, along with some close colleagues, created phantom investments to report to the Securities & Exchange Commission to avoid detection of their devious behavior. Ultimately, Madoff traded his "pin stripes for prison stripes" as he is now in federal prison for fraud.[36]

Only leaders who demonstrate integrity and values respected by all constituents of the company will be able to sustain effective outcomes over time. Those who engage in unethical or unlawful activities may go unrecognized or undetected for a time, but eventually they will fail. People working under the leader often demonstrate the same values in their actions that are evident in the leader's behavior. Thus, if the leader engages in unethical activities, the followers are likely to do the same. As a consequence, the leader will suffer from the poor performance that results from his/her own and others' unethical behaviors. However, when the leader displays integrity and strong positive ethical values, the firm's performance will be enhanced over time because the followers will do the same.[37] Opportunism and unethical activities evident in several companies in recent times clearly show the importance of having effective control systems, which are discussed next.

© AP Photo/Frank Franklin II

Public cynicism toward the business community is only one of many negative outcomes from cases of fraud and opportunism such as that perpetrated by Bernard Madoff.

Using Effective Controls

Controls are necessary to ensure that standards are met and that employees do not misuse the firm's resources. Control failures are evident in such dismal outcomes as exemplified by the bankruptcies of Bear Stearns, Lehman Brothers,

related-party transactions

paying a person who has a relationship with the firm extra money for reasons other than his or her normal activities on the firm's behalf

Enron, and Tyco. Unfortunately, in these cases, the strategic leaders with responsibility for implementing the controls violated them, and the weak governance in both firms was unable to identify and correct the problems until they became excessive and external entities expressed concern about them. However, the potential value of controls goes beyond preventing fraud and managerial opportunism. Properly formed and used controls guide managerial decisions, including strategic decisions. Effective strategic leaders ensure that their firms create and use both financial controls and strategic controls as guides in the strategic management process.

Financial controls focus on shorter-term financial outcomes. These controls help the firm stay on the right path in terms of generating sales revenue, maintaining expenses within reason, and remaining financially solvent. Of course, a prime reason for financial controls is to generate an adequate profit. However, if financial controls are overly emphasized to increase current profits, managers are likely to limit their expenditures more than is necessary. Too many expense reductions in certain categories (such as R&D) can damage the firm's ability to perform successfully in the future. Money spent on R&D helps the firm develop products that customers will want to buy.[38]

Alternatively, **strategic controls** focus on the content of strategic actions rather than on their outcomes. Strategic controls are best employed under conditions of uncertainty. For example, a firm may employ the correct strategy, but the financial results may be poor because of a recession or unexpected natural disasters or political actions (such as the global financial crisis experienced in 2008). To use strategic controls, the strategic leader or board must have a good understanding of the industry and markets in which the firm or its units operate in order to evaluate the accuracy of the strategy. Using strategic controls encourages managers to adopt longer-term strategies and to take acceptable risks while maintaining the firm's profitability in the current time period.[39] Firms without good strategic controls often have significant growth stalls. For example, Dell and Starbucks recently brought back their former CEOs Michael Dell and Howard Schultz, respectively, to reverse problems of slow growth and execution.

Michael Dell returned in 2007 and has made 10 acquisitions and cut 10,000 jobs as well as hiring other management team executives from Motorola and Nike to improve the company's growth prospects. Dell bought Perot Systems for $3.6 billion in 2009, to expand its growth opportunities in services. HP and IBM have pursued this same computing services strategy. However, in the same period, these latter firms' stocks have increased 11 percent while Dell's stock has fallen 42 percent since 2007. To overcome the problem, Michael Dell has recently considered taking the company private to get better strategic control of its operations. Its strategic positioning in services is not as strong as HP and IBM, and this hurts its stock price because this is a higher margin business in which Dell's competitors are better positioned. It also has not been able to position itself well in the tablet computer market, where Apple has continued to outperform. In the server market, Cisco is angling to get a piece of Dell's server business. Accordingly, much better strategic positioning through improved strategic control is required to perform effectively. These issues are determined by the strategic control system in place among the top managers and board of directors of the firm.[40]

The most effective system of controls is balanced using strategic *and* financial controls as illustrated. Controlling financial outcomes is important while simultaneously looking to the longer term and evaluating the content of the strategies used. To obtain the desired balance in control systems, many firms use a **balanced scorecard**,[41]

financial controls

focus on shorter-term financial outcomes

strategic controls

focus on the content of strategic actions rather than on their outcomes

balanced scorecard

provides a framework for evaluating the simultaneous use of financial and strategic controls which provides a framework for evaluating the simultaneous use of financial and strategic controls.

A balanced scorecard focuses on four areas—*financial* (profit, growth, and shareholder risk), *customers* (value received from the firm's products), *internal business processes* (asset utilization, inventory turnover), and *learning and growth* (a culture that supports innovation and change). In addition to helping implement a balanced control system, the balanced scorecard allows leaders to view the firm through the eyes of stakeholders such as shareholders, customers, and employees. The company's management system is the important link between strategy and operational execution. The company must necessarily begin with a strategic statement and then translate this statement into specific objectives and initiatives that serve as a guide for all employees, especially top management. The plan should map out operations and execution as well as the resources necessary to achieve the objectives. Through the control systems implemented, managers and employees monitor and learn from the strategy performance results and execution of the plan. Periodic assessment and updating of the strategic plan are necessary as emerging strategies show potential and necessitate adaptation and change. Thus, continuous strategic assessment and analysis are required to refine the vision and mission of the corporation that will guide the changes in strategy and execution.[42]

SUMMARY

The primary purpose of this chapter is to explain strategic leadership and emphasize its value to an organization. In doing so, we examined the following topics:

- **Strategic leadership** involves developing a vision for the firm, designing strategic actions to achieve this vision, and empowering others to carry out these strategic actions. Establishing the firm's vision (and mission), developing a management team and planning for succession, managing the resource portfolio, building and supporting an entrepreneurial culture, promoting integrity and ethical behavior, and using effective organizational controls are the actions of strategic leadership.

- Strategic leaders, those practicing strategic leadership, develop a firm's vision and mission. The vision contains at least two components—a statement describing the firm's DNA and the "picture" of the firm as it hopes to exist in the future. The mission of the firm focuses on the markets it serves and the goods and services it provides and defines the firm's core intent and the business or businesses in which it intends to operate.

- A **top management team** is the group of managers responsible for developing and implementing the firm's strategies. A heterogeneous team usually develops more effective strategies than a homogeneous team because it holds a greater diversity of knowledge, considers more issues, and evaluates more alternatives. Managerial succession is important for the maintenance of the firm's health. Individuals should be developed and prepared to undertake managerial roles throughout the firm's hierarchy.

- **Human capital** includes the knowledge and skills of those working for the firm. Employees' knowledge and skills are an important resource to all organizations. Another important resource is social capital. **Social capital** includes all internal and external relationships that help the organization provide value to customers and ultimately to its other stakeholders. Strategic leaders must help develop the skills within the firm's workforce, motivate employees to use those skills to implement strategies, and reward them when they successfully use their skills.

- Strategic leaders shape an organization's culture. In the current competitive environment, all firms need to be innovative to remain competitive. Therefore, building an entrepreneurial culture is of particular importance to strategic leaders. An **entrepreneurial culture** encourages employees to identify and exploit new opportunities. It encourages creativity and risk taking and tolerates failures that result from these activities.

● Strategic leaders develop standards of behavior among employees and serve as role models for meeting those standards. Integrity and ethical behavior are essential in today's business environment. Lack of integrity and unethical behavior can be serious and highly costly—to the firm and to individuals lacking integrity and behaving unethically. Ethical strategic leaders guard against managerial opportunism and fraudulent actions.

● Effective controls guide managerial decisions, including strategic decisions. **Financial controls** focus on shorter-term financial outcomes, whereas **strategic controls** focus on the content of the strategic actions rather than on their outcomes. An effective control system balances the use of financial controls and strategic controls. The **balanced scorecard** approach is a useful technique that can help balance these two types of control.

KEY TERMS

Balanced scorecard, 38
Entrepreneurial culture, 36
Financial controls, 38

Human capital, 33
Related-party transactions, 37
Social capital, 34

Strategic controls, 38
Strategic leadership, 26
Top management team, 29

DISCUSSION QUESTIONS

1. What is strategic leadership? Describe the major actions involved in strategic leadership.
2. How do a vision and a mission create value for a company?
3. What is a top management team? Why does a heterogeneous top management team usually formulate more effective strategies?
4. Why is it important to develop managers for succession to other managerial jobs?

5. What do the terms *human capital* and *social capital* mean? What is the importance of human capital and social capital to a firm?
6. How can a strategic leader foster an entrepreneurial culture, and why is such a culture valuable to a firm?
7. Why are managerial integrity and ethical behavior important to a firm?
8. Why should strategic leaders develop a control system that balances strategic controls and financial controls?

STRATEGY TOOLBOX

Introduction

Strategic management is the study of how business leaders take their organizations to new heights. A key player in this process is the Chief Executive Officer (CEO). Chapter 2 provides the foundation for the strategic analysis the CEO must perform. With that in mind, we offer for the Strategy Toolbox a "CEO Strategy Checklist" for completion of this awesome responsibility.

"CEO Strategy Checklist"

Key Question	Assessment
Develop—Do we have a strategy that leads to differentiation or low cost position in the marketplace?	Low – Medium – High
Understand—Could our employees articulate our mission and vision?	Low – Medium – High
Accept—Do our employees believe in our organizational strategy?	Low – Medium – High
Implement—Are our employees making decisions consistent with our strategies?	Low – Medium – High
Modify—Do we have adequate feedback mechanisms to track progress?	Low – Medium – High

MINI-CASE

Strategic Leadership Made the Difference at Priceline.com

Priceline.com, an auction and travel discounter focused on a name-your-own-price travel service, started in the dot-com boom, but in 2001, four years after its founding, it was near bankruptcy. It had tried to diversify into other online businesses besides travel such as name-your-own-price groceries and gasoline. However, this had caused it to burn through cash at an increasing rate, and Wall Street was in no mood to provide additional funding. Interestingly, in April 1999 during the boom, the stock price had reached a split-adjusted high of $974 per share. However, by October 2002 it had fallen to a mere $7 per share, when management sought a reverse one-for-six split. By 2010, however, Priceline had recovered and jumped 27 times its low to $185. If you had invested $10,000 in Priceline in March 2005, your stock value would have been $101,000 five years later.

After the September 11, 2001, terrorist attacks, the entire travel industry experienced a significant downturn, and the business models of many online travel brokers like Priceline were in doubt. Jeffrey H. Boyd became the CEO of Priceline in 2002 and sought to change Priceline's fortune. Instead of continuing its focus on airline tickets, Boyd sought to rebuild the brand around hotel bookings and expand into Europe. Although many airlines were spiraling toward bankruptcy (United Air and U.S. Air both sought protection in the bankruptcy courts), the lodging and hotel business was not as bleak. Priceline cultivated stronger relationships with important brands such as Marriott and Starwood and gained control of TravelWeb, a joint venture owned by major hotel chains. This increased Priceline's access to over 10,000 hotels. Priceline also lowered the fee that it received from hotels for facilitating bookings relative to other travel agents/brokers.

At the same time, Priceline sought to have William Shatner become the company spokesman. He had been a spokesman on their radio ads, but now they were moving into television ads. The ad campaign changed to focus on the "negotiator" ads. The character seems to do almost anything to get a bargain, and that has apparently resonated with the consumer.

Additionally, Boyd began focusing more on Europe through both new investment and acquisitions. For example, in 2004 Priceline purchased Britain's Active Hotels, an online discount booking agency, and a year later purchased Booking.com, a Netherlands' based booking agent. Big hotel chains were not as dominant in Europe, creating

© Alija, iStock

few larger pricing blocks and hence competitive openings for smaller travel agents. Priceline gave the smaller hotels an opportunity for broader coverage in the market at a cheaper price than other booking agents.

In 2007, Boyd sought to carry out a similar strategy in Asia as accomplished in Europe and purchased Agoda.com, a Bangkok-based online travel company specializing in discount hotel bookings across Asia and Australia, the Middle East, and Africa. By 2009, 61 percent of Priceline's revenue came from international bookings in Europe and Asia, which far exceeded Expedia and Orbitz, its dominant online competitors.

Interestingly, its revenues shot up in 2008 as the economy began its downturn; because of the recession and due to its discount approach, demand actually increased for Priceline. Further expansion opportunities may be found in South America and the Middle East; however, the downturn in Europe, given the government debt crises, may present some financial turmoil for Priceline. However, "Priceline's revenues are expected to grow 20 percent in 2010, compared with 11 percent at Expedia and 4 percent at Orbitz." Thus, the future appears quite bright for Priceline even in poor economic times.

Sources: A. R. Elliott, 2010, Did Priceline's slide overstate Euro's impact?, *Investor's Business Daily*, June 17, B03; E. Levy and R. Farzad, 2010, How Priceline became No. 1 on the Bloomberg BusinessWeek 50, *Bloomberg BusinessWeek*, June 21–June 27, 57–58; S. Morrison, 2010, Priceline shifts model in Asia, *The Wall Street Journal*, March 24, B6; C. Rose, 2010, Charlie Rose talks to William Shatner, *Bloomberg Business-Week*, June 21–27, 59; C. Anderson, 2009, Setting prices on Priceline, *Interfaces*, 39(4): 307–315; D. Fisher, 2009, Cheap seats, *Forbes*, August 24, 102–103; T. Wang, E. Gal-Or, and R. Chatterjee, 2009, The name-your-own-price channel in the travel industry: An analytical exploration, *Management Science*, 55(6): 968–979; G. Zuckerman, 2009, Priceline's differences appeal, *The Wall Street Journal*, April 20, C6.

Questions

1. What did Jeffrey H. Boyd, CEO of Priceline, and his management team do to turn around the business to make it profitable after the downturn in 2001?
2. What aspects of strategic leadership found in this chapter are emphasized in the mini-case on Priceline.com?
3. If you were the CEO of Priceline, what challenges would you need to overcome in the future given the knowledge you have gained through studying the concepts in this chapter?

EXPERIENTIAL EXERCISES

Exercise One: Building an Entrepreneurial Culture

In this chapter we discussed one of the important strategic leadership actions, building an entrepreneurial culture. An entrepreneurial culture encourages the identification and exploitation of new opportunities, encourages creativity and risk taking, and tolerates failures.

In Small Groups

Each group should choose one of the following five firms. These firms were identified in a recent issue of *Fast Company* as the top five of the 50 most innovative companies in the world. Your group should investigate what the firm does to build an entrepreneurial culture.

- Google
- Apple
- Facebook
- General Electric
- Ideo

Answer the following questions:

1. Does the firm do what was suggested in the chapter? For example, does it encourage risk taking? Does it tolerate failures?
2. What are some examples of how the firm encourages employees to identify or exploit new opportunities? How does the firm encourage risk taking?
3. Does the firm have some other ways of building an entrepreneurial culture that are not discussed in the chapter?

Whole Class

The groups should then compare answers to the questions. What are the similarities and differences in how these innovative companies build an entrepreneurial culture?

© vndrpttn, iStock

Exercise Two: Codes of Ethics

Many types of organizations try to define expectations and deal with the behavior of their leaders, employees, agents, and perhaps even business partners by establishing codes of ethics. The content of codes can vary greatly and is often linked to the mission of the organization. Explore http://

www.e-businessethics.com, especially the Ethics Links. Be prepared to discuss the prevalence and importance of ethics dialogues across various business, government, and professional organizations.

ENDNOTES

1. V. Souitaris & B. Maestro, 2010, Polycronicity in top management teams: The impact on strategic decision processes and performance of new technology ventures, *Strategic Management Journal*, 31: 652–678; R. Osborne and R. Marion, 2009, Contextual leadership, transformational leadership and the performance of international innovation seeking alliances, *Leadership Quarterly*, 20(2): 191–206; J. Uyoo, R. Reed, S. Shin, & D. Lemak, 2009, Strategic choice and performance in late movers: Influence of the top management team's external ties, *Journal of Management Studies*, 46(2): 308–335.

2. 2010, Market transactions wait for no one, *Business Today*, May 2, 88–91.

3. P. Burrows, 2010, Apple's endlessly expanding universe, *Bloomberg BusinessWeek*, April 26–May 2, 92–99.

4. J. Stein, 2009, VW's global push gains credibility, *Automotive News*, August 17, 8.

5. Y. Ling & F. Kellermanns, 2010, The effects of family firm specific sources of TMT diversity: The moderating role of information exchange frequency, *Journal of Management Studies*, 47(2): 322–344; A. M. L. Raes, U. Glunk, M. G. Heijltjes, & R. A. Roe, 2007, Top management team and middle managers, *Small Group Research*, 38: 360–386.

6. S. Nielsen, 2009, Why do top management teams look the way they do? A multilevel exploration of the antecedents of TMT heterogeneity, *Strategic Organization*, 7(3): 277–305.

7. R. Milne & J. Reed, 2010, Ghosn sees use of scale as crucial to success, *Financial Times*, June 2, 17.

8. A. Karaevli, 2007, Performance consequences of new CEO "outsiderness": Moderating effects of pre- and post-succession contexts, *Strategic Management Journal*, 28: 681–706; W. Shen & A. Cannella, 2002, Revisiting the performance consequences of CEO succession: The impacts of successor type, post succession, senior executive turnover, and departing CEO tenure, *Academy of Management Journal*, 45: 717–734.

9. D. Ulrich & N. Smallwood, 2007, Building a leadership brand, *Harvard Business Review*, 85(7/8): 93–100.

10. J. J. Marcel, 2009, Why top management team characteristics matter when employing a chief operating officer: A strategic contingency perspective, *Strategic Management Journal*, 30(6): 647–658.

11. J. Reingold, 2009, The $79 billion handoff, *Fortune*, December 7, 80.

12. A. Dutra & J. Griesedieck, 2010, Succession success, *Leadership Excellence*, 27(5): 14.

13. W. Shen & A. A. Cannella, 2003, Will succession planning increase shareholder wealth? Evidence from investor reactions to relay CEO successions, *Strategic Management Journal*, 24: 191–198.

14. L. Greiner, T. Cummings, & A. Bhambri, 2002, When new CEOs succeed and fail: 4-D theory of strategic transformation, *Organizational Dynamics*, 32: 1–16.

15. T. Foremski, 2004, Motorola's new boss aims for Zander-du, *Financial Times*, http://www.ft.com, May 9.

16. Y. Zhang & N. Rajagopalan, 2010, Once an outsider always an outsider? CEO origin, strategic change and firm performance, *Strategic Management Journal*, 31(3): 334–346.

17. C. Holahan, 2008, eBay's new tough love CEO; John Donahoe will concentrate on winning back users, even at investors' expense, *BusinessWeek*, February 4, 58.

18. J. L. Bower, 2007, Solve the succession crisis by growing inside-outside leaders, *Harvard Business Review*, 85(11): 90–96.

19. G. Kristandl & N. Bontis, 2007, Constructing a definition for intangibles using the resource-based view of the firm, *Management Decision*, 45(9): 1510–1524; M. Reitzig, 2004, Strategic management of intellectual property, *MIT Sloan Management Review*, 45(3): 35–40.

20. R. Cheng, 2010, Corporate news: TiVo claims dismissed—patent office ruling hands Dish, Echostar a rare victory, *The Wall Street Journal*, June 9, B7.

21. L. Gomes, 2010, The end of the TiVo era, *Forbes*, April 26, 36.

22. B. Breen, 2004, Hidden asset, *Fast Company*, March, 93.

23. S. Brown, 2008, Learning from failure, *Director*, February, 31; S. Finklestein, 2003, *Why Smart Executives Fail: And What You Can Learn from Their Mistakes*, New York: Penguin Group.

24. M. Makri & T. Scandura, 2010, Exploring the effects of creative CEO leadership on innovation in high-technology firms, *Leadership Quarterly*, 21(1): 75–88; B. A. Ready and J. A. Conger, 2007, Make your company a talent factory, *Harvard Business Review*, 85(6): 68–77.

25. J. Champ, 2003, The hidden qualities of great leaders, *Fast Company*, November, 139.

26. C. Manz, F. Shipper, & G. Stewart, 2009, Everyone a team leader: Shared influence at W. L. Gore & Associates, *Organizational Dynamics*, 38(3): 239–244.

27. D. W. Yiu & C. M. Lau, 2007, Corporate entrepreneurship as resource capital configuration in emerging market firms, *Entrepreneurship Theory and Practice*, 32(1): 37–57; J. Nahapiet & S. Ghoshal, 1998, Social capital, intellectual capital and the organizational advantage, *Academy of Management Review*, 23: 242–266; R. D. Ireland, M. A. Hitt, & D. Vaidyanath, 2002, Alliance management as a source of competitive advantage, *Journal of Management*, 28: 413–446.

28. A. Jung, 2004, You will stand on our shoulders (keynote address at the WWIB Conference), Knowledge @ Wharton, http://knowledge.wharton.upenn.edu, November 5.

29. C. Stephenson, 2008, Dorothy Gale: A compassionate leader, *Financial Times*, January 28, 5.

30. Yiu & Lau, Corporate entrepreneurship as resource capital configuration in emerging market firms; R. A. Baron & G. D. Markman, 2003, Beyond social capital: The role of entrepreneurs' social competence in their financial success, *Journal of Business Venturing*, 18: 41–60.

31. S. D. Anthony, N. W. Johnson, & J. B. Sinfield, 2008, Institutionalizing innovation, *MIT Sloan Management Review*, 49(2): 45–50; R. D. Ireland, M. A. Hitt, & D. Sirmon, A model of strategic entrepreneurship: The construct and its dimensions, *Journal of Management*, 29: 963–989.

32. J. Jargon, 2008, General Mills sees wealth via health: New recipe for profit, sales growth: More whole grains, less salt, fat, *The Wall Street Journal*, February 25, A9.

33. M. Cording, J. D. Harrison, & R. E. Hoskisson, 2010, Implicit contracts and ex post settling up: Performance effects of employee responses to organizational authenticity, *Paper presented at the Strategic Management Society Conference*, Rome, September 13.

34. R. B. Adams, B. E. Hermalin, & M. S. Weisbach, 2010, The role of boards of directors in corporate governance: A conceptual framework and survey, *Journal of Economic Literature*, 48(1): 58–107; S. Mishra, 2008, Counting

progress: The state of boards five years after Sarbanes-Oxley, *The Corporate Governance Advisor*, January/February, 12; R. E. Hoskisson, M. A. Hitt, R. A. Johnson, & W. Grossman, 2002, Conflicting voices: The effects of ownership heterogeneity and internal governance on corporate strategy, *Academy of Management Journal*, 45: 697–716.

35. M. Kohlbeck & B. W. Mayhew, 2010, Valuation of firms that disclose related party transactions, *Journal of Accounting and Public Policy*, 29(2): 115–137.

36. G. Farrell & B. Masters, 2009, How Madoff concealed the $65bn fraud, *Financial Times*, August 12, 14.

37. A. Carmeli & Z. Sheaffer, 2009, How leadership characteristics affect organizational decline and downsizing, *Journal of Business Ethics*, 86: 363–378; D. Pastoriza, M. A. Arino, & J. E. Ricart, 2008, Ethical managerial behavior as an antecedent of organizational social capital, *Journal of Business Ethics*, 78: 329–341.

38. J. T. Macher & D. C. Mowery, 2009, Measuring dynamic capabilities: Practices and performance in semi-conductor manufacturing, *British Journal of Management*, 20: S41–S62.

39. N. Plambeck & K. Weber, 2010, When the glass is half full and half empty: CEOs' ambivalent interpretations of strategic issues, *Strategic Management Journal*, 31(7): 689–710; K. Bogjin, M. L. Burns, & J. E. Prescott, 2009, The strategic role of the board: The impact of board structure on top management team strategic action capability, *Corporate Governance: An International Review*, 17(6): 728–743.

40. C. Guglielmo & A. Ricadela, 2010, Mulling options, Dell considers going private, *Bloomberg BusinessWeek*, June 21–27, 37–38.

41. H. Sundin, M. Granlund, & D. A. Brown, 2010, Balancing multiple competing objectives with a balanced scorecard, *European Accounting Review*, 19(2): 203–246; R. S. Kaplan & D. P. Norton, 2008, Mastering the management system, *Harvard Business Review*, 86(1): 62–77.

42. Kaplan & Norton, Mastering the management system.

PART 2
Analyzing Environments

CHAPTER 3
Analyzing the External Environment

KNOWLEDGE OBJECTIVES

Reading and studying this chapter should enable you to:

1. Explain the importance of analyzing the firm's external environment.

2. Identify and describe the categories of trends in the general environment that create opportunities or threats for the firm.

3. Describe the five forces of an industry analysis.

4. Understand how to complete a competitor analysis.

5. Identify potential reactions to significant strategic moves by competitors.

6. Understand how complementors support value creation for the firm in a competitive situation.

GameStop Is Formulating a New Strategy in a Game-Changing Environment

GameStop Corporation is a video, game products, and personal computer entertainment software retailer. It sells both new and used games including video software games and video game accessories, including controllers, memory cards, and other add-ons. The company sells its products through its 6,500 stores in the United States, Australia, Canada, and Europe, as well as through an electronic commerce Web site.

Although GameStop could be considered the most successful retail operator with a particular focus in the segment mentioned above, it has a number of environmental changes that could be "game changers." Best Buy has announced that it will open a specialty shop within 700 of its stores, offering a wide assortment of game and entertainment software products, accessories, and services that will challenge the prowess of GameStop in this segment. Accordingly, Best Buy, as a relatively new specialty entrant in this segment, will have to upgrade its expertise because GameStop's associates will be seen as expert solely in gaming. Furthermore, Best Buys are located in more distant malls, whereas GameStop has more specialty stores that are likely located closer to many of the home markets of gamers.

An additional threat is the online gaming market, which is growing. Electronic Arts, Take Two Interactive, and other game developers are expanding into the digital game add-ons as well as many sequels to games and pursuing online delivery. This approach would disrupt GameStop's business model, which would be comparative to the online delivery of music and thereby challenge brick and mortar music business retailers focused on CDs and tapes. This is also similar to the challenge of online movie delivery for retailers such as Blockbuster, focused on retail CD movie rental business.

To combat this threat, GameStop has recently signaled that it will buy Kongregate, which is a gaming social network site. Paul Rains, CEO of GameStop, has said, "Kongregate is a first-step building block in advancing GameStop's digital strategy by providing a unique platform for developers and consumers of free-to-play mobile and browser games." Kongregate offers 30,000 free games that players can dabble in for a few minutes at a time, compared to hardcore titles like *Halo* and *Grand Theft Auto* produced by game producers such as Electronic Arts.

In summary, the environment of GameStop is changing. Many of its gaming suppliers are forward integrating through online electronic games that are directly sold to consumers through producer Web sites, and new entrants are coming from the electronic retail segment (Best Buy). Furthermore, the online gaming segment represents a substitute product that is akin to the online distribution of digital musical business for the CD delivery of music. Whether GameStop can survive these changes will depend on how it assesses its environment and manages its strategy in the future.

Sources: 2010, GameStop Corporate Profile, http://www.gamestop.com, July 30; C. Edwards, 2010, GameStop is bulking up to battle new rivals, *Bloomberg BusinessWeek*, http://www.businessweek.com, July 26; V. Godinez, 2010, GameStop buys Kongregate to gain an online edge, *Dallas Morning News Online*, http://www.dallasnews.com, July 28; P. Sellers & J. P. Mangalindan, 2010, How gaming became the future of social media, *Fortune*, http://www.fortune.com, July 29; N. Wingfield, 2010, GameStop to acquire online distributor, *The Wall Street Journal*, July 28, B5.

Recall from Chapter 1 that the external environment is the set of conditions outside the firm that affects the firm's performance. As the opening *Focusing on Strategy* suggests, the external environment can indeed affect the firm's choice and use of strategy. Clearly, GameStop chose to acquire Kongregate to deal with changes in its competitive environment; in particular, the trend toward online game entertainment. To pursue an opportunity or to protect itself against a threat, a firm might choose to change how it is implementing a current strategy or change to a different strategy. GameStop's shift to online digital gaming represents such a change.

In this chapter, we examine the three parts of a firm's external environment: the general environment, the industry environment, and the competitor environment (see Figure 3.1). Firms analyze their external environment to collect information that will help them select a strategy. For example, conditions in the external environment influence whether a firm might choose to pursue a certain opportunity or to take action to avoid an impending threat. The firm's decisions are also affected by the firm's resources and capabilities, as we discuss in the next chapter. The actual choice of a strategy is a function of conditions in the firm's external environment and the internal conditions of the firm.

As mentioned in Chapter 1, being able to identify opportunities and threats is an important reason why firms study their external environment.[1] *Opportunities* are conditions in the firm's general, industry, and competitor environments that enable the firm to use its core competencies to achieve its vision. *Threats*, on the other hand, are conditions in the firm's general, industry, and competitor environments with the potential to prevent the firm from successfully using its core competencies.[2] Firms evaluate trends in their general environment, assess the effects of competitive forces in the industry in which they compete, and study competitors to identify the opportunities and threats they face.

Figure 3.1 **External Environment Analysis**

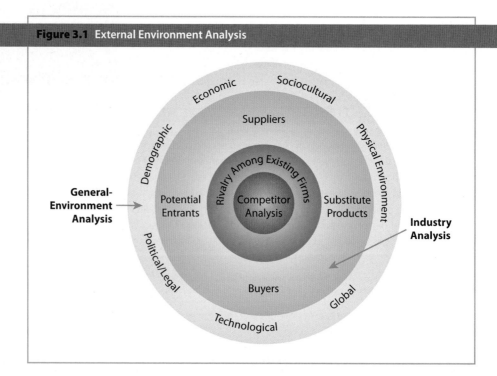

Firms should not rely on personal opinions and casual observations to assess their external environment. In-depth study is required, and it is important to ask the right questions. Studying all parts of the firm's external environment—the general, industry, and competitor environments—is essential. Beginning with the general environment, we discuss each analysis the firm performs to understand the conditions in its external environment.

Analyzing the General Environment

The **general environment** is composed of trends in the broader society that influence an industry and the firms in it. Firms must pay attention to seven factors in the general environment: demographic, economic, political/legal, sociocultural, technological, global, and physical trends. Each category has conditions that affect the firm's choice of strategy. Conditions in the general environment are outside the firm's direct control; no firm can control demographic trends, for example. Yet, they are important for the company to consider in deciding on its strategy. Think about how conditions in each trend could influence different types of firms and their strategies.

Demographic Trends

Demographic trends are changes in population size, age structure, geographic distribution, ethnic mix, and income distribution. Analysis of these trends is important to determine whether the firm might be able to serve additional customer groups with its products. For example, increasing population rates in international markets might represent opportunities for a firm to sell its products to a new set of consumers. As the largest economies in the world, China and India offer enticing opportunities for a number of firms to use their products to satisfy new customer groups' needs. By 2015, it is predicted that the world population will grow to 7.2 billion, up from 6.1 billion in 2000.

Change in the average age of a population is another important demographic trend. Consider the prediction that the number of Americans over age 65 will increase to 55 million by 2020, up 56 percent from 2000. This prediction could signal an opportunity for pharmaceutical companies to increase their revenues through product innovations.[3]

"As baby boomers get older, they're increasingly going to be less 'do-it-myself' and more 'do-it-for-me,'" and so The Home Depot's and Lowe's customer installation service business is growing more rapidly than their other business segments. This trend has also led to firms increasing their advertising for this segment including new Web sites focused on the aging populations. "There's (now) talk about boomers and 'zoomers' (boomers with active lifestyles) as the latest trend."[4] Other demographic trends such as changes in a population's ethnic mix can affect the opportunity to enhance diversity in the workforce and also affect patterns of consumer demand.[5] For example, the increasing Hispanic population in the United States and the simultaneous increase in their purchasing power will influence firms' decisions about the customers they seek to serve and the types of products they sell to serve those needs.

Shifts in the geographic distribution of a population can also affect firms. As fertility rates in developed countries slow and those in developing countries slow at a lower rate, this has significant implications for developed countries. One demographer suggests the following: "The proportion of global GDP [gross

general environment

the trends in the broader society that influence an industry and the firms in it

demographic trends

changes in population size, age structure, geographic distribution, ethnic mix, and income distribution domestic product] produced by Europe, the United States, and Canada fell from 68 percent in 1950 to 47 percent in 2003 and will decline even more steeply in the future. If the growth rate of per capita income (again, adjusted for purchasing power parity) between 2003 and 2050 remains as it was between 1973 and 2003—averaging 1.68 percent annually in Europe, the United States, and Canada and 2.47 percent annually in the rest of the world—then the combined GDP of Europe, the United States, and Canada will roughly double by 2050, whereas the GDP of the rest of the world will grow by a factor of five."[6] This suggests that the opportunities for future business will continue to be in developing countries.

Economic Trends

Economic trends concern the direction of the economy in which a firm competes or may choose to compete. Gross national product, interest and inflation rates, income growth or decline, savings rates, and currency exchange rates in countries across the globe are examples of economic factors that firms examine to understand current future economic trends. Of course, economic trends also affect customers' purchasing decisions. Your current and expected income influences what you decide to buy and from whom.

In addition, economic trends affect the broader society, such as when a deep recession occurs like the one that occurred recently. The deep worldwide recession in 2008 through 2010 has affected many firms' strategies. For example, consumers focused on price and chose store-branded products over branded products such as those produced by P&G. However, P&G was able to claw back some profits by lower prices, heavy advertising, and new products to entice consumers with improved product value. One analyst offered the following examples: "Its Duracell line will offer bigger battery packs without higher prices. Its Pampers diapers will boast a new absorbent technology—which P&G calls its biggest diaper innovation in 25 years—without costing more than existing products."[7] When facing less-than-favorable economic trends, firms must decide how to allocate their resources so they will be positioned to grow when domestic and/or global economies improve.

Political/Legal Trends

Political/legal trends pertain to changes in organizations and interest groups that compete for a voice in developing and implementing the body of laws and regulations that guide interactions among firms and nations. Because political conditions affect how business is conducted, firms try to influence legislation in ways that benefit them through political strategy.[8] The means used to influence political and legal trends must be ethical, moral, and consistent with the laws of the land.

Increasingly, privatization of government-owned and government-regulated businesses has transformed many state-owned enterprises to private firms (as in eastern Europe) and has deregulated formerly regulated businesses (such as Toll Motorways in Europe);[9] consequently, the global competitive landscape is increasingly dynamic (open to competition) and deregulated. This trend is being fostered by admittance of countries (such as China) to the World Trade Organization (WTO). The Geneva-based WTO helps establish trade rules in the global environment. China's entry into the WTO in late 2001 signaled a significant trend in emerging market countries. Since its entry into the WTO, China has reduced a number of trade barriers and allowed firms from other countries to enter Chinese markets in multiple industries such as telecommunications, banking, automobiles, and professional services.

economic trends
the direction of the economy in which a firm competes or may choose to compete

political/legal trends
the changes in organizations and interest groups that compete for a voice in developing and implementing the body of laws and regulations that guide interactions among firms and nations

Managers must carefully examine political trends in antitrust, taxation, and industry regulations as well as labor laws because of their potential importance to the implementation of strategies. Legal and regulatory constraints reduce the discretion of managers in the strategies that they can select.[10] Often, firms develop political strategies before establishing competitive positions within an industry.

Specific regulatory bodies frequently oversee industry activities. The airline industry in the United States is greatly affected by the Federal Aviation Administration (FAA), and the food and drug industries are strongly influenced by the Food and Drug Administration (FDA). The influence of regulations and antitrust laws on a firm is important. For example, every merger between large firms is scrutinized by the Federal Trade Commission and the Justice Department.

Regulations in place to reduce systematic risk in our financial system failed in 2008 and sparked the financial crisis. One commentator suggested that "recent events show that our 21st-century financial markets need improved financial rules and procedures to offset the growing level of systemic risk and 'to protect ourselves from our most self-destructive tendencies.'"[11] Accordingly, regulations also can create economic stability and protect against economic bubbles like that experienced in the residential real estate markets, not only in the United States but around the world. This is illustrated in the *Focusing on Strategy* example examining the subprime mortgage crisis, which threatened the global financial system and led to the bankruptcy of storied investment banks Bear Stearns and Lehman Brothers.

© AP Photo/Donald Stampfli

The admittance of emerging market countries such as China to World Trade Organization (WTO) is an important step toward increasing the overall global market for goods and services.

Sociocultural Trends

Sociocultural trends deal with changes in a society's attitudes and cultural values. Clearly, national cultures tend to affect managerial work values and thus differ across countries such as the United States, Japan, China, and Russia.[12] Likewise, the emphasis on saving the environment is relatively strong in Europe and throughout the developed world; however, until recently, these issues have been less important in emerging economies such as Russia, India, China, and Latin America. Health consciousness is also a trend that has become increasingly important in many countries around the world. Another factor, especially in the United States, is that more women are entering the workforce rather than remaining in traditional family roles, providing new human capital that a firm can hire to pursue an opportunity. What sociocultural trends do you see that you believe are important for U.S. businesses? What should firms do to be prepared to successfully deal with these trends?

sociocultural trends

changes in a society's attitudes and cultural values

Technological Trends

Technological trends concern changes related to creating new knowledge and translating that knowledge into new products, processes, and materials. Some firms require a thorough examination of technological trends because of swift technological changes and shortened product life cycles in their industries. In

technological trends

changes related to creating new knowledge and translating that knowledge into new products, processes, and materials

The Subprime Crisis and the Financial Services Industry

Subprime loans became popular with what was hailed as financial innovation. Subprime mortgages are essentially high-interest loans designed for people with prior credit problems. This innovation allowed millions of people to own homes who could not do so otherwise, and mortgage debt in the United States grew from about $6 trillion in 1999 to almost $13 trillion in 2008. However, many of the subprime loans issued during 2004–2006 involved adjustable interest rates that increased after a short term (e.g., two to three years). With the housing boom, prices of homes were escalating. With the increase in prices, homeowners were able to refinance their mortgages when the short-term balloon payments were due.

Could more strigent financial regulations and enforcement have prevented the subprime mortgage fiasco and damaging economic recession it spawned?

The loans were then repackaged and sold. Some financial services packaged many of these loans into groups of supposedly varied risk levels and sought investors. Early in the process, many lenders and, in turn, investors made large profits from these mortgages and packages of loans, respectively. Unfortunately, the whole process was similar to a huge pyramid scheme. When some of these securitized subprime loans became delinquent, the whole debt security was suspect. And since some of these packages of loans were in many securities, the crises expanded across a range of securities that held a portion of these bad loans. The only way it could continue to succeed was for housing prices to regularly increase. When the housing bubble burst, a full-scale financial crisis took hold because of the subprime loans. Even though subprime adjustable rate loans represent only 6.8 percent of the total number of loans, they accounted for approximately 43 percent of the foreclosures in 2007. About 2 million people with subprime loans faced foreclosure in 2008 and many more in 2009 and 2010.

A number of smaller and newer lenders that entered the market to service the subprime market have gone out of business. Many of the larger financial service firms that were major players have also suffered bankruptcies, including venerable Wall Street banks Bear Stearns and Lehman Brothers; others had significant negative write-offs. The CEOs at Citigroup and Merrill Lynch lost their jobs over losses their firms suffered because of their investments in the sub-prime market. The crisis also reached outside the United States and caused problems for foreign financial services firms such as Credit Suisse and Deutsche Bank.

The U.S. Federal Reserve had to lower interest rates to keep the economy afloat, and other leading agencies established policies creating stricter mortgage and lending requirements. These restrictions require lenders to certify that loan applicants have the appropriate income and ability to repay the loans granted. Further, they proposed restrictions on hidden fees by lenders and on their ability to refinance these loans. Hopefully, these actions and more reasonable strategies by lenders will disallow future crises such as this one in the financial services industry.

Sources: S. Bergsman, 2010, A capacity problem for special servicers, *Mortgage Banking*, May, 74–79; A. Dymi, 2010, Market focuses on still-high strategic defaults, *National Mortgage News*, July 12, 6; R. Farzad & P. Dwyer, 2010, When it comes to its role in the financial crisis, Goldman Sachs has a message for the world: Not guilty. Not one little bit, *Bloomberg BusinessWeek*, April 12, 30–38; D. Issa & J. Jordan, 2010, Cleaning up the mortgage mess, *The Wall Street Journal*, August 25, A13; B. Keys, T. Mukherjee, A. Seru, & V. Vig, 2010, Did securitization lead to lax screening? Evidence from subprime loans, *Quarterly Journal of Economics*, 125(1): 307–362; F. Longstaff, 2010, The subprime credit crisis and contagion in financial markets, *Journal of Financial Economics*, 97(3): 436–450; C. Mollenkamp & S. Ng, 2010, How a little subprime lending had a big impact, *The Wall Street Journal*, May 3, C1, C3.

© PAUL J. RICHARDS/AFP/Getty Images

© kimeveruss, iStock

Table 3.1 Five Important Global Trends

1. **The advent of nanotechnology.** Advances in manipulating organic and inorganic material at the atomic and molecular levels will lead to the ability to create smaller, stronger products. Even though nanotechnology is predicted to usher in a new industrial revolution with effects on global trade and intellectual property, simultaneous developments in information technology and biotechnology will also have substantial effects on standards of living and economic trends.

2. **Globalization.** One of the consequences of globalization is an increasing gulf between rich and poor countries. It has been predicted that many corporations will play an increasingly paternalistic role in Third World countries, developing infrastructure and stepping in where governments have failed. But perhaps the largest development over the next 20 years will be the growth and impact of emerging markets in China, India, and the like.

3. **Global warming.** Earth's average surface temperature has risen by about 1°F in the past century, with accelerated warming during the past two decades, largely due to the buildup of greenhouse gases.

Climate change will affect everything from human health and agriculture to forests and water supplies.

4. **Water and other resource shortages.** Population growth will increase pressure on water and energy supplies. "Blue gold" (water) is in short supply throughout much of the world. Water and shortages are likely to lead to greater political tensions, particularly in drier regions of the world (e.g., the Middle East). In other regions, energy may be the resource in short supply. Thus, the management and conservation of potable water and energy resources will become increasingly important.

5. **The human capital power shift.** Depending on economic conditions, projections suggest that Europe and Japan will lack human capital based on lack of population growth. Asia, Africa and Latin America will account for virtually all population growth. Although Europe and Japan will out distance these future middle income economies, the lack of available human resources will stifle economic growth, depending of the availability of education opportunities in these now emerging economy areas.

Source: L. Pratt, 2003, The 5 most important global trends, *Profit*, December, 24; 2008, Global trends 2025, National Intelligence Council, http://www.dni.gov/nic/NIC_globaltrend2015.

particular, Internet technology has played an increasingly important role in domestic and global technological change. Furthermore, the Internet is an excellent source of data on the three parts of the external environment. Significant changes in communications technology, especially wireless communications technology, have provided opportunities for many firms. For example, new industries have been created by combining handheld devices and wireless communications equipment in a variety of network-based services. This technology enables individuals to use their handheld computers (such as mobile phones) for scheduling and to send e-mail or conduct Web-based transactions (such as online purchases of stock and other investments).

As suggested earlier, firms study technological trends to identify opportunities and threats. Recent research suggests that new technologies often are applicable across a range of markets. However, new technologies are generally underutilized early in their existence because either firms are deterred by expected competition or they do not realize their full value and applicability to their industry.[13] So those firms that effectively analyze technological trends and identify opportunities with new technologies can achieve an advantage over their competitors.

Global Trends

Global trends concern changes in relevant emerging and developed country global markets, important international political events, and critical changes in cultural and institutional characteristics of global markets. Table 3.1 lists five important global trends that some expect to significantly influence global markets in future years.

global trends

changes in relevant emerging and developed country global markets, important international political events, and critical changes in cultural and institutional characteristics of global markets

Examining trends such as the ones shown in the table helps the firm identify opportunities and threats outside its domestic market. Undoubtedly, increasing globalization is having a profound effect on national economies and on major political decisions around the world.[14] A major factor increasing globalization has been the rapid development of some emerging markets such as China and India. They represent markets for multinationals based in developed markets, and firms from emerging market countries are increasingly entering international markets.[15] Therefore, managers developing a global mind-set to identify opportunities and threats from global trends can help their firms to grow by pursuing opportunities in other countries.

Global trends can also present significant threats both from foreign competitors and the complexity involved in competing in different countries. Companies must understand the sociocultural and institutional differences in global markets in order to be successful. Significant changes in currency and political risks because of war and nationalization of assets also need to be considered.[16]

Physical Environment Trends

An increasingly important dimension of the general environment focuses on **physical environment trends.** These trends refer to the changes in the physical environment and business practices that are intended to sustain it.[17] Table 3.1 notes that one of the major global trends is "global warming." Global warming, for example, is the reason that many glaciers such as those in the Los Glaciares National Park in Argentina are melting at an alarming rate.[18] Exemplifying the concern for the environment, Ireland implemented a tax on plastic bags, and in a short period of time, the use of plastic bags decreased by 94 percent. In fact, many people in Ireland now carry cloth bags in which to carry home grocery purchases. Irish citizens support this law and look askance at the few people who still use plastic bags.[19] Because of the growing concern for sustaining the physical environment around the world, many companies are developing environmentally friendly policies. Some refer to these as "green" policies. Coca-Cola Company is a good example. Coke's former Board Chairperson and CEO, Neville Isdell, recently stated: "Among businesses, the economy is going to separate the 'wheat from the chaff.' It is already separating the businesses that are really serious about a sustainability agenda from those that are merely, in environmental terms, 'greenwashing' and that make changes only in search of cost benefits rather than long-term sustainability."[20] Coke's management seeks to establish an environmental philosophy to minimize the firm's environmental footprint.

Firms commonly focus on the future when studying the general environment. However, that future must take place within a particular context. An **industry,** which is a group of firms producing similar products, is the context within which a firm's future is experienced. Firms analyze the industry environment to understand the profitability potential of a particular industry or of a segment within an industry. For example, the financial services industry is not an attractive one in the near term because of poor potential for profitability (see discussion of the industry in *Understanding Strategy: Learning from Failure*). We discuss how firms study an industry in the next section.

Analyzing the Industry Environment

Michael Porter developed a framework for classifying and analyzing the characteristics of an industry's environment.[21] His five forces model of competition examines competitive forces that influence the profitability potential in an

physical environment trends

changes in the physical environment and in the business practices that are intended to sustain it

industry

a group of firms producing similar products

Figure 3.2 The Five Forces Model

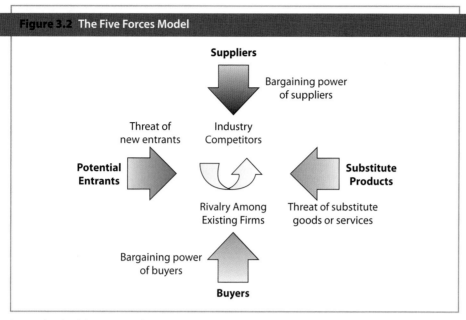

industry or of a segment within an industry. Each force can reduce the probability that a firm can earn profits while competing in an industry. As shown in Figure 3.2, potential entrants, substitute products, suppliers, buyers, and rivalry among existing firms are the five forces that affect the profitability potential of an industry. Firms competing in an industry want to understand these forces so they can position themselves in the industry to maximize their ability to earn profits. Firms thinking of entering an industry need to understand these forces to decide whether the industry's profitability potential is sufficient to support entry into that industry.

Potential Entrants

Potential entrants can be a threat to firms already competing in an industry; by entering that industry, new firms can take market share away from current competitors. Potential entrants also pose a threat to existing competitors because they bring additional production capacity. If this additional production leads to overcapacity in the industry, prices for consumers will be reduced but will also cause lower returns for industry firms. On the positive side, new entrants may force incumbent firms to learn new ways to compete. For example, initiating a new Internet-based distribution channel has been important for established pharmacy competitors such as Walgreens, given new Internet drug distributors in the United States and Canada.

In the highly competitive airline industry, Delta Airlines and American Airlines have been weakened by new entrants such as JetBlue. As smaller, more nimble, and more focused competitors (e.g., Southwest Airlines and JetBlue and Ryan Air in Europe) increased market share, old-guard (legacy) airlines with traditionally high cost structures have had to dramatically change their strategies and their implementation to survive. American, unlike United, barely managed to avoid bankruptcy by bargaining for concessions from labor unions and by cutting

Table 3.2 Barriers to Entry into an Industry

Barrier	Description
Economies of scale	Without economies of scale, potential new entrants are likely to be at a cost disadvantage relative to established competitors with economies of scale.
Capital requirements	If the amount of financial capital needed isn't available, a firm may not be able to enter an industry at all or may lack the resources to compete against an established competitor.
Switching costs	A firm thinking of entering an industry would want to determine how costly it would be for an industry's customers to buy from a new firm compared with continuing to buy from an established competitor.
Differentiation	If customers decide that an established firm's product uniquely meets their needs, then it may be difficult for a new firm to enter that segment of the market.
Access to distribution channels	If established firms have developed relationships majority of distribution channels, potential entrants may find it difficult to gain access because a change may create switching costs for a distributor.
Government policy	Some industries are more regulated than others and require a government license or permit before business can be conducted; entry then becomes more difficult.

costs significantly. Though bankruptcy is no longer an immediate threat, American continues to face numerous challenges (such as rising fuel costs). Despite the airline industry's significant barriers to entry by new firms, new market entrants have changed the nature of competition in the airline industry.[22]

Entry barriers make it difficult for new firms to enter an industry and often place them at a competitive disadvantage even when they are able to enter. Therefore, existing competitors try to develop barriers that new firms must face when deciding whether to enter an industry. The barriers we will discuss next are briefly described in Table 3.2.

Economies of Scale **Economies of scale** are the improvements in efficiency from incremental increases in the size of a firm's operations. Economies of scale can be realized through increased efficiencies in almost all business functions such as marketing, manufacturing, research and development, and purchasing. Importantly, economies of scale reduce the costs the firm incurs to produce additional units of its products. Often, new entrants do not have economies of scale and thus are at a cost disadvantage trying to compete against established competitors.

Capital Requirements A significant amount of financial capital is often needed for a firm to establish operations in an industry. Financial capital enables the entering firm to build or lease physical facilities, purchase supplies, support marketing activities, and hire talented workers (human capital) who know how to

economies of scale

the improvements in efficiency from incremental increases in the size of a firm's operations compete in a particular industry. If the amount of financial capital needed isn't available, a firm may not be able to enter an industry or it may do so at a competitive disadvantage (because it lacked the capital to build or acquire what is needed to successfully compete against established competitors).

Switching Costs **Switching costs** are the one-time costs that customers incur when they decide to buy a product from a different supplier. Switching costs can be low, high, or anywhere in between. Think of the costs you would incur to fly with one airline instead of a competing airline. Assuming the ticket costs are about the same, it costs you essentially nothing to check in at a different ticket counter after arriving at the airport and to land at a different terminal or a different part of a terminal at your destination city. On the other hand, deciding to transfer as a last-semester senior from one college to another university or college could be quite costly because most educational institutions require students to complete the last 60 or so hours of course work on site. So the cost to switch to another university or college as a last-semester senior can be substantial. Existing competitors try to create switching costs for customers, such as airline frequent-flyer plans. A firm thinking of entering an industry should determine how costly it would be for an industry's customers to buy from a new firm compared with continuing to buy from an established competitor.

Differentiation Over time, customers may decide that an established firm's product uniquely meets their needs. Such perceptions of uniqueness are defined as *differentiation* (see Chapter 5 for a more formal definition). Even in a commodity-type business such as soft drinks, firms such as Coca-Cola and PepsiCo have been effective at establishing customer loyalty through strong marketing programs. In these circumstances, a potential entrant must invest significant resources to overcome existing customer loyalties. Often, this means entering with low-end products that compete on price rather than brand image. However, low-end products often require lower prices because of incumbent firms' economies of scale. New entrants may have difficulty in matching the low prices because it is difficult to achieve similar economies of scale. Thus, to match the low prices may require the firm to lose money on the products sold (until economies of scale arc achieved).

Access to Distribution Channels Over time, established firms learn how to build and use effective distribution channels. Often, relationships develop between firms and their distributors, creating switching costs for the distributors. Thus, potential entrants frequently find it difficult to gain access to distribution channels. Price breaks and cooperative advertising allowances might be proposed by a potential entrant. But if taken, these actions can be expected to reduce the new entrant's profit. However, most firms already competing in the industry likely will be able to match these actions.

Government Policy Entry can also be limited by government policy through licensing and permit requirements. Some industries are more regulated than others. Liquor retailing, banking, and trucking, for example, are highly regulated. Substantial regulations limit entry by new firms. The Federal Communications Commission (FCC) grants licenses to radio and television stations. In 1997, the FCC took bids on licenses for satellite radio, and only two licenses were granted to bidders. From these licenses, only two competing companies were formed: XM Radio and Sirius Radio. In early 2007, XM Radio and Sirius Radio announced a merger agreement between the two firms. In early 2008, the two firms

switching costs

the one-time costs customers incur when they decide to buy a product from a different supplier

© Justin Sullivan/Getty Images News/Getty Images

Even though the iPod has been on the market for over a decade, the music industry is still struggling to adjust to a world where fewer and fewer consumers are purchasing CDs.

applied with the FCC to operate under one license. They received approval from the Antitrust Division of the U.S. Department of Justice and the FCC in August 2008.[23] It should be noted that even though regulations may protect established competitors from the challenges of new entrants, excessive regulations generate costs that reduce the industry's profitability potential.

Substitute Products

Substitute products also have the potential to influence an industry's profitability potential. Substitute products are goods or services that perform functions similar to an existing product. For example, the music industry has experienced a number of substitute products over the years. Cassette tapes became substitutes for phonograph records, and compact discs (CDs) became substitutes for tapes. More recently, MP3 and other digital formats are being substituted for CDs. In general, product substitutes present a strong threat to an incumbent firm when the substitutes are more effective and sold at a lower price. Interestingly, one of the reasons that the XM Sirius Radio merger was approved is because the demand for the product is "dynamic," meaning that it is in flux. One of the reasons that it is in flux is because there are serious substitutes such as cheaper Internet radio channels that stream over broadband services. Pandora has the largest number of subscribers in this segment with over 60 million registered users.[24] Thus, the product performance relative to the price is the relevant concern, especially if the incumbent firms' products lack switching costs. However, if the incumbent firms can differentiate the existing product in ways that customers value (such as after-sales service), a substitute product's attractiveness will be lower.

Bargaining Power of Suppliers

Suppliers' actions can also reduce the ability of firms to earn profits while competing in an industry.[25] For example, if a supplier can either increase the price of its product or reduce the quality while selling it at the same price, the effect on established firms' profitability is negative. A supplier that can do one of these things is considered to be a powerful supplier. Suppliers tend to be powerful when

- There are a few large suppliers and the buying firms' industry is not concentrated.
- Substitute products are not available to the buying firms.
- The buying firms are not a significant customer for the suppliers.
- The suppliers' goods are essential to the buyers' marketplace success.
- The suppliers' products have high switching costs for the buyers.
- The suppliers pose a credible threat to integrate forward into the buyers' industry.

Interestingly, a number of new entrants came into the financial services industry to handle the subprime loans because demand for them was high (see *Understanding Strategy: Learning from Failure*). However, they did not have strong access to supplies of capital and many of the new entrants went out of business when problems were experienced with the subprime loans. The only firms receiving infusions of capital were the larger and more established firms (e.g., Citigroup, Bank of America).

substitute products

goods or services that perform functions similar to an existing product

Bargaining Power of Buyers

Firms selling a product want to enjoy high profitability, while their customers (buyers) want to buy high-quality products at a low price. These goals mean that buyers try to reduce their costs by bargaining with selling firms for lower prices, higher quality, and greater levels of service. In contrast, firms try to offer value to customers at prices that clearly exceed the costs of providing that value. Of course, powerful customers have the potential to reduce the profitability potential of an industry. Buyers or customers tend to be powerful when

- They buy a large portion of the selling firm's total output.
- The selling firm is dependent on the buyers for a significant portion of its sales revenue.
- They can switch to another seller's product with few switching costs.
- The selling industry's products are undifferentiated or similar to a commodity.
- They present a credible threat to integrate backward into the sellers' industry.

Certainly, firms want to provide significant value to their customers, value that exceeds that offered by competitors.[26] Yet, their owners (shareholders) also expect them to earn profits and create value as well. So firms must balance the value created for each group and contend with the buyers' power. For example, the average consumer does not have a strong preference to buy, for example, a Nokia phone instead of a Motorola phone. Phone service companies often lure customers with cell phone giveaway programs; customers' indifference to cell phone brand makes this possible. Unless cell phone manufacturers have sufficient market share to maintain the scale of their operation and keep costs low, their ability to earn profits likely will be reduced because of the power of their main customers.[27]

Rivalry Among Existing Firms

Competitive rivalry is the set of actions and reactions between competitors as they compete for an advantageous market position.[28] For example, competitive rivalry is highly visible and intense in the airline industry. When one airline lowers its prices in a market, that action is likely to affect a competitor's business in that market; so the tactical action of reducing prices by one airline invites a competitive response by one or more of its competitors. Competitive rivalry is likely to be based on dimensions such as price, quality, and innovation. Next, we discuss conditions that influence competitive rivalry in an industry.

Degree of Differentiation Industries with many companies that have successfully differentiated their products have fewer rivals, resulting in lower competition for individual firms and less of a negative effect on the industry's profitability potential. This stability usually happens when competing companies have established brand loyalty by offering differentiated products to their customers. Differentiated products to which customers are loyal cannot be easily imitated and often earn higher profits.[29] Yet, competitors will try to imitate successful competitors, as did many digital camera producers after early entry by Kodak and Sony.[30] And when buyers view products as undifferentiated or as commodities, rivalry intensifies. Intense rivalry leads to buyers making purchasing decisions mainly on the basis of price. In turn, intense price competition negatively affects an industry's profitability potential.

Switching Costs The lower the buyers' switching costs, the easier it is for competitors to attract them. High switching costs partially protect firms from rivals' efforts to attract customers. Interestingly, the government has lowered the switching costs

competitive rivalry

the set of actions and reactions between competitors as they compete for an advantageous market position of cell phone carriers by reducing regulation of phone numbers. Consumers can now transport their old cell phone number to a new cell phone service provider, which reduces the switching cost for the customer. However, lower switching costs for customers increase rivalry among cell phone service providers.[31]

Numerous or Equally Balanced Competitors Intense rivalries are common in industries in which competing firms are of similar size and have similar competitive capabilities. An intense rivalry has evolved between Boeing and Airbus. These large competitors are battling to gain a dominant position in the global commercial jet aircraft market. In particular, the competition between different giant wide-body jet designs has created heated rivalry. The A380 (Airbus design) and the 787 Dreamliner (Boeing's design) seem to be in a significant horse race as to which competitor will win in this market. To a lesser extent the single-aisle Boeing 737 and Airbus A320 jets, with seating capacity between 120 and 180 seats, are also jockeying for competitive position. For years these firms have been equal competitors. However, because of the airlines' push for better fuel efficiency and because of tighter margins, more recent competitors such as Bombardier in Canada and Embraer in Brazil have been making important progress in the single-aisle planes with smaller seating capacity. This increased competition in smaller jets has made the two large producers think about reshaping their older options such as Boeing's 737 model or even making new aircraft designs in order to compete with the increased competition from the smaller players.[32]

Slow Industry Growth Growing markets reduce the pressure to attract competitors' customers. However, when sales growth declines, the only way to increase sales for current products is to take market share from competitors. Therefore, rivalry usually increases in no-growth or slow-growth markets. The battle often intensifies as firms react to actions by competitors to protect their market shares. One of the worst economic downturns since the depression occurred between 2007 and 2010. This has led to significant increased rivalry among many industries. The economic slowdown was particularly acute in financial services (as noted in *Understanding Strategy: Learning from Failure*) and home building. In these situations, firms with abundant resources often are able to take advantage of the weaker firms.

In industries such as air travel, the level of competitive rivalry is extreme and companies such as Italy's Alitalia can ill-afford to make missteps especially with decreasing demand for their services and an increasing number of lower-cost competitors.

High Strategic Stakes Competitive rivalry tends to be high when it is important for competitors to perform well in their chosen market(s). For example, the competition for global market share between Boeing and Airbus represents high strategic stakes for both firms. Similarly, as airlines compete with lower demand for their services and with the growth of low-cost airlines, many larger carriers are not as competitive as they once were. Alitalia, the flagship Italian airline, has been losing money for a long time. Besides mismanagement and political problems due to government involvement, Alitalia must compete against a number of low-cost carriers such as Ryanair.[33] Although several bidders sought to acquire the firm in 2007, government requirements and political interference caused all bidders to eventually drop out of the process. Because of the importance of the Italian market to Alitalia and its competitors, continued significant competitive rivalry can be expected.

© ALESSANDRO GAROFALO/Reuters/Landov

High Fixed Costs or High Storage Costs When fixed or storage costs are a large part of total costs, companies try to spread costs across a larger volume of output. However, when many firms attempt to better utilize their capacity, excess capacity often results in the industry. Therefore, firms try to reduce their inventory by cutting the price of their product. Alternatively, they may offer rebates and other special discounts. This practice is quite common in the automobile industry and leads to more intense competition. This pattern is also often found in perishable goods industries; as perishable goods inventory grows, intense competition follows, with price cutting used to sell products and avoid spoilage, further increasing rivalry.

High Exit Barriers Firms facing high exit barriers often continue competing in industries even when their performance is less than desirable. In such industries, intense competition often leads firms to make desperate choices to survive. Barriers to exiting from an industry include the following:

- Specialized assets (assets with values linked to a particular business or location)
- Fixed costs of exit (such as labor agreements)
- Strategic interrelationships (relationships of mutual dependence, such as those between one business and other parts of the company's operations, including shared facilities and access to financial markets)
- Emotional barriers (aversion to economically justified business decisions because of fear for one's career, loyalty to employees, and so forth)
- Government and social restrictions (more common outside the United States; often based on government concerns for job losses and regional economic effects)[34]

The airline industry has high exit barriers because of the specialized assets associated with air travel, agreements with airports and other partners, government restrictions, and unions. Satellite radio firms such as XM and Sirius have high exit barriers as well.

With an understanding of the potential of each of the five competitive forces to influence an industry's profitability, the firm can determine the attractiveness of competing in that industry. In general, the stronger the competitive forces the less attractive the industry. An industry characterized by low barriers to entry, strong suppliers, strong buyers, the potential for product substitutes, and intense rivalry among competitors has low potential for firms to generate significant profits. On the other hand, an industry characterized by high entry barriers, suppliers and buyers with little bargaining power, few potential substitutes, and moderate rivalry suggests that the profitability potential of that industry is strong.

A competitor analysis is the final part of assessing the external environment that firms must undertake to fully recognize their opportunities and threats. The purpose of the competitor analysis is to fully understand the firm's competitors.

Competitor Analysis

Studying competitors is often the most important part of the external environment analysis (see Figure 3.1 on page 48). Answering the questions in Table 3.3 can help a firm recognize its most important current and future competitors.

Table 3.3 Basic Questions for Conducting an Industry Analysis to Screen Key Competitors

Threat of new entrants:
- Which firms have developed economies of scale, and how strong are they?
- How differentiated are the industry's products and services?
- Would buyers encounter switching costs to purchase from a new entrant?
- Which firms pose the most significant threat of potential new entry?

Substitute products:
- What product functionalities can be duplicated in some other fashion?
- Are there lower-cost alternatives to current products?

Bargaining power of suppliers:
- Is the supply chain dominated by only a few companies?
- How important is the industry to its suppliers?
- How differentiated are suppliers' products?
- Do suppliers pose a threat of forward integration into the industry?

Bargaining power of buyers:
- Are there large concentrations of buyers in the industry?
- Are products a high percentage of buyers' costs?
- Do buyers pose a threat of backward integration into the industry?

Rivalry among existing competitors:
- How many competitors are there?
- How differentiated are they?
- What are the exit barriers?
- Which competitors are most likely to respond to a specific competitive move?

Armed with a list of critical competitors, the firm is prepared to conduct a thorough analysis of each, focusing on the competitor's strategic intent, current strategy, and major strengths and weaknesses.

We describe the intense competition in the pharmaceutical industry and how Teva Pharmaceutical is managing it in *Understanding Strategy: Learning from Success*. As explained in the segment, Teva has been winning the battle globally by pursuing its generic drug strategy aggressively in the United States and Europe and in many of the markets across the world. After reading about Teva, decide whether you believe it will continue to be successful over the next ten years and what will happen to its larger competitors such as Pfizer and Merck, as traditional drug producers, as well as other generic drug competitors.

Competitor Strategic Intent

Strategic intent is the firm's motivation to leverage its resources and capabilities to reach its vision. Understanding a competitor's strategic intent increases a firm's ability to predict how that competitor will react to a competitive action. Teva can be assessed to have a vigorous strategic intent as noted in *Understanding Strategy: Learning from Success*.

The strength of strategic intent can be gauged by examining important competitor characteristics such as the competitor's market dependence. Market

---

strategic intent

the firm's motivation to leverage its resources and capabilities to reach its vision

Teva Pharmaceuticals Is Feared as the Top Generic Drug Producer

In 2010, Eli Hurvitz was replaced by Dr. Phillip Frost as Chairman of the Board of Directors of Teva Pharmaceutical Industries Ltd. Shlomo Yania will continue as Teva's president and CEO. Headquartered in Israel, Teva is the world's lead producer in the generic drug market. Phillip Frost came to be a Board of Directors member at Teva when the firm purchased Ivax Corporation in 1987. Dr. Frost was the Chairman of the Board and CEO of Ivax at the time of the purchase. In 1985, Teva had only $91 million in sales, but the company's global revenues were projected to be over $31 billion in 2015; at least this is what its strategic leadership is striving to realize. The company has become a "feared competitor" by "challenging brand patents, routinely suing rivals, vigorously defending its market share, and acquiring competitors and suppliers to remain the world's largest generics company."

To accomplish this, it pursues strategic discipline by seeking to increase its market share in key markets, aiming to double its product portfolio, improving customer service, creating a focus on biotechnology, and by becoming an innovator in business processes and supply chain management.

Its market aggressiveness has become legendary because of its cunning and perhaps, as considered from their competitors' point of view, "ruthlessness." It has filed numerous "Abbreviated New Drug Applications (ANDAs)," which are applications to pursue a generic drug for a current branded product when its patent expires. It has over 130 lawyers who file these drug applications seeking to be the first to ambush a brand when patent expiration occurs.

Teva also vigorously defends its own patented drugs and seeks to prevent potential generic competitors from reproducing them. It has its own patented drug called Copaxone, which provides relief for multiple sclerosis patients. Teva filed multiple patent infringement lawsuits against Sandoz and

Teva has proven to be an important competitor in the highly competitive global pharmaceutical market by aggressively moving on multiple fronts, including, the expansion of its product portfolio, defense of its patented drugs, introduction of operational innovations, and acquisition of key geographic competitors.

Mylan in order to protect the patents on this particular drug. It's also aggressively trying to acquire competitors to expand geographically. In the last two decades it has acquired 15 companies, including Ivax, Barr, and most recently Ratiopharm. For example, Ratiopharm, Germany's largest generic drug company, outbid Pfizer and thereby expanded its generic market share in Europe significantly. Similarly, it is seeking to protect its market share by dealing with new powerful providers such as biotechnology companies. Teva has integrated backward to supply some of its own active pharmaceutical ingredients by its joint venture and partial acquisition of Lonza, a biogeneric supplier.

Furthermore, Teva has been an innovator in supply chain management, information technology, and manufacturing practices. As such, it has produced advances in information technology, sourcing, packaging, and manufacturing techniques. These innovations have enhanced Teva's competitiveness by dramatically improving delivery reliability and reducing customer costs. In summary, Teva has sought to strengthen its position relative to more legacy pharmaceuticals as well as other generic drug producers who are rivals. It has sought to protect itself against substitutes who are producing new drugs through biotechnology as well as to deal with suppliers and buyers in as cost efficient a manner as possible. Accordingly, it is an efficient competitor, and its strategy deals rather successfully with all five competitive forces illustrated earlier in this chapter.

Sources: 2010, New era beckons for Teva, *Business Middle East (Economist)*, April 1, 4; S. Bernard, 2010, Big pharma's most feared competitor, *Pharmaceutical Executive*, July, 30–31; A. Dearment, 2010, The biggest little pharma in the world, *Drugstore News*, March, 39; T. Gryta, 2010, Teva takes aim at Europe, *The Wall Street Journal*, March 24, B–5; N. Kresge, 2010, As the pill turns 50, a rivalry heats up, *BusinessWeek*, April 25, 55; M. Schifrin, 2010, Teva believer, *Forbes*, March 15, 44; K. Mina, 2009, The king of low cost drugs, *Fortune*, August 17, 88–92; A. Weintraub, 2009, A push for generic biotech drugs, *BusinessWeek*, August 10, 30.

© Greg Epperson, iStock

© Martin Jenkinson/Alamy

dependence is the extent to which a firm's revenues or profits are derived from a particular market. Competitors with high market dependence are likely to respond strongly to attacks threatening their market position.[35] Boeing is not as dependent on the commercial aircraft business as it once was; the firm has diversified into military aircraft and other defense-related equipment, as well as a space and satellite-launching business, to reduce its dependence on commercial aircraft production. Understanding Boeing's strategic intent in the commercial aircraft business can help Airbus formulate its strategy to compete with Boeing. Understanding the strategic intent and actions of competitors clearly contributes to the firm's ability to compete successfully.[36]

Current Competitor Strategy

Gathering data and information to understand a competitor's current strategy is critical to conducting an effective competitor analysis. Meaningful information about a competitor's current strategy helps the firm predict that competitor's behavior. Despite the importance of studying competitors, evidence suggests that only a relatively small percentage of firms use formal processes to collect and disseminate such information. Some firms overlook analyzing competitors' future objectives as they try to understand their current strategies, thereby yielding incomplete insights about those competitors.[37] Even if research is inadequate, appropriate interpretation of that information is important. "Research found that how accurate senior executives are about their competitive environments is indeed less important for strategy and corresponding organizational changes than the way in which they interpret information about their environments."[38] Thus, although competitor scanning is important, investing money to appropriately interpret that information may be just as important as gathering and organizing it. Therefore, assessing whether a competitor represents an opportunity or a threat and evaluating that competitor's strengths and weaknesses are extremely important. This information is critical in the development of the firm's own strategy and its ability to respond to competitors' strategic actions.[39]

Strengths and Weaknesses of the Competitor

Assessing a competitor's strengths and weaknesses is the final component of a competitor analysis. Understanding a competitor's resources can help a firm formulate a strategy to gain a competitive advantage.[40] Firms with few or competitively unimportant strengths may not be able to successfully respond to a competitor's actions. Boeing has a number of strengths and resources that have enabled it to respond to Airbus's introduction of the A380 jumbo jet. But smaller jet producers such as Bombardier may be unable to respond to this action. Basic areas that firms study to understand where a competitor is strong and where it is weak are financial resources, marketing capability, human resource management, and innovation capability. A firm will want to avoid attacking a competitor where it is strong and instead attack where it is weak.[41]

Complements to Competitive Interaction

When a product is sold, complementary products may be necessary to facilitate the sale or to increase the functionality of the product as it is used.[42] **Complementors** are the network of companies that sell goods or services that

complementors
the network of companies that sell goods or services that are complementary to another firm's good or service

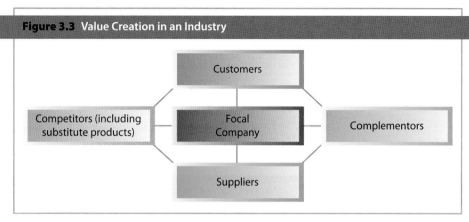

Figure 3.3 Value Creation in an Industry

Source: From *Co-opetition* by Adam M. Brandenburger & Barry J. Nalebuff. Copyright © 1996 by Adam M. Brandenburger & Barry J. Nalebuff. Used by permission of Doubleday, a division of Random House, Inc., and Barry Nalebuff, Adam Brandenburger, and Helen Rees Literary Agency, Boston, MA.

are complementary to another firm's good or service. If a complementor's good or service adds value to the sale of a firm's good or service, it is likely to create value for that firm. For example, a range of complements is necessary to sell automobiles, such as financial services to arrange credit and luxury options (stereo equipment, extended warranties, and so forth). Personal computers are complemented by peripheral devices and services such as printers, scanners, digital telephones, operating systems, software and games, and Internet service providers. Digital cameras are complemented by digital storage disks, software that creates usable and storable digital images, and printers and services for printing digital photographs.

As illustrated in Figure 3.3, complementors are a part of understanding the nature of value creation in an industry. A firm can increase its chances of achieving value creation by paying attention to customers, suppliers, competitors, and complementors.

SUMMARY

The primary purpose of this chapter was to describe what firms do to analyze the three parts of their external environment: the general, industry, and competitor environments. In doing so, we examined the following topics:

● Although the firm's external environment is challenging and complex, examining it is important. Careful analysis of the external environment enables a firm to identify opportunities and threats. The firm cannot directly control its external environment; however, the firm can use information about the external environment in developing its strategies.

● The external environment has three major parts: (1) the general environment (trends in the broader society that affect industries and their firms); (2) the industry environment (forces that influence a firm in relation to its buyers and suppliers and current and potential competitors); and (3) the competitor environment (in which the firm analyzes each major competitor's current and potential strategic actions).

● The general environment has seven categories of trends that need to be analyzed: demographic, economic, political/legal, sociocultural, technological, global, and physical.

● The five forces model of competition examines the threat of entry, the power of suppliers, the power of buyers, product substitutes, and the intensity of rivalry among competitors. By studying these forces, the firm can identify an attractive position in an industry. Compared to the general environment, the industry environment has a more direct effect on the firm's strategic actions.

● Competitor analysis informs the firm about the strategic intent, current strategies, and strengths and weaknesses of its major competitors. Competitor analysis

helps the firm understand how its competitors likely will compete in its chosen industry.

● Understanding how complementors' products or services add value to the sale of the focal firm's product or service will help the focal firm improve its competitive position.

KEY TERMS

Competitive rivalry, 59
Complementors, 64
Demographic trends, 49
Economic trends, 50
Economies of scale, 56

General environment, 49
Global trends, 53
Industry, 54
Physical environment trends, 54
Political/legal trends, 50

Sociocultural trends, 51
Strategic intent, 62
Substitute products, 58
Switching costs, 57
Technological trends, 51

DISCUSSION QUESTIONS

1. Why is it important for a firm to study and understand the external environment?
2. What are the seven segments of the general environment that are important to study? Explain the relationships and differences among them.
3. How do the five forces of competition in an industry affect its attractiveness?

4. What three components are necessary to conduct a competitor analysis?
5. When would a competitor likely respond to a strategic competitive move?
6. How can complementors add value to a firm's competitive situation?

STRATEGY TOOLBOX

Introduction

Successful strategic management is based on the ability to navigate the turbulent waters of the macro environmental and competitor seas. Data to assist in the strategic management process are plentiful. In fact, the advent of the Internet and electronic databases makes available a plethora of data that can be used in ways never imaginable 20 years ago. This chapter's tool is designed to provide special guidance in searching for critical data to be used in analyzing external environments in a focused and efficient manner.

© Jan Paul Schrage, iStock

Business Intelligence

Competitor Data	Industry Data	Market Trends

• Factiva
  • General news
  • Detailed company reports
  • Daily newspapers
• Mergent Online
  • Deep data on firms
  • Downloadable financials
• Hoover's Online
  • Company profiles
  • Comprehensive reports
	• Datamonitor
	  • Consumer market reports
	  • Quick hits on key trends within industries
	• S&P NetAdvantage
	  • Outstanding industry data
	  • Company comparisons and industry outlooks
	• Frost & Sullivan
	  • Full industry reports
		• Reuters Business Insight
		  • Global market reports
		  • Includes healthcare, IT, transportation, and others
		• Investext Plus
		  • Full text research reports
		  • Prepared by industry research specialists
		• Government Data
		  • Census.gov
		  • Fedstats.gov
		  • BLS.gov

MINI-CASE

The Multi-Industry Battle for Digital Living Room Entertainment

The next round of the battle over digital living room entertainment was recently kicked off by Apple and Google. Google introduced "Google TV"; it is a set-top box provided by Logitech, which may become a default way for you to look at TV shows, that comes between the cable box and your TV. It lets you search TV listings, Web video sites, and will eventually have an application (app) store. The next player is Apple that just released its second version of "Apple TV" costing $100, or two-thirds less than the first Google TV set-top box. It is basically a DVD player that includes movie and TV rentals from iTunes, allows playback of other iTune videos, and provides an outlet for Netflix movie streaming. Furthermore, it will allow wireless beaming of video and audio to and from an iPad, iPhone, or iPod Touch. Although Apple has not announced such plans, it is expected that an app store will be available on Apple TV. Because of the lower price point, Apple may have a

much easier time convincing people to give Apple TV a try compared to Google TV. Although Google's approach is a little riskier, over time, if it can get some set-top box makers, cable companies, and other producers to use Google TV as a basis for their devices (it will become as if it were operating system software), then people will get Google TV in their homes without realizing it.

Other competitors are using game boxes as an entry point for media. Microsoft Corporation has revamped its online Xbox Live service with new features such as movies streaming from Netflix. It also has a social network facility called Xbox Live Party that allows users to create a "party" where eight people online can share photos and play games together. Likewise, Sony, through its online world for PlayStation 3 owners called PlayStation Home, allows similar relationship communication and gaming. PlayStation Home is a virtual-reality environment where gamers can shop virtually through shopping malls, shoot pool with friends, or strike up a conversation. These online services are capitalizing on the popularity of social networking and virtual-reality services such as Facebook and Second Life. Xbox Live was originally launched by Microsoft in 2002, and now has more than 14 million active users, more than half of the 25 million Xbox 360 owners in 2010. Most users pay $50 a year for premium access. Interestingly, all of Sony's networking services are offered free. Sony plans to sell special goods within the virtual world to realize revenue off its online services.

Amazon and Netflix, which have home-streaming movie services, are girding for new competition. Major telecomm and cable companies are seeking to establish new rules in the digital living room. However, some forecasters are signaling that the next generation of the living room may be lost by broadcasters and that cable will have a diminished role because of these new specialized services. They suggest that Apple, for example, is aiming to disrupt the TV market, as it has the music business. Apple has revolutionized the PC, music, and mobile-phone markets; however, at this point, both Apple and Google need broadband providers to deliver their content. But a new hybrid type of broadband providers, meaning Apple, Google, Amazon, and Netflix, have opportunity to make Apple TV and like products much more successful than their earlier failures in this market.

Because Apple has so many devices that work together in all segments of the market, it appears that they have a huge advantage in regard to distributing content over many devices. However, it remains to be seen how this battle will play out and who will win. There are other providers of content such as Hulu. Hulu provides streaming videos and television through desktop and laptop computers. It may not be a replacement for living room television, but both Google and Apple may supersede the need for services such as Hulu. Again, who is going to win this battle will be determined by the market forces across many of the service providers in this multi-industry complex of forces.

Sources: 2010, Microsoft at the edges, *Financial Times*, June 24, 16; P. Burrows, 2010, Don't rule out Apple ruling your living room, *Bloomberg BusinessWeek*, September 6, 1; P. Elmer DeWitt, 2010, How Apple took the high ground in the battle for the global digital living room, *Fortune*, http://www.cnnmoney.com, October 1; D. Frommer, 2010, Apple wins first round of TV war with Google, *Business Insider*, http://www.businessinsider.com, October 7; S. Gustin, 2010, Tech titans' new battlefield: Your living room, *Dailyfinance*, http://www.dailyfinance.com, September 9; E. Gruenwedel, 2009, VOD migrating to the living room, *Home Media Magazine*, October, 3; M. Learmonth, 2009, Maybe Hulu really wants to take over the (TV) world, *Advertising Age*, June 19, 3, 19.

Questions

1. What trends in the general environment have influenced these changes in the associated media, hardware and software producer, and broadband provider industries?
2. From the point of view of Apple as the focal firm, which of the five forces seem to be having the most influence on Apple's decision to enter with the Apple TV product? Justify your answer.
3. What competitive reactions do you expect broadband providers (cable and telecomm in particular) to pursue as a result of the entry by Apple TV and Google TV?
4. What actions would you recommend that Microsoft take to remain competitive in the television and entertainment delivery services covered in this mini-case?

EXPERIENTIAL EXERCISES

Exercise One: Competitor Analysis

Studying competitors is an important part of the external environment analysis and consists of a determination of the competitor's strategic intent, the competitor's current strategy, and the main strengths and weaknesses of the competitor.

In Small Groups

The instructor will assign each group a pair of firms from the following list. Perform a competitor analysis for each firm in the pair by answering these questions:

1. What is the competitor's strategic intent? To answer this question, examine the competitor's market dependence. Competitors with high market dependence are likely to respond aggressively to threats to their market position.
2. What is the current competitor strategy? In answering this question, consider the competitor's future objectives.
3. What are the main strengths and weaknesses of the competitors? Firms with few or insignificant strengths will not be able to respond to a competitor's actions.
4. Which of the two firms in your competitor pair will be more successful in the near future? Give support for your choice.

Whole Class

Each group should present to the class its findings about strategic intent, current strategy, and main strengths and weaknesses. The groups should also present their choice for which firm will be more successful based on the competitor analysis.

Competitor Pairs

- CVS, Walgreens
- Delta Air Lines, AirTran Airways
- SABMiller, Anheuser-Busch
- Toyota, General Motors
- Walmart, Target

Exercise Two: Five Forces and Pharmaceuticals

The pharmaceutical industry in the United States is one of the most publicly discussed and least understood. The pharmaceutical market has several unique traits. Products must be ordered by physicians, not by consumers. The party paying for the prescription may be the patient, but more often today it is a pharmaceutical benefits management (PBM) firm. PBMs work with managed-care organizations to acquire drugs at lower costs by using formularies, which list preferred drugs for any given malady. Many drugs are similar to other drugs in their effectiveness and likelihood to cause side effects, so these products should compete against each other based largely on price. But patients cannot choose one drug over another based on price; they have to take what the doctor prescribed. PBMs try to create this missing price competition by telling pharmaceutical firms that if they offer the PBM's managed-care partners a lower price, the PBM will pressure doctors to write prescriptions for the firm's product. The PBMs also encourage patients to use formulary drugs by charging a lower copayment for using these "preferred" products.

Developing new drugs is a major undertaking, particularly for truly unique drugs. Although the FDA tries to "fast-track" the approval of important new drugs, the time between identifying a molecule that may be a valid "drug target" and approving a new drug may be seven to ten years or more. By that time, a firm may have invested more than $400 million in development. Most approved drugs will not earn that much in gross revenues. In addition, most drug targets never get to market, leaving the few successful drugs to cover their costs as well. Research expenses are a drug's main cost, as the product is often mass-produced in bulk with basic chemical inputs.

One reason people are so interested in the pharmaceutical industry is that it directly affects their health. Most illnesses that pharmaceuticals treat effectively today were not treated effectively just a century ago by any medical product or procedure. As a result, drugs have an almost mystic quality for consumers who look to their pills and potions as the key to good health.

Using the information provided about the pharmaceutical industry, systematically examine the industry using the five forces model as well as industry complementors such as physicians and PBMs.

ENDNOTES

1. D. Grégoire, P. Barr, & D. Shepherd, 2010, Cognitive processes of opportunity recognition: The role of structural alignment, *Organization Science*, 21(2): 413–431; M. H. Anderson & M. L. Nichols, 2007, Information gathering and changes in threat and opportunity perceptions, *Journal of Management Studies*, 44: 367–387.

2. B. McCann & G. Vroom, 2010, Pricing response to entry and agglomeration effects, *Strategic Management Journal*, 31(3): 284–305.

3. Z. Caliskan, 2009, The relationship between pharmaceutical expenditure and life expectancy: Evidence from 21 OECD countries, *Applied Economics Letters*, 16(16): 1651–1655.

4. E. Howell, 2009, Advertising for senior-somethings, *Ottawa Business Journal*, August 24, 9.

5. 2009, Boomers & Millennials define the new workplace, *Trends Magazine*, October, 17–22; S. E. Page, 2007, Making the difference: Applying a logic of diversity, *Academy of Management Perspectives*, 21(4): 6–20.

6. J. Goldstone, 2010, The new population bomb, *Foreign Affairs*, 89(1): 31–43.

7. E. Byron, 2010, P&G meets frugal shoppers halfway, *The Wall Street Journal*, January 29, B1–B2.

8. F. R. Baumgartner, J. M. Berry, M. Hojnacki, D. C. Kimball, & B. L. Leech, 2009, *Lobbying and Policy Change: Who Wins, Who Loses, and Why*, Chicago: University of Chicago Press; A. J. Hillman, G. D. Keim, & D. Schuler, 2004, Corporate political activity: A review and research agenda, *Journal of Management*, 30: 837–857.

9. D. Albalate, G. Bel, & X. Fageda, 2009, Privatization and regulatory reform of toll motorways in Europe, *Governance*, 22(2): 295–318; M. Delmas, M. V. Russo, & M. J. Montes-Sancho, 2007, Deregulation and environmental differentiation in the electric utility industry, *Strategic Management Journal*, 28: 189–209.

10. M. Peteraf & R. Reed, 2007, Managerial discretion and internal alignment under regulatory constraints and change, *Strategic Management Journal*, 28: 1089–1112.

11. A. Lo, 2009, The opportunities brought to you by distress, *MIT Sloan Management Review*, 50(3): 53–57.

12. M. Naor, K. Linderman, & R. Schroeder, 2010, The globalization of operations in Eastern and Western countries: Unpacking the relationship between national and organizational culture and its impact on manufacturing performance, *Journal of Operations Management*, 28(3): 194–205; D. A.

Ralston, D. H. Holt, R. H. Terpstra, & Y. Kai-Cheng, 2008, The impact of national culture and economic ideology on managerial work values: A study of the United States, Russia, Japan and China, *Journal of International Business Studies*, 39: 8–26.

13. G. Clarkson & P. Toh, 2010, 'Keep out' signs: The role of deterrence in the competition for resources, *Strategic Management Journal*, 31(11), 1202–1225; E. Daneels, 2007, The process of technological leveraging, *Strategic Management Journal*, 28: 511–533.

14. Y. Rizopoulos & D. Sergakis, 2010, MNEs and policy networks: Institutional embeddedness and strategic choice, *Journal of World Business*, 45(3): 250–256.

15. S. R. Gubbi, P. S. Aulakh, S. Ray, M. B. Sarkar, & R. Chittoor, 2010, Do international acquisitions by emerging-economy firms create shareholder value? The case of Indian firms, *Journal of International Business Studies*, 41(3): 397–418; D. E. Thomas, L. Eden, M. A. Hitt, & S. R. Miller, 2007, Experience of emerging market firms: The role of cognitive bias in developed market entry and survival, *Management International Review*, 47: 845–867; Y. Luo & R. L. Tung, 2007, International expansion of emerging market enterprises: A springboard perspective, *Journal of International Business Studies*, 38: 481–498.

16. S. Knight, 2010, Divested interests: Globalization and the new politics of exchange rates, *Business & Politics*, 12(2): 1–28.

17. L. Berchicci & A. King, 2008, Postcards from the edge: A review of the business and environment literature, in J. P. Walsh & A. P. Brief (Eds.), *Academy of Management Annals* (New York: Lawrence Erlbaum Associates), 513–547.

18. D. Browning, 2008, The melting point, *The New York Times*, http://www.nytimes.com, February 2.

19. E. Rosenthal, 2008, Motivated by a tax, Irish spurn plastic bags, *The New York Times*, http://www.nytimes.com, February 2.

20. N. Isdell, 2010, Connected capitalism: How business can tackle twenty-first-century challenges, *Thunderbird International Business Review*, 52(1): 5–12.

21. M. E. Porter, 1980, *Competitive Strategy*, New York: Free Press.

22. F. Gillette, 2010, The Duke of Discomfort, *Bloomberg BusinessWeek*, September 6, 58–61.

23. J. G. Sidak & H. J. Singer, 2008, Evaluating market power with two-sided demand and preemptive offers to dissipate monopoly rent: Lessons for high-technology industries from the antitrust division's approval of the XM-Sirius satellite radio merger, *Journal of Competition Law & Economics*, 4(3): 697–751.

24. A. Hampp, 2010, Who listens to radio these days, anyway? Doesn't everyone use their iPods and iPhones to hear music? *Advertising Age*, September 27, 50.

25. A. Hecker & T. Kretschmer, 2010, Outsourcing decisions: The effect of scale economies and market structure, *Strategic Organization*, 8(2): 155–175; A. Camuffo, A. Furlan, & E. Rettore, 2007, Risk sharing in supplier relations: An agency model for the Italian air-conditioning industry, *Strategic Management Journal*, 28: 1257–1266.

26. R. Verganti, 2010, Changing the rules of competition by delighting customers, *Ivey Business Journal* (online), March/April; R. L. Priem, 2007, A consumer perspective on value creation, *Academy of Management Review*, 32: 219–235.

27. P. Kirby, 2009, Critics of Verizon AT&T praise reported probe of large telecomm carriers' practices, *Telecommunications Reports*, July 15, 3–6; R. O. Crockett, A. Reinhardt, & M. Ihlwan, 2004, Cell phones: Who's calling the shots? *BusinessWeek*, April 26, 48–49.

28. D. Sull, 2010, Competing through organizational agility, *McKinsey Quarterly*, January, 48–56; M. J. Chen, K. H. Su, & W. Tsai, 2007, Competitive tension: The awareness-motivation-capability perspective, *Academy of Management Journal*, 50: 101–118.

29. D. Sull, 2009, How to thrive in turbulent markets, *Harvard Business Review*, 87(2): 78–88; D. M. De Carolis, 2003, Competencies and imitability in the pharmaceutical industry: An analysis of their relationship with firm performance, *Journal of Management*, 29: 27–50.

30. S. Thompson, 2009, Price competition in the presence of rapid innovation and imitation: The case of digital cameras, *Economics of Innovation and New Technology*, 18(1), 93–106; S. D. Dobrev, 2007, Competing in the looking-glass market: Imitation, resources, and crowding, *Strategic Management Journal*, 28: 1267–1289.

31. B. Stone, 2003, Cutting the (phone) cord, *Newsweek*, December 8, 103.

32. 2010, Plane poker, *The Economist*, October 2, 72; 2010, Another nose in the trough, *The Economist*, September 18, 77–78.

33. 2010, All Alitalia redux, *Aviation Week & Space Technology*, April 19, 51.

34. C. Decker & T. Mellewigt, 2007, Thirty years after Michael E. Porter: What do we know about business exit? *Academy of Management Perspectives*, 21(2): 41–55.

35. J. Boyd & R. Bresser, 2008, Performance implications of delayed competitive responses: Evidence from the U.S. retail industry, *Strategic Management Journal*, 29(10): 1077–1096; K. G. Smith, W. J. Ferrier, & C. M. Grimm, 2001, King of the hill: Dethroning the industry leader, *Academy of Management Executive*, 15(2): 59–70.

36. W. Kang, B. Bayus, & S. Balasubramanian, 2010, The strategic effects of multimarket contact: Mutual forbearance and competitive response in the personal computer industry, *Journal of Marketing Research*, 47(3): 415–427; G. McNamara, R. A. Luce, & G. H. Thompson, 2002, Examining the effect of complexity in strategic group knowledge structures on firm performance, *Strategic Management Journal*, 23: 153–170.

37. T. Laseter, C. Lichtendahl, & Y. Grushka-Cockayne, 2010, Cleaning the crystal ball: How intelligent forecasting can lead to better decision making, *Strategy + Business*, http://www.strategy-business, May 25; L. Shanling, J. Shang, & S. Slaughter, 2010, Why do software firms fail? Capabilities, competitive actions, and firm survival in the software industry from 1995 to 2007, *Information Systems Research*, 21(3): 631–654; L. Fahey, 1999, Competitor scenarios: Projecting a rival's marketplace strategy, *Competitive Intelligence Review*, 10(2): 65–85.

38. K. M. Sutcliffe & K. Weber, 2003, The high cost of accurate knowledge, *Harvard Business Review*, 81(5): 74–82.

39. M. Kunc & J. Morecroft, 2010, Managerial decision making and firm performance under a resource-based paradigm, *Strategic Management Journal*, 31(11): 1164–1182; T. Yu & A. A. Cannella, 2007, Rivalry between multinational enterprises: An event history approach, *Academy of Management Journal*, 50: 665–686.

40. L. Capron & O. Chatain, 2008, Competitors' resource-oriented strategies: Acting on competitors' resources through interventions in factor markets and political markets, *Academy of Management Review*, 33: 97–121.

41. Kang, Bayus, & Balasubramanian, The strategic effects of multimarket contact: Mutual forbearance and competitive response in the personal computer industry.

42. G. B. Dagnino, 2009, Coopetition strategy: A new kind of interfirm dynamics for value creation, in G. B. Dagnino & E. Rocco (Eds.), *Coopetition Strategy: Theory Experiments and Cases*, London: Routledge; A. Brandenburger & B. Nalebuff, 1996, *Co-opetition*, New York, Currency Doubleday.

CHAPTER 4
Analyzing the Firm

KNOWLEDGE OBJECTIVES
Reading and studying this chapter should enable you to:

1. Explain how to use an internal analysis to identify the firm's strengths and weaknesses.

2. Define resources, capabilities, and core competencies and explain their relationships.

3. Describe the four characteristics that core competencies must have to be competitive advantages.

4. Explain the value chain and describe the differences between primary activities and support activities.

5. Define outsourcing and describe its advantages and disadvantages.

© Chris Sattlberger/Culture/Getty Images

McDonald's: Where Being "Better" Is Proving Superior to Trying Only to Be "Bigger"

I take considerable pride in our people and performance. We're determined to keep stretching our business, increasing traffic, and going to where our customers are headed. And we will continue to work hard to deliver sustainable business results for the long-term benefit of our shareholders.

Jim Skinner, CEO, McDonald's

A well-known and recognized global corporation, McDonald's is the world's largest restaurant company. Toward the end of 2010, McDonald's operated and franchised roughly 32,500 units in 117 countries, employed more than 1.5 million people, and was serving 60 million customers daily. The extent of McDonald's market penetration is shown by the fact that its sales revenue is several times larger than that of its closest competitors, Burger King, and Wendy's.

McDonald's financial performance over the last few years is quite positive and impressive, even during 2009, a year that featured many challenges in economies throughout the world. Comments from the firm's 2009 Annual Report describe its success during a difficult year: "In 2009, global comparable sales increased 3.8 percent, fueled by solid gains in the United States (+2.6 percent); Europe (+5.2 percent); Asia/Pacific, Middle East, and Africa (+3.4 percent); Latin America (+5.3 percent); and Canada (+5.8 percent). Earnings per share for the year increased 9 percent to $4.11 ... while consolidated operating income increased 6 percent." Positive financial results such as these suggest that a firm is creating value (defined later in this chapter) for customers.

The firm claims that providing "great value" to customers has been a "hallmark" of the McDonald's experience since its founding in 1955. As is true with all companies, McDonald's relies on its resources, capabilities, and core competencies to create value. (Defined in Chapter 1, we fully describe these parts of the internal analysis—resources, capabilities, and core competencies—in this chapter.)

© AP Photo/Kin Cheung

McDonald's claims to have several capabilities, including its employees and the training experiences provided to them. *Fortune* magazine's selection of McDonald's in 2010 as the 14th Most Admired Corporation in the world is some evidence of the value the firm places on its employees and on developing their talents. Product innovation skills are another capability. A global food vision and a stable of full-time chefs in studios located in Hong Kong, Munich, and Chicago are examples of the resources that are combined to form the firm's product innovation capability. In turn, production innovation is a core competence for McDonald's.

Making all of this work is the firm's organizational structure (this structure may be a core competence and perhaps even a competitive advantage for the firm). McDonald's has never used a rigid hierarchical organizational structure. Instead, based on its "freedom within a framework" mantra, McDonald's uses a highly decentralized business model. This model gives local managers throughout the world a great deal of leeway to make their own decisions. This decision-making flexibility is at the core of the different menu items and different store layouts you see in various nations' McDonald's units. South Korea's Bulgogi Burger (a pork patty marinated in soy-based sauce), the Netherlands' McKroket (a deep-fried patty of beef ragout), and Taiwan's Rice Burger (shredded beef between two rice patties) are examples of the locally oriented products resulting from McDonald's use of its decentralized organizational structure. The firm has a décor design studio in Grenoble, France. This group works with local units to choose a store layout design that will appeal to each unit's customers.

Collectively, McDonald's uses its resources, capabilities, and core competencies to focus on becoming "better" rather than to concentrate only on becoming "bigger." And it appears that one way McDonald's is becoming "better" is by creating value for customers by offering localized menu options and locally appealing store layouts and options.

Sources: 2010, Our company, McDonald's, http://www.mcdonalds.com, September 14; 2010, McDonald's Corp., *Standard & Poor's*, http://www.standardandpoors.com, September 25; B. Paynter, 2010, Making over McDonald's, *Fast Company Online*, http://www.fast-company.com, October 1; B. Polino, 2010, McDonald's: CEO Skinner's Plan to Win, http://www.seekingalpha.com, July 1; T. Stynes, 2010, McDonald's raises quarterly dividend 11%, *The Wall Street Journal Online*, http://www.wsj.com, September 23; 2009, *McDonalds Annual Report*, http://www.mcdonalds.com; L. Light & J. Kiddon, 2009, Brand revitalization: Background to the Turnaround at McDonald's, Wharton School Publishing, http://www.whartonsp.com, February 18.

In Chapter 3, we noted that a firm must be concerned with its competitors' actions as well as with other conditions in the external environment. At the same time, though, the firm must be concerned about its *internal organization,* which we defined in Chapter 1 as the set of conditions (such as strengths, resources, capabilities, and so forth) inside the firm affecting the choice and use of strategies. The reason managers must devote attention to understanding their firm's internal organization is that any strategy a firm chooses must be based on its resources. For example, McDonald's intention of creating more value for customers as a path to becoming "better" rather than focusing only on becoming "bigger" won't be fulfilled if the firm lacks appropriate types and levels of resources.

In *Focusing on Strategy*, we noted that McDonald's is using the skills of its human resources as the foundation for producing a number of new products to serve local customers' culinary interests and to design restaurants that are aesthetically appealing at the local level. Angus Snack Wraps, McCafe Real Fruit Smoothies, and McCafe Frappes are examples of new products being introduced in the United States and to which customers are responding positively.[1] To satisfy local tastes, a range of wraps was developed in Austria that is appealing to customers throughout Europe.[2] Using the principles of feng shui to design a restaurant in Hacienda Heights, California, is an example of using the firm's design skills. (Feng shui is the ancient Chinese practice of arranging numbers and objects with the purpose of promoting health, prosperity, and harmony. Feng shui was used to design this restaurant because the majority of the unit's clientele are Asian.)[3]

In Chapter 1, we defined *resources* as the tangible and intangible assets held by a firm. To implement a strategy, managers integrate or combine different resources so the firm will be able to complete different work-related tasks. We also defined *capabilities* in Chapter 1, noting that *capabilities* result when the firm integrates several different resources in a way that allows it to effectively and efficiently complete a task or a series of related tasks. As we described in *Focusing on Strategy*, McDonald's integrates its training programs with its human capital to develop its employees' talents. As a capability, talented employees contribute to product innovation and design as core competencies for McDonald's.

We described how to conduct an external analysis (analysis of the firm's external environment) in Chapter 3. In this chapter, we discuss how to complete an internal analysis of the firm. To discuss this topic, we first describe how resources are integrated to create capabilities and how some capabilities are then developed into core competencies. Core competencies that satisfy certain conditions are also competitive advantages for a firm. We describe these important conditions in this chapter as well. The chapter closes with discussions of two additional aspects of an internal analysis: the value chain and outsourcing.

Conducting an Internal Analysis

To develop and implement the best strategy, managers need to understand what the firm's resources, capabilities, and core competencies make possible. Indeed, as we noted earlier, a firm cannot successfully implement any strategy without being able to use the appropriate set of resources, capabilities, and core competencies. Think of it this way: A U.S.-based firm that wants to begin selling its products in Mexico won't be able to do so unless it has the resources needed to properly distribute its products in the country, the financial capital to support the distribution channel, the manufacturing capacity to produce additional quantities of its products, the capability to sell its products in a market outside the United States, and so forth.

Therefore, because of the importance of resources, capabilities, and core competencies to the success of all strategies, managers complete an internal analysis to identify and understand them as a precursor to selecting a strategy.[4] Through an internal analysis, the firm discovers many things, including its strengths and weaknesses. As defined in Chapter 1, *strengths* are resources and capabilities that allow the firm to complete important tasks. **Weaknesses** are resource and capability deficiencies that make it difficult for the firm to complete important tasks. In general terms, *strengths* suggest possibilities while *weaknesses* suggest constraints. Think of a firm in your local community. In your opinion, what are its strengths and weaknesses? Do you think the owners are aware of their firm's strengths and weaknesses? Do those owners rely on their firm's strengths as the foundation for creating value for you as a customer?

The analysis of a firm's internal organization focuses on resources, capabilities, and core competencies. We discuss these important concepts next.

Resources, Capabilities, and Core Competencies

Resources

Firms deal with two kinds of resources—tangible and intangible. **Tangible resources** are valuable assets that can be seen or quantified, such as manufacturing equipment and financial capital. **Intangible resources** are assets that contribute to creating value for customers but are not physically identifiable. Intangible resources often accumulate within a firm and become more useful over time. Reputation, brand name, know-how, and organizational culture are examples of intangible resources. Both tangible and intangible resources play important roles in creating value for customers. **Value** is judged in terms of the satisfaction a product (a good or a service) creates for customers and is measured by the price customers are willing to pay to buy that product.[5]

Tangible resources such as financial capital are important for acquiring other physical assets (such as technology). Financial capital is also necessary to obtain human capital. Tangible resources alone, however, typically do not create value for customers. Intangible resources play a critical role in the value creation

weaknesses

resource and capability deficiencies that make it difficult for the firm to complete important tasks

tangible resources

valuable assets that can be seen or quantified, such as manufacturing equipment and financial capital

intangible resources

assets that contribute to creating value for customers but are not physically identifiable

value

the satisfaction a product (a good or service) creates for customers and is measured by the price customers are willing to pay to buy that product

© STR/AFP/Getty Images

Even global mega-brands like Coca-Cola can suffer from deficiencies in human capital, particularly at the executive level. With new leadership in place starting in 2004, the company began to quickly emerge from a period of stagnation it experienced earlier in the decade.

process. For example, manufacturing equipment must be operated by employees (human capital) or by computers programmed by and using software developed by human capital. In fact, human capital is likely the most valuable intangible resource for most firms,[6] largely because of the important role human knowledge plays in shaping capabilities and core competencies.[7]

Human capital at upper managerial levels can have a strong influence on a firm's performance, as demonstrated by Coca-Cola. Claiming that "refreshment is a language everyone understands, and no one speaks it better than Coca-Cola" and pursuing a mission "To Refresh the World . . . in body, mind, and spirit,"[8] this company owns a well-known global brand name with much potential to create value for customers. However, as evidenced by a languishing price of its stock, this potential was not being fully realized in the early 2000s. During this period of time, the poor performance was attributed largely to the firm's human capital in the form of its CEO and top management team. Analysts criticized the two successive CEOs and management teams that governed the firm after the death of former CEO Roberto Goizueta. Articles detailing the poor strategies, indecisiveness, and political infighting among Coca-Cola's top executives and board of directors left little doubt that the firm suffered from a weakness of strategic leadership for a number of years. However, Coca-Cola's fortunes improved almost immediately following the appointment in 2004 of E. Neville Isdell as CEO. Decisions to expand the firm's presence in global markets and to improve its distribution system are thought to be major contributors to the change in the firm's performance. Muhtar Kent succeeded Isdell as the firm's CEO in 2008 and is emphasizing the pursuit of Vision 2020, which for the company is "...a deep commitment to best serve our consumers, and customers everywhere by continuously improving and evolving our global franchise system."[9] Thus, human capital remains an important intangible resource at the Coca-Cola Company that is contributing to the firm's strong performance.

Managers constantly take action to acquire resources, including human capital. The full set of resources a firm holds is called a *resource portfolio*. McDonald's believes that the firm's success depends on the ability of its employees, affectionately known as those who work "under the arches." The firm's "people principles" (guidelines that validate individuals' importance and the value McDonald's places on their growth and development) and the firm's array of training programs are aspects of the McDonald's operations that help it manage resources as a part of the firm's resource portfolio.[10] In other cases, firms purchase companies to add needed resources to their resource portfolio. Halliburton Corporation is an oil field services company. Its acquisition of Boots & Coots is an example of a firm buying another company to have access to needed resources, in that Halliburton bought Boots and Coots to gain access to that firm's expertise in well intervention services.[11]

Firms such as McDonald's and Halliburton hope that their actions will shape an effective resource portfolio—an important move, in that failing to do so can limit a firm's ability to implement its strategy. For example, some analysts concluded that General Motors' (GM) inability to use its resources in ways that allowed it to consistently make money producing small cars hampered the firm's attempt to successfully implement its strategies. Recently though GM rededicated itself to finding ways to use its resources to produce a lineup of smaller, fuel-efficient cars such as the planned compact sedan for the Buick brand.[12]

Intangible resources require constant attention to retain and extend their value. For example, employees' skills should be continuously updated so that the firm's human capital can perform at peak levels. Intangible resources such as brand names also must be reinforced with customers or their value will diminish. The need for reinforcement is why firms such as McDonald's and Coca-Cola continuously advertise their brands even though both of them have an iconic status with customers throughout the world.

Additionally, managers must understand that negative events can harm a firm's reputation, another important intangible asset. For example, consumer products giant Johnson & Johnson's Healthcare unit encountered manufacturing problems during 2010 that led to a massive recall of children's Tylenol and other over-the-counter medicines. Recognizing that "...customers were smarting from the recalls," the firm's CEO vowed to do everything to regain customers' trust and confidence as a means of preventing serious damage to Johnson & Johnson's reputation. Creating a quality position that reports directly to the CEO and is responsible for overseeing quality in all of the firm's manufacturing operations is an action taken to deal with the problem.[13] More effective management of Johnson & Johnson's resource portfolio might have prevented problems with the quality of parts of the firm's manufacturing operations and in turn, the potentially negative effect on its reputation.

Although it may seem easy to identify strengths and weaknesses (which are products of the firm's resources and capabilities), it generally is somewhat difficult for several reasons. First, managers need full information about the firm's resources and capabilities to accurately evaluate them. Tangible resources (such as plants and equipment) aren't hard to identify, but intangible resources (such as organizational culture, brand name, and reputation) are more challenging to identify and evaluate. Tangible resources—financial resources, for example—are usually identified in the firm's accounting system and audited and certified by an external accounting firm. Physical resources can be visually identified and values placed on them by standard (accepted) practices. Yet a firm's intangible resources, such as human capital, brand names, and reputation, are harder to evaluate. Ultimately, the judgment about the worth of a tangible or intangible resource is made in terms of that resource's ability to help the firm create value for customers.

Resources as Options Resources may be acquired or developed to use at a future time, in which case the resources are thought of as *options*. For example, a firm may purchase a piece of land and hold it for future expansion. The land can be used as a location for a facility such as a plant. In this instance, the firm holds the purchased land as an *option* to expand. Some refer to these as *real options* because without the land, for example, the firm could not expand in that particular location if it decided to do so. Buying land in a current time period allows a firm the option to use it later to expand its operations. The thought is that the land will be more expensive later, which is why the firm took out an option on the land by buying it at a lower price today.

Real options create strategic flexibility for firms. When executed effectively, real options typically hold their value or may even increase in value. Therefore, if the firm decides not to use the resource being held as an option, it can be sold to recoup the original investment and possibly additional returns. In this way, real options represent investments having value and provide options to support the firm's future strategies.[14]

Resources acquired as real options can be especially useful for firms competing in highly uncertain environments, which is the case for pharmaceutical companies. These firms (such as Pfizer, Merck, and Johnson & Johnson) invest large sums of money in research and development (R&D) as the foundation for developing a number of new drug compounds, some of which are used as real options. In other words, they invest to develop a variety of drugs that are intended to treat different illnesses even though the firms know that many of the drugs won't succeed. These firms do not focus on only one drug or on a few drugs because of the uncertain success of new products (drugs) and the highly competitive nature of their industry. Each firm's competitors are also investing heavily to discover the next "blockbuster" drug. Investing to develop a variety of drugs provides the firm with a portfolio of potential drugs that can be developed and marketed.

Many firms in technology-intense industries also use their resources to create options. They invest in the development of a variety of technologies to provide flexibility to use if needed, given conditions in their highly competitive environments.[15] Today for example, automobile manufacturers are taking options in fuel-efficient, more sustainable technologies (e.g., hybrid and all-electric) as a foundation for isolating the "best" technology to which additional resources can be committed in the future.[16]

Some firms competing in highly uncertain industries even invest in resources that provide options to move into totally new industries. Firms take these actions to maintain flexibility in case the industry changes dramatically and they find themselves lacking the resources needed to adapt to those changes.[17] U.S. Steel, for example, was once only a steel manufacturer; but the firm now uses its resource portfolio to compete in a range of other businesses such as coal mining, transportation, real estate development, and mineral resource management. U.S. Steel initially took options in these different fields because of the intense competition it faced as a steel manufacturer. The same type of description can be given for Rolls Royce in that this firm has not produced high-end luxury automobiles since it sold its car unit to BMW in 1998. Today, Rolls Royce notes that it is "a global business providing integrated power systems for use on land, at sea, and in the air." Civil aerospace, defense aerospace, marine, energy, and services are the divisions through which the firm offers integrated power systems to customers in over 50 countries. The firm took options in these business areas while still building and selling its luxury marquee cars.[18]

However, regardless of whether resources are held as options or are designed for current use only, simply having them is not enough to build a competitive advantage.[19] The true value of a firm's resources emerges when they are integrated to form capabilities.[20] Some capabilities are developed into core competencies, which are the ultimate source of value creation for customers. We show the link among resources, capabilities, and core competencies in Figure 4.1.

Figure 4.1 Managing Resources to Develop Capabilities and Core Competencies

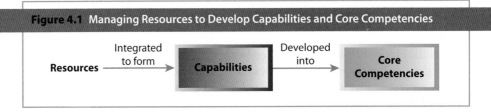

Capabilities

As we said earlier, capabilities are a product of integrating several different resources to complete a task or a series of related tasks. Commonly, capabilities are part of organizational functions such as marketing, manufacturing, finance, and so forth. Apple, for example, is thought to have a capability in the R&D function. People, work teams, equipment, and financial resources are some of the resources that Apple integrates to complete various R&D tasks. Similarly, as we explain in *Understanding Strategy: Learning from Success* about Ford Motor Company, this firm is integrating some of its tangible resources (e.g., financial capital, manufacturing equipment) with

© Gero Breloer/Newscom

some of its intangible resources (e.g., the knowledge possessed by employees) to form several capabilities (e.g., manufacturing controls) as the foundation for seeking to again become a successful company. Honda, another automobile manufacturer, uses its capabilities in product design, engineering, and manufacturing to build a wide variety of engines. Honda produces many different consumer products while competing in three divisions—automobiles, motorcycles, and power products. The engines in all of these products are thought to create value for Honda's customers.[21]

Leveraging broad capabilities in product design, engineering, and manufacturing, Honda is able to effectively compete in numerous product categories where its engines create significant value for its customers.

Several insights about capabilities are important to remember, and those trying to use a firm's resources to create capabilities must understand them. First, most capabilities are based on the knowledge held by the firm's employees (its human capital).[22] For example, Apple's new products are developed based on ideas from the software engineers and designers working in the firm's R&D function. Honda provides another example of human capital as the foundation for many capabilities. In this firm, engineers and others are given a great deal of free time to "tinker" with various aspects of product design and manufacturing to discover how things work. The discoveries they make while "tinkering" add to their stock of knowledge—knowledge that facilitates their work on various projects. In this sense, Honda employees are encouraged to "dream" about what is possible in the future. "One Team" is an important aspect of Ford's new mission (called One Ford Mission). One Team is defined as "people working together as a lean, global enterprise for automotive leadership, as measured by: Customer, Employee, Dealer, Investor, Supplier, Union/Council, and Community Satisfaction."[23] Thus, human capital is critical to developing Ford's capabilities and to reaching the One Ford Mission.

A second important insight about capabilities is that each of them is a product of deliberate attempts to integrate several resources with the purpose of completing one or more work tasks. By this we mean that capabilities do not spring to life by themselves; rather, capabilities result when people (employees) think carefully about which combination of resources will allow the firm to create a capability with potential to become a core competence. Thus, while each core competence is grounded in a capability, not every capability becomes a core competence, and not every core competence is also a competitive advantage.

Ford Motor Company: Using Capabilities as the Foundation for Seeking to Return to Long-Term Success

Ford's current success "…isn't just happenstance; it's a combination of benefits from not taking a bailout, unassailably high quality and an interesting, exciting product lineup. Ford is in the driver's seat now."

John Wolonowicz, analyst at HIS Global Insight

An iconic firm, Henry Ford and 11 associates established Ford Motor Company on June 16, 1903. Quickly, the firm's moving assembly line (an innovation when introduced) became a value-creating core competence in that the line greatly improved manufacturing efficiency. Being able to sell products to consumers at a price lower than competitors' prices was a major benefit produced by the efficient moving assembly line. A number of tangible resources (e.g., manufacturing facilities and equipment) and intangible resources (e.g., unique work procedures) were integrated to design and use the moving assembly line as a key source of the firm's success.

Multifaceted capabilities including market analysis focused on better understanding customer purchasing decisions, vendor relationships which enable more effective supply chain management, and manufacturing controls and procedures that have led to increased product quality and production flexibility have allowed Ford to outpace other US-based automakers and to gain ground on its major foreign competitors.

© AP Photo/Richard Drew

Fast-forward to the beginning of the 21st century and we find a completely different company. Along with major U.S.-based competitors, GM and Chrysler Corporation, Ford was struggling to produce cars that customers wanted to buy. In 2006, Ford made a "…literal bet-the-company decision to borrow $23.6 billion putting even the company's fabled blue logo up as collateral." Two major benefits resulted from this decision: (1) Ford was able to invest more rapidly than GM and Chrysler to quickly bring out new lines of more fuel-efficient cars, and (2) the company had a cash cushion to support its operations when the market for new cars weakened substantially in 2008.

Armed with its borrowed financial resources, new CEO Alan Mulally decided that the firm had to focus its efforts on developing a smaller number of more fuel-efficient cars that would appeal to customers on a worldwide basis. Supporting

this focus were efforts to reduce costs, increase product quality, and add technological capabilities to the firm's products (for example, current plans call for Ford to put "social networking, Web browsing, and iPod-style thumb controls in 80 percent of models by 2015").

These actions are yielding the types of benefits Ford sought. In 2010, *Consumer Reports* said that Ford's products had "world-class" reliability and that the Fusion (one of the company's new, fuel-efficient cars) topped Toyota Motor Corporation's Camry in quality. Selling more models the firm now produces at lower costs helped Ford earn $2.6 billion in 2010's second quarter; and Mulally predicted at the time that Ford would have more cash than debt at the end of 2011.

Capabilities are the foundation for Ford's resurgence. We'll mention a few here. As is commonly the case, the firm's human capital plays a critical role in forming each capability. Through a capability in market analysis, the firm is able to more clearly understand what consumers want when they buy a car or truck. A capability in vendor relationships facilitates the firm's efforts to effectively and efficiently manage its supply chain. A capability in manufacturing controls is the foundation for enhancing the quality of the products the firm produces. Finally, a capability with manufacturing procedures allows Ford to develop global platforms through which it is able to produce cars (with slight modifications) that appeal to consumers throughout the world.

Sources: C. Idifore, 2010, Ford turnaround picks up speed, *CNNMoney.com*, http://money.cnn.com, July 23; C. Idifore, 2010, Turnaround for big three automakers? Not so fast, *CNNMoney.com*, http://money.cnn.com, April 30; K. Naughton and I. King, 2010, Ford's tremendous progress, *Bloomberg/BusinessWeek Online*, http://www.businessweek.com, January 7; J. Palmer, 2010, Ford, a U.S. auto maker hitting on all cylinders, *The Wall Street Journal Online*, http://www.wsj.com, August 8; *News.com*, http://www.cellular-news.com, April 25.

© Greg Epperson, iStock

Core Competencies

Defined in Chapter 1, *core competencies* are capabilities the firm emphasizes and performs especially well while pursuing its vision. When the firm's core competencies are different from those held by competitors, they may be referred to as *distinctive competencies*,[24] another term we defined in Chapter 1. When core competencies allow the firm to create value for customers exceeding the value competitors create for them, it has a *competitive advantage.*

Product innovation is a core competence and appears to be a distinctive competence for Apple and Honda. The iPhone (Apple) and the 1975 CVCC engine (using fuel-combustion technology, Honda designed this engine to meet U.S. clean-air standards) are examples of innovative products associated with each company's product innovation core competence. Ford's market analysis capability is foundational to its brand management core competence. Evidence suggests that the brand is well known throughout the world and that in general, consumers have a positive image of the firm. As a capability, vendor relationships support the firm's supply chain management core competence. Long-term and productive relationships with steel, glass, and other vendors result in efficiencies that in turn allow Ford to reduce its supply chain costs. As a capability, manufacturing controls are critical to the significant improvements Ford has recently made in the quality and reliability of its products.

So what causes a core competence also to be a competitive advantage? Is the core competence of product innovation a competitive advantage for Apple or Honda? Are Ford's brand management and supply chain management core competencies also competitive advantages? As you will see in the following materials, a core competence must satisfy four characteristics in order to be a relatively sustainable competitive advantage. We summarize these characteristics in Table 4.1. (Remember Ford's moving assembly line that it used in its early days? There is little doubt that this line satisfied these criteria and as such, was a competitive advantage.)

1. Core competencies must be *valuable.* Valuable competencies help the firm create value for the customer, exploit market opportunities, or neutralize threats. For example, firms with a product innovation core competence develop new products that exploit opportunities in the external environment. These opportunities represent customer needs that haven't been satisfied. Apple's iTunes digital music store provides a substantial selection of music at reasonable prices with easy access for customers, satisfying their need to listen to the music they prefer at a time that is convenient for them. Ford's supply chain management core competence facilitates efforts to control the costs of its supplies; in turn,

Table 4.1 Characteristics of Core Competencies That Lead to a Competitive Advantage	
Valuable	They contribute to value creation for customers by exploiting new opportunities or neutralizing threats.
Rare	They are held by few if any competitors.
Difficult to imitate	They are difficult to re-create because intangible resources or their specific contribution to the capability cannot be easily identified.
Nonsubstitutable	No resources/capabilities exist that can complete the tasks and provide the same value to customers.

controlling costs makes it possible for the firm to reduce the price of its products to consumers.

2. Core competencies must be *rare*. Rarity means that few if any competitors have the competencies needed to complete a task or a set of tasks with the same quality as the focal firm. The firm holding a core competence that is valuable but not rare (i.e., the competence is held by at least some and perhaps many of the firm's competitors) has a competence that is a source of competitive parity rather than a source of competitive advantage.[25] As an example of this situation, think about Coca-Cola and PepsiCo. Both of these firms have a core competence in terms of global distribution channels and practices. Even though this competence is valuable, it is not rare in that both firms are using capabilities in ways that yield a core competence when it comes to distributing products globally. In contrast, Honda's ability to produce an array of engines is valuable and may also be rare. Because of its concentration on designing and producing multiple types of engines that are used in a variety of applications, Honda is often thought of as an engine company rather than as a car company.

3. Core competencies must be *difficult to imitate*. Competitors want to imitate another firm's valuable and rare core competencies. However, doing so may be difficult. Think of product innovation as an example here. LG Electronics is thought to have a product innovation core competence that it uses to produce cell phones. (The talents of its designers and engineers, the way those individuals work together as well as the systems and procedures they use to design and produce mobile phones are the capabilities on which this core competence is based.) Being able to fully understand (and certainly to imitate) how LG uses its capabilities to create a product innovation core competence is a challenge for competitors such as Motorola, Nokia, and Samsung.[26] Today, LG (along with Motorola, Nokia, and Samsung) is being challenged to develop a viable competitor to Apple's iPhone.[27] Obviously, LG's product innovation core competence is critical to developing a successful response to this challenge. Apple's product innovation core competence is based on several capabilities, including the culture and environment that CEO Steve Jobs and other long-tem employees established and continue to nurture, as well as the way the firm organizes its R&D activities. Given the lack of full visibility of Apple's and LG's product innovation core competence to competitors and the difficulty competitors would have in attempting imitation, it is likely that the product innovation core competence for Apple satisfies the first three criteria to become a competitive advantage. Consider the possibility that a failure to develop a viable competing product to Apple's iPhone might suggest that LG needs to reinvest in product innovation if it is to remain a core competence.

4. Core competencies must be *nonsubstitutable*. For a core competence to be a competitive advantage, a competitor that can perform the same function must not possess equivalent competencies. A core competence in customer service is an example of a core competence with no equivalent substitutes. When customers want service on the products they have purchased, the firm cannot use its design skills (for example) to satisfy the customer.

Firms selling products that are expensive relative to other offerings sometimes attempt to develop after-sales service as a competence. Lexus automobiles (manufactured by Toyota) may be a product for which after-sales service is a core competence lacking substitutes. The use of a free loaner automobile while the customer's car is being serviced and the ability to schedule an appointment to have a representative from the Lexus dealer come to a distant location to obtain a customer's car and then return it after it has been serviced are examples of a core competence that creates value and has no substitutes.

As we see, capabilities clearly influence the selection of a firm's strategy, particularly its business-level strategy (see Chapter 5). The reason for this influence is that capabilities are what the firm performs especially well and what the firm emphasizes while producing its products. However, firms must continuously invest in and support capabilities in order for them to generate maximum value as a source of core competencies. (Recall that we previously mentioned that Apple continues to nurture its R&D activities given that they are the foundation for its product innovation core competence.) Stated a bit differently, capabilities, and the core competencies they help form, can atrophy or lose their value when firms fail to consistently invest in them.

This may be the case with product quality at Toyota Motor Corporation. We discuss in the *Understanding Strategy: Learning from Failure* how the firm's product quality core competence appears to have lost its value during the last few years. We also describe what the firm is doing to reestablish product quality as a core competence and to restore the firm's reputation with customers for producing high-quality, reliable cars and trucks.

Competitive Advantages

Having a competitive advantage means that the firm is using its resources, capabilities, and core competencies in ways that create more value for customers compared to the value competitors' products create for those customers. In terms of the four criteria discussed earlier, firms with valuable and rare core competencies are able to achieve competitive advantages over their rivals, but likely for a relatively short period of time. Core competencies that are difficult to imitate and that are nonsubstitutable as well as valuable and rare often produce competitive advantages that last longer—that is, the advantages are more sustainable. However, no competitive advantage can be sustained forever; competitors eventually learn how to imitate another firm's core competencies or how to use their own capabilities to form competencies and competitive advantages that allow them to produce products that create more value for customers.

Competitive advantages are important because they enable firms to capture larger shares of the market and to increase their returns. When they do so, they also create value for their owners and other stakeholders (having already created superior value for customers). As a result, managers are continuously searching for ways to develop core competencies that are valuable, rare, difficult to imitate, and nonsubstitutable. Managers must understand, though, that competitors will try to imitate their firm's competitive advantages or to create different advantages that create more value for customers. Firms can try to imitate a core competence that is also a competitive advantage in many ways. For example, even though a production innovation core competence is difficult to imitate, firms might acquire a company with an established R&D competence. Similarly, a firm could develop an alliance with companies having complementary capabilities that, when integrated with their own, form a core competence that is valuable and rare (and perhaps difficult to imitate and nonsubstitutable as well).

Next, we examine how firms use the value chain to understand the activities in which they can create value for customers. In actuality, capabilities and core competencies are combinations of activities that are required to complete one or more work tasks that collectively form the entire value chain.

Toyota Motor Corporation: Trying to Regain Its Reputation for Product Quality

Toyota has made significant progress in recent months to help ensure that customers can have complete confidence in the quality, safety, and reliability of their vehicles, and our latest initiatives build on those accomplishments.

Steve St. Angelo, Chief Quality Officer for Toyota North America

An individual without access to news during the latter part of 2009 and through 2010 might be shocked to read this statement from a Toyota official. The reason for this is that Toyota Motor Corporation has long been known for the quality and reliability of its products. In fact, for many years, product quality was a core competence and a competitive advantage for this firm as it rose to global prominence, becoming the world's largest automobile manufacturer (both in sales volume and number of units sold) in 2009. GM had long been the world's largest car company prior to losing this distinction to Toyota.

Originally called "just-in-time production," the Toyota Production System (TPS) was

Did Toyota's ascent to the title of world's largest automobile manufacturer lead to a loss of focus on product quality as a core competence? Regardless of the cause, during 2009 – 2010, the company paid a heavy price in the recall of millions of vehicles and reduction in customer confidence.

foundational to Toyota's initial success. TPS, through which manufacturing and logistics' activities are carefully integrated with the purpose of eliminating waste and inconsistencies in production processes and outcomes as well as preventing overburdening different parts of the production process at different times, was unique in the automobile manufacturing industry when Toyota established it. Firmly committed to the value of TPS, Toyota worked on continuously improving this set of techniques that eventually led to the "lean manufacturing" system for which Toyota became known in markets throughout the world (and especially in North American markets during the 1970s and 1980s). By concentrating on lean manufacturing principles (e.g., continuous improvement, respect for people, long-term philosophy, and the right process will produce the right results), Toyota became a world leader in terms of the quality and hence the reliability of its products.

The events of 2009 and 2010 surfaced a different picture of Toyota. From roughly November 2008 through September 2010, Toyota recalled over 8.5 million vehicles to deal with a variety of problems. Issues with some engines' electronic control units, faulty engine components, and accelerator pedals sticking to the floor are examples of the problems confronting Toyota during these years. The effects on Toyota were immediate and dramatic in that the value of the firm's stock declined 17 percent during the first three quarters of 2010 and its U.S. market declined from 16.6 percent to 15.2 percent in 2010's first eight months.

Toyota officials quickly announced that the firm was fully committed to correcting all problems that consumers experienced. In addition to providing appropriate levels of customer service, it seemed that the firm's actions were also taken to reestablish product quality as a core competence and potentially as a competitive advantage as well. Among the host of corrective, quality-driven actions Toyota was taking are the following: (1) established the North American Center for Quality Excellence, (2) organized SMART (Swift Market Analysis Response Teams) with the purpose of responding to a customer's complaint within 24 hours, (3) instituted new training procedures to assure quality work, and (4) increased the amount of time new models are physically tested before entering them into production.

Toyota appears to be responding aggressively to deal with the significant number of product recalls it faced. By late 2010, the firm indicated that roughly 65 percent of the repairs required by the full set of recalls had been completed. Additionally, company officials continuously reiterated that moving forward, the firm would be "ultra careful" in all of its activities as the foundation for again producing high-quality cars in which customers could have complete confidence.

Sources: 2010, Complimentary maintenance plans now standard on new Toyota and Scion models, Toyota Motor Corp., http://www.toyota.com, October 6; 2010, Toyota announces new quality leadership initiatives, Toyota Motor Corp., http://www.toyota.com, October 4; N. Bunkley, 2010, Toyota says 65% of recall repairs are completed, *The Wall Street Journal Online*, http://www.wsj.com, October 4; P. R. LaMonica, 2010, Investors bid sayonara to Toyota, *CNNMoney.com*, http://money.cnn.com, September 14; M. Ramsey & N. Shirouzu, 2010, Toyota is changing how it develops cars, *The Wall Street Journal Online*, http://www.wsj.com, July 5; H. Yousuf, 2010, Toyota recalls 1.33 million cars, *CNNMoney.com*, http://money.cnn.com, September 7.

The Value Chain

The **value chain** is the structure of activities the firm uses to implement its business-level strategy (we discuss business-level strategies in the next chapter). Firms analyze their value chain to better understand the activities that contribute most strongly to creating value for customers and the cost incurred to complete each activity. Of course, to succeed, the firm must create value that exceeds the costs incurred to produce, distribute, and service products for customers.[28]

Based on the firm's analysis of its value chain activities, it can compare them to those of competitors. Benchmarking is a common means of making these comparisons. **Benchmarking** is the process of identifying the best practices of competitors and other high-performing firms, analyzing them, and comparing them with the organization's own practices.[29] Through these comparisons, firms sometimes identify better ways to complete activities that create greater value for customers. For example, FedEx studied the activities and best practices of transportation companies to invent the overnight-delivery business. Other firms may develop means of handling the value chain activities differently from competitors because they could not complete the activity in a comparable way. For example, when founded, personal computer manufacturer Dell decided to handle distribution activities differently from its competitors. As we know, Dell decided to sell its computers directly to customers rather than through retail outlets. At the time of its founding as a very small venture it would have been highly difficult for Dell to obtain the needed retail agreements with companies to sell its products. The growth and popularity of the Internet greatly enhanced Dell's ability to reach customers and sell its products using the direct-sales approach. Today however, virtually all PC manufacturers know how to configure the value chain in order to deliver products directly to customers. In this sense, Dell's value chain innovations in terms of distribution have been imitated. (For a period of time, Dell's build-to-order distribution methods were a competitive advantage. The fact that competitors have imitated these methods demonstrates that no competitive advantage lasts permanently.)

The focus of value chain analysis is on primary and secondary activities. **Primary activities** include inbound logistics (such as sources of parts), operations (such as manufacturing if dealing with a physical product), sales and distribution of products, and after-sales service. Therefore, primary activities are directly involved in creating value for the customer. **Support activities** provide support to the primary activities so that they can be completed effectively. Support activities, then, are only indirectly involved in creating value for the customer as they support the primary activities. Next, we examine primary and support activities to more fully explain the value chain.

Focusing on the primary activities, the product moves from raw-material suppliers to operations, to finished-goods inventory, to marketing and distribution, and finally to after-sales service. These activities are shown in Figure 4.2. Each stage of the value chain's primary activities adds costs, but hopefully creates value as well.

Knowledge of the customer is a critical component of actions taken to use the value chain.[30] This knowledge must be injected into each stage of activities to increase the probability that activities are being used in ways to create value for customers. For example, using knowledge about customers, the firm ensures that its raw materials are of appropriate quality to build a product that meets or exceeds customer needs. These materials should be delivered in a timely matter so that the firm can provide the finished product on the dates required by the

value chain

the structure of activities the firm uses to implement its business-level strategy

benchmarking

the process of identifying the best practices of competitors and other high-performing firms, analyzing them, and comparing them with the organization's own practices

primary activities

inbound logistics (such as sources of parts), operations (such as manufacturing if dealing with a physical product), sales and distribution of products, and after-sales service

support activities

provide support to the primary activities so that they can be completed effectively

Figure 4.2 The Value Chain

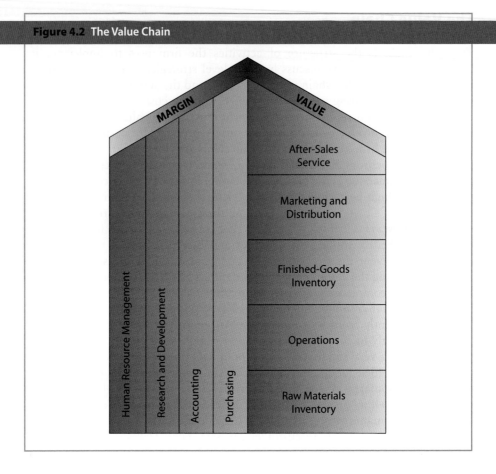

customer. Of course, the firm must be able to transform the raw materials into a high-quality finished product. These products are then sent to inventory so that marketing can distribute them to the customer when needed at the lowest possible distribution cost. Marketing develops sales and promotion campaigns to attract customers and to ensure that they understand the value provided by the product. Finally, after-sales service helps customers use the product and makes certain that the product meets the customers' standards. The value provided is reflected in the size of the margin as shown in Figure 4.2.

Support activities are important even though their effect on creating customer value is indirect. As shown in Figure 4.2, human resource management, research and development, accounting, and purchasing are examples of support activities (information technology is yet another support activity). The human resource management function is responsible for recruiting the human capital needed to complete all primary and support activities. Research and development helps to create the new products that are produced and provided to customers through the primary activities. Shareholders and investors pay close attention to the reports provided by accounting to determine whether the firm is performing well and whether they want to make additional investments in the firm. This discussion emphasizes the necessity of the support functions and shows their effect on a firm's ability to create value for customers through the primary activities. With today's new technologies, some primary and support activities are being performed in new and more efficient ways. For example, firms can use the Internet

Figure 4.3 **Outsourcing the HRM Function**

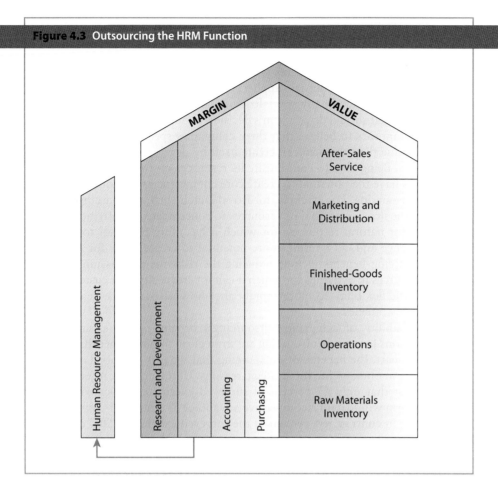

to communicate with customers, track deliveries, and learn more about customers' needs.

Firms analyze their value chain continuously to find ways to operate more efficiently as a means of creating additional value for customers. Continuous analysis of the value chain is a prerequisite to developing a competitive advantage and sustaining it against substantial competition. In fact, analysis of the value chain has led to a significant amount of outsourcing of support activities and even some primary activities. When a firm identifies serious inefficiencies in how it completes one or more activities, those activities are candidates for outsourcing.

Outsourcing

Outsourcing involves acquiring a capability from an external supplier that contributes to the focal firm's ability to create value for customers.[31] Outsourcing is a popular strategic management tool that is being used by firms throughout the world, including a number of U.S. companies.

In Figure 4.3, we show hypothetically how a support activity—human resource management—might be outsourced. Of course, a firm could choose to outsource the entire human resource management activity or only certain parts of it. Information technology (IT) is another support activity that some firms choose to outsource. Recently for example, Royal Dutch Shell announced plans

outsourcing

acquiring a capability from an external supplier that contributes to the focal firm's ability to create value for customers to outsource the majority of its IT activities to three companies—Electronic Data Systems (EDS) (Hewlett-Packard paid $13.9 billion to acquire EDS in 2008), AT&T, and T-Systems.[32]

Firms seek one or more benefits when they decide to outsource the performance of an activity to an external supplier. Being able to create more value for its customers by using a company specializing in completing a particular activity is the key benefit that should drive a firm's decision to outsource. Royal Dutch Shell, for example, appears to believe that three companies specializing in IT can generate more value than the firm can create itself by developing and using its own IT operations. Being able to concentrate its resources on the activities for which the firm does have the potential to create core competencies is another important benefit of outsourcing. For example, for Royal Dutch Shell, outsourcing IT activities enables the firm to marshal its resources to concentrate on activities (perhaps exploration for natural resources) for which it has more potential to develop a core competence and, as a result, more potential to create value for customers. Other outsourcing benefits include reducing the risks the firm assumes when it allocates resources to activities for which it cannot create superior customer value and having the flexibility to more rapidly alter how activities are being used to implement its strategies.

The probability of achieving outsourcing's benefits increases significantly when the reasons for using outsourcing are strategic in nature rather than tactical. For the most part, the benefits of outsourcing that we just described accrue to a firm engaging in outsourcing for strategic reasons. Unfortunately, recent research results suggest that only 27 percent of surveyed executives indicated that they hoped their firm would gain a competitive advantage as a result of their outsourcing decisions. In contrast, 64 percent of the surveyed executives cited cost reduction as the primary motive for their firm's outsourcing decisions.[33]

As a tactical decision, reducing costs is clearly an important objective. But cost reductions that are not part of a robust plan as to how the firm's entire resource portfolio is to be managed to create superior value for customers by developing and effectively using core competencies is not the path to long-term success. Another way of thinking about this is to say that tactical outsourcing decisions (such as cost reductions that are not sought within the context of a strategic set of decisions) typically prevent the firm from gaining access to the most important benefits associated with outsourcing (such as those discussed earlier). Thus, the challenge for managers is to make certain that their firm's outsourcing decisions are the product of deliberate analyses about how outsourcing certain activities will allow the firm to better manage its resources in order to develop value-creating core competencies.[34]

Those studying the firm's internal organization must also know that outsourcing is not risk free. For example, the quality of the work completed by the company to which a firm outsources an activity may fall short of expectations. This can happen even when the outsourcing firm diligently tries to assess the quality of the work produced by the other company. Another risk is that the outsourcing firm may have to share quite a bit of information about how it produces its product. While necessary to support the work of the firm to whom an activity is being outsourced, revealing too much competitively relevant or sensitive information can be risky. Timing is another risk. Here, the concern is that the firm completing the outsourced activity will fail to meet the delivery deadline to which it agreed. If this happens, a firm's entire production process can be negatively affected. Miscommunication is a final risk we'll mention. After experiencing product quality problems (see *Learning from Failure*), Toyota brought some activities that had been outsourced back in-house. According to Toyota officials, the reason for this is that some outsourcing contracts "...led to a breakdown in communication and potential misunderstandings"[35] about the level of quality Toyota expected. Effective outsourcers are aware of these types of risks and try to fully assess them prior to finalizing an agreement with another company.

SUMMARY

The primary purpose of this chapter is to explain how a firm's resources and capabilities can be managed to develop one or more core competencies that are also competitive advantages. In doing so, we examined the following topics:

- To develop and implement the most effective strategy, managers need to understand the firm's resources and capabilities. To reach this understanding, managers complete an internal analysis to identify the firm's strengths and weaknesses. **Strengths** are resources and capabilities that allow the firm to complete important tasks. **Weaknesses** are resources and capability deficiencies that make it difficult for the firm to complete important tasks.

- Firms have two types of resources—**tangible** and **intangible.** Tangible resources are valuable assets that can be seen or quantified, such as manufacturing equipment and financial capital. Intangible resources are assets that contribute to creating value for customers but are not physically identifiable.

- Resources may be acquired or developed to use in the future. These resources are considered *real options.* Resource options provide firms with strategic flexibility, or the ability to deal with issues as they surface. These options normally hold their value and may even increase in value.

- Capabilities are formed by integrating several resources with the intent of accomplishing a major task or series of related tasks. Capabilities are normally based on the knowledge held by the firm's employees (its human capital).

- **Core competencies** are capabilities the firm emphasizes and performs especially well while pursuing its vision. If these core competencies are different from those held by competitors, they may be referred to as distinctive competencies. When core competencies allow the firm to create more value for customers compared to the value competitors' products create for them, it has a competitive advantage. To be a relatively sustainable competitive advantage, a core competence must be valuable, rare, difficult to imitate, and nonsubstitutable.

- The **value chain** is the structure of activities the firm uses to implement its business-level strategy. A firm analyzes its value chain to better understand the activities that contribute most strongly to creating value for customers and the costs of using each activity. This analysis yields information and insights the firm requires to wisely (i.e., efficiently) use its resources. The value chain includes both **primary** and **support activities. Value** can be created when using primary activities to produce, sell, distribute, and service a product and when using support activities to support wise use of the firm's resources.

- **Outsourcing** involves acquiring a capability from an external supplier that contributes to the focal firm's ability to create value for customers. Even though risks are associated with its use, outsourcing has many benefits and as such, is becoming more common.

KEY TERMS

DISCUSSION QUESTIONS

1. What are strengths and weaknesses and how does the firm identify them?
2. What are resources, capabilities, and core competencies? How are these concepts related?
3. What four characteristics of core competencies are necessary for them to be competitive advantages?
4. How would you explain the value chain to a classmate? What are primary and support activities?
5. What is outsourcing? How can outsourcing create value for the firm? What are the potential problems with outsourcing?

STRATEGY TOOLBOX

Introduction

After examining the external environment for opportunities to move a company forward, strategic leaders must carefully examine their firm's internal organization to identify capabilities. A vision that is disconnected with the reality of internal capabilities is doomed to failure. One of the most common elements of this analysis is a review of the value chain and an honest assessment of how the company compares to the competition. This chapter's tool summarizes how to systematically complete this review.

The Value Chain Assessor

ACTIVITY	IMPORTANCE (low, medium, or high)	COMPARISON OF COMPANY'S COMPETENCE TO KEY COMPETITORS				
		SIGNIFICANTLY LOWER	SOMEWHAT LOWER	NEITHER HIGHER/ LOWER	SOMEWHAT HIGHER	SIGNIFICANTLY HIGHER
After-Sales Service						
Marketing and Distribution						
Finished-Goods Inventory						
Operations						
Raw Materials Inventory						
Human Resource Management						
Research and Development						
Accounting						
Purchasing						

STRATEGY TOOLBOX · STRATEGY TOOLBOX · STRATEGY TOOLBOX · STRATEGY TOOLBOX · STRATEGY TOOL

Netflix: Entering a Brave New World

The Epix deal is an example of the innovative ways in which we're partnering with major content providers to broaden the scope and freshness of choices available to our members to watch instantly over the Internet.

Ted Sarandos, Chief Content Office, Netflix

Netflix was founded in 1997 as a more conventional rental service with online offerings. The firm grew rapidly, particularly beginning in 1999 when it eliminated due dates to return rented products and the "late" fees associated with returning items after the due date. These actions were especially popular with customers who were disenchanted by the late fees they sometimes incurred when renting from firms such as Blockbuster.

Fast-forward to late 2010 and we find that Netflix had 15 million subscribers. To serve these customers, Netflix shipped an average of over 2 million DVDs per day. The company had become the world's largest subscription service streaming movies and TV episodes over the Internet and shipping DVDs by mail. Supporting the firm's success and continued growth was its customer service core competence (we identify other capabilities and core competencies below). Evidence that customer service is a core competence for this firm is provided by the fact that in February 2010, "…the American Customer Satisfaction Index named Netflix the number one ecommerce company for customer satisfaction." From an operational perspective, Netflix notes that 90 percent of its members say they are satisfied with the firm's service and that they recommend the company to family and friends.

Netflix's success was in stark contrast to Blockbuster's fortunes. This surprised some observers in that, in 2005, some took the position that Blockbuster was poised to outperform Netflix as a result of a decision to integrate online and in-store rentals. (Through this system, customers could rent online but return the product to a Blockbuster store and immediately select another rental.) However, Blockbuster never achieved the synergies it anticipated through the efforts to integrate "bricks" (i.e., the storefront locations) with "clicks" (i.e., online rentals). According to an analyst, "Blockbuster's experience shows that executing a bricks-and-clicks strategy entails a high degree of difficulty, managing not just two very different kinds of businesses, with dissimilar domains of expertise, but also a third challenge: integrating two separate systems." Rather than integrating two systems (bricks and clicks), Netflix's strategy finds the firm concentrating solely on online and streaming opportunities. In light of its competitive difficulties and poor performance, Blockbuster filed for bankruptcy in September 2010, partly with the objective of overcoming nearly $1 billion in debt.

Several capabilities stimulate and support Netflix's success. Information technology is a capability and a core competence as well for this firm. Netflix allocates a significant amount of resources to build its own proprietary IT systems, which are the source of another capability—data management. By carefully analyzing rental patterns, Netflix provides a great deal of supportive information to its customers including recommendations for movies that are consistent with previous rentals. Vendor relationships are a capability and likely a core competence, too, in that the firm works tirelessly with content providers to gain access to their products and with distributors to find avenues for delivering the content it has available. In fact, as Chief Content Officer, Ted Sarandos' (quoted at the beginning of this mini-case) primary responsibility is to find additional ways for Netflix to gain access to content (such as the deal with Epix) that can be distributed through multiple channels. The deal with Epix, for example, gives Netflix exclusive rights to new releases and older films from Paramount, Lionsgate, and MGM "…on its site 90 days after Epix first debuts the films to its premium pay and on-demand subscribers." In terms of distribution channels, by late 2010 customers were able to use multiple devices such as Sony's PS3 and Nintendo's Wii consoles and Internet TVs from LG, Sony, and VIZIO to view Netflix's products.

Although successful, Netflix is not without competitive challenges. Instead of competing against storefront operators such as Blockbuster, Netflix now finds itself facing well-financed companies with impressive technologies. Apple,

Amazon, and Google are examples of the competitors Netflix will now likely face in the battle to deliver innovative content to customers through a variety of channels.

Sources: 2010, Netflix Inc., *Market Edge Research*, http://www.marketedge.com, October 4; V. G. Kopytoff, 2010, Shifting online, Netflix faces competition, *The New York Times Online*, http://www.nytimes.com, September 26; S. Kurczy, 2010, Blockbuster fizzles in US, but renters overseas haven't switched to Netflix—yet, *The Christian Science Monitor Online*, http://www.csmonitor.com, September 23; D. Nosowitz, 2010, Netflix's mobile invasion continues: Android, you're next, *Fast Company.com*, http://www.fastcompany.com, April 9; C. Salter, 2010, "12 Netflix, *Fast Company.com*, http://www.fastcompany.com, February 17; R. Stross, 2010, Why bricks and clicks don't always mix, *The New York Times Online*, http://www.nytimes.com, September 18.

Questions

1. Some of Netflix's capabilities and core competencies are mentioned in the case. Go to the firm's Web site (http://www.netflix.com) and use other information sources as well to see if you can identify additional capabilities and core competencies. Do you think the core competencies mentioned in the case and/or the ones you found are valuable, rare, difficult to imitate, and nonsubstitutable and as such, are also competitive advantages? Why or why not?

2. What do you believe are the primary competitive challenges facing Netflix today? What capabilities and core competencies does the firm require to successfully deal with those challenges?

3. The value chain is explained in this chapter. Use the primary activities and support activities (see Figure 4.2) to determine where Netflix creates value. In which primary activity and which support activity do you believe the firm creates the largest amount of value for customers? Why?

EXPERIENTIAL EXERCISES

Exercise One: Value Chains and Competencies

Organize into at least five groups (if you need more groups, have different groups do the same company), making sure that members in each group represent the different functional discipline majors (accounting, marketing, finance, management, information systems, and so forth).

Each group should draw the value chain of the following five companies:

- Disney
- General Motors
- Nike
- McDonald's
- Starbucks

Highlight any elements of each value chain that you think represent areas in which the firm has a core competence. Determine whether any of the firm's core competencies are valuable, rare, difficult to imitate, and nonsubstitutable and as such are a competitive advantage. Also, identify any activities the firm has outsourced and explain the firm's decision to do so.

When the class reassembles, compare value chains and defend your choices.

Exercise Two: Intangible Resources

According to the chapter, intangible resources contribute to creating value for customers but are not physically identifiable. Intangible resources include reputation, brand name, know-how, and organizational culture. The value (satisfaction created by a firm's products) created by intangible resources can be measured by the price customers are willing to pay for the firm's products. Organize into groups and choose one firm in each of the following industries (or any other industry your instructor chooses) that has successfully used intangible resources to create value. Explain the intangible resources and show how the firm used those resources to create value for its customers.

- Airlines
- Banking
- Apparel
- Personal computers
- Cell phones
- DVD rentals

ENDNOTES

1. L. Damast, 2010, McDonald's execs discuss Angus snack wraps and smoothies, *Slash Food*, http://www.slashfood.com, June 3.

2. 2010, It's a wrap, *Food Chain*, http://www.foodchain.com, August 31.

3. 2008, McDonald's tries feng shui makeover, *AOL Money & Finance*, http://www.money.aco.com, February 25.

4. D. G. Sirmon, M. A. Hitt, R. D. Ireland, & B. A. Gilbert, 2011, Resource orchestration to create competitive advantage: Breadth, depth and life cycle effects, *Journal of Management*, in press.

5. J. W. Webb, R. D. Ireland, M. A. Hitt, G. M. Kistruck, & L. Tihanyi, 2011, Where is the opportunity without the customer? An integration of marketing, entrepreneurship, and institutions, *Journal of the Academy of Marketing Science*, in press; D. G. Sirmon, M. A. Hitt, & R. D. Ireland, 2007, Managing firm resources in dynamic environments to create value: Looking inside the black box, *Academy of Management Review*, 32: 273–292.

6. J. Kraaijenbrink, J. C. Spender, & A. J. Groen, 2010, The resource-based view: A review and assessment of its critiques, *Journal of Management*, 36: 349–372; C. O. Trevor & A. J. Nyberg, 2008, Keeping your headcount when all about you are losing theirs: Downsizing, voluntary turnover rates, and the moderating role of HR practices, *Academy of Management Journal*, 51: 259–276.

7. H. Yang, C. Phelps, & H. K. Steensma, 2010, Learning from what others have learned from you: The effects of knowledge spillovers on originating firms, *Academy of Management Journal*, 53: 371–389; D. J. Miller, M. J. Fern, & L. B. Cardinal, 2007, The use of knowledge for technological innovation within diversified firms, *Academy of Management Journal*, 50: 308–326.

8. 2008, Behind the brand, Coca-Cola, http://www.thecoca-colacompany.com, May 12.

9. 2009, From our leadership, *Coca-Cola Annual Report*, http://www.cocacola.com.

10. 2010, McDonald's Corporation, McDonald's, http://www.mcdonalds.com/cor/values/people/opportunity.html, May 12.

11. 2010, Halliburton completes acquisition of Boots & Coots, 2010 Press Releases, http://www.halliburton.com, September 17.

12. S. Terlep, 2010, GM plans compact car for Buick, *The Wall Street Journal Online*, http://www.wsj.com, October 6.

13. J. D. Rockoff, 2010, J&J, bruised by recalls, aims higher, *The Wall Street Journal Online*, http://www.wsj.com, August 19.

14. R. G. McGrath, 2010, Business models: A discovery driven approach, *Long Range Planning*, 43: 247–261; R. E. Hoskisson, M. A. Hitt, R. D. Ireland, & J. S. Harrison, 2008, *Competing for Advantage*, 2nd ed., Mason, OH: Thomson South-Western, Chapter 13; R. G. McGrath & A. Nerkar, 2004, Real options reasoning and a new look at R&D investment strategies of pharmaceutical firms, *Strategic Management Journal*, 25: 1–21.

15. R. Oriani & M. Sobrero, 2008, Uncertainty and the market valuation of R&D within a real options logic, *Strategic Management Journal*, 29: 343–361; C. M. Scherpereel, 2008, The option-creating institution: A real options perspective on economic organization, *Strategic Management Journal*, 29: 455–470; K. D. Miller & A. T. Arikan, 2004, Technology search investments: Evolutionary, option reasoning, and option pricing approaches, *Strategic Management Journal*, 25: 473–485.

16. A. Avadikyan & P. Lierena, 2010, A real options reasoning approach to hybrid vehicle investments, *Technological Forecasting and Social Change*, 77: 649–661.

17. N. Li, W. Boulding, & R. Staelin, 2010, General alliance experience, uncertainty, and marketing alliance governance mode choice, *Journal of the Academy of Marketing Science*, 38: 141–158; M. S. Olson, D. van Bever, & S. Verry, 2008, When growth stalls, *Harvard Business Review*, 86(3): 51–61; T. B. Folta & J. P. O'Brien, 2004, Entry in the presence of dueling options, *Strategic Management Journal*, 25: 121–138.

18. 2010, Rolls-Royce, http://www.rollsroyce.com, October 1; B. Clanton, 2008, Rolls-Royce name lives on—as supplier, *The Houston Chronicle Online*, http://www.chron.com, May 8.

19. R. D. Ireland & J. W. Webb, 2007, Strategic entrepreneurship: Creating competitive advantage through streams of innovation, *Business Horizons*, 50: 49–59; Sirmon, Hitt, & Ireland, Managing firm resources.

20. R. Bruehl, N. Horch, & M. Orth, 2010, Improving integration capabilities with management control, *European Journal of Innovation Management*, 13: 385–408; H. Lee & D. Kelley, 2008, Building dynamic capabilities for innovation: An exploratory study of key management practices, *R&D Management*, 38: 155–168.

21. 2010, Honda, http://www.honda.com, September 28.

22. I. Barreto, 2010, Dynamic capabilities: A review of past research and an agenda for the future, *Journal of Management*, 36: 256–280; T. Felin & W. S. Hesterly, 2007, The knowledge-based view, nested heterogeneity, and new value creation: Philosophical considerations on the locus of knowledge, *Academy of Management Review*, 32: 195–218.

23. 2010, About Ford, http://www.ford.com, October 1.

24. F. Damanpour & R. M. Walker, 2009, Combinative effects of innovation types and organizational performance: A longitudinal study of service organizations, *Journal of Management Studies*, 46: 650–675; C. Quintana-Garcia & C. A. Benavides-Velasco, 2008, Innovative competence, exploration and exploitation: The influence of technological diversification, *Research Policy*, 37: 492–507; M. A. Hitt & R. D. Ireland, 1985, Corporate distinctive competence, strategy, industry and performance, *Strategic Management Journal*, 6: 273–293.

25. H. K. Christensen, 2010, Defining customer value as the driver of competitive advantage, *Strategy & Leadership*, 38: 20–25; J. Barney, 2001, Is the resource-based view a useful perspective for strategic management research? Yes, *Academy of Management Review*, 26: 41–56.

26. J.-A. Lee, 2010, LG Electronics unveils plan for revamp, *The Wall Street Journal Online*, http://www.wsj.com, November 30; M. Ihlwan, 2008, LG closes in on Motorola, *BusinessWeek*, May 19.

27. M. Kim & H. Jin, 2010, LG Electronics names new CEO as mobile business struggles, *Reuters*, http://www.reuters.com, September 17.

28. M. A. Hitt, R. D. Ireland, & R. E. Hoskisson, 2011, *Strategic Management: Competitiveness and Globalization*, 9th ed., Mason, OH: Cengage Learning; R. Adner & R. Kapoor, 2010, Value creation in innovation ecosystems: How the structure of technological interdependence affects firm performance in new technology generations, *Strategic Management Journal*, 31: 306–333; D. P. Lepak, K. G. Smith, & M. S. Taylor, 2007, Value creation and value capture: A multilevel perspective, *Academy of Management Review*, 32: 180–194.

29. M. A. Hitt, J. S. Black, & L. W. Porter, 2011, *Management*, 3rd ed., Upper Saddle River, NJ: Pearson Prentice Hall; T. Kollat, 2008, *Strategy*, Atlasbooks.com.

30. M. Reimann, O. Schilke, & J. S. Thomas, 2010, Customer relationship management and firm performance: The mediating role of business strategy, *Journal of the Academy of Marketing Science*, 38: 326–346; R. J. Harrington & A. K. Tjan, 2008, Transforming strategy one customer at a time, *Harvard Business Review*, 86(3): 62–72.

31. O. E. Williamson, 2008, Outsourcing: Transaction cost economics and supply chain management, *The Journal of Supply Chain Management*, 44(2): 5–16; F. T. Rothaermel, M. A. Hitt, & L. Jobe, 2006, Balancing vertical integration and strategic outsourcing: Effects on product portfolio, product success, and firm performance, *Strategic Management Journal*, 27: 1033–1056.

32. R. Marshall, 2008, Shell could miss out in new outsourcing deal, *Accountancy Age*, http://www.accountancy.age.com, January 4.

33. A. Van Der Luijt, 2008, Outsourcing is about more than just money, *Director of Finance Online*, http://www.dofonline.co.uk, February 15.

34. S. D. Vivek, D. K. Banwet, & R. Shankar, 2008, Analysis of interactions among core, transaction, and relationship-specific investments: The case of offshoring, *Journal of Operations Management*, 26: 180–197; M. J. Leiblein, J. J. Reuer, & F. Dalsace, 2002, Do make or buy decisions matter? The influence of organizational governance and technological performance, *Strategic Management Journal*, 23: 817–833.

35. M. Ramsey & N. Shirouzu, 2010, Toyota is changing how it develops cars, *The Wall Street Journal Online*, http://www.wsj.com, July 5.

PART 3
Strategy

CHAPTER 5
Business-Level Strategy

KNOWLEDGE OBJECTIVES
Reading and studying this chapter should enable you to:

1. Define business-level strategy.

2. Define and explain the differences among the five business-level strategies.

3. Describe how to successfully use each business-level strategy.

4. Identify the risks of each business-level strategy.

5. Explain the structures to best implement each business-level strategy.

FOCUSING ON STRATEGY

Walmart's Evolving Strategy

In 2010, Walmart was the largest corporation with sales of almost $405 billion. Walmart has more than 8,300 stores worldwide and employs 2.1 million associates, with 1.4 million of them in the United States. It has operations in 15 other countries and is expanding its supplier network globally. Walmart's scale of operations is unrivaled by any competitor. It serves more than 200 million customers per week and because of the huge market it serves, suppliers will do almost whatever Walmart asks because of the exceptionally large quantities of goods the firm purchases. It continues to reaffirm its goal to offer its customers the lowest price available and therefore clearly uses a cost leadership strategy.

Yet even with its market power and reaffirmation of its cost leadership strategy, Walmart has been making changes in its strategic approach. The greatest change in recent years is the focus on global growth. For example, approximately 25 percent of its total annual revenue comes from its international operations. And, 48.2 percent of its stores are located outside the United States. Walmart plans to add approximately 500,000 employees by 2015. The company uses its global scale to reduce its costs and improve the quality of the goods it sells. The firm expects to increase its online sales as well. In fact, its current plans are to increase the number of customers served from 200 million per week to one billion per week by 2030, a major portion of which will represent online sales.

Walmart has also initiated a major sustainability program. Walmart has instituted a number of "green" policies designed to have a more positive impact on the physical environment. The company intends to measure and reduce its greenhouse gas emissions and has announced plans to make all of its suppliers do the same. For example, Walmart expects to reduce 20 million metric tons of greenhouse gases from its suppliers by 2015. This represents a massive reduction; it is equivalent to eliminating the use of 3.8 million autos during one year. Walmart also plans to develop a sustainability index for each product that represents its environmental impact. The index will be published on the label of each product it sells. And, this strategy has other benefits. For example, it saved approximately $100 million in 2009 by using recyclable cardboard in shipments to its U.S. stores. After using it, the cardboard is sold to a recycler rather than paying to transport the used materials to a landfill.

Therefore, even though Walmart has not abandoned its low-cost strategy, it is making other changes that allow it to compete even more effectively with its rivals.

© s70/ZUMA Press/Newscom

Sources: S. N. Bhanoo, 2010, Products that are earth-and-profit friendly, *The New York Times*, www.nytimes.com, June 11; M. Bustilo, 2010, Walmart's chief pledges to pick up the pace online, *The Wall Street Journal*, www.wsj.com, June 5; S. Clifford & S. Rosenbloom, 2010, With backdrop of glamour, Walmart stresses global growth, *The New York Times*, www.nytimes.com, June 4; S. Rosenbloom, 2010, Walmart unveils plan to make supply chain greener, *The New York Times*, www.nytimes.com, February 26; K. Rockwood, 2010, Will Walmart's "sustainability index" actually work? *Fast Company*, www.fastcompany.com, February 1; Corporate facts: Walmart by the numbers, 2010, www.walmart.com, March 31; Walmart leverages global scale to lower costs of goods, accelerate speed to market, improve quality of products, 2010, www.walmart.com, January 28; Corporate facts, 2008, www.walmart.com, February 23; Out in front, 2008, www.walmart.com, February 23; M. Kabel, 2008, Walmart says it likely will profit off hard times, *Houston Chronicle*, www.chron.com, February 19.

In Chapter 1, we defined strategy as an action plan designed to move an organization toward achievement of its vision. The different types of strategies firms use to meet this goal are shown in Figure 1.1 in Chapter 1.

Business-level strategy, the topic of this chapter, is one of the types of strategies firms develop to achieve their vision. A **business-level strategy** is an action plan the firm develops to describe how it will compete in its chosen industry or market segment. A business-level strategy describes how the firm will compete in the marketplace on a day-by-day basis and how it intends to "do things right."[1] Walmart's primary strategy has been one of cost leadership. Its increasing focus on international sales is actually improving costs through global scale of operations. However, in recent times, Walmart has been adding services and approaches that differentiate it from its primary competitors. Of critical importance is Walmart's strong new emphasis on sustainability. And, it is not only introducing into its own operations (e.g., the use of recyclable cardboard containers for shipping), it is providing incentives for its suppliers to do the same. Its efforts are expected to lead to major reductions in greenhouse gas emissions. Its sustainability index should be useful to consumers in the selection of greener products. Thus, while its primary strategy is that of cost leadership, it has integrated some elements of a differentiation strategy as well.

A firm's main objective in using a business-level strategy is to consistently provide a good or service to customers that they will buy because it creates more value (in the form of performance characteristics or price) for them than does a competitor's good or service. This approach is illustrated in the opening *Focusing on Strategy* in this chapter, which describes Walmart's cost leadership strategy. In fact, Walmart's market research suggests that about 90 percent of citizens in the United States shop at Walmart (an extremely high percentage) and that 91 percent of these shoppers give the firm positive favorability ratings.[2] A business-level strategy is most successful when everybody in the firm fully understands the chosen strategy[3] and when it is implemented with zeal and efficiency.[4] In other words, firms must be precise in describing what they seek to accomplish with their strategy. The strategy must "connect" with the target customers as well. Of course, as is the case with all of the firm's strategies, ethical practices should guide how the business-level strategy is used.[5] Often, a firm's intended ethical practices are made public by recording them in written documents such as a code of ethics, a code of conduct, and a corporate creed. The statements in these documents signal to stakeholders how the firm intends to interact with them. They also set the expectation that a firm's employees adhere to the behaviors specified in these documents.

A business-level strategy is intended to help the firm focus its efforts so it can satisfy a group of customers.[6] This strategy is intended to create a defensible competitive position in the market allowing the firm to gain a competitive advantage.[7] To contribute to a competitive advantage, a business-level strategy must have a clear statement of the value to be created for customers. This point is illustrated by the founding of Walmart. Through the strategic leadership of Sam Walton, its founder, Walmart initially used a business-level strategy to offer a large assortment of many different products at low prices to consumers living in towns with a population no greater than 25,000.[8] Thus, early Walmart customers received the value from the opportunity to buy goods at prices that were always lower than the prices of those goods from locally owned stores. Everyone working at Walmart understood the value the firm was creating for its customers, which helped the firm effectively implement its business-level strategy. In addition, by comparison shopping and then buying from Walmart, customers discovered the

business-level strategy

an action plan the firm develops to describe how it will compete in its chosen industry or market segment value the firm was providing in the form of lower prices on a wide assortment of items. Interestingly, Walmart still follows this strategy and has achieved considerable success with it.

We fully discuss five business-level strategies in this chapter. These five strategies are sometimes referred to as generic because they are used in all industries and by all types of firms. A properly chosen business-level strategy favorably positions the firm relative to the competitive forces we discussed in Chapter 3. Being effectively positioned enables the firm to simultaneously create value for customers and returns for shareholders.[9] We also use the value chain (see Chapter 4) to show the primary and support activities that are required to successfully use each business-level strategy. And, the firm must have the resources and capabilities (also see Chapter 4) to implement the strategy successfully.[10] Therefore, in formulating the firm's business-level strategy, strategic leaders must ensure that the strategy fits well with the investments made in resources and their deployment along with the firm's business model in order to achieve the highest performance.[11] In this chapter, we also describe the particular organizational structure (defined later in the chapter) that should be used to effectively implement each generic strategy. Because it affects the behavior of individual employees, the responsibilities assigned to them, and the leadership style they experience, organizational structure is an important aspect of how business-level strategies are implemented.

As the Walmart example shows, a firm's business-level strategy should be regularly evaluated and updated or revised as needed to stay ahead of competition. As an action plan, a business-level strategy is a living entity that is constantly subject to changes based on opportunities and threats emerging in the firm's external environment as well as changes in the competitive advantages that are a product of the resources, capabilities, and core competencies in the firm's internal environment.

Types of Business-Level Strategies

Firms choose from five business-level strategies: cost leadership, differentiation, focused cost leadership, focused differentiation, and integrated cost leadership/differentiation (see Figure 5.1). As shown in this figure, the firm's business-level strategy has two key dimensions: competitive advantage and competitive scope. The business-level strategy the firm chooses is a function of the basis for the competitive advantage (either cost or uniqueness) that it seeks to achieve or maintain (if it already has an advantage over competitors)[12] and the breadth (either broad or narrow) of the target market it wishes to serve. When using the cost leadership or differentiation strategy, the firm seeks to apply its competitive advantage in many customer segments. When using either focused cost leadership or focused differentiation, the firm uses its cost advantage or its uniqueness advantage in more narrow market segments. Specifically, with focus strategies, the firm "selects a segment or group of segments in the industry and tailors its strategy to serving them to the exclusion of others."[13]

Procter & Gamble's Tide soap is an example of a product that has a broad target market, while Porsche's 911 Carrera is designed to serve the needs of a

Luxury brands such as Porsche are clearly focused on specific target markets consisting of customers with both a desire for the quality and status of their products as well as the spending power to attain them.

© AP Photo/Str/Porsche AG

Figure 5.1 Five Business-Level Strategies

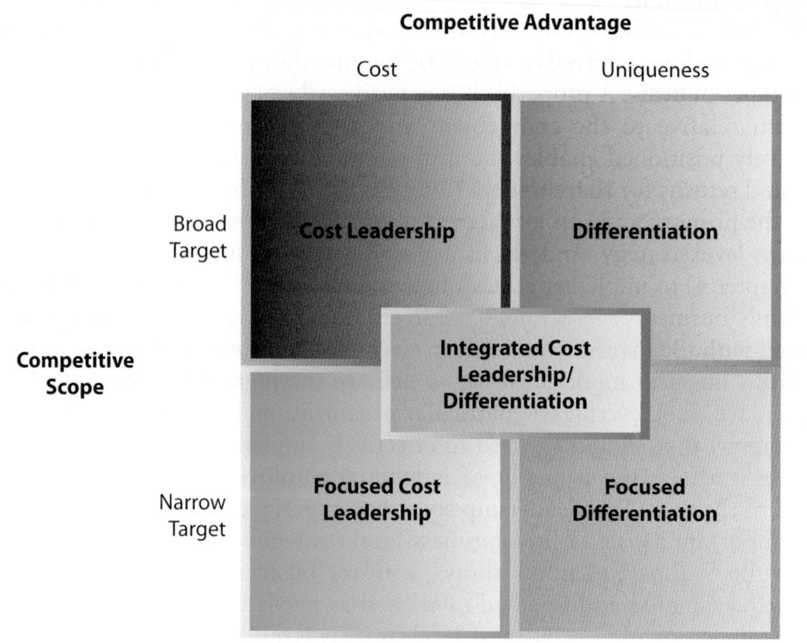

Source: Adapted with the permission of Free Press, a Division of Simon & Schuster, Inc., from *Competitive Advantage: Creating and Sustaining Superior Performance* by Michael E. Porter. Copyright © 1985, 1998 by Michael E. Porter. All rights reserved.

narrow group of customers. Each firm's decision about competitive scope (broad or narrow) is influenced by opportunities and threats in its external environment. A market segment is a group of people with similar needs with respect to certain variables such as price, quality, and product features. Segmenting markets into smaller groups with similar needs can be a threat to firms with a relatively standardized product serving the needs of multiple customer segments. Tide, for example, is designed to fit a broad target market. Simultaneously, though, being able to identify people with a specific need that isn't being satisfied by the product aimed at a broad target market creates opportunities for other firms. A number of smaller companies develop specialty laundry detergent and soaps for specific market segments (e.g., hypoallergenic cleansing products for people who want to avoid the types of chemicals in products such as Tide).

In general, a firm's capabilities and core competencies enable it either to produce standardized products at lower costs than those of their competitors or to produce unique products that differ from competitors' products in ways that create superior value for customers. In the first instance, the firm has a competitive advantage based on costs; in the second instance, it has a competitive advantage based on uniqueness (see Figure 5.1).

Standardized products are widely available and have a large customer demand, such as automobile tires. We all need tires for our vehicles, and Cooper Tire & Rubber is known for producing relatively inexpensive (yet reliable) tires for cars and trucks. Cooper can charge lower prices because its production, distribution, and service costs are lower than those of its rivals (i.e., Michelin, Goodyear, and

Pirelli). Cooper remains committed to being lean in all of its operations as a way of continuously holding its costs down relative to competitors' costs.[14]

Unique products have features different from or in addition to the standardized product's features. For example, although more expensive than beers designed for the broad target market, Guinness beers are popular with segments of the population (especially in Ireland). Guinness beers are more expensive because Guinness targets customers who are willing to pay more for what some perceive to be a distinctive taste—a taste that is more expensive to produce.[15]

We now turn our attention to learning about each of the five generic business-level strategies.

Cost Leadership Strategy

A **cost leadership strategy** is an action plan the firm develops to produce goods or services at the lowest cost.[16] Producing at the lowest cost enables the firm to price its product lower than competitors can and therefore gain a larger share of its target market. Firms using the cost leadership strategy typically sell standardized products to the industry's "average" customers because they are usually the largest target segment. Thus, Cooper Tire & Rubber targets the customer with "average" or "typical" needs in selling its tires. Successful use of the cost leadership strategy across time results when the firm continuously reduces its costs relative to competitors' costs by constantly examining how the costs of its primary activities and support activities can be lowered without damaging the functionality of its products. Firms using a cost leadership strategy commonly have economies of scale because of the large quantities of standardized products produced.[17] Firms implementing the cost leadership strategy generally have strong process engineering skills, emphasize manufacturing processes that permit efficient production of products, have performance evaluation systems that reward employees on the quantity of their output, and know how to buy raw materials needed to produce their products at low costs. For example, some firms are able to achieve low costs by manufacturing modular products in which parts may fit several different product variations.[18] For example, it has been recently noted that the rapid growth of local Chinese auto manufacturers is not due to low labor costs. Rather, it is because of unique product designs that have allowed them to manufacture cars with similar features and attributes as Western car makers but at a substantially lower price.[19]

In Chapter 4, we described how firms use value-chain analysis to identify the primary activities and support activities in which they are able to create value. A firm's value chain can be managed to achieve low costs.[20] In Figure 5.2, we show how the cost leader could create value in each primary activity and in each support activity. A firm does not need to outperform competitors in every one of these activities to successfully use the cost leadership strategy; however, the more primary and support activities in which the firm can outperform its competitors, the more likely that its costs will be lower than its competitors' costs.

Effective use of the cost leadership strategy positions the firm in the marketplace in a way that enables it to create value for customers, especially through lower prices. In recent years, such a strategy has been effective for reaching unique markets with low income levels not previously considered by many firms.[21] Also, as we describe in the next five subsections, effectively implementing the cost leadership strategy enables a firm to establish a strong market position relative to the five competitive forces we introduced in Chapter 3.

cost leadership strategy

an action plan the firm develops to produce goods or services at the lowest cost

Figure 5.2 Examples of Value-Creating Activities Associated with the Cost Leadership Strategy

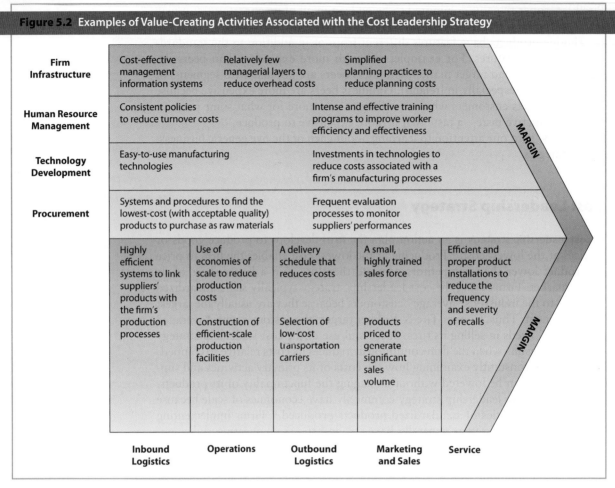

Rivalry with Existing Competitors

Competitors find it extremely difficult to compete against the cost leader on the basis of price. To meet the cost leader's sales price, a competing firm must reduce its profit margins when selling its products. In turn, lower margins leave that firm with less capital to invest to improve its operational efficiency. Therefore, competing on the basis of price against the cost leader places a competitor in a cycle of falling farther behind in terms of efficiency and cost reductions. Kmart encountered this competitive circumstance when trying to compete against cost leader Walmart on the basis of price. Kmart's cost structure, compared to Walmart's, was higher. The higher cost structure prevented Kmart from being able to offer products at prices as low as Walmart's. Having emerged from bankruptcy, Kmart no longer attempts to compete against Walmart on the basis of costs and product prices. Instead, the firm changed its product mix to reduce the degree to which it competes directly with cost leader Walmart. In fact, after it was acquired by Sears in 2004, Kmart's strategy changed further and the Sears holding company has performed reasonably well since that time. Kmart had an increase in sales in 2009, its first since 2005.[22]

Many rivals now compete with each other across markets, including different product markets and especially different geographic markets.[23] This multimarket competition is more complex because a rival may respond differently to a competitor's action in a given market compared with the same actions in another market. For example, a firm may be strong in one geographic market (e.g., the United States) and therefore take an action (e.g., reduce prices) to increase its market share. A primary rival may then respond with a competitive action in a different geographic market where it is stronger (e.g., reduce prices in the European Union). As such, the firm taking the initial action may have to lose market share in Europe in order to gain market share in the United States.[24]

Bargaining Power of Buyers (Customers)

As buyers, customers can exercise power against the cost leader under several conditions, but especially if they purchase a large quantity of the cost leader's output. For example, as a buyer, Walmart exhibits significant power because it often purchases large quantities and a substantial amount of a firm's output. The cost leader successfully positions itself against buyers' potential power by selling to a large number of buyers to avoid becoming dependent on any one customer for a significant portion of its sales. Regardless, firms should always be conscious of the customer's potential power to avoid a competitive blind spot in which they become vulnerable to competitors who might take away good customers.[25]

Bargaining Power of Suppliers

A supplier can exercise power over the cost leader if it provides a significant amount of a key input to the cost leader's production process. Firms dependent on key natural resources to produce their products when sources of supply are limited may have to pay higher prices. Airline companies, for example, are highly dependent on aviation fuel, a product sold by a relatively small number of firms. Successfully positioned cost leaders try to develop long-term contracts with a number of suppliers at favorable rates to reduce the potential of suppliers raising their prices, which would affect the cost leader's position in terms of costs. Cost leader Southwest Airlines has been quite savvy about forming long-term contracts with fuel suppliers. These contracts have often kept Southwest's fuel costs lower than those of its competitors.

Potential Entrants

The favorably positioned cost leader operates at a level of efficiency that can't be matched by firms thinking of entering the industry in which the cost leader is well established. The cost leader's ability to continuously drive its costs lower and lower while still satisfying customers' needs makes it difficult for potential entrants to the market to compete against the cost leader. JetBlue is one of the few successful entrants in the airline industry, especially when competing with Southwest for the low-cost segment of the market.

Product Substitutes

A product substitute is a product that can replace the focal product because it has essentially the same functionality. For example, NutraSweet is a replacement or substitute for sugar. To compete against a cost leader, though, a substitute must offer something in addition to the same functionality. This "something different" could be a lower purchase price (which is unlikely when competing against the cost leader) or a feature that customers value that isn't a part of the cost leader's product. (As you know, NutraSweet's "something different" is a taste similar to that of sugar but without sugar's calories.) The successfully positioned cost leader commonly responds to product substitutes by reducing the purchase price of its product, which makes it difficult for a substitute to attract and capture the cost leader's customers.

Competitive Risks of the Cost Leadership Strategy

The cost leadership strategy has three major risks. First, competitors' innovations may enable them to produce their good or service at a cost that is lower than that of the cost leader. For the price-conscious "typical" consumer, the lower cost is attractive. Second, concentrating too much on reducing costs may eventually find the cost leader offering a product at low prices to customers who are less inclined to purchase it. Even though the cost leader must keep its costs down, it can't lose contact with its customers and fail to identify and understand changes in customers' expectations relative to the product in terms of price and features. At some point, for example, customers wanting to buy low-cost products may become willing to pay more for additional features such as increased product safety and extended product warranties. The cost leader must stay in close touch with its customers so it will be able to detect changes in their needs.

The third competitive risk is that of a supplier becoming a competitor. This is especially the case when a firm outsources a critical function such as manufacturing in order to maintain its cost leadership position. In this case, the supplier is very powerful and could become a competitor stealing its buyers/customers.[26]

Differentiation Strategy

A **differentiation strategy** is an action plan the firm develops to produce goods or services that customers perceive as being unique in ways that are important to them. The "uniqueness" a firm provides when using the differentiation strategy may be physical or psychological. It can be created by the way in which the firm uses one or more of either the primary activities or the support activities. Product durability, ease of repair, and superior installation services are examples of physical sources of differentiation. Perceptions of the quality of service after the sale and of the courtesy of salespeople are examples of sources of psychological differentiation. Blockbuster captured the market with differentiated service that customers originally perceived to be superior. But, it maintained its original formula too long and competitors entered the market with differentiated services that customers found to be of value. As a result, Blockbuster lost major market share to competitors such as Netflix and Redbox. Blockbuster went into a decline that it was unable to turn around even with major changes to its line of services. Eventually, its market value declined so low that it was delisted from the New York Stock Exchange.

The cost leader commonly serves an industry's typical customer. In contrast, the firm using the differentiation strategy serves customers who want to buy a good or service that is different from the good or service purchased by an industry's average customer. The goods offered by Ralph Lauren provide examples of differentiated items. The logo appearing on many of the firm's clothing products is used to differentiate these goods from those made for the clothing industry's typical customer. In addition to the logo, the firm's dress shirts for men are made

differentiation strategy
an action plan the firm develops to produce goods or services that customers perceive as being unique in ways that are important to them

How to Lose While Holding a Winning Hand: Blockbuster's Decline

Blockbuster was once the industry leader in the video-rental market. At one time, it had over 4,500 stores. In 2005, Blockbuster had a market capitalization of $2 billion and by March of 2010, it had declined to about $50 million. Unfortunately, because of its poor prospective, its stock price continued to decline to 35 cents per share in July 2010 and its stock was delisted from the New York Stock Exchange. What happened? How could the number one firm in the market fall so far?

Well, Blockbuster's decline occurred over many years and was at least partly because it failed to adapt to changes in its environment and it did not adjust its business model when needed. It stayed too long with the formula that made it successful. Technology changed,

Failing to recognize and adjust quickly enough to changing customer expectations, Blockbuster has watched as competitors such as Netflix and Redbox gained competitive advantage by offering differentiated services that better meet customer's evolving needs.

customers' desires changed and new competitors entered the market. Blockbuster failed to respond to these changes until it was too late. The primary competitor that did the most damage was Netflix. Netflix entered the market offering a subscription system sending videos through the mail each month. And, importantly, it did not charge late fees. At one time, late fees (extra fees charged to customers for returning their video rental late) composed 40 percent of Blockbuster's revenues. So, Blockbuster was not really unhappy that customers returned the video late. Yet, customers evidently did not like the late fees and many of them moved to Netflix. Also Redbox entered the market with a different model, providing video rentals through vending machines in popular locations (e.g., McDonald's restaurants) renting videos for one dollar.

In 2009 and 2010, Blockbuster implemented a number of actions designed to turn around its performance. It started closing unprofitable stores, for example, 374 in 2009 and more than 500 in 2010. But, it began doing so much later than it should have and still had 3,500 stores operating at the beginning of 2011. It began offering movies by mail (similar to Netflix) and digitally (Netflix also offers videos through the Internet). Blockbuster also signed an agreement with movie studios to sell first-run movies through Blockbuster outlets. But few observers expect these actions to fend off the failure of the company. One analyst compared the collapse of Blockbuster to a "slasher" movie in slow motion which is very painful to watch. Essentially, Blockbuster's competitors offered differentiated services that obviously provided more value to customers. Blockbuster did too little too late.

Sources: M. Murphy, 2010, Blockbuster will be delisted, *The Wall Street Journal*, www.wsj.com, July 2; A. Carr, 2010, Blockbuster CEO Jim Keyes on Bankruptcy, Netflix, and becoming the next Apple, *Fast Company*, www.fastcompany.com, June 18; A. Carr, 2010, Blockbuster CEO Jim Keyes on Competition from Apple, Netflix, Nintendo, and Redbox, *Fast Company*, www.fastcompany.com, June 8; M. Marcus, 2010, The sun has not yet set on Blockbuster, *Forbes*, www.forbes.com, May 18; T. Kary, 2010, Blockbuster bondholders betting company will collapse (update 1), *BusinessWeek*, www.businessweek.com, May 7; J. Birchall, 2010, Blockbuster strikes deal to ensure DVD supply, *Financial Times*, www.ft.com, April 7; R. Grover, 2010, The last picture show at Blockbuster? *BusinessWeek*, www.businessweek.com, March 25; K. Swanekamp, 2010, Blockbuster running out of cards to play, *Forbes*, www.forbes.com, March 17; Blockbuster, 2010, *Financial Times*, www.ft.com, March 17; A. Sattariano & R. Grover, 2010, Blockbuster seeks to cut DVD costs, may file chap. 11 (update 2), *BusinessWeek*, www.businessweek.com, March 16.

of high-quality raw materials and lack a pocket. The logo, the materials, and the absence of a pocket are differentiated features that create value for customers desiring to wear something other than a "typical" dress shirt.

Think about goods and services (e.g., cars and clothes) that you believe are different from those serving the typical customers in an industry. Doing so suggests that the ways goods and services can differ from one another are virtually endless. Different tastes, responsive customer service, product design, alternative distribution methods, and customer loyalty programs are but a few examples of how goods or services can offer unique value to customers.

Many firms offer unique products by emphasizing innovation in their organization.[27] In doing so, they continuously introduce new and unique products that provide value to customers. Some firms offer a special service or identity with a segment of the market. Some develop new technology on which to build new products that may even create new markets.[28] For example, banks from Latin America have established subsidiaries in Miami, Florida, and focus on serving the large Hispanic community in the area.[29] Other firms try to differentiate the value provided to customers through their after-sales service. In fact, recent research shows that firms can closely monitor their customers' satisfaction after the sale and any returns of products in order to develop information to improve their products and gain a competitive advantage.[30]

The value chain can be used to highlight the primary and support activities where value should be created to use the differentiation strategy. Through this approach, the firm emphasizes the primary and support activities shown in Figure 5.3 to create more value than competitors can create for customers. The

Figure 5.3 Examples of Value-Creating Activities Associated with the Differentiation Strategy

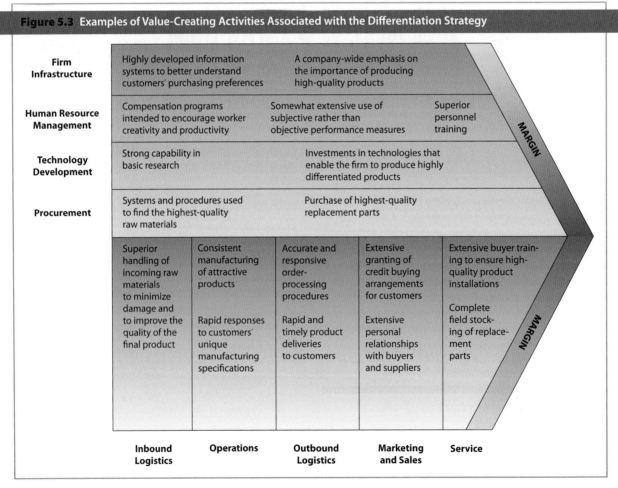

firm using the differentiation strategy wants to develop core competencies in one or more of the primary and support activities.[31] The more unique value the firm can create for customers, the more likely the firm will be able to successfully use the differentiation strategy.

Next, we explain how the firm effectively using the differentiation strategy is able to position itself in the marketplace. In the next five subsections, we explain how an effective differentiation strategy results in a strong market position for the firm by countering each of the five competitive forces discussed in Chapter 3.

Rivalry with Existing Competitors

Customers tend to be loyal buyers of products that create unique value for them. For this reason, firms using the differentiation strategy do everything they can to increase the loyalty of their customers by providing them greater benefits than do rivals.[32] With increasing loyalty, customer sensitivity to the price of the product they are buying is reduced. Reducing price sensitivity is important because the firm using the differentiation strategy needs to establish large profit margins on its products to afford the resources required to continuously reinvest in its products so that the valued sources of difference can be maintained.[33] Think of it this way: providing differentiated goods and services can be expensive. The firm needs to earn high returns on what it sells to be able to pay for the costs of creating differentiated features while producing its products.

Bargaining Power of Buyers (Customers)

The uniqueness of a differentiated good or service reduces customers' sensitivity to the product's price. Firms using the differentiation strategy continuously stress the uniqueness of their products to customers (often through advertising campaigns) to reduce customers' sensitivity to price. For example, the Lexus slogan of "The Relentless Pursuit of Perfection" by Toyota, the manufacturer of Lexus products, signals to the customer that even though the product's price is higher than that of cars aimed at the typical customer, the Lexus is a superior product because it is made by people seeking perfection in their work. When a firm's effort to emphasize product uniqueness is successful, customers' sensitivity to price is reduced, thus enabling the firm to continue selling its products at a price that permits constant reinvestment in the products' differentiated features.

Bargaining Power of Suppliers

The firm using the differentiation strategy typically pays a premium price for the raw materials used to make its product. In this way, the supplier is more willing to make investments to provide higher quality goods in the quantity needed to support the firm's differentiated strategy.[34] For a good, a premium price means that some of the raw materials will be expensive (e.g., high-quality cotton used to make expensive, yet differentiated clothing items). Alternatively, for a service, the firm may pay a premium price to hire highly talented employees. For example, the consultants McKinsey & Company must hire skilled and knowledgeable employees to provide differentiated service to its clients. However, the returns earned from a premium sales price of a differentiated good or service yield the funds the firm needs to pay its suppliers' higher prices (because of the higher valued resources that they use).[35] In addition, a firm providing goods or services that create differentiated value to customers may be able to pass supplier price increases on to its satisfied and loyal customers in the form of higher prices.

Potential Entrants

Customer loyalty and the need to provide customers with more value than an existing firm's product provides to them are strong challenges for potential rivals that are considering competing against a firm successfully using the differentiation strategy. Customer loyalty is difficult to earn. Often, a firm must consistently meet people's needs for quite some time before they become loyal to it, meaning that a new entrant typically faces a long battle. In addition, the established firm has the margins necessary to reinvest in ways that will further enhance the differentiated value it creates for customers, making it even more difficult for a new competitor to compete against it.

Firms also try to establish barriers to entry to reduce the number of potential entrants.[36] For example, in some industries, firms use patents on their unique products to stop potential rivals from imitating them.[37] Yet patents are sometimes difficult to defend, and smart competitors make enough changes in their products to avoid legal patent violations.

Product Substitutes

It is difficult for competitors to create substitute products that will satisfy loyal customers of a firm that provides them differentiated value from a good or service. Perceived unique value is difficult to replace, even when a product substitute has a better performance-to-price ratio that favors substitution. It will generally take a lot to get most of us to switch to a substitute when we are satisfied with the product we've been buying for a long time. Thus, firms with loyal customers tend to be largely insulated from competitors' substitute products that are intended to provide different value to the focal firm's customers.

Competitive Risks of the Differentiation Strategy

The differentiation strategy is not risk free.[38] The first risk is that customers may decide that the price they are paying for a product's differentiated features is too high. This situation can happen especially when a cost leader learns how to add some differentiated features to its product without significantly raising the product's price, as JetBlue did in its early years in the industry. The customers buying the differentiated product may decide that the value received is too expensive relative to the combination of some differentiation and low price of the cost leader's good or service. A second risk is that the source of differentiation being provided by the firm may cease to create value for the target customers. For example, men buying Ralph Lauren dress shirts might conclude that the logo, lack of a pocket, and high-quality cotton no longer provide value for which they are willing to pay. For this reason, some firms go to great lengths to continuously innovate and bring new and improved products to the market (to stay ahead of competition). As part of their efforts, these firms may form joint ventures with other firms to obtain access to unique knowledge and skills, thereby enriching their innovations.[39]

Customer experiences are the third risk; by using a differentiated product and comparing its performance with lower-cost alternatives, the customer may conclude that the cost of the differentiation isn't acceptable. When first introduced, the IBM brand name enabled the firm to charge premium prices for its personal computers (PCs). However, through experience, many customers learned that the performance of competitors' lower-priced products was virtually equivalent to that of the IBM PC. Finally, differentiated products run the risk of being somewhat effectively counterfeited. Although of much lower quality, the counterfeit product that looks like "the real thing" can be appealing, even for the customer capable of buying the true differentiated product. Here, the customer thinks about why he or she should pay the higher price for "the real thing" when the counterfeit product looks about as good.

Whole Foods Market implements a differentiation strategy explained in *Understanding Strategy: Learning from Success*. As the world's largest retailer of natural and organic foods, it emphasizes the unique products and services it provides to customers. These are described in the five values presented in the firm's Declaration of Interdependence. With more than 200 stores and $5.6 billion-plus in sales, its success is unequaled in the natural and organic foods market.

Focus Strategies

A **focus strategy** is an action plan the firm develops to produce goods or services that serve the needs of a specific market segment. Therefore, focus strategies serve a more narrow segment within a broader market.[40] Firms using the focus strategy intend to serve the needs of a narrow customer segment better than their needs can be met by the firm targeting its products to the broad market (see Figure 5.1). A particular buyer group (such as teenagers, senior citizens, or women working outside the home), a specific segment of a product line (such as professional painters rather than "do it-yourself" painters), and particular geographic markets (such as the West Coast or the East Coast of the United States) are examples of different target market segments on which a firm might focus. As noted in *Understanding Strategy: Learning from Success,* many of Whole Foods' competitors follow a focus differentiation strategy by serving a specific geographic region (e.g., FreshDirect's focus on the New York City market). Firms can use either the focused cost leadership strategy or the focused differentiation strategy to successfully serve the needs of a narrow market segment.

Focused Cost Leadership Strategy

The **focused cost leadership strategy** is an action plan the firm develops to produce goods or services for a narrow market segment at the lowest cost. Based in Sweden, IKEA uses the focused cost leadership strategy.

IKEA is a global furniture retailer with locations in 39 countries. IKEA targets younger customers desiring style at a low cost.[41] IKEA offers home furnishings with good design and function and acceptable quality at low prices to young buyers who, according to IKEA's research, aren't wealthy, work for a living, and want to shop at hours beyond those typically available from firms serving the broad furniture market.

To successfully use its focused cost leadership strategy, IKEA concentrates on lowering its costs and understanding its customers' needs. To keep the firm's costs low, IKEA's engineers design low-cost modular furniture that customers can easily assemble. To appeal to young buyers who often are short of time and are inexperienced when it comes to buying furniture, IKEA arranges its products by rooms instead of by products. These configurations enable customers to see different living combinations (complete with sofas, chairs, tables, and so forth) in a single setting.[42]

focus strategy

an action plan the firm develops to produce goods or services that serve the needs of a specific market segment

focused cost leadership strategy

an action plan the firm develops to produce goods or services for a narrow market segment at the lowest cost

Whole Foods Market: Differentiation the Organic Way

The Whole Foods Market is the largest natural foods retailer in the world. Whole Foods sells natural and organic food products in all types of food categories, such as meat, produce, and baked and prepared foods. The company now has more than 280 stores, employs about 54,000 associates, and generates annual sales of $7.95 billion. It is the most successful natural and organic food retailer. Although competitors existed, Whole Foods was the first to build a larger supermarket that carried all natural and organic foods. So it gained first mover advantages.

Whole Foods now has a number of competitors that try to imitate its products and services. As such, Whole Foods encourages its managers and associates to be innovative in the development of new products and services it can provide customers. Each store is organized into self-directed work teams with each team responsible for a category of products (e.g., prepared foods, meats and poultry, and customer service). Team members go through a rigorous selection process and are highly trained to do their jobs. These actions are necessary for Whole Foods to continue to command a premium price for its products. Because compensation is partly based on individual, team, and store results, associates are motivated to ensure that customers are highly satisfied with the products and service they receive.

Whole Foods implements its differentiation strategy through its "Declaration of Interdependence." This declaration explains Whole Foods' five primary values:

- Providing only high-quality foods
- Satisfying and delighting customers
- Promoting team member excellence and happiness
- Creating wealth through profits and growth
- Caring about communities and the environment

The values are designed to show the interdependence among Whole Foods' stakeholders (e.g., customers, associates, shareholders, and communities) and the intent to work with all of them in an effective manner.

Despite being the largest and most successful natural and organic food retailer, Whole Foods Market is continually reinforcing and evolving those attributes that differentiate it from its competitors. From implementing policies requiring supplies to prove that their products are indeed organic to empowering their individual work teams to focus on innovation, the company remains focused defining what success looks like in this market.

Yet, Whole Foods continues to maintain its differentiation as the number one retailer of organic goods. In 2010, the company announced that suppliers would have to prove that their products were organic in order to be sold through Whole Foods. Evidently, personal care product companies make claims about organic products but they do not have to adhere to regulatory policies as do food manufacturers and suppliers. However, analysts believe that they will meet Whole Foods requirements because they want their products sold in the firm's stores.

In an attempt to increase its differentiation from competitors, Whole Foods invited specialty street vendors to sell their foods through Whole Foods stores. However, they also had to meet all of the company's standards. Thus, it will likely be difficult for many of the vendors to accept the invitation. Yet, some have agreed to partner with Whole Foods and are selling their goods at one or two stores.

Whole Foods carefully monitors its competitors even though it is much larger than most of them. In fact, Whole Foods has acquired several of its competitors including the purchase of its largest competitor Wild Oats. Many of its competitors serve only regional markets similar to FreshDirect, an online marketer of quality foods in the New York City market. Thus, Whole Foods benefits from its national reputation and name recognition. And, Whole Foods performance has regained momentum after the recession in 2008 and 2009 and its stock price increased by healthy amounts in 2010.

Sources: A. Schwartz, 2010, Whole Foods invites street-food vendors into stores, *Fast Company*, www.fastcompany.com, June 10; S. Ju, 2010, Whole Foods cracks down on organic claims, *Forbes*. www.forbes.com, June 24; M. Marcus, 2010, Whole Foods gains on healthy profits, *Forbes*, www.forbes.com, February 17; S. Cendrowski, 2009, What about Whole Foods? *Fortune*, July 20: 26; 2007, Whole Foods Market. *Wikipedia*, www.wikipedia.com, September 2; 2007, Whole Foods closes buyout of Wild Oats, *New York Times*, www.nytimes.com, August 29; 2007, Our core values, Whole Foods Market Web site, www.wholefoodsmarket.com, April 29; 2007, Declaration of interdependence, Whole Foods Market, www.wholefoodsmarket.com, April 29.

Focused Differentiation Strategy

The **focused differentiation strategy** is an action plan the firm develops to produce goods or services that a narrow group of customers perceive as being unique in ways that are important to them. Thomas Pink is a business unit of LVMH Moet Hennessy Louis Vuitton, which uses the focused differentiation strategy. For example, Thomas Pink introduced men's shirts made of 170-count cotton. This count of cotton is quite high and is the main way the product is differentiated in the marketplace (in comparison, a T-shirt from Old Navy is made of 18-count cotton). When introduced, these shirts were priced at $195 each. Thus, this shirt is targeted to a narrow market: men who have a high income and who often have achieved a great deal of success in corporate settings.[43] Whole Foods also uses a focused differentiation strategy selling Darjeeling Tea and Ginger Cured Smoked Salmon for $39.96 per pound and dried morel mushrooms at a price that works out to be $1,280 per pound.[44] The firm is also targeting a select market of people with high incomes.

To successfully use either focus strategy, a firm must perform many of the value chain's primary and support activities in ways that enable it to create more value than competitors can create for a narrow group of target customers. The specific activities required to successfully use the focused cost leadership strategy are identical to those shown in Figure 5.2, while the activities needed to be successful with the focused differentiation strategy parallel those shown in Figure 5.3. The difference is that each activity in the value chains shown is performed with a narrow market instead of a broad market segment in mind. Therefore, Figures 5.2 and 5.3 and the text regarding the five competitive forces describe how a firm successfully using one of the focus strategies is favorably positioned against the five competitive forces. However, to maintain its favorable position, when using the focused cost leadership strategy, the firm must continually drive its costs lower compared to competitors'. In addition, when using the focused differentiation strategy, the firm must continue to differentiate its product in ways that are meaningful to the target customers. Whole Foods is continuing its differentiation forcing suppliers to prove their products are organic and having specialty street-food vendors sell their products in Whole Foods stores.

Competitive Risks of Focus Strategies

Using a focus strategy carries several risks. First, a competitor may learn how to "outfocus" the focusing firm. For example, Charles Tyrwhitt Shirts is trying to outfocus Thomas Pink in men's high-quality dress shirts. Tyrwhitt introduced a 180-count cotton shirt priced at $160, creating significant competition for Thomas Pink.[45] Second, a company serving the broad target market may decide that the target market being served by the focusing firm is attractive. Ralph Lauren, for instance, could introduce a dress shirt with a cotton count lower than that used by Thomas Pink and Charles Tyrwhitt and a slightly lower price. Ralph Lauren could rely on its brand image to entice its competitors' customers to try its dress shirt. Finally, the needs of the narrow target customer may change and become similar to those of the broad market. For example, increases in their disposable income and experience with buying furniture might change some of IKEA's young buyers' needs such that they can be satisfied by a firm serving the broad market.

focused differentiation strategy

an action plan the firm develops to produce goods or services that a narrow group of customers perceive as being unique in ways that are important to them

Integrated Cost Leadership/Differentiation Strategy

The **integrated cost leadership/differentiation strategy** is an action plan the firm develops to produce goods or services, with strong emphasis on both differentiation and low cost. With this strategy, firms produce products that have some differentiated features (but not as many as offered by firms using the differentiation strategy) and that are produced at a low cost (but not at a cost as low as those of the firm using the cost leadership strategy). This strategy can be used to serve the needs of a broad target market or a narrow target market. McDonald's uses this strategy to serve the needs of a broad market, while Anon uses it to focus on the needs of a narrow target market. (Anon makes semi-customized rooftop air-conditioning systems for large customers such as The Home Depot, Walmart, and Target.) Because the integrated cost leadership/differentiation strategy requires firms to be somewhat differentiated while producing at relatively low costs, firms must develop the flexibility needed to serve both of these objectives. They have to achieve a balance between the two objectives.[46]

Lenovo, which acquired IBM's PC business, must attempt to maintain this balance as well. It must invest in R&D to continuously develop new technology and designs such as its new LePad tablet designed to compete with Apple's iPad. Yet because personal computers have become a commodity, Lenovo must also keep its costs low in order to compete effectively in the PC market worldwide.

The possibility of being "neither fish nor fowl" is the main risk of using the integrated cost leadership/differentiation strategy. In other words, when a firm fails to produce somewhat differentiated products at relatively low costs, it becomes stuck in the middle.[47]

Implementing Business-Level Strategies

To be successful, business-level strategies must not only match the needs of the marketplace, they also need to be implemented effectively. Organizational structure is an important dimension of implementing strategies. An **organizational structure** specifies the firm's formal reporting relationships, procedures, controls, and authority and decision-making processes.[48] Matching the right structure with the chosen strategy enhances firm performance.

Three major types of organizational structure are used to implement strategies: a simple structure, a functional structure, and a multidivisional structure.[49] Only the simple structure and the functional structure can be used to implement business-level strategies. A **simple structure** is an organizational structure in which the owner/manager makes all of the major decisions and oversees all of the staff's activities. This structure has few rules, depends on informal relationships, and has a limited task specialization. The work is coordinated through frequent informal communications between the owner/manager and staff. This type of structure is best suited for use in a small business. The **functional structure** is an organizational structure consisting of a CEO and a small corporate staff. Here, the managers of major functional areas usually report to the CEO or a member of the corporate staff. This structure is based on functional specialization and facilitates active information sharing within each function. However, the functional orientation sometimes makes it difficult to communicate and coordinate across functions.

integrated cost leadership/ differentiation strategy

an action plan the firm develops to produce goods or services, with a strong emphasis on both differentiation and low cost

organizational structure

specifies the firm's formal reporting relationships, procedures, controls, and authority and decision-making processes

simple structure

an organizational structure in which the owner/ manager makes all of the major decisions and oversees all of the staff's activities

functional structure

an organizational structure consisting of a CEO and a small corporate staff

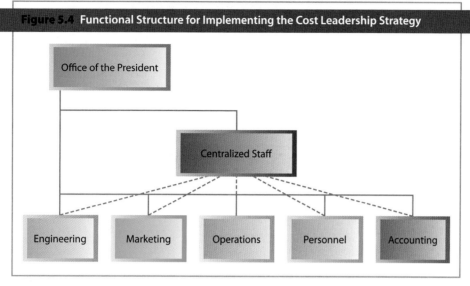

Figure 5.4 Functional Structure for Implementing the Cost Leadership Strategy

Notes: • Operations is the main function.
        • Process engineering is emphasized rather than new product R&D.
        • Relatively large centralized staff coordinates functions.
        • Formalized procedures allow for emergence of a low-cost culture.
        • Overall structure is somewhat rigid, causing job roles to be relatively structured.

Implementing the Cost Leadership Strategy

Firms implementing the cost leadership strategy use a functional structure with highly centralized authority in the corporate staff (see Figure 5.4). Recall that with a cost leadership strategy, the firm produces a relatively standardized product that is sold to the industry's average customer. To ensure that the product is produced at low costs and with standard features, the firm's structure entails a strong centralized authority. To create efficiency, jobs are highly specialized and organized into homogeneous subgroups and highly formalized rules and procedures are established. The substantial efficiency resulting from this structure helps firms keep their costs low. The operations function is important in this structure to ensure that the firm's product is produced at a low cost.

Implementing the Differentiation Strategy

The functional structure used by firms implementing the differentiation strategy differs from the one used by firms implementing the cost leadership strategy. In this version of the functional organizational structure, the R&D and marketing functions are more important. R&D is emphasized so the firm can continuously differentiate through innovations in products and designs that create value for customers, and marketing is emphasized so customers will be aware of the unique value being created by the firm's products (see Figure 5.5). Authority is decentralized in this structure so employees closest to the customer can decide how to appropriately differentiate the firm's products. Jobs in this structure have low specialization, and employees work without a large number of formal rules and processes. The characteristics of this form of the functional structure enable employees to frequently communicate and to coordinate their work. Communication and coordination are vital parts of being able to understand customers' unique needs in order to produce unique products to satisfy those needs.

Figure 5.5 Functional Structure for Implementing the Differentiation Strategy

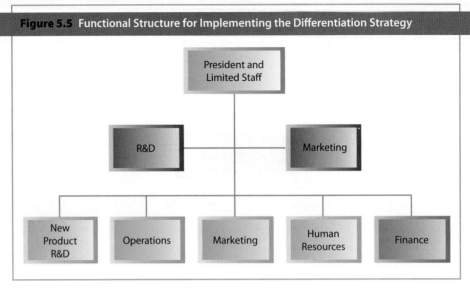

Notes: • Marketing is the main function (to track new product ideas).
        • New product R&D is emphasized.
        • Most functions are decentralized, but R&D and marketing may have centralized staffs that work closely with each other.
        • Formalization is limited so that new product ideas can easily emerge and change is more readily accomplished.
        • Overall structure is relatively flexible, causing job roles to be less structured.

Implementing the Focus Strategies

When firms following a focus strategy have only a single product line and operate in a single geographic market, a simple structure is effective for implementing the strategy. These firms are often small, and the focus is direct. However,
in firms that are larger and more complex (i.e., those with several product lines
or that operate in multiple geographic markets), a functional structure usually
is more effective. The type of functional structure used is matched to the type of
strategy. Firms using a focused cost leadership strategy should use a centralized
functional structure that emphasizes efficiency. However, firms using a focused
differentiation strategy should use a functional structure that is decentralized and
encourages interaction across functions to create innovation that continuously
differentiates the firm's products.

Implementing the Integrated Cost Leadership/
Differentiation Strategy

Because of the competing demands of the cost leadership strategy's concern
with efficiency and the differentiation strategy's concern with innovation, an
integrated cost leadership/differentiation strategy is difficult to implement. To
satisfy these competing demands, a firm using this strategy needs a structure in
which decisions are partly centralized and partly decentralized. Jobs are semi-
specialized, and some formal rules and procedures are needed, as well as the
flexibility to engage in some informal activity. This strategy requires efficient
processes to maintain lower costs. Yet, the ability to change is also important in
order to develop and maintain differentiated goods or services. Flexible manufacturing systems, quality-control systems, and sophisticated information systems
can all contribute to simultaneous efficiency and flexibility. For example, Target,
a major competitor of Walmart, uses an integrated strategy. It buys in volume,

and with its many outlets, it builds economies of scale. Additionally, it tries to maintain nice but efficient stores to keep costs at manageable levels. To differentiate its products, it has developed alliances with brand-name companies such as Eddie Bauer (camping and outdoor equipment) and Mossimo (apparel), among others. Of course, Walmart's recent changes to customize stores and merchandise to local communities are designed to compete more directly with the differentiation part of Target's strategy.

Business-Level Strategy Success Across Time

As we've described in this chapter, a business-level strategy is based on the firm's capabilities and competencies and designed to achieve competitive advantages. This strategy is used to position the firm favorably in the marketplace relative to its rivals. After it is developed and implemented, though, the firm must continuously evaluate its business-level strategy and change it as needed to create more value for customers. The changes in the strategy should be designed to help the firm reach its vision and satisfy the mission, as explained in Chapters 1 and 2. Sometimes, major changes in strategy or the implementation of new strategic actions are needed to turn around a firm's performance when its business-level strategy is unsuccessful.[50]

© Andrew Harrer/Bloomberg / Getty Images

For many years, Hershey depended on the quality of its products and its reputation for producing excellent candies (especially chocolate) to differentiate its products from those of rivals. This strategy was effective for a long time. However, other firms began developing new chocolate candies and eroding Hershey's market share. Rather than develop new candies, top executives at the firm depended on acquisitions to add new product lines (e.g., Reese's Peanut Butter Cups). In 2008, the Hershey company experienced declines in its financial performance and thus considered potential options such as a merger with another major company such as Cadbury Schweppes. And, Cadbury was a continuous target for about two years. Hershey entered into a bidding war with Kraft to acquire Cadbury and eventually lost with Kraft buying Cadbury in 2010. Yet, Hershey has also taken other strategic actions to turn around its performance. For example, it has introduced some new candy products to compete more effectively with its major rival, Mars, and entered new international markets such as China.[51] In 2010, Hershey announced improved performance with an expected growth in sales of 7 percent over 2009.[52]

Facing increasing pressure from competitors along its traditional lines of differentiation, Hershey has had to adjust its business level strategy. Growing its product lines both organically and through acquisition as well as focusing on entering new international markets such as China have led to improvements in the company's overall performance.

Recent research suggests that both innovation and internationalization have potential to turn around a firm's performance.[53] Another way the firm can learn how to create more value for customers by using its business-level strategy is to ask them how it can do so. Sam Walton was known for recommending that firms trust their customers and frequently talk to them to find out what they want.

Diversified firms with multiple businesses competing in many industries and market segments develop business-level strategies for each of their business units. For example, GE has more than a dozen business units, each of which develops a business-level strategy to describe how it intends to compete in its industry or market segments. In the next chapter, we describe the multiproduct strategies that firms such as GE use.

Unlike GE, non-diversified firms that compete in a single product market develop only one business-level strategy. A neighborhood dry-cleaning store and favorite locally owned restaurant are examples of firms with a single business-level strategy. Every firm needs a business-level strategy, and diversified firms need multiple business-level strategies plus a multiproduct strategy (see Chapter 6) as well as an international strategy (see Chapter 8) if they compete in more than a single country's markets.

SUMMARY

The primary purpose of this chapter is to explain the different business-level strategies firms can use to compete in the marketplace. In doing so, we examined the following topics:

- Business-level strategy is an action plan the firm develops to compete in its chosen industry or market segment. A business-level strategy details how the firm intends to compete in the marketplace on a continuous basis to satisfy customers' needs.
- The five business-level strategies are referred to as *generic* because they can be used by any firm regardless of the industry. Opportunities and threats in the external environment and the firm's capabilities and core competencies suggest the business-level strategy the firm should implement to achieve a competitive advantage.
- Each business-level strategy has two dimensions: competitive advantage (either a cost advantage or a uniqueness advantage) and competitive scope (either broad or narrow). The cost leadership and differentiation strategies are used to serve a broad market, while the focused cost leadership and focused differentiation strategies serve the specialized needs of a narrow market. The integrated cost leadership/differentiation strategy strikes a balance between the competitive advantage and competitive scope dimensions.
- When using the cost leadership strategy, a firm produces standardized products that are intended to satisfy the needs of the typical or "average" customer, which is usually the largest market segment. These products are produced at costs lower than those of competitors. To use this strategy successfully across time, the firm must continuously drive its costs lower

than competitors' costs so it can sell its products at lower prices.

- Firms use the differentiation strategy to produce products that customers consider unique in ways that are important to them. Target customers for this strategy are willing to pay for product uniqueness that creates value for them. Uniqueness can be physical (e.g., superior reliability) or psychological (e.g., perceived status). Earning margins that are sufficient to support continuous reinvestment in sources of differentiation that customers value is the key to long-term success with this strategy.
- Focus strategies (cost leadership and differentiation) rely on either the cost or uniqueness advantage to better serve the specialized needs of a narrow target market, as compared to serving a broad target market.
- Firms use the integrated cost leadership/differentiation strategy to produce products that have some differentiation at a relatively low price. Because low cost and differentiation are sought simultaneously, the firm must be flexible to successfully use this strategy and avoid becoming stuck in the middle. The main risk of the integrated cost leadership/differentiation strategy is being outperformed by firms successfully using either the cost leadership or differentiation strategy.
- Two versions of the functional structure are best suited to implement the cost leadership strategy and the differentiation strategy. These two versions differ in their degree of centralization, specialization, and formalization. To promote efficiency, the functional structure for the cost leadership strategy holds decision-making authority in centralized staff functions, is highly specialized, and uses formal rules and procedures. In contrast, the functional structure used

to implement the differentiation strategy is decentralized to different organizational functions. The emphasis here is on R&D and marketing to promote innovation. This structure requires less specialization, greater use of cross-functional teams, and fewer formal rules and procedures. Structures for the focus strategies largely match the structures used to implement the cost leadership or differentiation strategy. However, if a firm using a focus strategy is small, a simple structure is used. The structure for the integrated cost leadership/differentiation strategy is more complex. It must be flexible, with some centralization and some decentralization in order to promote efficiency and innovation simultaneously. Use of flexible manufacturing systems, quality-control systems, and sophisticated information systems contribute to the flexibility.

KEY TERMS

Business-level strategy, 98
Cost leadership strategy, 101
Differentiation strategy,104
Focus strategy, 109

Focused cost leadership
   strategy, 109
Focused differentiation strategy, 111
Functional structure, 112

Integrated cost leadership/
   differentiation strategy, 112
Organizational structure, 112
Simple structure, 112

DISCUSSION QUESTIONS

1. What is a business-level strategy? Why is a business-level strategy important to a firm's success?
2. What are the definitions of the five business-level strategies discussed in this chapter? What are the differences among the five business-level strategies?
3. What specific actions should a firm take to effectively use each business-level strategy?

4. What risks are associated with using each business-level strategy?
5. What organizational structures should be used to implement each of the business-level strategies?

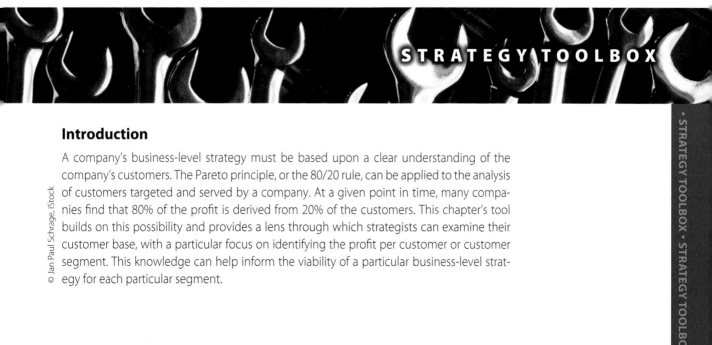

STRATEGY TOOLBOX

Introduction

A company's business-level strategy must be based upon a clear understanding of the company's customers. The Pareto principle, or the 80/20 rule, can be applied to the analysis of customers targeted and served by a company. At a given point in time, many companies find that 80% of the profit is derived from 20% of the customers. This chapter's tool builds on this possibility and provides a lens through which strategists can examine their customer base, with a particular focus on identifying the profit per customer or customer segment. This knowledge can help inform the viability of a particular business-level strategy for each particular segment.

© Jan Paul Schrage, iStock

Customer Value Analysis

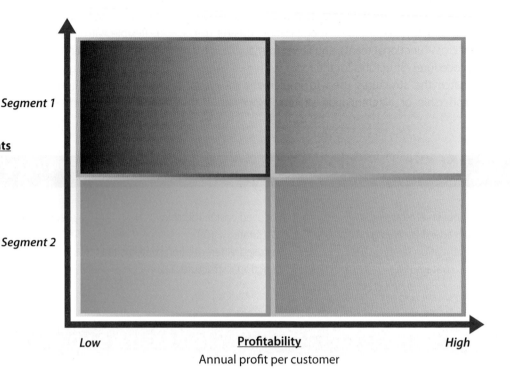

Meaningful Segments
- Demographic
- Preferences
- Purchase History

MINI-CASE

Krispy Kreme: Will Dough Continue to Flow to Shareholders?

Launched in 1937, Krispy Kreme Doughnuts is a branded specialty retailer of premium doughnuts. Its Original Glazed doughnut is the firm's most recognizable product. However, Krispy Kreme's commitment to innovation results in frequent tests of potential new doughnuts such as its whole wheat 180-calorie doughnut introduced in 2007. More recently (2010), it has introduced the triple chocolate doughnut and two new doughnuts with banana flavor, the Banana Pudding doughnut and the Banana Caramel Cake doughnut. New products that are well received by customers are then added to the stores' inventory of doughnuts. The variety of flavors Krispy Kreme can incorporate into its doughnuts is virtually endless.

As this brief discussion suggests, Krispy Kreme uses a differentiation strategy. It seeks to sell its premium doughnuts to customers who value the doughnuts' uniqueness. The firm's Doughnut Theatre is a source of differentiation between Krispy Kreme and its competitors. The Doughnut Theatre is the in-store manufacturing process customers can watch to see employees make doughnuts.

Are Krispy Kreme doughnuts really significantly different from competitors' offerings? As we noted earlier in this chapter, some differentiation is tangible, while other differentiation may be more psychological in nature. Some believe that Krispy Kreme's uniqueness is more psychological than tangible. One analyst even suggested, "It isn't what's inside a Krispy Kreme doughnut that creates the demand. It's what's inside the customer's head that makes a Krispy Kreme a Krispy Kreme." Regardless of the nature of the differentiation, Krispy Kreme achieved great success with its differentiation strategy for many decades.

However, the situation began to change for Krispy Kreme in 2004. Essentially, Krispy Kreme over-expanded, taking on significant debt in the process. One indicator of the seriousness of the change is the firm's stock price. After hitting a high of more than $50 in March 2003, it fell to roughly $7.50 per share in February 2005.

We noted in Chapter 3 that firms can't control events in the external environment, but those events can significantly affect a firm's performance. The diet craze and the desire to be more physically fit is a trend in the general environment that is having a major effect on Krispy Kreme. Stated simply, the firm's doughnuts are high in fat, high in carbohydrates, and high in sugar. In addition, Krispy Kreme was investigated for alleged accounting irregularities. The firm tried to respond to the problems with appropriate actions. It brought in a turnaround specialist for a stint as CEO, and a new permanent CEO was named in 2006. Additionally, the whole wheat doughnut was a response to concerns about high calories. Finally, the company removed all grams of trans fat from its products. Yet, its sales continued to decline. After the stock price fell to a new all-time low of under $3 per share, the CEO resigned in January 2008. Some investors suggested that Krispy Kreme should expand further into international markets. Yet it already has stores in 10 foreign countries outside the United States. The new CEO, James Morgan, hired thereafter faced significant challenges to decide what strategic actions can be taken to turn around the once highly successful company. He announced plans to improve the customers' experience in the stores, making them more family oriented. He also explained that the firm was working on improving the shelf life of its doughnuts. His actions seem to be working as the company announced that it achieved breakeven performance in fiscal 2010. In fiscal 2011, it plans to open about 55 more stores to add to its current set of 582 stores. Finally, a profit is projected for fiscal 2011.

Sources: L. LaMotta, 2010, New filling for Krispy Kreme, Forbes, www.forbes.com, June 23; 2010, Krispy Kreme reports net income for the fourth quarter and breakeven results for the physical year ended January 31, 2010, Krispy Kreme Doughnuts Inc., www.krispykreme.com, April 15; 2010, Krispy Kreme goes bananas and puts a flavorful twist on a southern classic, Krispy Kreme Doughnuts Inc., www.krispykreme.com, March 3; 2010, Celebrate the season of love with Krispy Kreme's irresistible heart and chocolate treats, Krispy Kreme Doughnuts Inc., www.krispykreme.com, January 20; 2008, Krispy Kreme's CEO resigns, *The Wall Street Journal*, online.wsj.com, January 8; 2008, Krispy Kreme's Chief Executive Officer quits amid turnaround, *New York Times*, www.nytimes.com, January 8; M. Linder, 2007, Krispy Kreme fills its hole, for now, *Forbes*, www.forbes.com, September 9; M. Umy, 2007, The way we live now; the hole is healthy, *Financial Times*, www.ft.com, February 27; F. Norris, 2006, Krispy Kreme names a chief executive, and its shares jump nearly 21%, *New York Times*, www.nytimes.com, March 8.

Questions

1. Go to the Krispy Kreme Web site (www.krispykreme.com) and read about how the firm operates. Based on what you read, prepare a list of each source of differentiation the firm is using to make its doughnuts and the way the firm sells them that is unique relative to its competitors.
2. Using the information collected in responding to the first question, determine the sustainability of Krispy Kreme's differentiation strategy. Are the firm's sources of differentiation sustainable over the next 10 years? Why or why not?
3. If you were appointed CEO of Krispy Kreme, what actions would you take and why?

EXPERIENTIAL EXERCISES

Exercise One: Focus Cost Leadership Strategy Falters in Countering Forces in the U.S. Airline Industry

In March and April 2008, four discount carriers—ATA Airlines, Champion Air, Skybus Airlines, and Frontier Airlines—declared Chapter 11 bankruptcy, ceased operations, or announced plans to do so. Frontier Airlines, unlike the others, declared bankruptcy but planned to continue service for the near future. These small carriers used the focused cost leadership strategy, competing in a limited market segment with a low-cost strategy. In contrast, discount carriers Southwest Airlines, JetBlue, and AirTran have continued to perform strongly. Of the most recent new entrants, Skybus (started May 2007) was the first to fail. In contrast, another recent low-cost entrant, Virgin

© vndrpttn, iStock

America Inc. (started in August 2007) continues to operate and plans to add 30 planes in 2008 and 20 more in 2009. U.S. and British investors plan to inject $100 million of additional funds into Virgin America to keep it operating.

Were these failures a result of the inability of the airlines' strategies to counter the forces in the industry? Your assignment is to choose one failing discount airline (or any other recently failed discount carrier) such as Skybus and one successful airline such as JetBlue to determine why one strategy was successful against the industry forces while the other was not. Was the airline failure a result of poor strategy formulation? If so, what could have been done differently?

Sources: Susan Carey, 2008, Low-cost carrier Skybus closes down business, *The Wall Street Journal*, April 5; Susan Carey, 2008, Champion Air plans to shut down, *The Wall Street Journal*, March 31; Susan Carey & Melanie Trottman, 2008, ATA shutdown signals discount carrier woes, *The Wall Street Journal*, April 4; Paulo Prada, 2008, Virgin America investors to inject $100 million, *The Wall Street Journal*, April 12; Melanie Trottman, 2008, Frontier to fly amid bankruptcy filing, *The Wall Street Journal*, April 12.

Exercise Two: Competitive Risks of Walmart's Cost Leadership Strategy

Walmart is frequently cited as an example of a firm that has successfully implemented a cost leadership strategy. This exercise requires you to investigate whether that strategy is sustainable given the pressures that Walmart exerts on its suppliers to lower their costs and prices. Do some research to determine whether Walmart's power over its suppliers has caused them to lower the quality of some of the products in the name of the cost leadership strategy. What effect might this factor have on the success of Walmart's strategy? Look at business publications such as *Fast Company, Forbes, Fortune, The Wall Street Journal*, and *BusinessWeek*. Be sure to state your conclusions about whether this cost leadership strategy is sustainable in the long run.

ENDNOTES

1. M. E. Porter & E. Olmstead-Teisberg, 2004, Redefining competition in health care, *Harvard Business Review*, 82(6): 64–76.

2. M. Barbaro, 2008, Walmart: The new Washington, *New York Times*, www.nytimes.com, February 3.

3. M. Beer & R. A. Eisentat, 2004, How to have an honest conversation about your business strategy, *Harvard Business Review*, 82(2): 82–89.

4. G. Stalk, Jr., & R. Lachenauer, 2004, Hardball: Five killer strategies for trouncing the competition, *Harvard Business Review*, 82(4): 62–71.

5. L. K. Trevino & M. E. Brown, 2004, Managing to be ethical: Debunking five business ethics myths, *Academy of Management Executive*, 18(2): 69–81.

6. B. C. Skaggs & M. Youndt, 2004, Strategic positioning, human capital, and performance in service organizations: A customer interaction approach, *Strategic Management Journal*, 25: 85–99.

7. J. Grahovac & D. J. Miller, 2009, Competitive advantage and performance: The impact of value creation and costliness of imitation, *Strategic Management Journal*, 30: 1192–1212.

8. 2004, Becoming the best: What you can learn from the 25 most influential leaders of our times, Knowledge @ Wharton, www.knowledge.wharron.upenn.edu, February 11.

9. K. Z. Zhou, J. R. Brown, C. S. Dev, & A. Agarwal, 2007, The effects of customer and competitor orientations on performance in global markets: A contingency analysis, *Journal of International Business Studies*, 38: 303–319.

10. D. W. Voorhies, R. E. Morgan, & C. W. Autry, 2009, Product-market strategy and the marketing capabilities of the firm: Impact on market effectiveness and cash flow performance, *Strategic Management Journal*, 30: 1310–1334.

11. D. G. Sirmon & M. A. Hitt, 2009, Contingencies within dynamic managerial capabilities: interdependent effects of resource investment and deployment on firm performance, *Strategic Management Journal*, 30: 1375–1394; C. Zott & R. Amit, 2008, The fit between product market strategy and business model: Implications for firm performance, *Strategic Management Journal*, 29: 1–26.

12. F. F. Suarez & G. Lanzolla, 2007, The role of environmental dynamics in building first mover advantage theory, *Academy of Management Review*, 32: 377–392.

13. M. E. Porter, 1985, *Competitive Advantage*, New York: Free Press, 15; S. D. Dobrev, 2007, Competing in the looking-glass market: Imitation, resources, and crowding, *Strategic Management Journal*, 28: 1267–1289.

14. 2008, About Us, Cooper Tire & Rubber, www.coopertire.com, March 9.

15. 2008, Guinness, Wikipedia, http://en.wikipedia.org, March 9.

16. M. E. Porter, 1980, *Competitive Strategy*, New York: Free Press, 35–40.

17. J. Bercovitz & W. Mitchell, 2007, When is more better? The impact of business scale and scope on long-term business survival, while controlling for profitability, *Strategic Management Journal*, 28: 61–79.

18. M. Kotabe, R. Parente, & J. Y. Murray, 2007, Antecedents and outcomes of modular production in the Brazilian automobile industry: A grounded theory approach, *Journal of International Business Studies*, 38: 84–108.

19. H. Wang & C. Kimble, 2010, Low-cost strategy through product architecture: Lessons from China, *Journal of Business Strategy*, 31(3): 12–20.

20. T. Shervani, G. Frazier, & G. Challagalla, 2007, The moderating influence of firm market power on the transaction cost economics model: An empirical test in a forward channel integration context, *Strategic Management Journal*, 28: 635–652.

21. C. Seelos & J. Mair, 2007, Profitable business models and market creation in the context of deep poverty: A strategic view, *Academy of Management Perspectives*, 21(4): 49–63.

22. Kmart, 2010, Wikipedia, http://en.wikipedia.org, Accessed July 21; 2008, Message from the chairman, Sears Holdings, www.searsholdings.com, March 9.

23. H. R. Greve, 2008, Multimarket contact and sales growth: Evidence from insurance, *Strategic Management Journal*, 29: 229–249.

24. T. Yu & A. A. Cannella, 2007, Rivalry between multinational enterprises: An event history approach, *Academy of Management Journal*, 50: 665–686.

25. D. Ng, R. Westgren, & S. Sonka, 2009, Competitive blind spots in an institutional field, *Strategic Management Journal*, 30: 349–369.

26. C. Horng & W. Chen, 2007, From contract manufacturing to own brand management: The role of learning and cultural heritage identity, *Management and Organization Review*, 4: 109–133.

27. K. Z. Zhou & F. Wu, 2010, Technological capability, strategic flexibility, and product innovation, *Strategic Management Journal*, 31: 547–561; A. M. Kleinbaum & M. L. Tushman, 2007, Building bridges: The social structure of interdependent innovation, *Strategic Entrepreneurship Journal*, 1: 103–122.

28. J. Woolley, 2010, Technological emergence through entrepreneurship across multiple industries, *Strategic Entrepreneurship Journal*, 4: 1–21.

29. S. R. Miller, D. E. Thomas, L. Eden, & M. A. Hitt, 2008, Knee deep in the big muddy: The survival of emerging market firms in developed markets, *Management International Review*, 48(6): 645–666.

30. V. Jayaraman & Y. Luo, 2007, Creating competitive advantages through new value creation: A reverse logistics perspective, *Academy of Management Perspectives*, 21(2): 56–73.

31. M. J. Leiblein & T. L. Madsen, 2009, Unbundling competitive heterogeneity: Incentive structures and capability influences on technological innovation, *Strategic Management Journal*, 30: 711–735.

32. R. L. Priem, 2007, A consumer perspective on value creation, *Academy of Management Review*, 32: 219–235.

33. S. Jonsson & P. Regner, 2009, Normative barriers to imitation: Social Complexity of core competences in a mutual fund industry, *Strategic Management Journal*, 30: 517–536.

34. M.-P. Kang, J. T. Mahoney & D. Tan, 2009, Why firms make unilateral investments specific to other firms: The case of OEM suppliers, *Strategic Management Journal*, 30: 117–135.

35. C. C. De Fontenay & J. S. Gans, 2008, A bargaining perspective on strategic outsourcing and supply competition, *Strategic Management Journal*, 29: 819–839.

36. S. K. Ethiraj & D. H. Zhu, 2008, Performance effects of imitative entry, *Strategic Management Journal*, 29: 797–817.

37. B. B. Allred & W. C. Park, 2007, Patent rights and innovative activity: Evidence from national and firm-level data, *Journal of International Business Studies*, 38: 879–900.

38. A. Leiponen & C.E. Helfat, 2010, Innovation objectives, knowledge sources, and the benefits of breadth, *Strategic Management Journal*, 31: 224–236; T. J. Andersen, 2009, Effective risk management outcomes: Exploring effects of innovation and capital structure, *Journal of Business and Strategy*, 2: 352–379.

39. D. Li, L. Eden, M. A. Hitt, & R. D. Ireland, 2008, Friends, acquaintances, or strangers? Partner selection in R&D alliances, *Academy of Management Journal*, 51: 315–334.

40. G. Leask & D. Parker, 2007, Strategic groups, competitive groups and performance within the U.K. pharmaceutical industry: Improving our understanding of the competitive process, *Strategic Management Journal*, 28: 723–745.

41. K. Kling & I. Goteman, 2003, IKEA CEO Andres Dahlvig on international growth and IKEA's unique corporate culture and brand identity, *Academy of Management Executive*, 17(1): 31–37.

42. Welcome to IKEA.com, 2010, IKEA.com, http://www.ikea.com, accessed July 23; 2008, IKEA, *Wikipedia*, http://en.wikipedia.org, March 10.

43. 2008, Thomas Pink, LVMH Moet Hennessy Louis Vuitton, www.lvmh.com, March 10.

44. H. Miller, 2010, Whole Foods follies, Forbes.com, http://www.forbes.com, June 16.

45. 2008, Charles Tyrwhitt Shirts, www.ctshirts.co.uk, March 10.

46. F. T. Rothaermel, M. A. Hitt, & L. A. Jobe, 2006, Balancing vertical integration and strategic outsourcing: Effects on product portfolio, product success, and firm performance, *Strategic Management Journal*, 27: 1033–1056.

47. Porter, *Competitive Advantage*, 16.

48. B. Keats & H. O'Neill, 2001, Organizational structure: Looking through a strategy lens, in M. A. Hitt, R. E. Freeman, & J. S. Harrison (Eds.), *Handbook of Strategic Management*, Oxford, UK: Blackwell, 520–542.

49. R. E. Hoskisson, M. A. Hitt, R. D. Ireland, & J. S. Harrison, 2008, *Competing for Advantage*, Mason, Ohio: Thomson South-Western.

50. J. L. Morrow, D. G. Sirmon, M. A. Hitt, & T. R. Holcomb, 2007, Creating value in the face of declining performance: Firm strategies and organizational recovery, *Strategic Management Journal*, 28: 271–283.

51. J. Jargon, M. Karnitschnig, & J. S. Dublin, 2008, How Hershey went sour, *The Wall Street Journal*, online.wsj.com, February 23; J. Fishbein, 2008, Chocolatiers look to Asia for growth, *BusinessWeek*, www.businessweek.com, January 17.

52. Hershey announces second quarter results, 2010, *New York Times*, http://markets.on.nytimes.com, July 22; M. J. de la Merced & C. V. Nicholson, 2010, Kraft to acquire Cadbury in deal worth $19 billion, *New York Times*, http://www.nytimes.com, January 20.

53. Morrow, et al., 2007, Creating value in the face of declining performance.

CHAPTER 6
Multiproduct Strategies

KNOWLEDGE OBJECTIVES

Reading and studying this chapter should enable you to:

1. Define a multiproduct strategy.

2. Understand the differences between the levels of diversification.

3. Discuss the related diversification multiproduct strategy.

4. Explain the unrelated diversification multiproduct strategy.

5. Understand two motives that top-level managers have to diversify the firms they lead.

6. Describe the organizational structures used to implement the different multiproduct strategies.

Adding AirTran to the Mix: Does This Make Sense for Southwest Airlines?

As we approach our 40th anniversary of providing exceptional customer service at everyday low fares, the acquisition of AirTran represents a unique opportunity to grow Southwest Airlines' presence in key markets we don't yet serve and takes a significant step towards positioning us for future growth.

(Gary C. Kelly, Chairman, President and CEO, Southwest Airlines)

Launched on June 18, 1971, Southwest Airlines uses a single business multiproduct strategy (this strategy is fully discussed in this chapter). This strategy finds Southwest generating 95 percent or more of its revenue by providing air transportation as a service. By acquiring AirTran Holdings and its primary business AirTran Airways, Southwest is signaling that it intends to grow in a manner that differs from its historical growth pattern.

Pursuing its *mission* of being dedicated "…to the highest quality of customer service, delivered with a sense of warmth, friendliness, individual pride and company spirit" and relying on people as its main competitive advantage, Southwest historically has grown organically. In this respect, Southwest has grown by faithfully and consistently using its business model (and its cost leadership strategy—see Chapter 5) while avoiding partnerships and virtually avoiding acquisitions. (Prior to AirTran, Southwest had acquired only small competitors Muse Air in 1985, Morris Air in the 1993, and the now-defunct ATA Airlines earlier in this decade.) The business model through which Southwest grew organically includes several key components: (1) a point-to-point route system in which customers are moved from their point of origin to their final destination in a single flight. This is in contrast to the hub-and-spoke system used by many large carriers, a system in which passengers change planes in different airports in order to reach their final destination; (2) use of a single aircraft (Boeing 737s) in order to reduce costs related to maintenance and training of all employees working on the plane (e.g., pilots, mechanics, and flight crews); and (3) offering customers a single class of service, which means that business- and first-class seats are not available on Southwest flights. Given Southwest's historic success, why did the firm decide in September of 2010 to pay $1.4 billion to acquire AirTran instead of continuing to rely almost exclusively on organic growth?

© AP Photo/PRNewsFoto/
AirTran Airways

CEO Kelly describes the primary influence on Southwest's decision to acquire AirTran, saying, "As our competition changes, we don't live in a vacuum. That has to have an impact on our thinking." A key change facing Southwest is the ongoing merger and acquisition activity (such as the joining of Continental and United) in the airline industry. These large combinations make it increasingly difficult for smaller firms to remain competitive. Additionally, Southwest has reached a point where serving more business people and more markets is necessary for the firm to continue growing. Acquiring AirTran addresses these needs in that the deal makes Southwest a true national discount airline, allowing it to serve more business passengers by flying to a larger number of locations, while generating opportunities to serve international markets as well. Domestically, having AirTran's access to the Atlanta airport (at the time the acquisitions was announced, AirTran was the second-largest carrier in Atlanta) is significant in that this is the busiest U.S. airport. (Southwest itself does not serve Atlanta.) Internationally, Southwest will be able to serve markets in Mexico and four Caribbean destinations where AirTran was already established. Overall then, acquiring AirTran increases Southwest's capacity to serve a larger number of customers in a more diverse set of locations.

We discuss the difficulty of completing a successful acquisition in Chapter 7. Finding an appropriate firm to acquire and effectively integrating the acquired firm into the acquiring firm's operations are two of the difficulties we discuss in that chapter. In general though, analysts responded positively to Southwest's intention of acquiring AirTran with one individual saying, "This is one of those cases in which reward outweigh the risks."

Sources: J. Brancatelli, 2010, A Southwest strategy, *Portfolio.com*, www.portfolio.com, September 29; M. Esterl, 2010, Discount carriers Southwest, AirTran tie knot, *The Wall Street Journal Online*, www.wsj.com, September 28; M. Esterl, 2010, Southwest alters plan, *The Wall Street Journal Online*, www.wsj.com, September 29; J. Marte, 2010, What airline merger means for travelers, *The Wall Street Journal Online*, www.wsj.com, September 30; P. Sanders, 2010, Southwest looks likely to gain sway over Boeing, *The Wall Street Journal Online*, www.wsj.com, September 28; M. Schlangenstein & J. Hughes, 2010, Southwest CEO risks keep-it-simple strategy to reignite growth, *Bloomberg*, www.bloomberg.com, September 28.

A **multiproduct strategy** is an action plan the firm uses to compete in different product markets. Using a multiproduct strategy causes a firm to become more diversified to some degree. In this chapter, our focus is on how firms diversify by competing in different product markets; in Chapter 8, our focus is on how firms diversify by competing in different geographic locations. Of course, many firms, especially large established ones, diversify in terms of both products and geography.

The degree to which firms become more diversified varies among the multiproduct strategies we discuss in this chapter. As explained in *Focusing on Strategy*, Southwest Airlines uses a single business multiproduct strategy. By acquiring AirTran Airways, Southwest will serve additional domestic customers in a larger number of domestic markets, increasing the number of "product" markets it serves. Because Southwest will now serve international markets for the first time, it is also increasing its geographic diversity by acquiring AirTran. However, because air service will continue accounting for 95 percent or more of the firm's revenues, Southwest will still be using the single business multiproduct strategy.

The primary reason firms use multiproduct strategies is to improve their performance.[1] (In Table 6.1, we present other reasons firms use multiproduct strategies.) Multiproduct strategies result in performance improvements when their use allows firms to create operational relatedness, corporate relatedness, or financial economies. We define and discuss these terms later in the chapter.

Firms deal with two issues when choosing a multiproduct strategy: (1) What products (goods or services) are to be produced and sold? (2) How will the firm manage the different units it creates to make and sell its products?[2] Southwest Airlines, which offers a single set of services (answering the first of these two questions), uses a functional structure to implement its single business multiproduct

multiproduct strategy

an action plan the firm uses to compete in different product markets

Table 6.1 Reasons Firms Use Multiproduct Strategies to Diversify
• Achieve profitable growth
• Reduce the risk of being involved with a single product line
• Learn how to apply core competencies in other value-creating ways
• Gain exposure to different technologies
• Develop economies of scope
• Extend the firm's brand into additional product areas

strategy (answering the second question). In contrast, Hewlett-Packard (HP) uses the related constrained multiproduct strategy. This strategy finds HP producing an array of products that the firm offers to customers through seven business segments: "Services, Enterprise Storage and Servers, HP Software, the Personal Systems Group, the Imaging and Printing Group, HP Financial Services and Corporate Investments."[3] These segments share some resources and activities to make and sell their respective products, demonstrating that HP is indeed using a related constrained multiproduct strategy. Later in the chapter, we'll discuss this strategy type as well as the organizational structure firms such as HP use to support their implementation.

To explain multiproduct strategies, we first describe how diversified a firm becomes (from low to high) when it selects a multiproduct strategy. (Again, HP has a greater amount of product diversification than does Southwest.) Because firms use them frequently, we then examine two levels of product diversification (related and unrelated) in some detail. Following these discussions, we describe two motives that top-level managers have to diversify the firm in ways that may or may not create value. Closing this chapter are discussions of the different organizational structures firms use to implement the different multiproduct strategies.

Levels of Diversification

We show five levels of diversification (from low to high) in Figure 6.1. Firms using the single business multiproduct strategy are the least diversified, while companies using the unrelated diversification multiproduct strategy are the most diversified. A firm with a low level of diversification has a smaller total number of different products and generates a larger percentage of its sales from its dominant business. A firm with a high level of diversification has a larger number of different products and generates a smaller percentage of its sales revenue from its dominant business.

Low Levels of Diversification

As shown in Figure 6.1, the sources of a firm's sales revenue are used to determine its level of product diversification. This method of determining a firm's degree of product diversification is based on Richard Rumelt's classic work, *Strategy, Structure, and Economic Performance.*[4]

Single Business Multiproduct Strategy A firm pursuing low levels of diversification uses the single or a dominant business multiproduct strategy. With the single business strategy, the firm generates at least 95 percent of its sales revenue from sales generated within a single business. A *single business* is one in which the firm makes and sells a single good or service or a variety of that good or service. As we've noted, Southwest sells a single service (air transportation). By acquiring AirTran, the firm intends to increase the variety of the service it sells by increasing the number of domestic locations it serves and by adding international flights.

Kohl's, initially launched in Wisconsin in 1946 as a traditional grocery store, also uses the single business multiproduct strategy. With a mission of being "the leading value-oriented, family-focused, specialty department store," Kohl's operates close to 1100 stores in the United States. We discuss Kohl's continuing success in *Understanding Strategy: Learning from Success*. Given its success using the single business multiproduct strategy, can you imagine this firm choosing to become more diversified to the point of using the dominant business multiproduct

Figure 6.1 Levels of Diversification

Low Levels of Diversification

Single business:

More than 95 percent of revenue comes from a single business.

Ⓐ

Dominant business:

Between 70 and 95 percent of revenue comes from a single business.

Ⓐ
Ⓑ

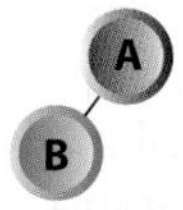

Moderate to High Levels of Diversification

Related constrained:

Less than 70 percent of revenue comes from the dominant business, and all businesses share product, technological, and distribution linkages.

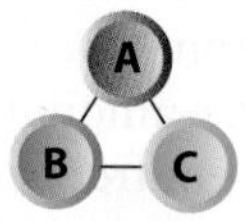

Ⓐ
Ⓑ—Ⓒ

Related linked (mixed related and unrelated):

Less than 70 percent of revenue comes from the dominant business, and only limited links exist between businesses.

Ⓐ
Ⓑ—Ⓒ

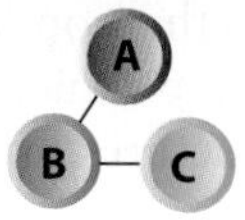

Very High Levels of Diversification

Unrelated:

Less than 70 percent of revenue comes from the dominant business, and no common links exist between businesses.

Ⓐ
Ⓑ Ⓒ

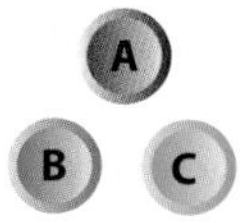

Source: Adapted from R. P. Rumelt, 1974, *Strategy, Structure, and Economic Performance,* Boston: Harvard Business School.

strategy? If so, what additional product markets do you think Kohl's might choose to enter and why?

Dominant Business Multiproduct Strategy A firm using the dominant business multiproduct strategy generates between 70 and 95 percent of its sales revenue from a single product group. Historically, United Parcel Service (UPS) used this strategy while competing in three business areas: U.S. Package Delivery, International Package, and Supply Chain Solutions. In 2005, the firm generated 74 percent, 17 percent, and 9 percent of its revenue, respectively, from those three product markets. Thus, the firm was using the dominant business strategy at the close of 2005.

The sources of the firm's sales revenue from 2009, however, show a change in UPS's multiproduct strategy in that Domestic Package Delivery accounted for 62 percent of revenue, International Package accounted for 21 percent of revenue, and Supply Chain Solutions accounted for 17 percent of revenue.[5] Those numbers show that UPS changed to a related multiproduct strategy. Contributing to this change in multiproduct strategies was the number of shipping-related opportunities in international markets relative to those in the firm's domestic U.S. market and its stronger focus on using technology to provide other companies with logistics and distribution services. Because of those opportunities, UPS was serving a larger number of international markets and providing additional logistics services to an increasingly diverse customer base. In essence then, UPS was becoming more diversified geographically by serving additional international markets and more diversified in terms of product offerings by providing additional types of logistics services.

Kohl's: Where Concentrating on a Single Business Area Is the Foundation to Success

If you've ever shopped one of our clean, bright department stores, you've already experienced our commitment to family, value, and national brands.

(Profile of Kohl's Corp.)

Telling them that they should "Expect Great Things," Kohl's wants to be the preferred shopping destination for busy women, the firm's target customer. Traditionally, these busy women are married and between 25 and 54 years of age. As suggested by the statement presented above, great brands, value, convenience, and strong customer service are the key benefits customers can expect from their shopping experience at one of Kohl's 1,089 locations in 49 U.S. states. Kohl's envisions itself as a "family-focused, value-oriented specialty department store offering moderately priced, exclusive and national brand apparel, shoes, accessories, beauty, and home products in an exciting shopping environment."

© Vicki Beaver

Are there opportunities for Kohl's to expand into other product markets or should they remain focused on the single business multiproduct strategy, which is the foundation of their current success?

Recall our discussion in Chapter 3 of "green" policies as part of how an increasing number of firms are interacting with their physical environment. Kohl's is strongly committed to green policies as demonstrated by the fact that it purchases 100 percent of its electricity from renewable sources such as wind and solar.

Selling an array of products that includes clothing, shoes, and accessories finds Kohl's competing in a single business. But Kohl's decision to organize its products into six major lines of business (men's clothing, women's clothing, children's clothing, footwear, home, and accessories) demonstrates the different types of products (all of which are highly related to

each other) the firm offers through a specialty department store format. To precisely serve customers' needs, Kohl's uses price and quality to batch its products into three categories— good, better, and best. Three distinct customer styles are served within each of the three categories: "the 'classic' customer who wants a coordinated look without bending the rules; the 'updated' customer who likes classic styles with a twist; and the more fashion-forward 'contemporary' customer."

One of the keys to Kohl's success while using the single business multiproduct strategy is its ability to offer recognizable brands at affordable prices. KitchenAid, Dockers, and Chaps by Ralph Lauren are examples. Kohl's sometimes forms partnerships with suppliers such as Ralph Lauren Company to offer exclusive versions of their products to Kohl's customers at affordable prices. For example, Kohl's has a multiyear contract with Vera Wang to create an exclusive premium fashion and lifestyle brand for the firm. Called Simply Vera, the collection that is exclusive to Kohl's includes sportswear, intimate apparel, and handbags, among other items. Some analysts conclude that Kohl's success is a result of its "…value pricing strategy, off-mall shopping convenience (of its stores), targeted expansion, and a growing e-commerce business."

Sources: 2010, Investor relations, *Kohl's Home Page*, www.kohls.com, November 1; 2010, Kohl's Corp., *Standard and Poor's Stock Report*, www.standardandpoors.com, October 23; R. Blitstein, 2010, Retailer Kohl's opens 37 stores, plans more for 2010, *Daily Finance*, www.dailyfinance.com, September 30; J. Jannarone, Kohl's mines for market share, *The Wall Street Journal Online*, www.wsj.com, September 18; C. Martin & K. Chipman, 2010, Intel, Kohl's lead U.S. in purchasing clean energy, *Bloomberg Businessweek*, www.businessweek.com, November 1; R. A. Smith, 2010, Vera Wang's idea of empire: Marry high, low, in between, *The Wall Street Journal Online*, www.wsj.com, September 17.

© Greg Epperson, iStock

UPS's experience with multiproduct strategies highlights two points. First, achieving additional successes in different product markets may cause a firm to become more diversified. Second, changing the multiproduct strategy a firm is using signals a need to change the organizational structure in place to support implementing that strategy.

Moderate to High Levels of Diversification

Related Diversification Multiproduct Strategy A firm generating less than 70 percent of sales revenue from its dominant business is using either the related or the unrelated diversification multiproduct strategy (see Figure 6.1). Let's look at the differences between these strategies.

Firms using a related diversification multiproduct strategy try to create economies of scope. **Economies of scope** are cost savings the firm accrues when it successfully shares some of its resources and activities between its businesses or transfers corporate-level core competencies into its businesses.

The differences between the two forms of the related diversification multiproduct strategy are subtle but important. With the *related constrained* multiproduct strategy, the firms' businesses are related to each other.[6] The relatedness between the groups occurs as they share some resources and activities to make and sell products.[7] As shown in Figure 6.1, the hypothetical firm using the related constrained strategy has three businesses (A, B, and C). The lines connecting all three businesses show hypothetically that they are somewhat constrained in the activities used to make their goods or services because they share some resources (e.g., raw materials as inputs to the manufacturing processes used to make the business's final product) and activities (e.g., capabilities that are used to develop advertising campaigns). Consumer product giant Procter & Gamble (P&G) uses the related constrained strategy as does UPS. (We describe an example of how P&G's businesses are related to one another in the upcoming paragraphs.)

In the *related linked* diversification strategy, only limited links or relationships exist between the firm's businesses. As shown in Figure 6.1, the hypothetical firm using the related linked strategy has three businesses (A, B, and C). The line connecting business A and business B reflects a hypothetical relationship, as does the line between business B and business C; notice though, that business A and business C are not related.

Resources and activities may be shared between some of the businesses that are a part of a firm using the related linked strategy. However, the focus in these firms is on transferring corporate-level core competencies into different businesses. **Corporate-level core competencies** are complex sets of resources and capabilities that link different businesses, primarily through managerial and technological knowledge, experience, and expertise. Typically, personnel in the diversified firm's corporate headquarters take the actions required to transfer core competencies into the firm's different businesses. An ability to price the firm's products effectively is an example of a corporate-level core competence that can create economies of scope when transferred from one of the firm's businesses to its other businesses.[8]

Unrelated Diversification Multiproduct Strategy A firm that does *not* try to transfer resources and activities between its businesses or core competencies into its businesses is using an unrelated diversification multiproduct strategy. Commonly, firms using this strategy are called *conglomerates*. The unrelated diversification multiproduct strategy is frequently used in both developed markets (e.g., the United Kingdom and the United States) and emerging markets. In fact, firms using this strategy dominate the private sector in Latin American countries and in China, Korea, and India.[9] Conglomerates account for the largest percentage of private firms in India.[10] Similarly, the largest business firms in

economies of scope

cost savings the firm accrues when it successfully shares some of its resources and activities between its businesses or transfers corporate-level core competencies into its businesses

corporate-level core competencies

complex sets of resources and capabilities that link different businesses, primarily through managerial and technological knowledge, experience, and expertise

Brazil, Mexico, Argentina, and Colombia are family-owned, highly diversified enterprises.[11]

We now turn our attention to discussing the related and unrelated diversification multiproduct strategies in detail and the way firms use them to generate economies of scope by achieving either operational relatedness or corporate relatedness. **Operational relatedness** is achieved when the firm's businesses successfully share resources and activities to make and sell their products. **Corporate relatedness** is achieved when corporate-level core competencies are successfully transferred into some of the firm's businesses. Most commonly, these transfers involve core competencies that are based on intangible assets such as marketing knowledge, design skills, and brand name.

Looking at Figure 6.2, notice that firms using the related constrained multiproduct strategy create economies of scope *primarily* by achieving operational relatedness (see cell 1 in Figure 6.2), while firms using the related linked multiproduct strategy create economies of scope *primarily* by achieving corporate relatedness (see cell 2 in Figure 6.2). Even though the firm using the related constrained multiproduct strategy emphasizes the sharing of resources and activities between its businesses as a means of creating economies of scope, it also tries to create economies of scope by transferring corporate-level core competencies between its businesses when it can do so. Similarly, although the firm using the related linked multiproduct strategy emphasizes transferring corporate-level core competencies into its businesses as a means of creating economies of scope, it also tries to create economies of scope through the sharing of resources and activities between its businesses when it can do so.

operational relatedness

achieved when the firm's businesses successfully share resources and activities to make and sell their products

corporate relatedness

achieved when corporate-level core competencies are successfully transferred into some of the firm's businesses

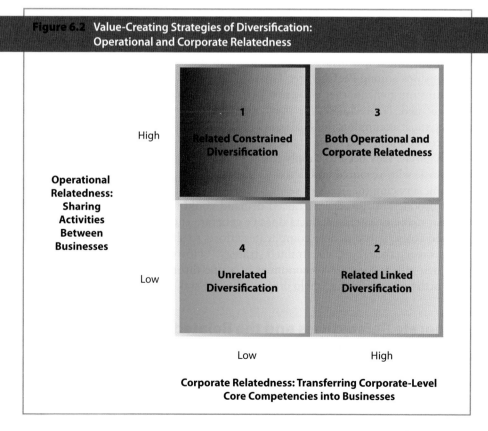

Figure 6.2 Value-Creating Strategies of Diversification: Operational and Corporate Relatedness

Operational Relatedness and the Related Constrained Multiproduct Strategy

Economies of scope are created through operational relatedness when the firm successfully shares primarily tangible resources (such as plant and equipment) and/or when a primary activity (such as inventory delivery systems) or a support activity (such as purchasing procedures) is successfully used in more than one of its businesses. We'll use Procter & Gamble (P&G) to describe how this operational relatedness is accomplished.

Currently, P&G has three global business units (GBUs)—Beauty & Grooming, Health and Well-Being, and Household Care—that share some resources and activities. Household Care is the largest of the three units, recently accounting for 48 percent of P&G's total sales revenues. Developing the overall strategy for brands' success is each GBU's primary responsibility. When developing these strategies, consider that in some form or fashion, paper is an important raw material input for products made by several of the GBUs. Accordingly, P&G operates a paper production facility that provides paper-based raw materials (in some form) to the GBUs; the paper-based raw material inputs (a tangible resource) that the GBUs need are similar enough that one facility can produce many if not most of those items. Because many of the GBUs' products are sold in some of the same outlets (grocery stores, for example), these products also share distribution channels (a primary activity) and networks of sales representatives.[12] The sharing of these resources (raw materials) and activities (distribution) enables P&G to generate economies of scope. Specifically, P&G reduces its overall costs by combining assets to produce similar raw materials in a single facility and then using similar channels to distribute the products produced with those materials. To show these relationships at P&G in Figure 6.1, we would use three circles (A–C) to represent P&G's GBUs. We would draw lines between the GBUs to demonstrate the links between them. Thus, the "hypothetical" relationships shown in Figure 6.1 to demonstrate a firm using the related constrained strategy actually depict the relationships among P&G's three GBUs.

Firms must ensure that efforts to share resources and activities are effectively implemented. For example, the people responsible for P&G's paper production facility must communicate successfully with personnel in the GBUs. Through these communications, those in the production facility learn about the quantity of raw materials they need to supply to each GBU.

A risk with resource and activity sharing is that the demand for the output of a unit servicing the needs of several of the firm's businesses may fall below the unit's production capacity. Reduced demand could lead to a situation in which the unit making shared products doesn't generate enough sales revenue to cover its fixed costs. This outcome complicates efforts to share resources and activities in firms using the related constrained strategy.[13] However, research evidence suggests that efforts to achieve economies of scope through operational relatedness are worthwhile in that they help create value for stakeholders.[14]

Corporate Relatedness and the Related Linked Multiproduct Strategy

Economies of scope are generated through corporate relatedness when the firm successfully transfers corporate-level core competencies into its different businesses. Let's see how GE uses corporate relatedness.

GE has five strategic business units, each with a number of divisions.[15] A **strategic business unit (SBU)** is a semi-autonomous unit of a diversified firm with a collection of related businesses. For example, Technology Infrastructure, one of GE's SBUs, has three divisions (aviation, healthcare, and transportation) while Energy has another three divisions (energy services, oil & gas, and power & water). Each division within each SBU has a set of identifiable product groups. Innovation is a corporate-level core competence that is transferred to each of GE's SBUs. In fact, GE allocated $5.2 billion to its research and development budget in 2009. The 2,370 U.S. patents the firm filed in 2009 indicate the

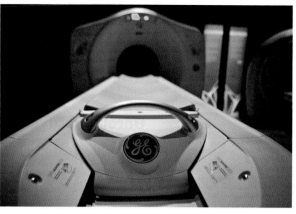

Insuring that innovation as a core competence permeates its entire organization is a top priority at GE. The company invests heavily in managerial and leadership training programs designed to transfer corporate-level competencies throughout its diverse businesses.

success the company achieves by transferring its innovation corporate-level core competence across its SBUs.

The knowledge individuals acquire by participating in managerial and leadership training programs is one way GE transfers corporate-level core competencies. In fact, one of the objectives of GE's executive education programs is for participating managers to develop knowledge that is imported into the firm's businesses. The importance of knowledge at GE is shown by the fact that the firm has provided learning and development opportunities to its employees for over 60 years and that it allocates approximately $1 billion annually to these activities.[16]

Simultaneously Seeking Operational Relatedness and Corporate Relatedness

As shown in cell 3 in Figure 6.2, firms can develop economies of scope by simultaneously seeking high levels of operational relatedness and corporate relatedness.[17] In this instance, the firm's multiproduct strategy is a hybrid with characteristics of both the related constrained and related linked multiproduct strategies.

Experience shows that achieving operational and corporate relatedness simultaneously is challenging.[18] Although sharing is difficult with tangible resources when primary and support activities are combined to achieve operational relatedness, transferring intangible resources that are the foundation for corporate-level core competencies is more challenging. Transferring intangible resources (such as knowledge about how to interpret market trends) between businesses to generate economies of scope by achieving corporate relatedness is more difficult because the potential outcome is less visible. (That is, it is difficult to know that an intangible resource is being transferred unless that resource is an individual manager.) So you can imagine how difficult it is for a firm to focus on *sharing* tangible resources and activities while simultaneously concentrating on *transferring* intangible core competencies.

Although it is challenging to attain operational relatedness and corporate relatedness simultaneously, evidence suggests that firms able to do so have developed a competitive advantage that is difficult for competitors to imitate.[19] The Walt Disney Company appears to be a firm that simultaneously achieves operational and corporate relatedness. Here's an example of how this works. Walt Disney Studios, one of Walt Disney Company's business units, can share resources and activities as it creates, produces, and promotes movies in its different studios

strategic business unit (SBU)

a semi-autonomous unit of a diversified firm with a collection of related businesses (such as Touchstone Pictures and Walt Disney Pictures). If Disney were to identify product promotion as one of its skills, it could share the activity with another part of Walt Disney Studios (e.g., Disney Theatrical Productions) to create operational relatedness and transfer the knowledge about how the skill was developed into other business units (e.g., Parks and Resorts)[20] to create corporate relatedness.

Unrelated Diversification Multiproduct Strategy

As indicated by cell 4 in Figure 6.2, firms using the unrelated diversification multiproduct strategy do not emphasize operational relatedness or corporate relatedness to create economies of scope. Instead, firms using the unrelated strategy emphasize financial economies to create economies of scope.

Financial economies are cost savings or higher returns generated when the firm effectively allocates its financial resources based on investments inside or outside the firm.[21] With respect to internal investments, the firm creates financial economies when it allocates its resources efficiently through the efforts of corporate headquarters personnel who represent a capital market for the entire organization. In terms of investments outside the firm, the company using the unrelated diversification multiproduct strategy creates financial economies when it is able to buy another firm, restructure that firm's assets in value-creating ways, and then (when and if appropriate) sell that company at a price exceeding its investment (price paid plus amount invested to increase the quality of the purchased company's assets). We consider each type of financial economy in greater detail in the next two sections.

Efficient Internal Capital Market Allocation

As you'll recall from your study of economics and finance in particular, capital markets are assumed to be efficient in allocating capital among competing investment opportunities. Efficiency results as investors take an equity position in firms by purchasing shares of stock in companies they believe have high future cash flow value. Efficient markets also allocate capital in the form of debt as shareholders and debt holders seek to improve the value of their investments by taking stakes in firms they believe have high growth and profitability prospects.

In companies using the unrelated strategy, corporate headquarters personnel allocate the firm's capital across its portfolio of divisions, each of which sells a variety of products. At United Technologies Corporation (UTC), for example, corporate headquarters personnel allocate capital across the firm's seven business units or divisions—Carrier, Otis, Pratt & Whitney, UTC Fire & Security, UTC Power Fuel Cells, Hamilton Sundstrand, and Sikorsky. (Pratt & Whitney accounted for the largest amount of UTC's sales revenue in 2009—24 percent.)[22] At UTC and other firms using the unrelated diversification strategy, capital is allocated on the basis of what headquarters personnel believe will generate the greatest amount of financial economies.

Internal capital market allocations in firms using the unrelated diversification strategy may be the basis for superior returns to shareholders compared to returns shareholders would receive as a result of allocations by the external capital market.[23] Access to information is the main reason for this possibility. Indeed, while managing the firm's portfolio of divisions, headquarters personnel may gain access to detailed information that isn't available to the external capital market

financial economies

cost savings or higher returns generated when the firm effectively allocates its financial resources based on investments inside or outside the firm about the ability of one or more of the firm's divisions to create value by growing its revenue and profitability streams.

Another potential benefit of internal capital market allocations is that those evaluating the performance of all of a firm's divisions can internally discipline poorly performing units by allocating fewer or different types of resources to them.[24] Disciplined divisional managers are likely to respond favorably by working hard to improve their units' performance as the first step to receiving a larger percentage of the entire firm's financial capital.

The external capital market relies on information produced by the firm to estimate the organization's ability to generate attractive future revenue and earnings streams. Annual reports, press conferences, and filings mandated by various regulatory bodies are the most common sources of information available to the external capital market. In these communication media, firms may overemphasize positive news while ignoring or deemphasizing negative news about one or more divisions. Firms may not want to divulge additional information when using these media because it might help competitors better understand and imitate the competitive advantages of product divisions within divisions. Therefore, in-depth knowledge about the positive and negative performance prospects for all of the firm's divisions creates a potential informational advantage for the firm relative to the external capital market.

Restructuring

A firm using the unrelated diversification multiproduct strategy can also produce financial economies by buying some or all of another company's assets. This process works two ways.[25] (These processes are called restructuring to denote that changes are made regarding the assets in question.) In one instance, a firm buys another's assets because it believes those assets would create more value if they were operated under its ownership. Prestige Brands Holdings uses this restructuring approach to create financial economies. Recognized as "a lifesaver in the business of resuscitating offloaded consumer product brands,"[26] Prestige buys branded products from other companies including P&G, Colgate-Palmolive, and Unilever. These products (such as Spic and Span, Right Guard deodorant, Chloraseptic, and Clear Eyes) are cast off because their former owner has lost faith in them or because they no longer fit with its portfolio of products. Prestige revitalizes them by devoting full attention to each product to enhance its market position, expand its distribution, and successfully launch product extensions.[27]

The second way restructuring can create financial economies is when a firm buys another company's assets with the intention of selling them as soon as it finds ways to make the assets more productive. Private equity firms such as the Carlyle Group, the world's largest firm of this type, use this multiproduct

While some brands may languish within firms where they no longer fit within its broader portfolio, with companies such as Prestige Brands Holdings they could see a rebirth. Through restructuring, Prestige purchases these types of brands and revitalizes them by devoting greater resources to their promotion, distribution, and expansion.

© Vicki Beaver

strategy. Some criticize private equity firms, seeing them as entities that focus on cutting costs without showing an appropriate amount of concern for those affected by the cost reductions.[28]

In general, it is easier to create financial economies by restructuring the assets of firms competing in relatively low-technology businesses because of the uncertain future demand for high-technology products. Moreover, firms seeking to create financial economies by buying and selling restructured assets must be able to restructure those assets at a cost below their expected future market value when they are sold to another company.

Managerial Motives to Diversify

In addition to the reasons for diversification that are shown in Table 6.1, top-level managers may have two additional motives to use a multiproduct diversification strategy. These motives may or may not be in the best interests of the firm's stakeholders.

Reducing the risk of losing their job is the first motive for top-level executives.[29] If a firm has multiple businesses and one business fails, total failure is unlikely if the other businesses are doing well. Therefore, additional diversification reduces the chance that top-level executives of a diversified firm will lose their jobs.

However, the managerial/leadership challenge increases greatly when a firm diversifies beyond the level of the single business multiproduct strategy. The risk here is that managers who believe that keeping their top-level positions depends on greater levels of product diversification may overdiversify the firm. Similar to business-level strategies, the multiproduct strategy used by the firm should be a function of opportunities in the firm's external environment. That strategy also should take into account the degree to which the firm has resources and activities that businesses can share or corporate-level core competencies that, when transferred from one business to another one in the firm's portfolio, can create value in product markets beyond its core product market. A firm's board of directors must ensure that the level of diversification top-level managers pursue is based on a match between opportunities in the external environment and the company's resources, activities, and corporate-level core competencies.

The relationship between firm size and executive compensation is the second managerial diversification motive. Research shows that as a firm's size increases, so does the compensation for top-level managers.[30] The strength of this relationship appears to be greater over the past few decades as compared to earlier times.[31] Of course, increasing a firm's level of diversification increases the firm's overall size.

The relationship between firm size and managerial compensation is perhaps not surprising in that larger, more diversified organizations are more difficult to manage than smaller, less diversified firms.[32] Common sense suggests that more complex and difficult work should be more highly compensated. Nonetheless, a board of directors should compensate managers in ways that will cause them to engage in value-creating diversification rather than compensate them simply on the basis of the firm's size.

In Chapter 5, we noted that organizational structure plays a major role in implementing a business-level strategy once it is chosen. Because of their importance, we next discuss the appropriate organizational structures for implementing the different multiproduct strategies.

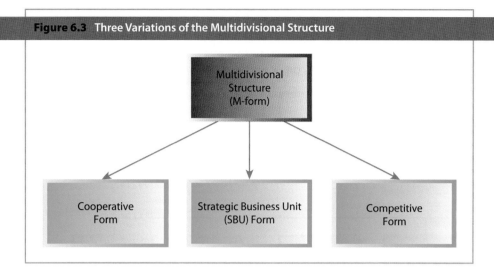

Figure 6.3   Three Variations of the Multidivisional Structure

Implementing Multiproduct Strategies

The **multidivisional (M-form) structure** is an organizational structure in which the firm is organized to generate economies of scope or financial economies. Thus, the M-form is the structure of choice for firms with moderate to high levels of product diversification. Firms using the single business and dominant business multiproduct strategies still rely on the different forms of the functional structure used to implement the business-level strategies we examined in Chapter 5. Each of the three versions of the M-form (see Figure 6.3) is used to support a different multiproduct strategy.

The Cooperative M-Form and the Related Constrained Multiproduct Strategy

The **cooperative M-form** is an organizational structure in which horizontal integration is used so that divisions can share resources and activities. Firms using the related constrained multiproduct strategy (such as P&G) adopt the cooperative M-form (see Figure 6.4). The divisions in a firm's M-form structure cooperate with one another to share resources and activities and generate economies of scope by achieving operational relatedness.[33] Earlier, we explained how P&G's three GBUs cooperate to share the outputs of the firm's paper production facility and distribution channels.

Success with the cooperative M-form is affected by how well divisions process information about the resources and activities they intend to share and how they intend to share them. *Horizontal linkages* are the mechanisms used to facilitate information sharing in these instances. Holding frequent meetings with division managers to discuss the goods or services they make and sell is an obvious horizontal linkage. In addition, managers can describe the resources that are available in their division and how those resources are used to form capabilities as the foundation for completing different activities in the value chain. Determining whether the different divisions' resources can be combined to create a new capability that can be shared among the divisions is a key objective of these discussions.

Temporary teams (sometimes called task forces) are a second horizontal integrating mechanism. Teams are typically formed for a project that requires sharing

multidivisional (M-form) structure

an organizational structure in which the firm is organized to generate economies of scope or financial economies

cooperative M-form

an organizational structure in which horizontal integration is used so that divisions can share resources and activities

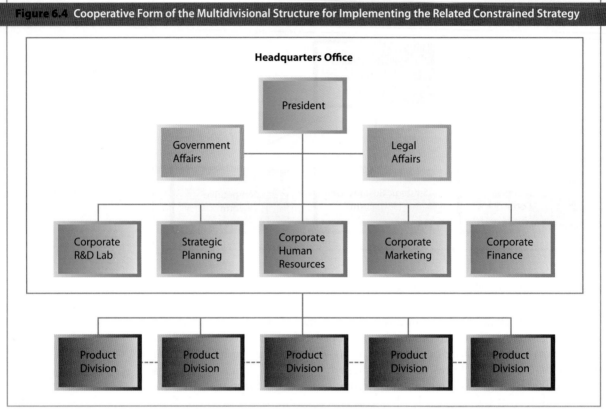

Figure 6.4 Cooperative Form of the Multidivisional Structure for Implementing the Related Constrained Strategy

Notes: • Structural integration devices create tight links among all divisions.
         • Corporate office emphasizes centralized strategic planning, human resources, and marketing to foster cooperation between divisions.
         • R&D is likely to be centralized.
         • Rewards are subjective and tend to emphasize overall corporate performance in additon to divisional performance.
         • Culture emphasizes cooperative sharing.

two or more businesses' resources and activities. Developing a new product and finding a way to create more value by completing one or more activities in the value chain are the objectives temporary teams seek.

An operational reality of the cooperative form of the multidivisional structure is that individual managers are held accountable for the performance of their division. For this reason, headquarters personnel should use compensation systems that reward sharing. When this is done, each manager's compensation might be based on a composite of his or her unit's performance as well as that of the other units, especially those that are cooperating on joint product development and management. This type of compensation signals that each manager's success is at least partly a function of the success of cooperation.

The SBU M-Form and the Related Linked Multiproduct Strategy

**strategic business unit
(SBU) M-form**

an organizational structure
in which corporate
headquarters personnel try
to transfer corporate-level
core competencies into the
firm's businesses

The **strategic business unit (SBU) M-form** is an organizational structure in which corporate headquarters personnel try to transfer corporate-level core competencies into the firm's businesses. Firms using the related linked multiproduct strategy (such as GE) adopt the SBU M-form (see Figure 6.5).

In the SBU M-form, each SBU is a profit center that corporate headquarters' evaluates and controls. Although both strategic controls and financial controls

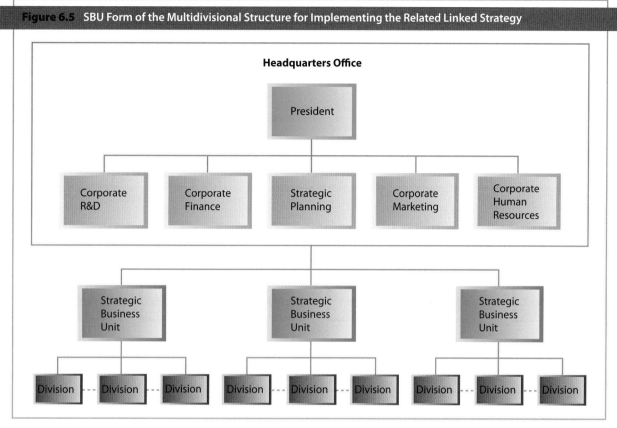

Figure 6.5 SBU Form of the Multidivisional Structure for Implementing the Related Linked Strategy

Notes: • Structural integration among divisions within SBUs, but independence across SBUs.
  • Strategic planning may be the most prominent function in headquarters for managing the strategic planning approval process of SBUs for the president.
  • Each SBU may have its own budget for staff to foster integration.
  • Corporate headquarters staff serve as consultants to SBUs and divisions, rather than having direct input to product strategy, as in the cooperative form.

are used (recall our discussion of these two types of controls in Chapter 2), financial controls are vital to headquarters' evaluation of each SBU. Strategic controls, on the other hand, are critical when those leading each SBU evaluate the performance of the divisions in their SBU. Strategic controls are also valuable to headquarters personnel as they try to determine whether the businesses the organization has chosen to enter (as shown by its collection of SBUs) are the right ones. As you can imagine, the SBU M-form can be a complex structure. Think of GE's size (five SBUs with multiple divisions in each SBU). It doesn't take much imagination to conclude that GE's organizational structure is immensely complicated.

The Competitive M-Form and the Unrelated Diversification Multiproduct Strategy

The **competitive M-form** is an organizational structure in which there is complete independence between the firm's divisions. Firms using the unrelated diversification multiproduct strategy adopt the competitive M-form structure (see Figure 6.6). Recall that with the unrelated diversification strategy, the firm seeks to generate financial economies rather than develop economies of scope through either operational relatedness or corporate relatedness.

competitive M-form

an organizational structure in which there is complete independence between the firm's divisions

Figure 6.6 Competitive Form of the Multidivisional Structure for Implementing the Unrelated Diversification Strategy

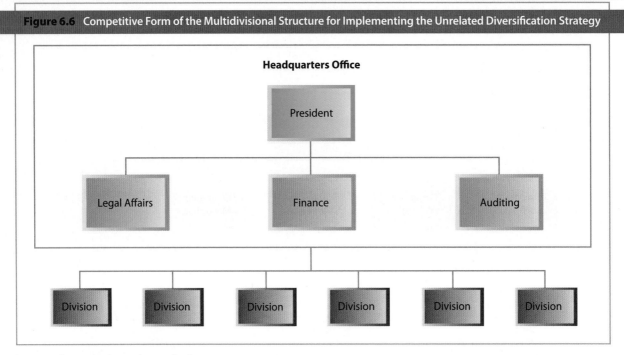

Notes: • Corporate headquarters has a small staff.
   • Finance and auditing are the most prominent functions in the headquarters office to manage cash flow and ensure the accuracy of performance data.
   • The legal affairs function becomes important when the firm acquires or divests assets.
   • Divisions are independent and separate for financial evaluation purposes.
   • Divisions retain strategic control, but cash is managed by the corporate office.
   • Divisions compete for corporate resources.

Divisions operating in a competitive M-form structure actually compete against one another for the firm's resources. Indeed, an efficient internal capital market allocates resources to the divisions with the greatest probability of generating excess returns on the firm's financial capital. Because of this focus, corporate headquarters personnel make no effort to find ways for resources and activities to be shared between divisions or for corporate headquarters personnel to transfer corporate-level core competencies into different divisions. Instead, the focus of the headquarters office is on specifying criteria that will be used to evaluate the performance of all divisions. For example, at Textron, a large conglomerate and the focus of this chapter's Mini-Case, return on invested capital is the primary performance criterion used by corporate headquarters personnel.[34]

With the competitive M-form, headquarters personnel rely on strategic controls to establish financial performance criteria; financial controls are then used to monitor divisional performance relative to those criteria. So the focus of headquarters is on performance appraisal, resource allocations, and long-range planning to ensure that the firm's financial capital is being used to maximize financial success.[35]

Regardless of the multiproduct strategy chosen and the multidivisional structure selected to support use of that strategy, performance declines suggest the need for change. This may be the case for Sears Holdings. Formed in 2005 and following Kmart's announcement that it intended to acquire Sears Roebuck & Company, Sears Holdings' financial performance has yet to reach expectations. As explained in *Understanding Strategy: Learning from Failure,* a decision was made to change the firm's organizational structure in order to improve its performance.

The Marriage of Kmart and Sears: What Lessons Can We Learn?

The (second quarter, 2010) results fell short of analysts' expectations as comparable-store sales at Sears U.S. Stores and the company's Kmart unit both fell, with the latter declining for the first time in three quarters.

(Karen Talley, The Wall Street Journal *reporter*)

Both Sears Roebuck and Kmart experienced declining performance during the 1990s and into the early years of the twenty-first century. Both firms were competing as full-line department stores as customers' sensitivity to price became a primary decision criterion when purchasing goods and services. Neither company possessed the capabilities needed to effectively compete against the likes of Walmart, Sam's, and Costco when dealing with price-sensitive customers.

Seeing underlying value in their brands, though, Edward S. Lampert's ESL Investments (a hedge fund) acquired Kmart in 2003 and Sears in 2005. Lampert then combined the two firms into Sears Holdings, a company in which ESL Investments has a 49.6 percent ownership stake. When formed, Sears Holdings was grouped into three business segments (or divisions) that operated independently:

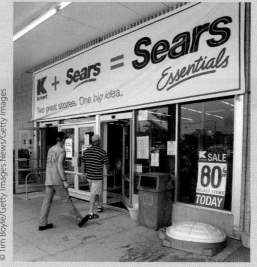

© Tim Boyle/Getty Images News/Getty Images

Did the application of the competitive form of the multidivisional structure to a collection of closely related businesses hinder the growth of Sears Holdings? Despite changes designed to correct the misalignment of strategy and structure, the firm continues to under perform.

Kmart, Sears Domestic, and Sears Canada. Thus, the competitive form of the multidivisional structure (see Figure 6.6) was in place and was intended to support Lampert's strategy of maintaining respectable sales growth while limiting capital expenditures in order to "generate prodigious cash flow."

It seems then that initially, Lampert (who today is the Chairman of the Board for Sears Holding but is no longer the CEO) sought to create financial economies by using a form of the multidivisional structure that is designed to facilitate implementation of the unrelated diversification strategy. Evidence suggests though that the decisions made initially with Sears Holdings as a means of creating financial economies were perhaps not as effective as they might have been. More

specifically, it may be that strategy and structure were not matched in this instance. (Remember that in Chapter 5, we noted that a firm's performance will decline when strategy and structure are not matched.) Let's consider this possibility further.

Combining Kmart and Sears resulted in a large firm that was essentially offering similar goods and services. In fact, some observers said that the structurally independent units were all trying to sell the same or similar major appliances (refrigerators, dishwashers, and so forth), home improvement/home repair services, auto repair services, and groceries, often to the same customer groups. The issue here is that the competitive form of the multidivisional structure is used to support the unrelated strategy—one in which the firm is highly diversified in terms of products it offers and customers it serves. It is difficult to generate financial economies by asking units offering essentially the same products to the same or similar customers to compete against one another for capital allocations.

In mid-2008, changes were made to Sears Holdings' organizational structure. Specifically, the firm was divided into five SBUs (with multiple divisions as part of each SBU): brands, real estate, support, online, and store operations. Commenting about this structural change, Lampert said that it was time "to empower individual businesses and teams to focus on the customer experience and performance. Stronger business units will be better able to support each other, build a stronger company, and be more attractive to partners and talent." Thus, Sears Holdings changed to the SBU form of the multidivisional structure—a structure that is designed to support use of the related linked diversification multiproduct strategy. Given that some indirect but relatively few direct relationships across the firm's newly formed business units were likely, it seems this change created a match between the firm's strategy and its organizational structure. Because of this match, the expecta- tion was that the firm's performance would improve as a result of the structural change made a few years ago.

To date, the performance improvements expected by developing an appropriate match between strategy and structure have not materialized. In late 2010, some analysts (who at this time issued a "sell" recommendation of Sears Holdings' stock) suggested that a key reason for this is that at least in their opinion, the Sears and Kmart brands lost their luster long ago, seriously undermining efforts to increase the firm's success. Nonetheless, the firm continues undertaking

actions that it hopes will result in improved performance. Converting some Kmart stores to a new midsize format called Sears Essentials and adding some Sears' branded products to Kmart locations are examples of these actions.

Sources: 2010, Chairman's letter, *Sears Holdings Investor Information*, Sears Holdings Home page, www.searsholdings.com, February 23; 2010, Sears Holding Corp, *Standard & Poor's Stock Reports*, www.standardandpoors.com, October 30; J. Hargett, 2010, A closer look at Dillard's Inc., Sears Holding Corp, and Nordstrom Inc., *Schaeffers Research*, www.schaeffersresearch.com, April 22; P. Eavis, 2008, The pain at Sears grows, *The Wall Street Journal Online*, www.wsj.com, May 30; 2008, Report: Sears Holdings to break into separate units, *Dallas Morning News Online*, www.dallasnews.com, January 19.

SUMMARY

The primary purpose of this chapter is to discuss the differ- ent multiproduct strategies that firms can use to enter new product markets. We examined the following topics:

- We noted that a **multiproduct strategy** is an action plan that the firm uses to compete in different prod- uct markets. When using multiproduct strategies, firms become more diversified in terms of the number and types of products they make and sell to customers.
- Five multiproduct strategies range from low levels of diversification (the single business and dominant business strategies) to moderate to high levels of di- versification (the related constrained, related linked, and unrelated diversification strategies). As a firm becomes more diversified, the number of products it offers and the number of product markets in which it competes increase.
- A firm using the single business multiproduct strategy makes and sells a single product or a variety of a single product line and generates at least 95 percent of its sales revenue from its dominant business or product line. As firms continue to develop the ways in which their resources and activities can be used to create additional products or to compete in different prod- uct markets, they may begin to pursue the dominant business strategy—a multiproduct strategy through

which the firm generates between 70 and 95 percent of its sales revenue from a single business.

- Firms using a related diversification multiproduct strategy try to create **economies of scope**, which are cost savings that result from the successful sharing of some resources and activities between the firm's businesses or from the transfer of corporate-level core competencies into its different businesses. In each of the two types of related diversification multiproduct strategies, the firm earns less than 70 percent of sales revenue from its dominant business.
- With the related constrained strategy, most or all of the firm's businesses share some resources (usually tangible resources) and activities (that are a part of the value chain) to generate economies of scope. Firms sharing resources and activities between their busi- nesses achieve **operational relatedness.**
- With the related linked strategy, few relationships exist between the firm's businesses. The focus with this strategy is on transferring corporate-level core competencies into the firm's different businesses to generate economies of scope. **Corporate-level core competencies** are complex sets of resources and capabilities that link different businesses, pri- marily through managerial and technological knowl- edge, experience, and expertise. Firms generating

economies of scope by transferring corporate-level core competencies achieve **corporate relatedness.**

- In the unrelated diversification multiproduct strategy, resources, activities, and corporate-level core competencies are not shared between the firm's divisions. Commonly, firms using this strategy are called conglomerates. With this strategy, the firm tries to create financial economies instead of economies of scope. **Financial economies** are cost savings or higher returns generated when the firm effectively allocates its financial resources based on investments inside or outside the firm. The firm's divisions compete against one another to gain access to a larger share of the entire organization's financial capital. Firms generate financial economies when they successfully allocate their own financial capital across their divisions or when they buy other companies, restructure those firms' assets, and then sell the acquisitions in the marketplace at a profit.

- Managers often have personal motives for increasing the level of their firm's diversification. For example, increasing the number of product markets in which the firm competes reduces managers' risk of losing their jobs (and balances firm performance across markets). Additionally, executive compensation is often related to firm size. Thus, growing the size of the firm through diversification may increase executives' pay. Engaging in a multiproduct strategy for these reasons may or may not create value for the firm's shareholders.

- It is important to match each multiproduct strategy with the proper organizational structure. Firms using the single business and dominant business strategies continue to use one of the functional structures we discussed in Chapter 5. However, the related and unrelated diversification strategies are effectively used only when supported by a version of the **multidivisional structure** (in which the firm is organized to generate economies of scope or financial economies). The **cooperative M-form** supports the related constrained strategy, the **SBU M-form** supports the related linked strategy, and the **competitive M-form** supports the unrelated strategy.

KEY TERMS

DISCUSSION QUESTIONS

1. What is a multiproduct strategy? Why do some firms use this strategy?
2. What are the different levels of diversification (from low to high) that firms experience when using a multiproduct strategy?
3. What is the related diversification multiproduct strategy? How can the firm create value by using this strategy?
4. What is the unrelated diversification multiproduct strategy? What are the ways that a firm can create value by using this strategy?
5. What are the two additional motives that top-level managers have to diversify their firms?
6. What organizational structure is used to implement each of the different multiproduct strategies?

STRATEGY TOOLBOX

Competitive analysis is a critical part of the strategic management process that firms use when selecting a multiproduct strategy. A competitive analysis includes identifying, profiling, and comparing the firm with all of its competitors'. All too often, those involved with a firm's strategic management process focus only on the *immediate* competitors, as these competitors tend to be well known throughout the firm and typically are already being studied. This chapter's tool takes competitor analysis two steps further by considering the firm's *impending*, and *invisible*, competitors. Analyzing the three types of competitors (immediate, impending, and invisible) facilitates a firm's efforts to carefully examine all types of competitors (current and potential) when selecting a multiproduct strategy.

© Jan Paul Schrage, iStock

3 I's Competitive Radar Screen

Invisible	• Large organizations considering an unanticipated move from other (unrelated) industrial segments into your market—in secret
	• Low knowledge base about these potential competitors
Impending	• Small organizations making a move for the purpose of growing and capturing market share
	• Major organizations from other (related) industrial segments announcing entry into your market
	• Medium knowledge base about these potential competitors
Immediate	• Existing major organizations in your particular industrial segment(s)
	• Public admission of competitive position and market share
	• High knowledge base about these current competitors

MINI-CASE

Textron: Achieving Success Using the Unrelated Diversification Multiproduct Strategy

In the coming year (2010), I look forward to executing a strategy that leverages the reputation of our brands; leads to long-term growth for our shareholders; creates career opportunities for our employees; and ensures a valued partner for our customers.

(Scott C. Donnelly, President and CEO, Textron)

Stakeholders likely are pleased by the nature of the outcomes Textron's President and CEO believes the firm will achieve in 2010. This firm's vision and the multiproduct strategy it uses to reach that vision are intriguing and are central to the firm's efforts to be successful.

Recall from Chapter 1 that a *vision* presents a picture of the firm as it hopes to exist in the future, while a *strategy* is an action plan designed to move a firm toward achieving its vision. "Textron's vision is to become *the* [italics in the

© Ailja, iStock

original document] premier multi-industry company, recognized for our network of powerful brands, world-class enterprise processes, and talented people." A diversified conglomerate, Textron uses the unrelated diversification multiproduct strategy as its action plan for becoming the premier multi-industry company.

Choosing to use the unrelated diversification multiproduct strategy means that Textron seeks to generate financial economies rather than operational relatedness or corporate relatedness to create value for customers and wealth (in the form of strong financial returns) for shareholders. Thus, Textron allocates its financial capital to pursue investment opportunities available inside the units it currently owns or to acquire assets from other companies that it can effectively restructure. As noted earlier in the chapter, Textron uses return on invested capital "as both a compass to guide every investment decision and a measure of Textron's success."

Currently, Textron has five operating segments—Bell Helicopter, Cessna, Textron Systems, Industrial, and Finance. During 2009, Cessna accounted for the largest percentage of the firm's sales revenue (32 percent) while Finance accounted for the smallest percentage (3 percent). In terms of organizational structure, Textron uses the competitive form of the multidivisional structure. Looking at Figure 6.6, visualize Textron's five operating segments with different product units being associated with each of them. (Textron uses the term "operating segments" rather than "divisions," the term we show in Figure 6.6. However, the terms are identical in what they represent.) For example, Textron Systems includes five product units: AAI, Textron Marine & Land Systems, Textron Defense Systems, Lycoming Engines, and Overwatch.

At the beginning of this chapter, we noted that companies using multiproduct strategies deal with two core issues: What goods or services will the company produce and sell? How will the firm manage the units it creates to produce and sell its goods and services? According to company documents, Textron's corporate-level personnel spend a great deal of their time dealing with the first of those two questions as they go about "identifying, selecting, acquiring, and integrating the right mix of businesses that will drive higher performance." With respect to the second issue, we have noted that Textron uses the competitive form of the multidivisional structure to manage its five operating segments or divisions.

Conditions in the global economy were challenging for Textron during 2009 and 2010. For example, sales at Cessna were declining, resulting in a decision to cut the workforce by 8.3 percent. Cessna was also dealing with aggressive competitive actions from competitors such as Bombardier's Learjet and Brazilian manufacturer Embraer. Offsetting Cessna's revenue decline however were increasing revenues from Bell Helicopter and Textron Systems. The relationship in revenues between these two segments highlights an outcome associated with using the unrelated diversification multiproduct strategy; namely, increasing revenues in one unit offset declining revenues on another unit.

Sources: 2010, Textron businesses, Textron Home page, www.textron.com, November 1; M. Jarzemsky, 2010, Textron to cut 700 more jobs at Cessna, *The Wall Street Journal Online*, www.wsj.com, September 21; M. Jarzemsky, 2010, United Technologies profit rises, *The Wall Street Journal Online*, www.wsj.com, October 20; P. Sanders, 2010, NetJets to order 50 Embraer jets, *The Wall Street Journal Online*, www.wsj.com, October 18; 2009, Textron annual report, Textron Home page, www.textron.com, September; 2009, Textron fact book, Textron Home page, www.textron.com, December.

Questions

1. Go to Textron's Web site (www.textron.com) to see whether the firm still operates with five operating segments or divisions. While at the Web site, determine whether Textron Systems has the same product units mentioned in the Mini-Case. If you find differences, what do you think influenced the decisions to make the changes you identified?

2. Use the Internet to find sources describing Textron's financial performance during the most recent quarter of the most recent year. Did sales revenue and earnings increase during the time period you examined relative to the same period the prior year? What do you think influenced the financial results you found?

3. What performance-related risks does Textron face while using the unrelated diversification multiproduct strategy? In your view, is the firm effectively managing those risks? Why or why not?

EXPERIENTIAL EXERCISES

Exercise One: Multiproduct Strategies at Novartis and in the Pharmaceutical Industry

Novartis AG, the Swiss pharmaceutical company, initially bought a 77 percent share in the eye care company Alcon from Nestlé SA for about $39 billion. In late 2010, Novartis acquired the remainder of Alcon, saying that the purchase was "the logical conclusion of our initial strategic investment…" The Alcon acquisition increases Novartis's presence in eye care by adding Alcon's glaucoma drugs and cataract surgery products. Novartis already had a presence in eye care through its Ciba Vision contact lens brand. Novartis is the world's fourth-largest drugmaker (2009 total sales of $44.3 billion) with products such as Diovan for blood pressure, Gleevec for certain kinds of cancer, and Trileptal for epilepsy. Novartis had previously diversified into other areas of the pharmaceutical industry. For example, in 2005, it acquired two generic drugmakers, and in 2006, it acquired Chiron, a company in the vaccine business. Despite these diversifications, prescription drugs still accounted for the majority of the firm's sales revenue in 2009.

Questions

1. What kind of multiproduct strategy (related constrained, related linked, or unrelated) is Novartis following? Explain your choice.
2. Search the Internet and other sources of information available to you to ascertain why Novartis chose to diversify into the eye care business. Relate the reasons to those given in Table 6.1.
3. How does the pattern of product diversification by Novartis compare to the patterns of diversification of other major firms in the pharmaceutical industry? Choose at least one major firm (e.g., Pfizer, GlaxoSmithKline, Sanofi-Aventis, or Roche Holdings) and investigate their recent patterns of diversification as the foundation for making a comparison with Novartis's actions. Classify the kinds of diversification according to whether they are related constrained, related linked, or unrelated. Look at sources such as *The Wall Street Journal*, *Bloomberg Businessweek*, *Fortune*, and *Forbes* to find the information needed to answer these questions.

Sources: 2010, Novartis to become global leader in eye care, with agreement of 100% merger with Alcon, Welcome to Novartis, http://www.novartis.com, December 15; R. Langreth, 2008, Why Novartis bought Alcon stake, Forbes.com, www.forbes.com, April 7; J. Whalen, 2008, Novartis picks up eye-care unit, *The Wall Street Journal Online*, www.wsj.com, April 8.

Exercise Two: Value-Creating Strategies at the Tata Group

The chapter notes that firms using the unrelated diversification multiproduct strategy dominate the private sector in Latin American countries as well as in China and Korea. Conglomerates also account for the greatest percentage of private firms in India. One such firm is the Tata Group, which was identified as the country's most valuable business group in 2010. Employing over 395,000 people worldwide, Tata operates in seven business sectors: communications and information technology, engineering, materials, services, energy, consumer products, and chemicals. At the close of 2010, the firm's market capitalization was approximately $100 billion. Tata generated over $67 billion in sales in 2009 with 57 percent of that total accruing from business operations outside of India.

The class should form into groups. Each group should take one of Tata's seven business sectors and provide a list of the companies in that sector and the date they were created or acquired (where possible). Then discuss how Tata creates value within this sector and across all sectors of the company. Each group should also discuss how Tata Motors (a subsidiary of the Tata Group) is likely to create value for the Land Rover and Jaguar divisions, which it acquired in March 2008 from Ford Motor Company. Refer to the chapter discussion of how diversified firms create value. Use the Internet, business publications sources such as *The Wall Street Journal*, *Forbes*, and *Bloomberg Businessweek* and the firm's Web site (www.tata.com) to obtain the information needed to complete these tasks.

Sources: 2010, Tata becomes India's most valued business group, *India Tribune*, www.indiatribune.com, December 18; 2010, Record gift to HBS from India's Tata Group, *Alumni Bulletin*, www.alumni.hbs.edu, December.

ENDNOTES

1. M. Goranova, R. Dharwadkar, & P. Brandes, 2010, Owners on both sides of the deal: Mergers and acquisitions and overlapping institutional ownership, *Strategic Management Journal*, 31: 1114–1135; M. F. Wiersema & H. P. Bowen, 2008, Corporate diversification: The impact of foreign competition, industry globalization, and product diversification, *Strategic Management Journal*, 29: 115–132.

2. R. E. Hoskisson, M. A. Hitt, R. D. Ireland, & J. S. Harrison, 2008, *Competing for Advantage*, 2nd ed., Mason, OH: Thomson South-Western; M. E. Porter, 1987, From competitive advantage to corporate strategy, *Harvard Business Review*, 65(3): 43–59.

3. 2009, HP annual report, 3–4.

4. R. Rumelt, 1974, *Strategy, Structure, and Economic Performance*, Boston: Harvard Business School.

5. 2010, United Parcel Service, Inc., *Standard and Poor's Stock Report*, www.standardandpoors.com, November 1.

6. P. David, J. P. O'Brien, T. Yoshikawa, & A. Delios, 2010, Do shareholders or stakeholders appropriate the rents from corporate diversification? The influence of ownership structure, *Academy of Management Journal*, 53: 636–654; M. A. Hitt, L. Tihanyi, T. Miller, & B. Connelly, 2006, International diversification: Antecedents, outcomes, and moderators, *Journal of Management*, 32: 831–867.

7. H. Bresman, J. Birkinshaw, & R. Nobel, 2010, Knowledge transfer in international acquisitions, *Journal of International Business Studies*, 41: 5–20; Rumelt, *Strategy, Structure, and Economic Performance*.

8. D. J. Teece, 2010, Business models, business strategy and innovation, *Long Range Planning*, 43: 172–194; S. Dutta, M. J. Zbaracki, & M. Bergen, 2003, Pricing process as a capability: A resource-based perspective, *Strategic Management Journal*, 24: 615–630.

9. S. Belenzon & T. Berkovitz, 2010, Innovation in business groups, *Management Science*, 56: 519–535; O. Beisheim & F. Guenther, 2008, Performance effects of firms' expansion paths within and across industries and nations, *Strategic Organization*, 6: 47–81.

10. R. Culpan & R. Chinta, 2010, Comparative analysis of entrepreneurial growth strategies of two multinational conglomerates in emerging markets, *International Journal of Business and Globalisation*, 5: 46–62; 2008, Chinese and Russian retailers break into world's top 250, according to Deloitte study, *Deloitte*, www.deloitte.com, January 19.

11. J. Cespedes, M. Gonzales, & C. A. Molina, 2010, Ownership and capital structure in Latin America, *Journal of Business Research*, 63: 248–254; J. Santiso, 2007, The emergence of Latin multinationals, *Deutsche Bank Research*, www.dbresearch.com, March 27.

12. 2010, P&G overview, Procter & Gamble Home page, www.procterandgamble.com, November 11.

13. M. A. Hitt, J. S. Harrison, & R. D. Ireland, 2001, *Mergers and Acquisitions: A Guide to Creating Value for Stakeholders*, New York: Oxford University Press.

14. V. Swaminathan, F. Murshed, & J. Hulland, 2008, Value creation following merger and acquisition announcements: The role of strategic emphasis alignment, *Journal of Marketing Research*, 45: 33–47; H. Tanriverdi & N. Venkatraman, 2005, Knowledge relatedness and the performance of multibusiness firms, *Strategic Management Journal*, 26: 97–119.

15. 2010, Fact sheet, GE Home page, www.ge.com, November 9; 2010, General Electric Co, *Standard and Poor's Stock Report*, www.standardandpoors.com, November 13.

16. 2010, How GE builds global leaders: A conversation with Chief Learning Officer Susan Peters, *Knowledge@Wharton*, www.knowledge.wharton.upenn.edu, November 2.

17. A. Kachra & R. E. White, 2008, Know-how transfer: The role of social, economic/competitive, and firm boundary factors, *Strategic Management Journal*, 29: 425–445; K. M. Eisenhardt & D. C. Galunic, 2000, Coevolving: At last, a way to make synergies work, *Harvard Business Review*, 78(1): 91–111.

18. A. Pehrsson, 2010, Business-relatedness and strategy moderations: Impacts on foreign subsidiary performance, *Journal of Strategy and Management*, 3: 110–133.

19. M. R. Haas & M. T. Hansen, 2007, Different knowledge, different benefits: Toward a productivity perspective on knowledge sharing in organizations, *Strategic Management Journal*, 28: 1133–1153; Eisenhardt & Galunic, Coevolving, 94.

20. E. Smith, 2010, Disney CEO turns slump into a springboard, *The Wall Street Journal Online*, www.wsj.com, November 8; 2010, The Walt Disney Company overview, Walt Disney Home page, www.waltdisney.com, November 2.

21. L. Capron & J.-C. Shen, 2007, Acquisitions of private vs. public firms: Private information, target selection, and acquirer returns. *Strategic Management Journal*, 28: 891–911; D. D. Bergh, 1997, Predicting divestiture of unrelated acquisitions: An integrative model of ex ante conditions, *Strategic Management Journal*, 18: 715–731.

22. 2010, United Technologies Corporation, *Standard and Poor's Stock Report*, www.standardandpoors.com, November 13.

23. M. A. Hitt, R. D. Ireland, & R. E. Hoskisson, 2011, *Strategic Management: Competitiveness and Globalization*, 9th edition, Cengage Learning; O. E. Williamson, 1975, *Markets and Hierarchies: Analysis and Antitrust Implications*, New York: Macmillan.

24. D. Bardolet, D. Lovallo, & R. Rumelt, 2010, The hand of corporate management in capital allocations; Patterns of investment in multi- and single-business firms, *Industrial and Corporate Change*, 19: 591–612; R. de Hass, 2010, Internal capital markets and lending by multinational bank subsidiaries, *Journal of Financial Intermediation*, 19: 1–25.

25. T. P. Moliterno & M. F. Wiersema, 2007, Firm performance, rent appropriation, and the strategic resource divestment capability, *Strategic Management Journal*, 28: 1065–1087; R. E. Hoskisson, R. A. Johnson, D. Yiu, & W. P. Wan, 2001, Restructuring strategies and diversified business groups: Differences associated with country institutional environments, in M. A. Hitt, R. E. Freeman, & J. S. Harrison (eds.), *Handbook of Strategic Management*, Oxford, U.K.: Blackwell, 433–463.

26. 2008, Prestige Brands Holdings, Inc., *Yahoo! Finance*, www.yahoo.com, June 1.

27. 2010, About us, Prestige Brands, Inc. Home page, www.prestigebrands.com, November 11.

28. L. A. Harris, 2010, A critical theory of private equity, *Delaware Journal of Corporate Law*, 35: 259–293; G. Morgenson, 2008, Questions of rent tactics by private equity, *The New York Times Online*, www.nytimes.com, May 9.

29. D. Miller, I. L. Breton-Miller, & R. H. Lester, 2010, Family ownership and acquisition behavior in publicly-traded companies, *Strategic Management Journal*, 31: 201–223; M. Larraza-Kintana, R. M. Wiseman, L. R. Gomez-Mejia, & T. M. Welbourne, 2007, Disentangling compensation and employment risks using the behavioral agency model, *Strategic Management Journal*, 28: 1001–1019.

30. P. M. Guest, 2008, The impact of mergers and acquisitions on executive pay in the United Kingdom, *Economica*, in press; J. J. Cordeiro & R. Veliyath, 2003, Beyond pay for performance: A panel study of the determinants of CEO compensation, *American Business Review*, 21(1): 56–66.

31. C. Frydman & R. E. Saks, 2010, Executive compensation: A new view from a long-term perspective, 1936–2005, *Review of Financial Studies*, 23: 2099–2138.

32. C. Lechner & M. Kreutzer, 2010, Coordinating growth initiatives in multi-unit firms, *Long Range Planning*, 43: 6–32; D. A. Garvin & L. C. Levesque, 2008, The multiunit enterprise, *Harvard Business Review*, 86(6): 106–117.

33. H. Gospel & M. Sako, 2010, The unbundling of corporate functions: The evolution of shared services and outsourcing in human resource management, *Industrial and Corporate Change*, 19: 1367–1396; C. C. Markides & P. J. Williamson, 1996, Corporate diversification and organizational structure: A resource-based view, *Academy of Management Journal*, 39: 340–367.

34. 2008, Textron profile, Textron, www.textron.com, June 1.

35. D. J. Teece, 2010, Alfred Chandler and "capabilities" theories of strategy and management, *Industrial and Corporate Change*, 19: 297–316; T. R. Eisenmann & J. L. Bower, 2000, The entrepreneurial M-form: Strategic integration in global media firms, *Organization Science*, 11: 348–355.

CHAPTER 7
Acquiring and Integrating Businesses

KNOWLEDGE OBJECTIVES

Reading and studying this chapter should enable you to:

1. Define acquisitions, takeovers, mergers, and acquisition strategy.

2. Discuss the five basic reasons that firms complete acquisitions.

3. Describe target screening, target selection, target negotiating, and due diligence.

4. Explain the importance and process of successful post-acquisition business integration.

5. Discuss the four major pitfalls of acquisitions and remedies for their prevention.

6. Describe the major restructuring strategies for failed acquisitions.

© Shannon Fagan, Getty Images

Big Pharma: More Acquisitions, Less Innovation

During the first decade of the 21st century, there were 1,345 mergers and acquisitions in the pharmaceutical industry. These deals were reportedly worth approximately $694 billion. Each of the 55 largest deals was valued at more than $1.5 billion. And, many of the largest acquirers completed multiple acquisitions (i.e., more than five) during this ten-year span. Consolidation and size (economies of scale) have driven many of the consolidations in other industries. Some of the same motivation existed in the pharmaceutical industry. For example, some firms announced their rationale for acquisitions included increases in market share and enhanced management efficiency. However, the primary reasons announced for a majority of the acquisitions in this industry were (1) to gain access to a blockbuster drug, (2) gain entry into a high growth therapeutic market segment, (3) to increase the productivity of the firm's R&D, and (4) to gain access to a new technology platform.

The large pharmaceutical companies have been turning to acquisitions as a way to achieve growth and gain access to innovative drugs because their sales and stock prices were not growing. And, the lack of growth has been due largely to weak innovation despite having invested significant financial resources in R&D. For example, in 2007 only 19 new drugs were approved by the Food and Drug Administration (FDA) for distribution to the public. And, only eight new drugs were brought to the market in 2008. This is especially sad as the pharmaceutical firms spent $65.2 billion on R&D during 2008. Therefore, large pharmaceutical firms were searching for targets with a pipeline of promising drugs to replenish their dwindling supply of new drugs. Faced with the prospect of current drugs' patents expiring and the reductions in sales revenue as a result, pharmaceutical firms use acquisitions as a short-term solution to their innovation problem.

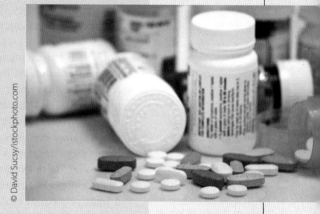

© David Sucsy/istockphoto.com

Large pharmaceutical firms have significant financial resources, are commonly effective at performing clinical trials and have good marketing and distribution systems. Their major weakness is not being creative and producing innovation. However, buying firms with promising drugs only helps in the short term. After acquiring them, they are integrated into the acquirer's bureaucratic R&D system and thus produce few new drugs. Andrew Witty, CEO of GlaxoSmithKline, refers to industrialization and bureaucratization of R&D. Creativity is lost to bureaucracy.

Some large pharmaceutical firms are working hard to change the way they conduct R&D. They decentralize the decisions in R&D and allow considerable discretion to the scientists working in small teams. Large pharmaceuticals are also attempting to partner with each other in joint ventures to create new innovative drugs. Partnering has several advantages in addition to producing more innovative drugs. It can also reduce costs, speed time to market, spread the risk and increase the market potential of new drugs.

Sources: P. Henske & T. van Biesen, 2010, Mega mergers can't cure the pharmaceutical industry, *BusinessWeek*, www.businessweek.com, July 26; K. Maggon, 2010, M&A review: Pharmaceutical & biotechnology industry, knol.google.com, July 11; M. Kimes, 2010, Sanofi's change agent, www.money.cnn.com, June 15; 2010, Ten-year data on pharmaceutical mergers and acquisitions, from dealsearchonline.com, reveals top deals and key companies, Irving Levin Associates Inc., www.pharmiweb.com, March 26; A. Abkowitz, 2009, Big pharma's new landscape, *Fortune*, www. money.cnn.com, March 12; C. Amst, 2009, The drug mergers' harsh side effects, *BusinessWeek*, www.businessweek.com, March 12; A. Weintraub, 2008, Cash-rich drugmakers eye mergers or acquisitions, *BusinessWeek*, www.businessweek.com, October 30.

Mergers and acquisitions (M&As) continue to be a popular strategy. For example, in 2007, global M&A activity reached a record $4.4 trillion. And, in this same year the value of M&As in Europe outstripped the value in the United States.[1] Furthermore, cross-border M&As have been increasing in recent years. In fact, research suggests that cross-border M&A activity completed by emerging market firms often creates more value than those undertaken by developed market firms.[2]

An **acquisition** is a transaction in which a firm buys a controlling interest in another firm with the intention of either making it a subsidiary business or combining it with its current business or businesses. It is important to understand that for some firms, an acquisition is a "one-time only" event. For example, a firm using a differentiation business-level strategy might decide to acquire only one other company because it has truly specialized skills that the focal firm requires to create unique value for its customers. It is rare, though, for a firm to complete only a single acquisition. Most firms involved with acquisitions develop an acquisition strategy. An **acquisition strategy** is an action plan that the firm develops to successfully acquire other companies. An effective acquisition strategy enables significant firm growth.[3] Firms pursue acquisitions for a number of other reasons. Many of the large pharmaceutical firms described in the *Focusing on Strategy* are using an acquisition strategy to increase their efficiencies, reduce costs, and especially to enhance their productivity of innovation.

A **takeover** is a specialized type of acquisition in which the target firm does not solicit the acquiring firm's offer. For instance, in 2007, US Airways made an unsolicited offer to buy (take over) Delta. The CEO of Delta reacted negatively to US Airways' bid. He proclaimed to senators and others that the proposed takeover would threaten the nation's transportation industry and lead to higher ticket prices and fewer flights from which customers could choose.[4] Even though these claims are likely an overstatement, Delta rejected the offer. When a target firm reacts negatively to a proposal, the proposed transaction is called a hostile takeover. Delta eventually acquired Northwest Airlines.

A **merger** is a transaction in which firms agree to combine their operations on a relatively equal basis. For example, DaimlerChrysler was created by the merger between Daimler-Benz and Chrysler and was originally described as a merger. However, as it turned out, Daimler actually acquired Chrysler and installed its own managerial team. Mergers are more common than takeovers, but acquisitions greatly outnumber mergers. Our emphasis in this chapter is on acquisitions and the acquisition strategy because of their frequency of use.

Relaxed regulations and improved trade relations among various countries are contributing to the growth of cross-border acquisitions described earlier. In the European Union, as more countries have been added, the number of regulations and restrictions between firms in these countries has been reduced. As home markets mature, governments are more motivated to facilitate the efforts of firms in their country to seek growth in other countries' markets. Yet these transactions are challenging as well. Among the challenges are the difficulties of screening firms, selecting an appropriate target firm, and then negotiating with target firm managers. Differences in languages and cultures require understanding and sensitivity from both sides of the transaction.

Figure 7.1 presents the framework used for discussion of acquisitions and the acquisition strategy. First, we describe the five major reasons that firms complete acquisitions. We then examine target screening and selection, target negotiating, and due diligence. In this discussion, we examine four questions firms should answer when engaging in due diligence. Our attention then turns to what should be

acquisition

a transaction in which a firm buys a controlling interest in another firm with the intention of either making it a subsidiary business or combining it with its current business or businesses

acquisition strategy

an action plan that the firm develops to successfully acquire other companies

takeover

a specialized type of acquisition in which the target firm does not solicit the acquiring firm's offer

merger

a transaction in which firms agree to combine their operations on a relatively equal basis

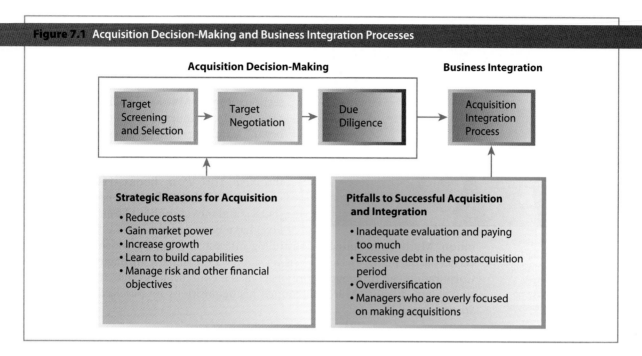

Figure 7.1 Acquisition Decision-Making and Business Integration Processes

Acquisition Decision-Making   **Business Integration**

Target Screening and Selection → Target Negotiation → Due Diligence → Acquisition Integration Process

Strategic Reasons for Acquisition

- Reduce costs
- Gain market power
- Increase growth
- Learn to build capabilities
- Manage risk and other financial objectives

Pitfalls to Successful Acquisition and Integration

- Inadequate evaluation and paying too much
- Excessive debt in the postacquisition period
- Overdiversification
- Managers who are overly focused on making acquisitions

done to successfully integrate the target firm into the acquiring firm. We discuss four major pitfalls to successful integration and the steps firms can take to avoid them. In spite of good intentions, acquisitions sometimes fail. We close the chapter with a discussion of what firms do when they face this failure.

Reasons for Acquisitions

Firms complete acquisitions and use an acquisition strategy for many reasons. We discuss five major reasons in the following sections.

Reduce Costs

Firms often use horizontal acquisitions to reduce costs. A **horizontal acquisition** is the purchase of a competitor competing in the same market or markets as the acquiring firm. An airline buying another airline (e.g., Delta acquiring Northwest) is an example of a horizontal acquisition.

Firms gain scale economies through horizontal acquisitions, which is one reason so many horizontal acquisitions take place in the pharmaceutical industry. As you might imagine, the ability to combine two firms' R&D skills is one reason for horizontal acquisitions between pharmaceutical firms as noted in *Focusing on Strategy*. The economies-of-scale increases from mergers are highly important in most industries.[5]

Horizontal acquisitions can also lead to increases in productivity, especially where firms have similar but some different resources that complement one another.[6] In addition, some firms acquire others to reduce the competition. Reducing the competition is part of the reason for the consolidation in the airline industry.[7] Additionally, the merger of XM and Sirius was clearly a desire on the part of each to reduce the competition. In fact, both were experiencing problems surviving when competing with each other.[8]

horizontal acquisition

the purchase of a competitor competing in the same market or markets as the acquiring firm

With the vertical acquisition of DirecTV, Rupert Murdoch's News Corporation has paired a mode of television distribution with its expansive array of media content.

A **vertical acquisition** is the purchase of a supplier or distributor of one or more of a firm's goods or services.[9] Vertical acquisitions can also be used to increase scale and to gain market power, which is discussed in the next section. Rupert Murdoch built News Corporation and continues to manage it today. He began acquiring British newspapers in the 1970s and then began an acquisition program in the United States in 1976 when he acquired the *New York Post*. Books (HarperCollins), magazines (*TV Guide*), television networks (FOX), and movie studios (Twentieth Century Fox) have been added to create News Corporation. Murdoch acquired a controlling interest in DirecTV which represents a vertical acquisition, as DirecTV is a satellite TV company through which News Corporation can distribute more of its media content: news, movies, and television shows. Finally, Murdoch capped his acquisitions by purchasing *The Wall Street Journal*.[10]

Gain Market Power

Market power exists when the firm sells its products above competitive prices or when its costs are lower than those of its primary competitors. Firms commonly use horizontal and vertical acquisitions to gain market power.[11] Horizontal acquisitions have been used in the business software industry. Declines in corporate spending because of the global economic malaise in the first decade of the 21st century influenced the use of horizontal acquisitions in this industry and later in the financial services industry. Acquisitions enable the acquiring firm to reduce overcapacity in the industry (reducing competition) by eliminating duplicate operations during the integration process. The acquisitions which created GlaxoSmithKline (discussed in *Focusing on Strategy*) were partly undertaken to increase the firm's market power and its goal was achieved.

However, pursuing market power can be problematic as well. Firms can pay too much for an acquisition as they compete to gain market power and the larger share of a market. When firms pay more than the current market value of a firm, it is referred to as a **premium**. Firms paying a premium assume that they can create synergy by merging the two firms, thereby increasing the value of the assets of the firm acquired. However, a number of firms do not create adequate synergy to earn returns beyond a premium. In these cases, executives of the acquiring firm often take more drastic steps to make the acquisition pay, such as selling off productive assets, laying off valuable employees to reduce costs, or buying additional businesses to integrate as they try to build synergy.[12]

Increase Growth

Some industries have significant fragmentation, with many small competitors of equal size. In these instances, some firms use an acquisition strategy to increase their growth rate relative to competitors. This strategy can be especially valuable if the acquiring firm is the first or one of the first to make such acquisitions in the industry. If they do so, it gives them an advantage in market power and position.[13] Firms often decide whether they can promote growth more effectively through internal development (e.g., creating innovative new products) or through

vertical acquisition
the purchase of a supplier or distributor of one or more of a firm's goods or services

market power
power that exists when the firm sells its products above competitive prices or when its costs are lower than those of its primary competitors

premium
occurs when firms pay more than the current market value to acquire another firm

acquisitions. Acquisitions produce much faster growth and entering new markets is often easier because the firm acquired is already operating in the desired market. But sometimes organic growth through innovation can provide more long-term value.[14]

Learn to Build Capabilities

Learning from a target firm and building new capabilities are more reasons that firms acquire other companies. Target companies often have unique employee skills, organizational technologies, or superior knowledge that are available to the acquiring firm only through acquisitions. Learning from acquired firms is common in cross-border acquisitions.[15] Although acquiring firms may gain new knowledge in several areas from the acquisition, they usually learn market-specific knowledge (e.g., about customers, distributors, suppliers, and government regulations).[16] A common goal of acquisitions in high technology industries is to obtain access to or learn new technological capabilities.[17] Additionally, pooling the companies' combined resources and capabilities may enable development of new "centers of excellence" for specialized products in new markets.[18] Cisco Systems, Microsoft, and Intel are examples of firms completing technology-driven acquisitions to build their capabilities.[19]

Building capabilities through acquisitions is a future-oriented reason to complete acquisitions. The three reasons for acquisitions of reducing costs, gaining market power, and increasing growth are about exploiting current advantages, while learning how to build the firm's capabilities is about exploring to create tomorrow's advantages. In general, exploitation was the rationale for many acquisitions in the 1980s and 1990s, while financial reasons (discussed next) influenced acquisitions in the 1970s. It appears that capability-building acquisitions are a dominant reason for many acquisitions in the first decade of the 21st century.[20]

As explained in the *Understanding Strategy: Learning from Success,* Schlumberger accomplished several purposes with its acquisition of Smith International. It increased its market power through increases in total market share and by increasing its breadth of services it provides to the market. In addition it added capabilities. In fact, integrating Schlumberger's current capabilities with those of Smith International should create synergy because the capabilities of the two businesses largely complement each other. Therefore, Schlumberger's acquisition is predicted to be a major success solidifying its leading position in its industry.

Manage Risk and Other Financial Objectives

Facing stiff competition, some firms use acquisitions to diversify their operations, thereby reducing their dependence on performance in an intensely competitive market. Many years ago, GE diversified away from the consumer electronics market into financial services to reduce its dependence on the consumer electronics area. Furthermore, GE has diversified into other service areas rather than base its revenue solely on industrial products.[21] At times, firms also make acquisitions to gain access to tax advantages or to reduce business or financial risk.[22] Of course, such acquisitions need to be done in a way that cannot be replicated by shareholders through portfolio diversification. In recent times, private equity firms amass financial capital from multiple investors and use this capital to make acquisitions. They usually acquire firms that they believe can provide significant and rapid returns on their investment. In particular, they search for undervalued assets.[23]

UNDERSTANDING STRATEGY
LEARNING FROM SUCCESS

Getting a Little of Everything from Acquisitions: Market Power, Growth, and New Capabilities

Schlumberger is the world's largest oil services company. And, it gained even more market power through its acquisition of Smith International. Prior to the acquisition, Schlumberger had annual revenues that were 50 percent higher than its nearest competitor, Halliburton. Schlumberger has gained market power partly because its market share has increased and the distance between it and its competitors is even greater now. In addition, while Schlumberger and Smith International have some overlapping activities and market segments served, they largely provided services to different market segments. Thus, Schlumberger now has a stronger position in the industry with a greater breadth of services provided to the market.

Smith International has been a leader in drilling for unconventional natural gas. In particular, Smith is strong in the drilling fluid and drill bit business and is one of the largest manufacturers of oil-field drill bits. Smith's technology in this area is considered to be "cutting edge." Because these technologies are used to drill for oil shale natural gas production, it can be very helpful to Schlumberger to compete against Baker Hughes, which acquired BJ Services. It also will be helpful in the future as unconventional fields are likely to be a major source of energy in future years. As such, Schlumberger has acquired new capabilities in unconventional drilling and technological capabilities as well. Because these capabilities complement Schlumberger's current set of capabilities, this acquisition is expected to produce significant synergies. Of

course, this is very important because Schlumberger paid a substantial premium to acquire Smith. Thus, the synergy must be obtained to produce greater value and recoup the premium paid.

Finally, the added market power and new capabilities along with the synergy expected are likely to produce additional growth for Schlumberger. Both Smith and Schlumberger provide services to some of the largest companies in the world. Schlumberger is likely to continue servicing its current customers while expanding sales to them by providing a broader array of services that they desire/need. Additionally, this acquisition may help to obtain new customers because of the breadth of services that they can now offer.

For these reasons, Schlumberger has announced that it does not intend to sell any of the Smith International businesses and will fully service all of Smith's current customers. Schlumberger was already the giant in the industry. This acquisition only made Schlumberger bigger, stronger, and better prepared for the future.

Sources: 2010, Statement on availability of Smith products and services, Schlumberger, www.slb.com/news, April 14; A. R. Sorkin, 2010, Behind Schlumberger's Smith deal: A big gas bet, *The New York Times*, www.nytimes.com, February 22; K. Swanekamp, 2010, Schlumberger snaps up Smith, *Forbes*, www.forbes.com, February 22; D. Wethe & E. Klump, 2010, Schlumberger sees Smith deal accelerating advances, *BusinessWeek*, www.businessweek.com, February 22; J. Jannarone, 2010, Smith deal drills into Schlumberger, *The Wall Street Journal*, www.wsj.com, February 22; 2010, Schlumberger and Smith International announce agreement, Schlumberger, www.slb.com/news, February 21; J. McCracken & B. Casselman, 2010, Schlumberger in talks to buy Smith International, *The Wall Street Journal*, www.wsj.com, February 19.

© Greg Epperson, iStock

Screening, Selecting, and Negotiating with Target Firms

Research suggests that financial acquirers (such as Kohlberg Kravis Roberts [KKR]) experience higher valuations in their acquisitions than do corporate acquisitions. Financial acquirers such as leveraged buyout (defined later in the chapter) firms often complete two or three acquisitions per year. However, these firms may explore as many as 400 or 500 possibilities and examine closely perhaps 25 targets before selecting the four or five target firms they'll attempt to acquire. Acquisition opportunities can come without warning and usually need to be evaluated quickly. Accordingly, it is important for firms to balance the need to think strategically with the need to react to an acquisition opportunity in a timely way. Firms whose stock is publicly traded have a great deal of data available to examine because regulations require that they make much of their financial data public. However, private firms whose stock is not traded on the stock exchange do not have to reveal much information. Therefore, while some private firms may be attractive, it is challenging for acquiring firms to obtain adequate information to evaluate the viability of the private firms as acquisition targets.[24] Cisco Systems has completed a large number of acquisitions; it may examine three potential markets and decide to enter only one of them and may evaluate five to ten candidates for each deal that it closes. This extra screening enables the acquiring party to identify the acquisition opportunities that exist while at the same time determining the appropriate price. Although this process takes time, it helps managers develop experience in screening, allowing them to increase the speed and effectiveness of the screening process over time. When managers do a careful and thorough job in screening potential targets, they are better able to select the best targets to acquire even in challenging situations such as cross-border acquisitions.[25]

Focusing too strongly on an "exciting" opportunity and setting aside the firm's basic strategy can be a major mistake. After the screening process is completed in a rational and strategic way, negotiations are initiated. Key issues requiring careful analysis should be identified early in the negotiating process. For instance, it is important to clarify what role the top executives will play in the newly combined organization. Determining the executive positions needed in the newly created firm and the people who will fill those positions is an important topic for negotiations.

Because most proposed transactions are greeted with skepticism by managers and employees in the target firm, acquirers with experience often try to develop a spirit of cooperation to negotiate a mutually beneficial agreement. A cooperative relationship between personnel in the acquiring and acquired firms is the foundation on which the most serious issues can be successfully negotiated. Thus, the negotiation process contributes strongly to the development of trust (or not) between the two parties.[26] Table 7.1 provides a list of suggestions that are helpful in the negotiation process. In particular, government officials may also need

---

Table 7.1 Considerations in Successful Acquisition (Including Cross-Border) Negotiation Processes

1. Be very clear about the strategic logic behind the proposed acquisition.

2. Be patient, acting decisively when needed but in a way that does not create emotion. Take a long-term view, which often runs counter to the strategic objective among participants in the negotiation process.

3. Seek to develop government, industry, and company contacts well before the transaction takes place.

4. Identify the potential players in the proposed deal-making process, including government administrators. Understand who will be for the deal and differentiate between those who will be unconditionally opposed and those whose objectives can be met in the negotiation process.

5. Understand who will defer to which group and sequence the negotiation process in a way that will maximize the chance of success.

6. Think about how you will negotiate with potential deal blockers and how you can give them a vision that meets your needs while enabling them to persuade others among their constituents of the transaction's value for their particular group's interests.

7. Act to ensure the sustainability of the deal. Remember that once the transaction is completed, negotiations are not finished. Integration between deal participants can be facilitated by taking a long-term view of the participants involved.

Sources: Adapted from J. K. Sebenius, 2002, The hidden challenge of cross-border negotiations, *Harvard Business Review*, 80(3): 76–85; J. K. Sebenius, 1998, Negotiating cross-border acquisitions, *Sloan Management Review*, 39(2): 27–41.

to be included in order to successfully negotiate a deal, especially in cross-border transactions.

Due Diligence

Due diligence is the rational process by which acquiring firms evaluate target firms. Due diligence is concerned with verifying that the reason for the proposed transaction is sound strategically and financially. To understand how to improve due diligence, Bain and Company, a strategy consulting firm, studied 20 companies, both private and public, known for the quality of their due diligence processes. We summarize the results of their research into four basic questions around which an acquiring firm's due diligence efforts should be framed.[27]

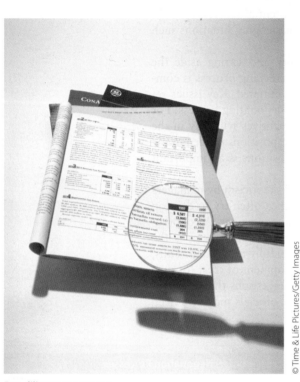

© Time & Life Pictures/Getty Images

Due diligence teams are formed by acquiring firms to analyze potential acquisitions. The teams focus on building a bottom-up view of targeted firm by studying their customers and suppliers, competitors, and overall capabilities.

What Is the Acquiring Firm Really Buying?

Acquiring firms frequently form a team to conduct due diligence. Rather than relying on potentially biased secondary sources for information, the due diligence team should build its own bottom-up view of the target firm and the industry. In this process, the team collects information from multiple parties, including customers, suppliers, and competitors as well as the target firm. This information helps the team carefully examine each assumption made by the acquiring firm regarding the target firm and its value.

Studying customers and suppliers enables the due diligence team to answer important questions about the target firm such as: Is the target customer group growing? Has the target firm fully explored the needs of its target customers? What distribution channels is the target firm using to serve customers? Are superior channels available? Does the target firm have favorable deals/relationships with its suppliers?

Analyzing competitors is another important source of information when it comes to understanding the target firm. Important questions in evaluating the target firm's competitors include the following: Is the target firm more profitable than its competitors? In what part of the value chain are most of the profits made? Is the target firm underperforming or outperforming its competitors in the key parts of the value chain? How will the target firm's competitors react to an acquisition, and how might this influence competition between the target and its competitors?

Finally, the due diligence team should assess the target firm's capabilities by considering a host of questions: Does the target have cost advantages relative to its competitors? How could the target's cost position help the acquiring firm's cost position? Could the target's capabilities (e.g., R&D) be integrated with those of the acquiring firm to create sources of differentiation?[28] If so, how valuable would those be and how long would it take to develop those new capabilities?

due diligence

the rational process by which acquiring firms evaluate target firms

The due diligence team's evaluation of the target firm is studied to ensure that no "deal breakers" exist and to verify that the proposed transaction is appropriate strategically. This evaluation likely provides information regarding the target firm's value.

What Is the Target Firm's Value?

Acquisitions can seem glamorous—a fact that sometimes biases decision makers to quickly conclude that a proposed acquisition is virtually without potential flaws. To thwart this bias, the due diligence team must assess the target's true financial value. True financial value is determined through an objective, unbiased process.

An objective analysis verifies the absence of accounting anomalies at the target firm. Accounting anomalies may signal problems and possibly past unethical actions as well. The team should consider rapid and significant increases in sales revenue as a possible accounting anomaly. For example, such changes may be a function of dramatically lower sales prices rather than true growth. Even though dramatically reducing prices to sell more products makes revenue look good in the current time period, such sales can't be sustained. Of course, the acquiring firm is most interested in future sales of a target firm. Another accounting anomaly occurs when the firm treats recurring items as extraordinary costs, thus keeping them off the profit and loss statement. These and other accounting anomalies must be revealed to understand the historical and projected cash flows. Thus, the due diligence team must extensively interact with target firm personnel about entries to the target's financial statements.

Where Are the Potential Synergies Between the Combined Firms?

Although evaluating the target firm to determine its actual value is wise, caution must be exercised when doing so. The due diligence team should also consider the synergies that might be created by integrating the target with the acquiring firm. This evaluation should identify potential synergies, the probability of realizing the synergies, and the time and investment required to do so. Acquisitions often fail because of an inability to obtain expected synergies, an outcome that highlights the importance of carefully studying proposed synergies and their costs.

What Is the Acquiring Firm's Walk-Away Offer Price?

The emotional pressure to make an acquisition can be significant. Think of the pressure that acquiring firm executives may encounter after a proposed acquisition is announced to the press. Extensive coverage highlights a transaction's visibility and can make it more difficult for the acquiring firm to walk away from the possible deal. However, successful acquisitions result from logical, unemotional decisions. To increase the probability that a rational decision will be made, the acquiring firm should decide on a purchase price it will not exceed. To do this, the acquiring firm must determine who makes the top-price decision and the decision criteria he or she will use. These determinations should be made before final negotiations begin. It may be especially helpful to avoid a bidding war with another firm competing to acquire the target firm. For example, HP and Dell entered a bidding war to acquire 3Par, a data storage company. The bid prices reached three times the market price of 3Par's stock prior to Dell's first offer to acquire the company, making the acquisition much more expensive than Dell expected.[29]

Based on the results of its due diligence process, the acquiring firm decides whether it will acquire the target firm. If the acquisition is completed, the focus shifts to what must be done to integrate the acquired firm into the acquiring firm's operations.

The failed acquisition between Prudential and AIG explained in *Understanding Strategy: Learning from Failure* emphasizes the importance of the initial phases of the acquisition process. This example, especially, shows the importance of target negotiating and due diligence. The activities leading to an acquisition decision (target screening, target selection, target negotiating, and due diligence) influence the success of individual acquisitions along with the acquisition strategies. However, in the final analysis, a particular acquisition will succeed or fail on the basis of how well the target firm and acquiring firm integrate their operations.[30] Integration success is more likely when an integration team, including employees from the acquiring firm and the acquired firm, is formed and charged with full responsibility to integrate the two companies to create value.

Although implementing acquisitions involves many challenges, as acquiring and target firms begin to integrate their operations, unanticipated opportunities for creating new value may be discovered. When firms are intent on learning from each other and when complementary assets are brought together in ways that enable such value creation, these value-creating opportunities are more likely to arise.[31] Still, to achieve the potential value will require that the change process involved in the integration be managed effectively.[32] If the integration process is carried out thoroughly and appropriately, opportunities are likely for increased growth as learning occurs. This is partly because the merged firm is able to avoid unwanted turnover among executives and talented employees.[33] Effective integration often allows the merged firm to leverage the capabilities (e.g., technological capabilities) of both firms to create enhanced value. Alternatively, poor integration of the two firms hinders the ability to leverage the special capabilities of the two firms, thereby producing lower value.[34] Effective integration is especially important when the acquiring firm pays a significant premium to buy the target firm. In this case, it must achieve the potential synergies of combining the businesses, making needed changes, in order to create new value that will return the premium paid.[35]

Pitfalls in Pursuing Acquisitions and Their Prevention

The importance of successful integration in the post-acquisition period cannot be overestimated.[36] Because combined firms often lose target firm managers through turnover, it is important to retain key executives and other valuable human capital, especially if the acquiring firm wants to gain new skills from the acquired firm.[37] In addition, because much of an organization's knowledge is contained in its human capital,[38] turnover of key personnel from the acquired firm should be avoided.[39] Involving these employees in the integration process reduces the likelihood that they will leave the newly combined firm.

History suggests that acquisitions are risky. However, learning how to deal effectively with prominent pitfalls increases the chance of acquisition success. Next, we discuss four major pitfalls.

Inadequate Evaluation and Paying Too Much

As we've discussed, effective due diligence is important in ensuring that a rational approach is used after negotiations begin. We also highlighted the importance of

Look Before You Leap: Prudential's Failed Acquisition of AIA

In March 2010, Prudential reached an agreement with American International Group (AIG) to acquire its Asian Insurance business, AIA Group, for a price of $35.5 billion. But, thereafter, Prudential's shareholders expressed concern about the acquisition and especially the price because of general declines in the stock market and the debt crisis brought on by Greece's substantial debt. In fact, two institutional investor shareholders, BlackRock and Fidelity Investments requested Prudential's CEO, Tidjane Thiam, to seek a reduction in the acquisition price because of the market declines. In turn, Thiam sought a $5 billion reduction in the acquisition price but AIG refused. Actually, AIG greatly desired to make this deal because it needed the revenue to pay off its debt to the U.S. government. So, the AIG CEO, Robert Benmosche, supported the change but AIG's Board of Directors rejected the request.

Failure to adequately grasp the appetite of key shareholders for the originally negotiated acquisition price for AIG's Asian insurance business, Prudential was eventually forced to abandon the deal, pay out related fees totaling $650 million, and slow the pace of its planned expansion into Asia.

As a result of the changing events and the AIG rejection of the request to reduce the offer price, Prudential decided to stop the acquisition. This change was not without costs, however. Several advisors had to be paid and the original agreement contained a termination fee which amounted to approximately $225 million. The fees in total were about $650 million. Therefore, the failed deal was very costly to Prudential. It paid substantial sums of money and received nothing in return. Because of this, Prudential shareholders are not pleased with Mr. Thiam and Harvey McGrath, chairman of the board. Both of these executives are fighting to save their jobs. To do so, they must develop a new strategy to replace the major acquisition. Essentially Prudential wants to expand its business in Asia. The acquisition would have helped the company expand in this region

quickly. Now, Prudential may have to take a more moderate and slower approach to expansion. This is a problem partly because by announcing the acquisition of AIA, some analysts suggested that Thiam and McGrath left the impression that the radical change (the acquisition would have doubled the size of the company) implied that the firm' current strategy was ineffective.

The executives on both sides of this acquisition deal are experiencing problems. Prudential experienced major problems with its shareholders and AIG's Board disagreed with the CEO on the reduction in price. Thus, even though AIG needed the revenue from the sell, it was left holding on to its Asian Insurance business. The CEO and Chairman of the Board for AIG experienced significant tension and conflict. Also, some analysts have suggested that Prudential should be broken up and some parts sold (e.g., its Asian business). Therefore, Prudential likely should have done more due diligence and negotiated a better acquisition price originally. Neither CEO understood well the evaluations and feelings of some of their firms' major shareholders. As a result, Prudential paid fees of $650 million and received nothing in return. And, AIG lost a sale and revenues that it dearly needed.

Sources: A. R. Sorkin, 2010, Tension said to grow between A.I.G. leaders, *The New York Times*, www.nytimes.com, June 25; K. Crowley & J. Menon, 2010, Prudential defends AIA bid, backs managers amid fury, *BusinessWeek*, www.businessweek.com, June 7; D. Cimilluca & N. Shah, 2010, Deal dead, Prudential's task is—what now? *The Wall Street Journal*, www.wsj.com, June 4; K. Crowley, 2010, Thiam misses Goodwin's lesson as Prudential bids fails, *BusinessWeek*, www.businessweek.com, June 2; C. Gutierrez, 2010, AIG in flux after Prudential backs off AIA buy, *Forbes*, www.forbes.com, June 2; 2010, AIG offloads Asian insurance business, *Forbes*, www.forbes.com, March 1.

© kimeveruss, iStock

© David Willis / Alamy

the acquiring firm's establishing a price above which it will not go. Notwithstanding due diligence and the use of investment bankers to help with this process, many firms still act too irrationally in acquiring the target, and as a result, they pay too much for it (the premium is too high). Research suggests that "a combination of cognitive biases and organizational pressures often causes managers to make overly optimistic forecasts in analyzing proposals for major investments" such as acquisitions.[40] Anchoring (quickly becoming committed to a position and being highly resistant to changing it) and overconfidence in one's opinion are two examples of cognitive biases that may surface during an acquisition process. Regardless of the causes, those evaluating a target firm as an acquisition candidate must ensure that the acquiring firm's evaluation of that target is complete and that the acquiring firm doesn't overpay to acquire the target. The example of Prudential's failed acquisition of AIG's AIA unit in the *Understanding Strategy: Learning from Failure* discussion shows the importance of thorough analysis before negotiating a deal. In fact, only a few months after completing the acquisition agreement, Prudential wanted to reduce the price by $5 billion. It realized that the price negotiated was too high. Because the deal failed, Prudential paid $650 million in fees and received nothing in return.

Excessive Debt in the Post-Acquisition Period

Many companies that make acquisitions have significant debt levels. When credit rating agencies, such as Moody's and Standard & Poor's, reduce a firm's credit rating, the firm will incur higher costs to obtain additional financial capital. This reduction is logical because firms with lower credit ratings are thought to be riskier investments. And investors expect higher returns from risky investments. An acquiring firm's managers should also understand that if its debt load becomes too high, it will have less cash to invest in R&D, human resources, and marketing.[41] Investments in these organizational functions are important parts of what the firm does to be successful in the long term.

Overdiversification

Frequent acquisitions help meet capital markets' expectations for the firm to grow and have the potential to increase top-level managers' salaries. Top-level managers' salaries tend to increase with growth in the firm's overall size. Therefore, capital markets and the relationship between organizational size and salaries for top-level managers may influence top-level managers to make frequent acquisitions. This behavior can be problematic, though, in that firms can become overdiversified. In the late 1990s and early 2000s, a number of media companies such as AOL Time Warner, Vivendi, and Bertelsmann completed several acquisitions that did not turn out well. A number of analysts concluded that these firms had become overdiversified, a condition that makes it difficult for the firm to effectively manage each successive acquisition. The response to overdiversification is for the firm to divest acquisitions that it can't successfully manage.[42] Another response has been for boards of directors to restructure the CEO's incentive compensation to avoid such problems in the future.[43]

Managers Who Are Overly Focused on Making Acquisitions

Acquisitions require significant managerial time and energy. Managers have opportunity costs for the time and energy spent searching for viable acquisitions, completing due diligence, preparing for and participating in negotiations, and managing the integration process after an acquisition is completed. Time and energy spent dealing with potential acquisitions obviously can't be invested in managing other aspects of the firm's operations. Furthermore, when acquisition negotiations are initiated, target firm managers often operate in "suspended animation" until the acquisition and integration processes are completed.[44] Therefore, it is important for managers to encourage dissent when evaluating an acquisition target. If failure occurs, leaders are tempted to blame it on others or on unforeseen circumstances. Rather, it is important that managers recognize when they are overly involved in the acquisition process. "The urge to merge is still like an addiction in many companies: doing deals is much more fun and interesting than fixing fundamental problems. So, as in dealing with any other addictions or temptations maybe it is best to just say no."[45] In fact, managers should treat acquisitions as one option from a series of alternatives. Acquisitions are successful only in selected instances and many fail to produce the necessary returns.[46]

In Table 7.2, we summarize the four major pitfalls of acquisitions and present possible preventive actions firms can take to avoid a pitfall or to reduce the negative consequences experienced because of a pitfall. As suggested in the table and as we've discussed, it is important for the firm to establish a rational due diligence process and to make certain that the walk-away offer price is fixed in order to thwart the temptation to surpass the rational price to pay for a target firm. Paying too much often happens when many bidders are involved; this tendency is called the "winner's curse" in the research literature.[47] Similarly, managers must ensure that the firm has enough cash on hand and debt capacity to complete the transaction at or below the established walk-away offer price. When faced with the possibility of becoming overdiversified, managers must fully understand the nature of synergy and the actions necessary to create it in the integration stage. Even with potential synergies and a transaction justified by its expected financial outcomes, a deal may not be good to execute due to lack of strategic fit with the acquiring firm's core strengths. Finally, it is important to establish a checks-and-balances system in which managers are challenged to support the acquisition decision, especially when a firm regularly uses an acquisition strategy. If these checks and balances can be established with integrity, they will likely protect managers from becoming overly focused on completing acquisitions to the detriment of other issues warranting managerial attention. When managers overcome the pitfalls and manage the process effectively, successful acquisitions result. Unfortunately, only a small number of firms appear to manage the acquisition process effectively.[48]

Table 7.2 Major Pitfalls of Acquisitions and Their Prevention

Pitfall	Prevention
Paying too much	Establish rational due diligence processes with a walk-away offer price and make certain that when this price is reached, managers involved do walk away.
Taking on too much debt	Ensure that the firm has adequate cash as well as debt capacity to complete the transaction at or below the walk-away offer price.
Becoming overdiversified	Understand fully the nature of synergy in the acquisition and the integration processes necessary to achieve it. Also, ensure that any unrelated transactions are justified based on strong financial rationales. However, even when such justification is in place, the deal may not be positive for strategic-fit reasons because it may lead to overdiversification. Therefore, make certain that strategic fit does not lead to overdiversification.
Managers who are overly focused on acquisitions	Establish checks and balances so that top managers are challenged by the board and other stakeholders regarding proposed acquisitions. These actions are especially important in firms making frequent acquisitions.

Acquisition Failure and Restructuring

Regardless of the effort invested, acquisitions sometimes fail. When they do, divestiture may be the best course of action. A **divestiture** is a transaction in which businesses are sold to other firms or spun off as independent enterprises. Some divestitures occur because the firm wants to restructure its set of businesses to take advantage of new opportunities.[49] Commonly, though, divestitures are made to deal with failed acquisitions. Sears, Roebuck is a famous example of a firm that failed with its acquisitions. In 1981, Sears acquired Dean Witter Reynolds to diversify into financial services and Coldwell Banker to diversify into real estate. At first, the results of these acquisitions seemed positive. Quickly, though, it became obvious that the synergies Sears expected among its retail, financial services, and real estate businesses would not materialize. The inability to rapidly create synergies caused Sears executives to focus too much time on trying to develop those synergies. The net result of these efforts was that Sears' core retail business received little managerial attention, causing it to lose market share and perform poorly. Pressured by institutional investors to correct the problems, Sears announced the divestiture of its financial services and real estate businesses so that it could concentrate on its retail business. Research suggests that despite initial gains over the period when Sears was diversified, the firm's shareholders suffered significant opportunity losses when compared to a portfolio of firms that maintained a focus on their core retailing sector.[50]

Leveraged buyouts are commonly used as a restructuring strategy to correct for managerial mistakes. A **leveraged buyout (LBO)** is a restructuring strategy in which a party buys all or part of a firm's assets in order to take the firm or a part of the firm private. After the transaction is completed, the company's stock is no longer traded publicly. Usually, significant amounts of debt are incurred to finance a buyout; hence the term *leveraged* buyout. To support debt payments, the new owners may immediately sell a number of assets in order to focus on the firm's core businesses.[51] Because leveraged buyout organizations (such as KKR) often control these firms, the intent is to restructure the firm to the point that it can be sold at a profit within five to eight years. However, in addition improving efficiencies, such buyouts can also represent a form of firm rebirth to facilitate entrepreneurial efforts and stimulate strategic growth. Equity firms have become more common in recent years.[52] Regardless, firms that engage in unsuccessful revisions often have to take actions to reverse the negative results. Some refer to this process as *merger repair*.[53]

divestiture

a transaction in which businesses are sold to other firms or spun off as independent enterprises

leveraged buyout (LBO)

a restructuring strategy in which a party buys all or part of a firm's assets in order to take the firm or a part of the firm private

SUMMARY

The primary purpose of this chapter is to describe the actions necessary to provide the foundation for an effective acquisition strategy. In doing so, we examined the following topics:

● An acquisition occurs when one firm buys controlling interest in another firm with the intention of either making the acquired firm a subsidiary business

or combining it with a current business. An acquisition strategy is an action plan that the firm develops to successfully complete acquisitions. A takeover is a specialized acquisition strategy in which a target firm does not solicit the acquiring firm's offer. Takeovers are often hostile transactions. A merger is a transaction in which firms agree to combine their operations on a relatively equal basis.

- Companies complete acquisitions for five basic reasons: (1) to reduce costs; (2) to gain market power; (3) to increase growth; (4) to learn and to build new capabilities; and (5) to manage managerial, financial, and risk-reduction objectives.

- Target screening, target selection, and target firm negotiations are activities necessary to complete an acquisition. Effective screening enables the acquiring firm to gain an overall sense of the acquisition opportunities that exist and helps to establish the appropriate price. After the screening and selection are completed, negotiating with target firm leaders begins. In negotiating, it is important to clarify the roles top executives of the acquiring and target firms will play in the new firm. Also, government officials may need to be consulted to conclude negotiations, especially in cross-border deals.

- Effective due diligence is critical to making the best decision about a possible acquisition. Four basic questions are answered when engaging in due diligence: (1) What is the acquiring firm really buying? (2) What is the target firm's true financial value? (3) Where are the potential synergies between the acquiring and acquired firms? (4) What is the acquiring firm's walk-away offer price?

- Efforts to integrate the acquired firm into the acquiring firm after the transaction is completed may have the strongest influence on acquisition success or failure. After a transaction is completed, it is critical to assess and improve, as required, the morale of all employees, but especially target firm employees. Building bridges between personnel in the target firm and personnel in the acquiring firm increases the likelihood that the firms will be effectively integrated.

- In addition to integration difficulties, acquisitions face other potential pitfalls: (1) inadequately evaluating the target firm and paying too much for the target, (2) taking on excessive debt in the post-acquisition period, (3) overdiversifying, and (4) having managers who are overly focused on making acquisitions.

- Acquisitions sometimes fail. When they do, firms divest businesses that are causing performance problems so that they might again focus on their core businesses. Leveraged buyouts are also used to restructure firms when particular acquisitions have failed or when a firm's whole acquisition strategy has failed.

KEY TERMS

Acquisition, 148	Horizontal acquisition, 149	Premium, 150
Acquisition strategy, 148	Leveraged buyout (LBO), 160	Takeover, 148
Divestiture, 160	Market power, 150	Vertical acquisition, 150
Due diligence, 154	Merger, 148	

DISCUSSION QUESTIONS

1. What are the definitions of an acquisition, takeover, merger, and acquisition strategy? Why are acquisitions important to understand?

2. What are the five basic reasons that firms make acquisitions? Over the next 10 years or so, do you think any of these reasons will become more important than the others? If so, why?

3. What are target screening, target selection, target negotiating, and due diligence? In your opinion, why do some firms fail to perform these activities effectively?

4. What process should be used to successfully integrate acquisitions, and why is integration important?

5. What are the four major pitfalls of acquisitions? How can these pitfalls be prevented?

6. What major restructuring strategies do firms use to deal with a failed acquisition? What are the trade-offs among the restructuring strategies?

Introduction

Acquisitions are one of the most common and most important strategic management tools in use today. The bad news is that most fail (the general rule of thumb is that up to 80%–85% do not achieve estimated synergies). Many times, acquisitions are not well thought out ahead of time or are the personal mission of CEOs. This chapter addresses many of the pitfalls and remedies, and this chapter's tool—The Acquisition Stoplight—is a guide for making an informed decision.

The Acquisition Stoplight

	Strategic	Financial	Operational
Stop	Offerings are redundant or not related to the strategic long-term vision of the company	Acquisition price clearly exceeds the discounted cash flows of incremental benefits	It is extremely unlikely that the acquirer possesses the ability to integrate new operations
Caution	Appears to offer additional offerings, but may cannibalize existing business	Cost/benefit calculations approximate zero	Acquisition would require additional resources for integrations
Proceed	Acquisition candidate is complementary to current offerings	Acquisition price clearly less than discounted cash flows of incremental benefits	Acquirer possesses the capacity and competencies necessary to integrate the new business

MINI-CASE

Credit Agricole Experienced Ups and Downs in the First Decade of the 21st Century

Agricole started a long-anticipated consolidation of European banks by acquiring Credit Lyonnais SA. Becoming the third-largest bank in the world, it was believed that Credit Agricole's actions might force a response from large European rivals such as Barclays Bank of the United Kingdom and Deutsche Bank. With the expansion of the European Union to include many new Eastern European countries, the scale of banking has become larger.

Because of limited growth opportunities in their mature home markets, many large European banks tried to expand by entering other countries. Furthermore, many of these banks' largest clients operate across borders in the European Union. Thus, banks follow and continue to serve their clients as they expand to new geographic areas. In 2003, Credit Agricole, with its 16 percent holding in Banca Intesa S.p.A., Italy's largest bank, was the only large European bank to own a position in a fairly large European rival.

Consolidation of European banks proceeded much more slowly in Europe than in the United States, where the banking industry continued to consolidate through acquisitions. Each European country's desire to have its own major bank has influenced decisions about acquisitions. Yet potential consolidation in the European banking sector picked up steam in 2007 and 2008 with the financial crises emanating from the United States. In fact, the largest acquisition in banking history was announced in 2007. A consortium of European banks, Royal Bank of Scotland, Banco Santander Central Hispano (Spain), and Fortis (Belgium-Dutch) acquired ABN Amro (Dutch) for $99.8 billion and agreed to split the ABN assets among themselves.

Alternatively, Agricole announced a fourth-quarter 2007 loss of $1.3 billion and decided in early 2008 not to make further acquisitions at the time. In fact, it sold some assets (e.g., its stake in a utility, Suez) for $1.6 billion to shore up its balance sheet. In 2009, the bank earned a profit but it was lower than expected and its CEO resigned.

In 2010, Credit Agricole experienced problems from the significant problems in its Greek unit accompanying the Greek financial crisis and is planning to restructure the unit. However, its first quarter net profit increased by more than 100 percent over its 2009 earnings during that period. Its performance was aided by a rebound in its investment banking unit. In June 2010, Agricole acquired 172 branches of the Italian bank Intesa for 740 million Euros. This acquisition provides Agricole with more than 900 branches in Italy making it the seventh-largest bank in Italy.

Sources: Laferty Ltd., 2004, Europe's banks commence mating season, *European Banker*, www.thebanker.com, February: 1; J. Wrighton, 2004, France's Credit Agricole is making its move; Carron faces challenge of turning bank into European powerhouse; regional holders may pose hurdle, *The Wall Street Journal*, www.wsj.com, June 3: C1; V. Ram, 2007, Sum of ABN's parts worth more than the whole, *Forbes*, www.forbes.com, October 5; D. Larner & A. Lagorce, 2008, Agricole sells Suez stake as banks bolster capital, *The Wall Street Journal*, www.wsj.com, January 15; A. R. Sorkin, 2009, Credit Agricole profits slide, and chief steps down, *The New York Times*, www.nytimes.com, November 11; J. Mullen, 2010, Credit Agricole reconsiders Greek plans, *The Wall Street Journal*, www.wsj.com, May 12; 2010, Update 3—Credit Agricole takes Greek unit hit, shares slide, *Reuters*, www.reuters.com, June 22; F. Benedetti-Valentini, 2010, Credit Agricole buys Intesa branches for about EU740 million, *BusinessWeek*, www.businessweek.com, June 22; 2010, Credit Agricole, SocGen lead bank surge as Basel committee softens rules, *Bloomberg*, www.bloomberg.com, June 28.

Questions

1. What would be the strategic motivations for a consolidation of large banks in the European Union?
2. What other issues in addition to strategic concerns are hindering or motivating banks that are considering acquiring other banks in the European Union?
3. What competitive reactions if any do you expect resulting from Credit Agricole's restructuring of its Greek unit and the acquisition of Intesa's Italian branches? Why or why not?
4. If you were the CEO of Agricole, would you pursue an acquisition target in the near future? Why or why not?

EXPERIENTIAL EXERCISES

Exercise One: 2008's Biggest Mergers and Acquisitions

The following list gives the top 10 mergers and/or acquisitions for 2008 taken from *CNNMoney.com* (http://money.cnn.com/news/deals/mergers/biggest.html). Select two of these firms and determine (a) whether the deal was a merger or an acquisition, (b) whether it occurred across borders and what the nationality of the target and acquirer was, (c) whether the deal was friendly or a takeover, and (d) how many of the five strategic reasons in Figure 7.1 were applicable to the deal. Provide supporting arguments for your conclusions.

Target Name	Acquirer Name	Deal Date	Value of Deal ($ millions)
Yahoo! Inc.	Microsoft Corp.	Feb. 1, 2008	43,711.60
Inmobiliaria Colonial SA	Investment Corp. of Dubai	Jan. 31, 2008	15,213.20
Rio Tinto PLC	Shining Prospect Pte Ltd	Feb. 1, 2008	14,284.20
Alcon Inc.	Novartis AG	Apr. 7, 2008	10,547.50
Bolsa de Valores de Sao Paulo	Bolsa Brasileira de Mercadorias	Feb. 20, 2008	10,309.10
Millennium Pharmaceuticals Inc.	Mahogany Acquisition Corp	Apr. 10, 2008	8,734.10
Citigroup Inc	Government of Singapore Investment Corp Pte Ltd	Jan. 15, 2008	6,880.00
Weyerhaeuser Co. (Containerboard Packaging and Recycling Business)	International Paper Co.	Mar. 17, 2008	6,000.00
MMX Mineracao e Metalicos SA (Certain Assets)	Anglo American PLC	Jan. 17, 2008	5,500.00
Scania AB	Volkswagen AG	Mar. 3, 2008	4,377.50

Exercise Two: Cisco Changes its Acquisition Strategy

According to the chapter, Cisco Systems, Microsoft, and Intel have used acquisitions primarily to build their capabilities. Cisco's approach has been to acquire small innovative firms rather than developing new technologies internally. These acquisitions have allowed Cisco to continuously generate new products. Cisco traditionally integrated these companies by installing Cisco managers and methods and removing the acquired company's name. But recently, Cisco has changed its acquisition strategy.

What are these changes in Cisco's acquisition strategy? Answer this question by looking at *The Wall Street Journal*, *BusinessWeek*, or *Forbes* as well as the company's Web site. Evaluate how these changes have affected the five reasons for acquisitions (reduce costs, gain market power, increase growth, build capabilities, and manage risk).

ENDNOTES

1. C. Moschieri & J. M. Campa, 2009, The European M&A industry: A market in the process of construction, *Academy of Management Perspectives*, 23(4): 71–87.
2. B. Aybar & A. Ficici, 2009, Cross-border acquisitions and firm value: An analysis of emerging-market multinationals, *Journal of International Business Studies*, 40: 1317–1338.
3. J. E. Ashton, F. X. Cook, Jr., & P. Schmitz, 2003, Uncovering hidden value in a midsize manufacturing company, *Harvard Business Review*, 81(6): 4–12.
4. J. Baer, 2008, Deals in the air: Rising costs force U.S. carriers to seek mergers, *Financial Times*, www.ft.com, February 18.
5. D. S. Siegel & K. L. Simons, 2010, Assessing the effects of mergers and acquisitions on firm performance, plant productivity, and workers: New evidence from matched employer-employee data, *Strategic Management Journal*, 31: 903–916; X. Yin & M. Shanley, 2008, Industry determinants of the "merger versus alliance" decision, *Academy of Management Review*, 33: 473–491.
6. R. Kapoor & K. Lim, 2007, The impact of acquisitions on the productivity of inventors at semiconductor firms: A synthesis of knowledge-based and incentive-based perspectives, *Academy of Management Journal*, 50: 1133–1155.

7. C. Marquis & M. Lounsbury, 2007, Vive la resistance: Competing logics and the consolidation of U.S. community banking, *Academy of Management Journal*, 50: 799–820.
8. A. R. Sorkin, 2007, When unequals try to merge as equals, *New York Times*, www.nytimes.com, February 25.
9. T. S. Gabrielsen, 2003, Conglomerate mergers: Vertical mergers in disguise? *International Journal of the Economics of Business*, 10(1): 1–16.
10. S. Ellison & M. Karnitschnig, 2007, Murdoch wins his bid for Dow Jones, *The Wall Street Journal*, http://online.wsj.com, August 1; A. Lashinsky, 2004, Murdoch's air war, *Fortune*, December 13: 131–138.
11. J. Haleblian, C. E. Devers, G. McNamara, M. A. Carpenter, & R. B. Davison, 2009, Taking stock of what we know about mergers and acquisitions: A review and Research Agenda, *Journal of Management*, 35: 469–502.
12. H. A. Krishnan, M. A. Hitt, & D. Park, 2007, Acquisition premiums, subsequent workforce reductions and postacquisition performance, *Journal of Management Studies*, 44: 709–732.
13. G. M. McNamara, J. Haleblian, & B. J. Dykes, 2008, The performance implications of participating in an acquisition wave: Early mover advantages, bandwagon effects, and the moderating influence of industry characteristics and acquirer tactics, *Academy of Management Journal*, 51: 113–130.

14. G. K. Lee & M. B. Lieberman, 2010, Acquisition vs. internal development as modes of market entry, *Strategic Management Journal*, 31: 140–158.

15. Z. Lin, M. W. Peng, H. Yang, & S. L. Sun, 2009, How do networks and learning drive M&As? An institutional comparison between China and the United States, *Strategic Management Journal*, 30: 1113–1132.

16. S.-F. Chen, 2008, The motives for international acquisitions: Capability procurements, strategic considerations, and the role of ownership structures, *Journal of International Business Studies*, 39: 454–471.

17. M. Makri, M. A. Hitt, & P. J. Lane, 2010, Complementary technologies, knowledge relatedness, and invention outcomes in high technology mergers and acquisitions, *Strategic Management Journal*, 31: 602–628; K. Ruckman, 2009, Technology sourcing acquisitions, *Journal of Strategy and Management*, 2: 58–75.

18. L. Wang & E. J. Zajac, 2007, Alliance or acquisition? A dyadic perspective on interfirm resource combinations, *Strategic Management Journal*, 28: 1291–1317.

19. A. L. Ranft & M. D. Lord, 2002, Acquiring new technologies and capabilities: A grounded model of acquisition implementation, *Organization Science*, 13: 420–441.

20. J. Gammelgaard, 2004, Access to competence: An emerging acquisition motive, *European Business Forum*, Spring: 44–48.

21. M. Warner, 2002, Can GE light up the market again? *Fortune*, November 11: 108–117.

22. D. Miller, I. Le Breton-Miller, & R. H. Lester, 2010, Family ownership and acquisition behavior in publicly-traded companies, *Strategic Management Journal*, 31: 201–223.

23. D. R. Dalton, M. A. Hitt, S. T. Certo, & C. M. Dalton, 2008, The fundamental agency problem and its mitigation: Independence, equity and the market for corporate control, in J. P. Walsh & A. P. Brief (Eds.), *The Academy of Management Annals*, New York: Lawrence Erlbaum Associates, 1–64.

24. L. Capron & J.-C. Shen, 2007, Acquisitions of private vs. public firms: Private information, target selection, and acquirer returns, *Strategic Management Journal*, 28: 891–911.

25. R. Chakrabarti, S. Gupta-Mukherjee, & N. Jayaraman, 2009, Mars-Venus marriages: Culture and cross-border M&A, *Journal of International Business Studies*, 40: 216–236.

26. M. Graebner, 2009, Caveat emptor: Trust asymmetries in acquisitions of entrepreneurial firms, *Academy of Management Journal*, 52: 435–472.

27. G. Cullinan, J.-M. Le Roux, & R.-M. Weddigen, 2004, When to walk away from a deal, *Harvard Business Review*, 82(4): 96–104.

28. M. Farhadi & G. Tovstiga, 2010, Intellectual property management in M&A transactions, *Journal of Strategy and Management*, 3: 32–49.

29. A. Vance, 2010, H.P.'s bidding war with Dell underscores the demand for data storage, *New York Times*, http://www.nytimes.com, August 23; I.I.P. raises its bid for 3Par again, topping Dell, 2010, *New York Times*, http://www.nytimes.com, August 27.

30. M. Y. Brannen & M. F. Peterson, 2009, Merging without alienating: Interventions promoting cross-cultural organizational integration and their limitations, *Journal of International Business Studies*, 40: 468–489.

31. M. Blyler & R. W. Coff, 2003, Dynamic capabilities, social capital, and rent appropriation: Ties that split pies, *Strategic Management Journal*, 24: 677–697.

32. A. E. Rafferty & S. L. D. Restburg, 2010, The impact of change process and context on change reactions and turnover during a merger, *Journal of Management*, 36: 1309–1338.

33. J. A. Krug, 2009, Brain drain: Why top management bolts after M&As, *Journal of Business Strategy*, 30(6): 4–14.

34. K. M. Ellis, T. H. Reus, & B. T. Lamont, 2009, The effects of procedural and informational justice in the integration of related acquisitions, *Strategic Management Journal*, 30: 137–161.

35. L. Capron & M. Guillen, 2009, National corporate governance institutions and post-acquisition target reorganization, *Strategic Management Journal*, 30: 803–833; T. Laamanen, 2007, On the role of acquisition premium in acquisition research, *Strategic Management Journal*, 28: 1359–1369.

36. Y. Weber & E. Menipaz, 2003, Measuring cultural fit in mergers and acquisitions, *International Journal of Business Performance Management*, 5(1): 54–72.

37. A. K. Bucholtz, B. A. Ribbens, & I. T. Houle, 2003, The role of human capital in post-acquisition CEO departure, *Academy of Management Journal*, 46: 506–514.

38. M. A. Hitt, L. Bierman, K. Uhlenbruck, & K. Shimizu, 2006, The importance of resources in the internationalization of professional service firms: The good, the bad and the ugly, *Academy of Management Journal*, 49: 1137–1157; M. A. Hitt, L. Bierman, K. Shimizu, & R. Kochhar, 2001, Direct and moderating effects of human capital on strategy and performance in professional service firms, *Academy of Management Journal*, 44: 13–28.

39. J. A. Krug, 2003, Why do they keep leaving? *Harvard Business Review*, 81(2): 14–15; H. A. Krishnan & D. Park, 2002, The impact of workforce reduction on subsequent performance in major mergers and acquisitions: An exploratory study, *Journal of Business Research*, 55(4): 285–292.

40. D. Lovallo & D. Kahneman, 2003, Delusions of success: How optimism undermines executives' decisions, *Harvard Business Review*, 87(5): 56–64.

41. M. A. Hitt & D. L. Smart, 1994, Debt: A disciplining force for managers or a debilitating force for organizations? *Journal of Management Inquiry*, 3: 144–152.

42. K. Shimizu, 2007, Prospect theory, behavioral theory, and the threat-rigidity hypothesis: Combinative effects on organizational decisions to divest formerly acquired units, *Academy of Management Journal*, 50: 1495–1514.

43. V. Bodolica & M. Spraggon, 2009, The implementation of special attributes of CEO compensation contracts around M&A transactions, *Strategic Management Journal*, 30: 985–1011.

44. M. L. A. Hayward, 2002, When do firms learn from their acquisition experience? Evidence from 1990–1995, *Strategic Management Journal*, 23: 21–39; M. A. Hitt, J. S. Harrison, & R. D. Ireland, 2001, *Mergers and Acquisitions: A Guide to Creating Value for Stakeholders*, New York: Oxford University Press.

45. J. Pfeffer, 2003, The human factor: Curbing the urge to merge, *Business 2.0*, July: 58.

46. K. D. Brouthers & D. Dikova, 2010, Acquisitions and real options: The Greenfield alternative, *Journal of Management Studies*, 47: 1048–1071.

47. N. P. Varaiya, 1988, The "winner's curse" hypothesis and corporate takeovers, *Managerial and Decision Economics*, 9: 209–219.

48. J. L. Morrow, D. G. Sirmon, M. A. Hitt, & T. R. Holcomb, 2007, Creating value in the face of declining performance: Firm strategies and organizational recovery, *Strategic Management Journal*, 28: 271–283.

49. O. Furer, J. R. Pandian, & H. Thomas, 2007, Corporate strategy and shareholder value during decline and turnaround, *Management Decision*, 45: 372–392; K. E. Meyer & E. Lieb-Doczy, 2003, Post-acquisition restructuring as evolutionary process, *Journal of Management Studies*, 40: 459–483.

50. S. L. Gillan, J. W. Kensinger, & J. D. Martin, 2000, Value creation and corporate diversification: The case of Sears, Roebuck & Co., *Journal of Financial Economics*, 55: 103–138.

51. M. F. Wiersema & J. P. Liebeskind, 1995, The effects of leveraged buyouts on corporate growth and diversification in large firms, *Strategic Management Journal*, 16: 447–460.

52. M. Wright, R. E. Hoskisson, & L. W. Busenitz, 2001, Firm rebirth: Buyouts as facilitators of strategic growth and entrepreneurship, *Academy of Management Executive*, 15(1): 111–125.

53. T. Galpin & M. Herndon, 2008, Merger repair: When M&As go wrong, *Journal of Business Strategy*, 29: 4–12.

CHAPTER 8
Competing Across Borders

KNOWLEDGE OBJECTIVES

Reading and studying this chapter should enable you to:

1. Explain four reasons why firms pursue international strategies.

2. Understand the two major pressures leading to three dominant international strategies.

3. Describe the four basic alternative contractual modes for entering international markets and explain the trade-offs of using each.

4. Discuss how three types of advantages affect the decision about which mode of entering international markets to use.

5. Explain the three alternative types of foreign direct investment and the strategic basis for each one.

6. Describe the organizational structures that are used to implement each of the international strategies.

© Shannon Fagan, Getty Images

FOCUSING ON STRATEGY

Apple is Rolling into China

For several years, Apple avoided entering the Chinese market when many competitors could not enter fast enough. In fact, with the largest consumer market in the world, many questioned Apple's decision to stay out of the market. But, in 2008, Apple opened its first retail store in Beijing and in the summer of 2010, it opened its second store in Shanghai. It plans to open a total of 25 stores in China by the end of 2011. Apple waited to move into the Chinese market until there were enough people with significant discretionary income to afford Apple's high-technology products.

China is the world's largest handset market and the second-largest personal-computer market. Therefore, the opportunity to sell products in these markets is high. But, there is also competition with Nokia as the market leader in handsets. Apple's unique products with high demand in other markets make it a formidable competitor. Apple is selling its iPhone 3G or 3GS and not the newer iPhone 4. But, the iPhone 4 with Wi-Fi is available on the gray market via Hong Kong. China Unicom which bargained to gain the distribution rights for Apple iPhones in China was unable to gain the concessions from Apple that it did from other manufacturers. Apple was a tough negotiator but it helped that it had a products that were in high demand. In fact, analysts estimate that approximately 2 million iPhones were purchased on the gray market in 2009. Analysts estimate that 26 million smartphones (of all brands) will be sold in China in 2010.

© Jerome Favre/Bloomberg/Getty Images

In 2010, Apple's sales increased by 900 percent to $1.3 billion, with about 2 million iPhones sold in the second quarter alone. This represented approximately 23 percent of Apple's global sales of the iPhone. Apple's unique products are in high demand because they are more than a communications device. They also provide entertainment. The Apple stores sell a large assortment of apps that can be added to increase the handset's functions and value to the owner. Interestingly, Apple's iPhones have many suppliers but are assembled in China by Foxconn Technology. Although outsourcing the manufacturing assembly to China has kept the costs lower, costs will be increasing because of higher labor costs and the increasing value of the Chinese currency. But, all of Apple's competitors are in the same situation so none will likely gain a cost advantage over Apple because of the increasing costs in China.

It appears that Apple is in the early stages of a major push into the Chinese market. Its sales there are likely to grow markedly in the next decade. Thus, Apple is on a roll!

Sources: L. Chao, 2010, Playing catch-up in China, Apple opens second store, *The Wall Street Journal*, www.wsj.com, July 11; P. Elmer-DeWitt, 2010, Apple plants its flagship in Shanghai, *Fortune*, www.fortune.com, July 10; M. Lee & A. Cang, 2010, Apple opens Shanghai store to spur sales in China, *BusinessWeek*, www.businessweek.com, July 10; D. Barboza, 2010, Supply chain for iPhone highlights costs in China, *The New York Times*, www.nytimes.com, July 5; P. P. Denlinger, 2010, For Apple, the best China strategy was not having one, *Forbes*, www.forbes.com, May 6; P. Elmer-DeWitt, 2010, Apple's Chinese iPhone sales explode, *Fortune*, www.fortune.com, April 21.

As *Focusing on Strategy* indicates, expanding international operations, especially in China, is increasingly important to Apple's strategic and financial performance as it enhances the Apple products it sells throughout the world. The increase in globalization mentioned in Chapter 3 is based on several historical changes in the global business environment. In the first half of the twentieth century, firms wanting to enter new markets were frustrated because of barriers against foreign trade and investments imposed by national governments. After World War I, many countries imposed tariffs and quotas on imported goods that favored local firms; as a result, international trade declined throughout the 1930s. These tariffs and quotas contributed to the severity of the U.S. depression.

However, after World War II, these policies were reversed as major trading powers negotiated reductions in tariffs and quotas and eliminated many barriers to foreign direct investment (FDI). **Foreign direct investment** is a process through which a firm directly invests (beyond exporting and licensing) in a market outside its home country.[1] These negotiations were embodied in the General Agreement on Tariffs and Trade (GATT) and its successor organization the World Trade Organization (WTO). Furthermore, regional trading agreements such as the European Union and the North American Free Trade Agreement (NAFTA) have also relaxed trade and investment barriers among member countries. Thus, globalization has become highly important in the world economy, but equally important has been the development of new technologies and the enhanced skills and capabilities they have facilitated.[2]

Investments in technology, particularly communications and transportation technologies, are making international transactions more feasible and more profitable by reducing the costs of transactions. Similarly, use of the Internet has increased international transactions by facilitating trade in services such as banking, consulting, and retailing, by making competition between large and smaller firms more reasonable regardless of the product sold, and by creating a more efficient networking capability among businesses.

These changes are producing a new global competitive landscape where emerging-market countries are playing an increasingly important role. Countries such as Brazil, Russia, India, and China (BRIC) are having a greater impact on the global economy and provide opportunities for multinational firms to market their products and to obtain resources (e.g., quality but cheaper labor). In fact, recent predictions suggest that the BRIC countries are likely to be among the top 10 in the size of their economies within the next 30 years.[3] As a result of these changes, managers must develop a global mind-set. A **global mind-set** is a cognitive model that motivates a manager to search for opportunities in foreign markets; to develop strategies that exploit those opportunities; and to coordinate units, tasks, and people in multiple geographic locations throughout the world.[4] Apple's managers are now developing a global mind-set as evidenced by their use of many foreign suppliers and their major entry into the Chinese market.

Even though significant trends have fostered growth in international business, the costs and risks of doing business outside a firm's domestic market can be significant.[5] These costs have been labeled as the **liability of foreignness**.[6] As Chapter 4 indicated, a firm must have resources that enable it to overcome these additional costs. In this chapter, we discuss firm-specific resources as well as location advantages that help to overcome these costs.

In summary, international strategies are becoming more widespread because of the environmental and technological changes taking place in the 21st century.[7] However, firms must still have the resources necessary to formulate and implement a strategy to overcome the continuing costs of the liability of foreign entry.[8]

foreign direct investment

a process through which a firm directly invests (beyond exporting and licensing) in a market outside its home country

global mind-set

a cognitive model that motivates a manager to search for opportunities in foreign markets; to develop strategies that exploit those opportunities; and to coordinate units, tasks, and people in multiple geographic locations throughout the world

liability of foreignness

the costs and risks of doing business outside a firm's domestic market

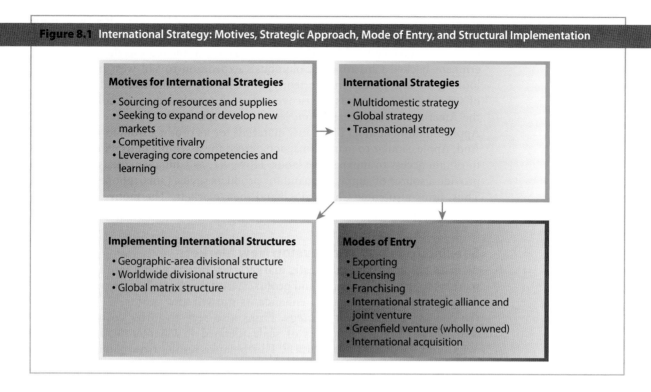

Figure 8.1 International Strategy: Motives, Strategic Approach, Mode of Entry, and Structural Implementation

Motives for International Strategies
- Sourcing of resources and supplies
- Seeking to expand or develop new markets
- Competitive rivalry
- Leveraging core competencies and learning

International Strategies
- Multidomestic strategy
- Global strategy
- Transnational strategy

Implementing International Structures
- Geographic-area divisional structure
- Worldwide divisional structure
- Global matrix structure

Modes of Entry
- Exporting
- Licensing
- Franchising
- International strategic alliance and joint venture
- Greenfield venture (wholly owned)
- International acquisition

In this chapter, as illustrated in Figure 8.1, we explore the reasons for and types of international strategies that firms use. We begin this important exploration by outlining the motives for using an international strategy. Next, we explore the basic international strategies employed by firms. After a strategy is chosen, managers must choose a mode of international entry. Finally, the firm must choose an organizational structure and accompanying processes to implement the chosen strategy.

Motives for International Strategies

A number of motives drive the use of international strategies. Next, we describe four of the most prominent motives.

Use of Current Resources and Access to New Resources

Commonly, companies seek to gain economies of scale and scope in the use of their current resources by expanding into new markets, increasingly foreign markets.[9] Firms may use their well-known products, such as those sold by Apple, to enter new international markets. Firms commonly use what is referred to as social capital—that is, partners in alliances and networks—to help them enter and compete effectively in international markets.[10] At times, some firms enter international markets to access new resources. For example, they may obtain access to valuable raw materials, specialized knowledge, or low-cost labor.[11] One resource commonly sought over the years has been valuable sources of supply.

During the Middle Ages, for example, Italy used its political and military strength in Venice, Genoa, and Florence as the foundation for its ability to be a major center of international commerce and banking. During this time, Italy was the major trading link between Europe and Asia. However, after these trade routes were severed by the Turks in 1453, European governments sought new ocean routes to the Far East. This situation is one of the reasons the Spanish government backed Christopher Columbus's expedition to sail west from Europe, looking for such routes. Inadvertently, as we know, Columbus found new sources of supply in the Americas, a discovery that ultimately led to the colonization of the Americas by European countries. As we explained in *Focusing on Strategy,* Apple obtains a number of the raw materials for its product from foreign sources. And, Apple, similar to many firms, outsourced the assembly of its iPhone to China to obtain access to inexpensive labor. However, as China's markets continue to provide a source of supply, demand for products such as smartphones is growing. Thus, firms also enter China to expand their markets. The motive to expand a firm's potential market is discussed next.

Seeking to Expand or Develop New Markets

As firms mature in their domestic market, they often expand into international markets to increase revenues and profits. Certainly, Apple has expanded further into international markets to enhance its growth and profits, as described in the opening *Focusing on Strategy.* Firms also seek to lower costs of production by developing economies of scale (defined in Chapter 3). International expansion balances a firm's risk.[12] This balance results from the firm's ability to sell in multiple markets, reducing its dependency on sales in any one market.[13] To show the magnitude of international strategies, think of how many of the products you use are made by a foreign company, such as your car, your stereo system, and your clothes. This clearly highlights the global nature of the world's economy.

Competitive Rivalry

Some businesses enter foreign markets to enhance their ability to compete with major rivals. They may do so to build economies of scale or scope, allowing them to compete better across all markets. Or they may do so to prevent or reduce a rival's competitive advantage.[14] For example, Coca-Cola and PepsiCo are both aggressively expanding their international operations. Of course, each firm is trying to prevent the other from gaining a competitive advantage in global markets.[15] If Pepsi or Coke gained a significant advantage in global markets, the additional profitability earned as a result of that advantage could be used to damage the competitor in the all-important U.S. market. About 40 percent of PepsiCo's revenues come from international markets.[16] The relationship between earth-moving equipment firms Caterpillar and Komatsu are similar as each firm actively competes against its rival in global markets.[17] This competitive rivalry exists to prevent a competitor from gaining a significant advantage in any one country or region.

Interestingly, other firms pursue international ventures to avoid domestic competition. In the local Japanese automobile market, competition is very intense because of the number of large firms competing in the local market, including Toyota, Honda, Nissan, Mazda, Mitsubishi, Suzuki, Subaru, Isuzu, and Daihatsu. Part of the reason for moving into the international market was the nature of domestic competition.[18] Japanese automakers have largely been successful in their international ventures, especially in the U.S. market, competing against the two primary U.S. auto firms, Ford and General Motors. Yet, as we learn in *Understanding Strategy: Learning from Failure,* Toyota has experienced some significant problems in recent years opening the way for a revival of Ford and General Motors in the U.S. market.

Leveraging Core Competencies and Learning

As we discussed in Chapter 4, firms invest heavily to develop core competencies. After a firm has developed a core competence that contributes to a competitive advantage in its domestic market, the firm may be able to use that competitive advantage in international markets as well. Research has shown that competitive advantages based on knowledge-based resources often contained in core competencies produce faster and larger international expansion than do physical asset-based advantages (e.g., property).[19] When the competitive advantage is in R&D, the firm may have the foundation needed to rely on innovation as the source of entry to international markets. We speak further on the use of innovation to enter new markets in Chapter 10.

Learning is also an important reason for international expansion. Firms often invest in countries that have centers of excellence in industries such as semiconductors. These firms enter international markets to gain access to product and manufacturing process knowledge.[20] For example, large pharmaceutical firms form alliances with foreign partners to learn about new drug research that could lead to developing and introducing new products into their domestic market.

As explained in *Understanding Strategy: Learning from Failure,* internalization actions are not always successful over time. Toyota experienced a lot of success, perhaps too much. It became insensitive to reports of defective products and the company's lack of response led to deaths and injuries for several of its customers, a recall of almost 8.5 million vehicles and a significant loss of reputation for the firm. The complexities of global operations and coordination difficulties are shown by its major delays in responding to reports of serious defects in its vehicles. Research supports the notion that international expansion causes difficulties for firms and sometimes is not profitable because of these challenges.[21]

We've discussed motives influencing firms to use strategies to compete in international markets, and we have learned the costs of international expansion as well. As you would expect, firms can choose from several different strategies to compete in international markets. We discuss these strategies in the next few sections.

International Strategies

Firms consider two important and potentially competing issues when choosing an international strategy: the need for global efficiencies and the need to customize a good or service for a particular host country market.[22] Generally, efficiency increases when the firm can sell its current good or service in multiple international markets. In contrast, the need for customization to serve international markets increases when the firm sells a good or service that must be adapted specifically to a particular local market.

Firms seeking global efficiency may decide to locate in countries where their production and distribution costs will be low. For example, a firm may locate in a country with low labor costs. It might also obtain economies of scale by building factories that can serve customers in more than a single country. Alternatively, by broadening their product line in countries they enter, firms can achieve economies of scope and thereby reduce their production and marketing costs for related products.

Toyota Cannot "Recall" its Glory Days Because It Colonized Instead of Globalized

Toyota received more than 2,000 complaints about unexplained acceleration in some of its vehicles but it responded to them slowly and with suggestions that it was due to loose floor mats. Yet, when an off-duty highway patrol officer and three members of his family were killed in a collision due to sudden acceleration and brake failure, Toyota executives finally decided that they had a problem and must respond. In fact, it became so serious that the President, grandson of the founder, took charge of dealing with the problem, beginning with a formal apology.

There seemed to be at least three basic problems leading to the tragic outcomes for customers and for the company. First, the former CEO, Katsuaki Watanabe, pressured the chief engineers, called shusas, to cut costs in order to increase profits. They did so, perhaps too aggressively in some cases because it led to quality problems. Second, the company left the foreign affiliates to their own devices in handling the problems. The international organizations were unable to provide feedback on the problems in design and manufacturing which needed to be corrected. So, the problems were not resolved. And, finally, the company executives seem to have become enamored with their success. They needed to practice humility but instead exhibited hubris. They did not

With failures in quality control, lack of oversight of foreign affiliates, and a slow response from corporate executives to the unfolding crisis, President Toyoda was forced to personally step in to manage the fallout from escalating reports of safety concerns with numerous Toyota vehicles.

listen to the problems. President Toyoda explained it this way: "It was as if we were engaged in car manufacturing in a virtual world and became insensitive to vehicle failings and defects in the market."

Unfortunately, much damage was done to Toyota's reputation. Ultimately, Toyota had to recall more than 8 million vehicles to fix the problems identified. Mr. Toyoda, the president, had to testify before a U.S. congressional committee and take other actions as well to mollify an angry public. In 2010, the company assigned 1,000 engineers to help analyze and correct quality problems before vehicles were taken to the market. Fortunately, the several steps taken seem to correct the problem and hopefully will prevent future ones like this from occurring. Only with time can we determine if the problems have been truly resolved and how much damage has been done to Toyota's reputation.

Sources: A. Taylor, III, 2010, How Toyota lost its way, *Fortune*, July 26, pp. 108–117; M. Ramsey, 2010, Toyota assigns 1,000 engineers to quality drive, *The Wall Street Journal*, www.wsj.com, July 7; S. Pope, 2010, A bad odor from Toyota, *Forbes*, www.forbes.com, February 19; 2010, The Toyota Recall: Understanding the real problem, *BusinessWeek*, www.businessweek.com, February 9; B. Vlasic, 2010, Toyota's slow awakening to a deadly problem, *The New York Times*, www.nytimes.com, February 1; A. Ohnsman & M. Kitamura, 2010, Is Toyota's reputation finished? *BusinessWeek*, www.businessweek.com, January 28.

In some international settings, firms can be more successful by customizing their products to meet local market tastes and interests. For instance, KFC adapted its restaurant foods to fit the culture and taste preferences of local markets. KFC offers more fish dishes in Asian countries and less chicken, for example. Language can also present challenges as the following indicates: "Pepsi-Cola went into Taiwan and carefully translated its slogan, 'Come alive with the Pepsi generation.'

Figure 8.2 International Strategies

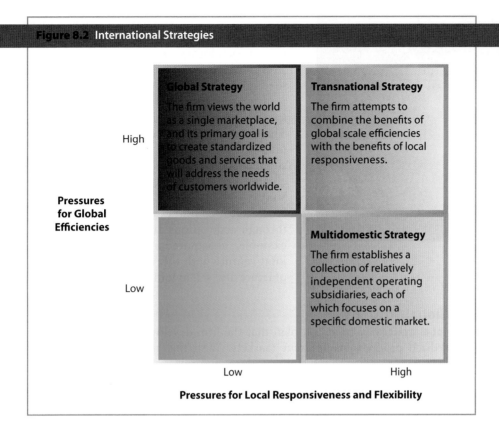

Global Strategy

The firm views the world as a single marketplace, and its primary goal is to create standardized goods and services that will address the needs of customers worldwide.

Transnational Strategy

The firm attempts to combine the benefits of global scale efficiencies with the benefits of local responsiveness.

Multidomestic Strategy

The firm establishes a collection of relatively independent operating subsidiaries, each of which focuses on a specific domestic market.

Pressures for Global Efficiencies — High, Low

Pressures for Local Responsiveness and Flexibility — Low, High

However, the translation came out as 'Pepsi will bring your ancestors back from the dead.' And, KFC's slogan 'Finger licking good,' in Chinese translates to, 'Eat your fingers off.'"[23]

As shown in Figure 8.2, the need for global efficiency and the need to satisfy a local host country market's unique needs result in a two-dimensional matrix that illustrates the different global strategies. We next describe the three international strategies shown in Figure 8.2.

The Multidomestic Strategy

The **multidomestic strategy** is an action plan that the firm develops to produce and sell unique products in different markets. To use this strategy, a firm establishes a relatively independent set of operating subsidiaries in which each subsidiary develops specific products for a particular domestic market. Each subsidiary is free to customize its products' marketing campaign and operating techniques to best meet the needs of local customers. The multidomestic strategy is particularly effective when clear differences between national markets exist; potential economies of scale for production, distribution, and marketing are low; and the cost of coordination between the parent and foreign subsidiaries is high. Because each subsidiary must be responsive to the local market, the parent usually delegates considerable power and authority to managers of host country subsidiaries. Many multinational corporations used the multidomestic strategy during World War II because it was difficult to communicate and transfer technologies. Many European firms also adopted this strategy because

multidomestic strategy

an action plan that the firm develops to produce and sell unique products in different markets

© AFP/Getty Images

Thales SA has become a local supplier of aerospace electronics in six countries outside of its home market in France through use of the multidomestic strategy.

of the cultural and language differences they needed to overcome in order to conduct business in each European country.

In the early part of the 21st century, the French defense contractor Thomson-CSF transformed into a global defense and aerospace electronics group called Thales SA. Thales won contracts worldwide by using a multidomestic strategy. It has become a local supplier in six countries outside France, including Britain, the Netherlands, Australia, South Africa, South Korea, and Singapore. However, it continues to expand its network through acquisitions and joint ventures. For example, it acquired Alcatel and formed a joint venture with the Samtel Group to manufacture and sell avionics systems in India.[24]

The Global Strategy

The **global strategy** is an action plan that the firm develops to produce and sell standardized products in different markets. With this strategy, a firm uses a central divisional office to develop, produce, and sell its standardized products throughout the world. A firm using a global strategy seeks to capture economies of scale in production and marketing, as well as economies of scope and location advantage. Because the global strategy requires worldwide coordination, the production and marketing strategies are usually centralized with decisions made at a division headquarters. Mercedes-Benz, a unit of Daimler, uses the global strategy to sell its products in many global markets. This strategy is successful for Mercedes-Benz because its products are known for their quality and reliability.[25] Toyota followed this strategy and it created problems because the design decisions were made in its home office in Japan and U.S. operations were unable to communicate the problems (or unable to get headquarters' managers to listen) to the home office managers. Thus, care must be taken with the global strategy.

Because of the importance of a particular location for access to critical customers and markets or access to financial resources, a firm may move its headquarters to a foreign setting.[26] It is important to note that at times, the global strategy presents difficulties in marketing the firm's standardized products to local consumer markets. For example, both Microsoft and Nintendo encountered difficulty using a global strategy to sell their platforms (Xbox for Microsoft; GameCube for Nintendo) outside their home markets.

The Transnational Strategy

The **transnational strategy** involves the firm producing and selling somewhat unique, yet somewhat standardized, products in different markets. With this strategy, the firm attempts to combine the benefits of global scale efficiencies with the advantages of being locally responsive in a country or geographic region; it requires both centralization and decentralization simultaneously. As such, managers have to think globally but also customize the products to the local markets as well.[27] IKEA, a worldwide furniture producer, employs the

global strategy

an action plan that the firm develops to produce and sell standardized products in different markets

transnational strategy

an action plan that the firm develops to produce and sell somewhat unique, yet somewhat standardized, products in different markets transnational strategy. In using this strategy, IKEA relies on standardization of products with global production and distribution, but it also has a system (called "democratic design") through which new designs for local markets are developed and introduced. Democratic design is helping IKEA produce products that meet the tastes of local customers. IKEA is a world leader in furniture production and distribution with 313 stores in 37 different countries in 2010.[28]

Although the transnational strategy is more difficult to manage and expensive to implement, it is often the most effective international strategy in facilitating learning. The balance of centralization and decentralization usually results in a corporate culture that promotes transfer of knowledge among subsidiaries and a transnational diffusion of organizational practices.[29] The multidomestic strategy uses a decentralized authority structure. This structure makes it difficult to transfer knowledge across subsidiaries. The global strategy, on the other hand, centralizes decision making, which hampers new knowledge development. When using the global strategy, the firm learns less from different host country markets because of its focus on exploiting the firm's current knowledge in each of the markets rather than learning from each market to adapt the products.

As suggested in *Understanding Strategy: Learning from Success,* Nestlé has been highly successful in global markets and is trying new ways of entering unique markets such as those in Brazil. The "floating stores" are a unique form of a greenfield venture. Nestlé continues to develop products and adapt them for new and existing markets in different parts of the world through its R&D centers and creative marketing programs. Its global success is evident as it is the largest food company in the world.

Modes of International Market Entry

After a firm decides to pursue an international strategy, it must choose a mode for entering new foreign markets. Factors affecting the choice of an entry mode are presented in Figure 8.3 (see p. 177).[30] These factors include firm-specific resource advantages, country-specific or location advantages, internal coordination or administrative advantages, need for control, and resource availability. We begin with an explanation of each mode of entry followed by a discussion of how each potential advantage affects the choice of entry mode.

Entry Modes

Exporting Perhaps the simplest and most common mode of entry is exporting domestic products to a foreign country. **Exporting** is the process of sending goods and services from one country to another for distribution, sale, and service. The advantage of exporting is that the firm can gradually enter an international market without taking too many risks. Exporting also has the advantage of helping the firm to acquire knowledge about a local market before making large investments.[31] But exporting isn't without problems. Firms exporting their products are vulnerable to tariffs and often encounter logistical challenges in getting products to an international market and especially to the ultimate consumer in those

exporting

the process of sending goods and services from one country to another for distribution, sale, and service

Globalized Nestlé Investing in Emerging Markets

Nestlé is the world's largest food company with operations in 86 countries and employs approximately 283,000 people. Even so, it continues to seek out new markets for its products. For example, Nestlé plans to obtain 45 percent of its total sales from emerging markets by 2020. In 2009 approximately 32 percent of its total sales came from markets in Asia, Latin America, and Africa. It continues to expand in these regions as well. For example, it recently launched a major effort in Brazil to provide branded goods to customers along the Amazon who do not have easy access to such products. To reach them, it is sailing a barge down the Amazon river and its tributaries with 300 different products for sale. The boat will sail to 18 small cities. Why is Nestlé taking this and similar actions in additional emerging market countries? Nestlé projects that almost one billion people will increase their incomes beyond the poverty level in these markets and thus will be able to afford the products. To make the sales feasible at this point, Nestlé has adapted the products to offer smaller packages that are cheaper. It has employed 7,000 saleswomen to market their goods to underprivileged groups in Brazil. The company adds vitamins to the foods it sells there to improve the health of the poorer people. Brazil, which is the largest economy in Latin America, grew by 9 percent in the first quarter of 2010. This growth is expected to continue for the foreseeable future.

The global nature of Nestlé, which is based in Switzerland, is observable in its recent action to increase the size of its regional R&D center in Singapore. This facility does research on various beverages, examining the opportunity to create more affordable and accessible versions of Nestlé's products. For example, Nestlé has developed a machine that dispenses smaller packets of its products than its normal packages. Its research on beverages, particularly coffee has significance because Singapore consumes 350 million cups of coffee mixes annually. Nestlé's pod coffee machines and single serving coffee pods (mixes) which have been popular in Europe represent a major opportunity for the Asian markets.

Nestlé is also taking the U.S. style diet plans to Europe hoping to capitalize on the global health craze. Its Jenny Craig business has been highly profitable since it was purchased in 2006. This business is expected to increase in importance because the World Health Organization predicts that 2.3 billion people will be overweight by 2015. Because weight problems are increasing in several European countries, Nestlé sees nutrition and dieting as a good business opportunity in the coming years. Therefore, Nestlé expects to continue its successful growth and profits over the next decade or more using these strategies.

Sources: 2010, Nestle sets up regional hub for innovation in Singapore, *Channel News Asia*, www.channelnewsasia.com, July 23; G. Mijuk, 2010, Nestle bets on emerging markets, *The Wall Street Journal*, www.wsj.com, June 22; T. Mulier & L. Dantas, 2010, Nestle to sail Amazon rivers to reach consumers, *BusinessWeek*, www.businessweek.com, June 17; M. Saltmarsh, 2010, *The New York Times*, www.nytimes.com, May 19; M. Saltmarsh, 2010, Nestle bringing American-style diet plans to Europe, *The New York Times*, www.nytimes.com, March 7; 2010, Nestle, *Wikipedia*, accessed January 25.

With a goal of obtaining nearly half of its total sales from emerging markets by 2020, Nestle is investing heavily to introduce and adapt its most successful brands to increasingly diverse groups of customers across the globe.

© Image Register 010 / Alamy

© Greg Epperson, iStock

markets. Exporting firms also are likely to be in conflict with local distributors who may want to distribute the firm's products instead.

Licensing is the process of entering an international market by leasing the right to use the firm's intellectual property—technology, work methods, patents, copyrights, brand names, or trademarks—to a firm doing business in

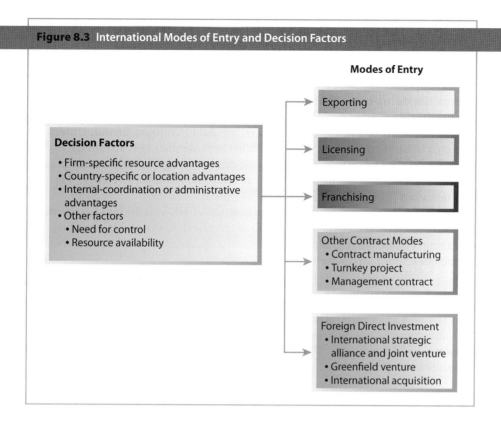

Figure 8.3 **International Modes of Entry and Decision Factors**

the targeted international market. The firm doing the leasing is the licensor, and the firm receiving the license is the licensee. Licensing is popular because it involves little direct cost or risk for the licensor. Electronic Arts successfully uses this strategy as it licenses games worldwide to game platform or hardware producers such as Sony (PlayStation), Nintendo (GameCube), and Microsoft (Xbox). These firms are willing to pay a license fee to Electronic Arts to have rights to the firm's innovative games and titles. Through licensing, Electronic Arts generates revenues and develops new video games, thereby stimulating further demand for its games and other products. The firm had sales revenue of approximately $3.7 billion in 2010.[32] Although licensing has low financial risks, it provides few opportunities for profit growth. Licensing may provide a low-cost means to assess market potential, but it also creates dependence on the licensee for exploiting that potential. Another risk is that the licensee can learn the technology and become a competitor of the licensor. Microsoft, for instance, is a software producer and has produced its own video games.

Franchising Franchising is a special form of licensing and is discussed further in Chapter 9 as a cooperative strategy. **Franchising** is the licensing of a good or service and business model to partners for specified fees (usually a signing fee and a percentage of the franchisee's revenues or profits). The franchisor provides trademarks, operating systems, and well-known products as well as service support such as advertising, specialized training, and quality-assurance programs. McDonald's has developed a successful global franchising system. Pizza Hut, KFC, and Taco Bell have also franchised restaurants worldwide.

licensing

the process of entering an international market by leasing the right to use the firm's intellectual property—technology, work methods, patents, copyrights, brand names, or trademarks—to a firm doing business in the targeted international market

franchising

the licensing of a good or service and business model to partners for specified fees (usually a signing fee and a percentage of the franchisee's revenues or profits)

Benetton uses franchised retail stores to distribute stylish clothing in more than 120 countries.

Other Contracting Modes Contract manufacturing is another popular contractual mode of entry. Large firms in Asia, such as Taiwan Semiconductor Manufacturing Company (TSMC), manufacture chips for large clients such as Hewlett-Packard (HP). TSMC and other big Asian contract manufacturers are expected to do better than smaller U.S. firms because their cost advantage in Asia has attracted large clients, such as HP, that can invest significant amounts of capital, thereby enabling the manufacturers to keep their competitive edge. The cost of a new chip plant requires more than $2 billion.

Similarly, turnkey projects, often construction projects to build large infrastructure facilities such as coal- or gas-fired electrical power plants, are done on a contractual basis. Management agreements to operate such facilities are handled on a contractual basis as well.

Approaches to Foreign Direct Investment With FDI entry modes, the firm has greater control of its destiny in the international market it enters, but FDI investments are not insulated from risk.[33] Next, we discuss three approaches to FDI: strategic alliances and joint ventures, greenfield ventures, and acquisitions.

International Strategic Alliances and Joint Ventures

International strategic alliances represent a cooperative agreement in which home and host country firms work closely together.[34] In the case of a joint venture, "working together" results in creating a separate company to promote the partners' mutual interests (joint ventures and strategic alliances are discussed further in Chapter 9).[35] Firms in emerging economies often want to form international alliances and ventures to gain access to sophisticated technologies that are new to them (learning from their partner).[36] This type of arrangement can benefit the foreign firm as well, providing access to a new market without the firm paying tariffs to do so (because of its local partner). However, the firm with the valuable technology needs to ensure that its partner doesn't copy it.[37] Therefore, in the selection of a partner, it is important to choose one that is reliable and trustworthy.[38]

Greenfield Venture

greenfield venture

a venture in which a firm buys or leases land, constructs a new facility and hires or transfers managers and employees, and then independently launches a new operation (commonly called a *wholly owned subsidiary*) without involvement of a partner

In a **greenfield venture**, a firm buys or leases land, constructs a new facility, and hires or transfers managers and employees, and then independently launches a new operation (commonly called a *wholly owned subsidiary*) without involvement of a partner. The firm maintains full control of its operations with a greenfield venture. More control is especially advantageous if the firm has proprietary technology. Research also suggests that "wholly owned subsidiaries and expatriate staff are preferred" in service industries where "close contacts with end customers" and "high levels of professional skills, specialized know-how, and customization" are required.[39] The major disadvantage with a greenfield venture launched in an international market is that it takes time to implement and gain acceptance in the market.[40] A lack of experience with and knowledge about the international local market makes it difficult for the greenfield venture to have rapid success. Therefore, firms establishing greenfield ventures in international markets need to be patient in order to achieve success with the venture.[41]

International Acquisition

The final FDI entry mode is one in which a firm acquires an existing host country firm. By acquiring a current business, the purchaser gains control over the acquired firm's assets, employees, technology, brand names, and distribution. Therefore, entry is much faster than by other modes. Walmart entered Germany and the United Kingdom by acquiring local firms.

Using the acquisition entry mode is not without risk. The main risk centers on the fact that the acquiring firm often assumes all of the acquired firm's liabilities.[42] Complicating cross-border acquisitions is the fact that the firms are commonly from countries with different cultures and institutional frameworks.[43] Thus, integrating the two firms can be more difficult.[44] This factor was one of the problems leading to the failure of the merger between Daimler (German firm) and Chrysler (U.S. firm). The risk in these acquisitions is also illustrated by Walmart's withdrawal from the German market only a few years after it entered.

We've explored the entry modes available to firms that want to enter international markets. Next, we consider the factors influencing the firm's choice of an entry mode, as illustrated in Figure 8.3.

Factors Affecting the Selection of Entry Mode

Firm-Specific Resource Advantages

Firm-specific resource advantages are the core competencies that provide a competitive advantage over a firm's rivals.[45] As we recall from our discussions in Chapter 4, core competencies are often based largely on intangible resources. When the success of a firm's entry into an international market relies on transferring core competencies, an entry mode involving an equity stake should be used.[46]

Therefore, a joint venture, an acquisition, and a greenfield venture represent the best entry mode choices in these cases because the firm retains more control over its competencies. However, if the firm-specific advantage is a brand name, which is protected by law, a licensing or franchising entry mode may be a better choice.

Country-Specific or Location Advantages

Country-specific or location advantages are concerned with the desirability of producing in the home country versus locating production and distribution assets in the host

country-specific or location advantages

advantages that are concerned with the desirability of producing in the home country versus locating production and distribution assets in the host country

With it advantageous location at the crossroads of Europe and Asia and cultural ties to surrounding markets, many firms have found great benefit in locating various assets in Turkey.

GNU Free Documentation License

country.[47] If country-specific advantages for production are stronger in the home country, exporting is likely the best choice for entering an international market. Such location advantages can be influenced by costs of production and transportation requirements as well as the needs of the intended customers. Many firms, for instance, have located their assets in Turkey because its geographic, religious, linguistic, and cultural ties provide opportunities to enter Central Asian markets of the former Soviet Union as well as markets in the Middle East.[48]

However, political risks such as the likelihood of terror or war, unstable governments, and government corruption may discourage direct investments in a host country. Government policies can also influence the mode of entry.[49] For example, high tariffs discourage exporting and encourage local production through direct investments. Similarly, economic risks such as currency fluctuations may create problems for international investment. If a currency is devalued, so are the assets invested through FDI in that country. When the dollar has a lower value than other currencies, such as the euro, it supports U.S. exports. However, the lower value of the dollar hurts foreign exporters coming into the United States from countries with a higher-valued currency. Cultural influences may also affect location advantages and disadvantages. A strong match between the cultures in which international transactions are carried out lowers the liability of foreignness in cases of greater cultural distance.[50]

Internal Coordination or Administrative Advantages

Internal coordination or administrative advantages make it desirable for a firm to produce the good or service rather than contracting with another firm to produce or distribute it.[51] When a firm outsources the manufacture and distribution of a product, it experiences transaction costs, or the costs of negotiating, monitoring, and enforcing the contract. If these costs are high, a firm may rely on some form of FDI rather than using exporting or contracting (such as licensing or franchising) as an entry mode. After choosing an appropriate entry mode, the firm must implement its international strategy. Next, we discuss the different organizational structures firms use to implement the multidomestic, global, and transnational international strategies.

Implementing the Multidomestic Strategy

The geographic-area divisional structure is used to implement the multidomestic strategy (see Figure 8.4). The **geographic-area divisional structure** is a decentralized organizational structure that enables each division to focus on a geographic area, region, or country.[52] This structure is particularly useful for firms selling products with characteristics that frequently change (such as clothing). The geographic-area structure facilitates managers' actions that tailor the product mix to meet the cultural or special tastes of local customers. However, cost efficiencies are often sacrificed when using the geographic-area structure. Indeed, economies of scale are difficult to achieve using this structure because each country has unique products. The disadvantage of this structure, then, is duplication of resources across the divisions; for example, each division has its own functional marketing specialists and production facilities. Coordination across divisions is also difficult and expensive due to the decentralization.[53]

internal coordination or administrative advantages

advantages that make it desirable for a firm to produce the good or service rather than contracting with another firm to produce or distribute it

geographic-area divisional structure

a decentralized organizational structure that enables each division to focus on a geographic area, region, or country

Figure 8.4 Using the Geographic-Area Divisional Structure to Implement the Multidomestic Strategy

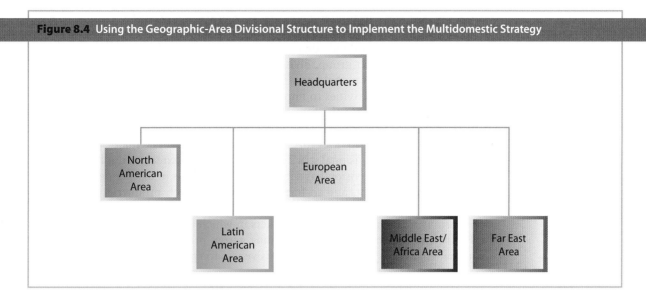

Implementing the Global Strategy

The worldwide divisional structure is used to implement the global strategy (see Figure 8.5). The **worldwide divisional structure** is a centralized organizational structure in which each product group is housed in a globally focused worldwide division or worldwide profit center.[54] In this structure, the first organizational

worldwide divisional structure

a centralized organizational structure in which each product group is housed in a globally focused worldwide division or worldwide profit center

Figure 8.5 Using the Worldwide Divisional Structure to Implement the Global Strategy

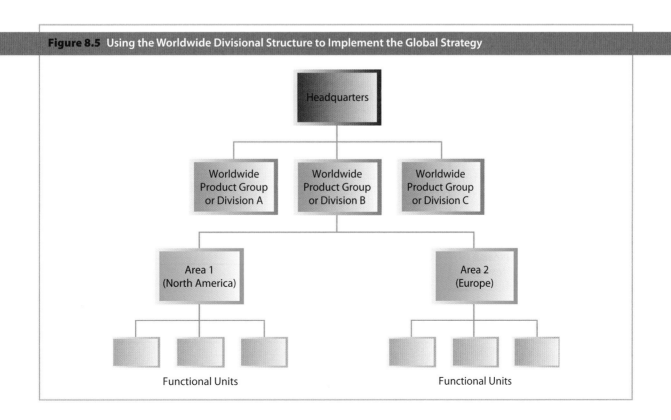

level below corporate headquarters is that of worldwide product divisions. The development and commercialization of new products for global markets is the responsibility of the worldwide division. Because a specific division focuses on a single product or product group, division managers are exposed to all aspects of managing products on a global basis. This experience helps managers learn how to integrate the firm's activities to improve manufacturing efficiency and responsiveness—abilities that help the firm adjust production requirements to fluctuating global demand. This approach requires global standardization in management practices, policies, and activities throughout the division.[55] The major disadvantage of the worldwide divisional structure is that it allows extensive duplication of activities because each division has similar functional skills in marketing, finance, information management, and so forth. Additionally, each product group must develop its own knowledge about the cultural, legal, and political environments of the various regional and national markets in which the various divisions operate. Furthermore, coordination and learning across product groups are difficult. These challenges also result in low responsiveness to specific country needs.

global matrix structure

an organizational structure in which both functional and product expertise are integrated into teams so the teams will be able to respond quickly to requirements in the global marketplace

Implementing the Transnational Strategy

The transnational strategy is usually implemented through a global matrix structure (see Figure 8.6).[56] The **global matrix structure** is an organizational structure in which both functional expertise and product expertise are integrated into teams

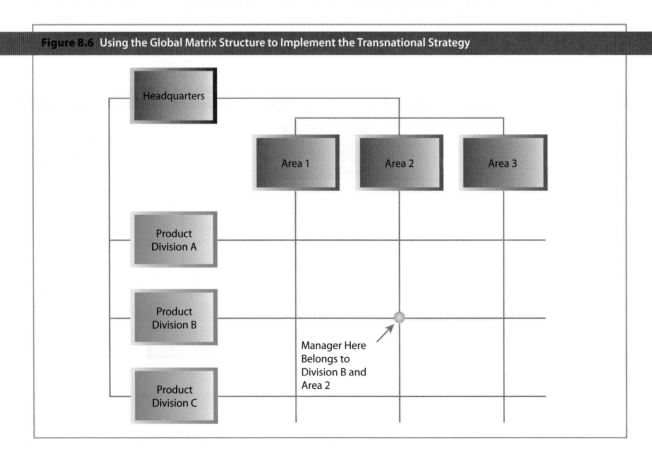

Figure 8.6 Using the Global Matrix Structure to Implement the Transnational Strategy

Headquarters

Area 1   Area 2   Area 3

Product Division A

Product Division B

Product Division C

Manager Here Belongs to Division B and Area 2

so the teams are able to respond quickly to requirements in the global market-place. The global matrix structure promotes flexibility in designing products and responding to customer needs from different geographical areas. However, employees are accountable to more than one manager. In fact, at any given time, an employee may be a member of several cross-functional or product or cross-geographical teams and may find it difficult to be loyal to all of them. Although the global matrix structure gives authority to managers who are most able to use it, the corporate reporting relationships are so complex and vague that it often takes longer to approve major decisions. This type of structure requires considerable coordination to ensure the sharing of knowledge within and across global teams.[57]

Most firms now operate in international markets. Therefore, international strategies and the organizational structures used to implement them are highly relevant to you.

SUMMARY

The primary purpose of this chapter is to examine firm strategies that extend across national borders. In doing so, we examined the following topics:

- The use of international strategies is increasing as firms seek to gain access to new markets and to valuable resources or to reduce their labor costs. The Internet and other technological innovations, such as those in logistics, facilitate global business transactions. Reduced regulations and tariffs also foster opportunities for the use of international strategies. These changes are producing a new global competitive landscape in which emerging market countries are playing an increasingly important role. Countries such as Brazil, Russia, India, and China (BRIC countries) are having a greater impact on the global economy. This changing global competitive landscape creates a need for managers to develop a global mind-set. A global mind-set is a cognitive model that motivates a manager to search for opportunities in foreign markets; to develop strategies that exploit those opportunities; and to coordinate units, tasks, and people in different geographic locations throughout the world.
- International strategies are driven by four major motives: (1) to reduce costs and secure resources, (2) to increase economies of scale and scope and

to capitalize on opportunities to secure desirable locations, (3) to respond to pressure by rivals that have moved into regions untapped by others, and (4) to seek learning and other advantages that provide new knowledge from international markets.
- Firms going abroad usually select one of three international strategies. Firms use a multidomestic strategy to sell products that are customized to the needs of individual host country markets. This international strategy works best when decision-making authority is decentralized to each business so it can operate freely in separate regions or countries. The decentralized authority allows the business to adapt its goods and services to the local geographic market. When global markets demand similar characteristics in a good or service, the firm uses a global strategy to sell standardized products to global customers with similar needs. Being able to operate efficiently is critical to the success of a global strategy. Finally, a transnational strategy combines characteristics of both multidomestic and global strategies to respond to pressures for local responsiveness and the need to globally integrate and coordinate operations for efficiency purposes.
- Firms can use several different modes to enter an international market. Entry modes requiring lower asset commitment include international exporting,

licensing, and franchising. These entry modes have less financial risk but also provide lower control over operations. They also reduce potential profits because they are shared with the licensee or franchisee. Other contract approaches include contract manufacturers, turnkey projects, and management contracts. These approaches require more investment by the licensee but also have similar advantages of reduced financial investment relative to the previously discussed contract approaches.

- FDI modes include joint ventures or strategic alliances, greenfield ventures, and acquisitions. Each FDI entry mode requires more up-front investment but allows for more control of the venture. A joint venture includes a separate entity in which control is shared with a local partner. A greenfield venture (new wholly owned subsidiary) allows more control and is most appropriate when proprietary technology needs to be protected. An acquisition is more appropriate when speedy entry is important. However, acquisitions often have significant challenges, including the difficulty of conducting due diligence in international settings and the complexities of integrating businesses from two different cultures and institutional environments.

- FDI strategies may encounter significant political and economic risks. Political risks include terrorism, wars, and nationalization of a private firm's assets by the host country. Economic risks include currency fluctuations and devaluations. Commonly, economic risks are accentuated in transition or emerging economies where the economy is less stable. Of course, political and economic risks are often interrelated.

- Implementing international strategies is often complex and can limit international expansion opportunities. The multidomestic strategy requires decentralization and therefore is implemented with a geographic-area divisional structure. The global strategy is implemented with a worldwide divisional structure. The transnational strategy requires both centralization and decentralization and is commonly implemented with a global matrix structure.

KEY TERMS

Country-specific or location advantages, 179
Exporting, 175
Foreign direct investment, 168
Franchising, 177
Geographic-area divisional structure, 180

Global matrix structure, 182
Global mind-set, 168
Global strategy, 174
Greenfield venture, 178
Internal coordination or administrative advantages, 180

Liability of foreignness, 168
Licensing, 177
Multidomestic strategy, 173
Transnational strategy, 174
Worldwide divisional structure, 181

DISCUSSION QUESTIONS

1. What are the basic reasons firms expand their operations internationally by employing international strategies?
2. What are the two primary pressures leading to three main international strategies?
3. What are the four contract-based international entry modes?
4. What major advantages influence the type of entry mode firms choose to enter international markets?

5. What are the three types of foreign direct investment (FDI), and what rationale supports the use of each one?
6. What structures are used to implement the multidomestic, global, and transnational strategies?

STRATEGY TOOLBOX

Introduction

When devising cross-border strategies, many business leaders fall into predictable, biased patterns of behavior known as blind spots. In the case of global expansion, for example, companies often base their strategies on what has worked in their own countries, without adequate consideration of the expansion territory context. This chapter's tool is designed to help executives break through the blind spots and avoid costly strategic mistakes.

Defending Against Blind Spots

Blind Spots	Remedies
• Overconfidence	• Checks and balances
• Invalid assumptions	• Extensive data analysis
• "Sending good news" bias	• External perspectives

MINI-CASE

The Olympic Games: An Opportunity for Growing International Businesses

The Olympic Games provide a way for outstanding national athletes to compete on an international stage. However, for global firms, the Olympics are a significant opportunity to increase global brand awareness. Firms such as Coca-Cola, Panasonic, Lenovo, and Samsung have the opportunity to market their products worldwide and in specific markets during the Olympic period by using a number of local and regional outlets to establish their global identities.

Likewise, large media firms seek to benefit from the potential advertising revenue associated with the Olympics. NBC, for example, commits significant sums of money to obtain the broadcast rights for the Olympic Games in North America. The network paid $1.27 billion for the broadcast rights of the 2000 Sydney Summer Games and the 2002 Salt Lake City Winter Games. Additionally, NBC paid $2.3 billion for the broadcast rights of the 2004, 2006, and 2008 Games and paid an additional $2.2 billion for the 2010 and 2012 Games even though the sites for these Games hadn't been determined at the time of the agreement (Vancouver was selected for the 2010 winter Olympics and London for the 2012 Summer Olympics). Additional broadcast rights for Europe, Australia, Asia, and the rest of the Americas go for smaller amounts but are still quite large for the local broadcasters in these areas. NBC and other local broadcasters pay so much for the broadcast rights to these Games because of the importance of international marketing and global mind-sets.

The Olympics are managed by the International Olympic Committee (IOC), based in Switzerland. Because of the high cost of running the Olympics, the IOC and national Olympic committees continually search for ways to offset the costs. Revenues received from firms for the rights to broadcast the Games are a great help in covering the Games' costs. In addition, the IOC uses the prestige and the marketing capability of the Games to sell high-profile corporate sponsorships. These sponsorships enable global corporations to capture the status and visibility of being associated with the Games. A worldwide partnership, the most expensive designation, costs $70 million or more. For the 2008 Olympic Games in Beijing, 12 companies paid to be worldwide sponsors: Coca-Cola, Samsung, Johnson & Johnson, GE, Atos Origin, Kodak, Manulife, McDonald's, Omega Watch Company, Panasonic, and Visa.

The primary advantage of a worldwide partnership with the IOC is that it provides advertising space during Olympic event broadcasts. For instance, Coca-Cola paid an additional $15 million to be one of the three sponsors for the Olympic torch relay. It is estimated that Coca-Cola spent approximately three times its front-end $90 million investment to advertise at the Olympics. In fact, the games provided a specific opportunity for Coca-Cola to market directly to the 1.3 billion Chinese consumers.

The Olympics also provide opportunities for local businesses in the area where the games are located. For example, the Southend Airport near the location for the 2012 Olympics in London is positioned as the gateway to the Games. The expectation is that it will increase the flow of traffic at the airport for many years after the end of the 2012 games. Several other firms also look to the London Olympics to enhance their business for several years into the future partly because of the infrastructure developed for the Olympics. Thus, the 2012 Olympic Games will serve as a catalyst for business growth throughout the Thames Gateway region.

In summary, the Olympic Games represent an opportunity for firms whose markets have become more global to advertise to the world during the two-week period of the Games. People across the world watch these games and global firms seek to advertise their products in increasingly international markets. The 2008 Olympic Games reached a cumulative audience of 40 billion people, so this event represents a significant opportunity for truly global marketing.

Sources: B. Sherwood, 2010, Business expects Olympics growth boost, *Financial Times*, www.ft.com, September 14; 2010, Vancouver 2010 winter games surplus medical/dental supplies/equipment bound for Haiti as part of Olympic Truce legacy, www.vancouver.2010.com, March 25; Advertising of 2007: Coke, Lenovo, and others have launched original campaigns that have engaged and entertained consumers, WSMV.com, www.wsmv.com, April 29; Beijing 2008, 2008, Beijing Olympic Broadcasting, www.en.beijing2008.com, April 29; 2008, Navigating Olympic sponsorship: Marketing your brand without alienating the world, Knowledge@Wharton, www.knowledge.wharton.upenn.edu, April 16; J. G. Collier, 2008, Coke takes neutral stance on Olympic protests, *Atlanta Journal-Constitution*, www.ajc.com, April 13; J. M. Higgins & S. McClellan, 2004, Welcome to the Olympics, *Broadcasting & Cable,* June 7, 1; J. Lafayette, 2004, Peacock crowing about Olympics, *TelevisionWeek*, August 30, 4; A. Romano, 2004, NBC plans to give local cable ads an Olympian push, *Broadcasting & Cable,* January 19, 35–36; P. McClintock, 2003, Ebersol's got games: NBC Sports chair's pact covers next 5 Olympics, *Daily Variety*, December 17, 7–9; B. Steinberg & Stefan Fatsis, 2003, NBC Olympics bid easily clears bar—GE agrees to pay $2 billion for rights to broadcasts, soaring past competition, *The Wall Street Journal*, June 9, B5.

Questions

1. If you wanted to build your firm's brand image at the Olympics and you were pursuing a global strategy, how would you market your products? Would you market your products differently if you were pursuing a multidomestic strategy? Describe the marketing approaches that you might use in advertising as well as local promotion at the Games.

2. What international strategy (multidomestic, global, or transnational) is NBC using to market in its region in North America (including the United States, Canada, and Mexico)? What are the characteristics of its international strategy?

3. What structure should be used to implement the particular strategy chosen in Question 2? Explain why the structure you chose was most appropriate.

EXPERIENTIAL EXERCISES

Exercise One: Top FDI and Trade Partners

The chapter discussed both FDI (a process through which a firm invests in a market outside the United States) and trade (exporting and importing). To complete this exercise, collect data on FDI and trade by looking at sources such as the *Survey of Current Business* and the U.S. Department of Commerce Web site. Then determine the top five countries that are recipients of U.S. FDI and the top five countries that invest in the United States. In addition, determine the top five trading partners of the United States, the top five recipients of U.S. exports, and the top five countries from which the United States imports. For the trade part of the exercise, consider only goods (not services). What conclusions do you draw from this exercise?

Exercise Two: International Strategy Choices of Emerging-Market Multinationals

A recent article in *The Economist* magazine referred to the following group of emerging-market multinationals as "a new breed of multinationals" and as "the challengers." In small groups, discuss the kinds of international strategies (i.e., global, multidomestic, or transnational) that these firms use to compete. Also, discuss the kinds of entry modes (i.e., exporting, licensing, and other contracting; joint venture; overseas acquisition; and greenfield) used to enter foreign markets. Based on what you read in the chapter, what are the differences in how these firms compete compared to firms from developed countries? Each group should choose one firm to investigate.

- Mittal Steel (India)
- Infosys (India)
- Tata Group (India)
- Chery Automobile (China)
- Haier (China)
- Lenovo (China)
- Embraer (Brazil)
- Sadia (Brazil)
- Cemex (Mexico)

ENDNOTES

1. D. Yan, J. Hong, & B. Ren, 2010, Determinants of outward foreign direct investment by Chinese enterprises, *Nakai Business Review International,* 1: 237–253; S. Mani, K. D. Antia, & A. Rindfleisch, 2007, Entry mode and equity level: A multilevel examination of foreign direct investment ownership structure, *Strategic Management Journal,* 28: 857–866.

2. G. A, Knight & D. Kim, 2009, International business competence and the contemporary firm, *Journal of International Business Studies,* 40: 255–273; A. S. Tsui, 2007, From homogenization to pluralism: International management research in the academy and beyond, *Academy of Management Journal,* 50: 1353–1364.

3. M. A. Hitt & X. He, 2008, Firm strategies in a changing global competitive landscape, *Business Horizons,* 51(5): 363–369.

4. M. Javidan, R. M. Steers, & M. A. Hitt (eds.), 2007, *The Global Mindset,* Amsterdam: Elsevier Ltd.; O. Levy, S. Beechler, S. Taylor, & N. A. Boyacigiller, 2007, What we talk about when we talk about "global mindset": Managerial cognition in multinational corporations, *Journal of International Business Studies,* 38: 231–258.

5. T. Hutzschenreuter & J. C. Voll, 2008, Performance effects of "added cultural distance" in the path of international expansion: The case of German multinational enterprises, *Journal of International Business Studies,* 39: 53–70; R. Mudambi & S. A. Zahra, 2007, The survival of international new ventures, *Journal of International Business Studies,* 38: 333–352.

6. L. Nachum, 2010, When is foreignness an asset or a liability? Explaining the performance differential between foreign and local firms, *Journal of Management,* 36: 714–730; E. W. K. Tsang & P. S. L. Yip, 2007, Economic distance and the survival of foreign direct investments, *Academy of Management Journal,* 50: 1156–1168.

7. J. W. Spencer, 2008, The impact of multinational enterprise strategy on indigenous enterprises: Horizontal spillovers and crowding out in developing countries, *Academy of Management Review,* 33: 341–361; M. A.

Hitt, L. Tihanyi, T. Miller, & B. Connelly, 2006, International diversification: Antecedents, outcomes, and moderators, *Journal of Management,* 32: 831–867.

8. D. G. Sirmon, M. A. Hitt, R. D. Ireland, & B. A. Gilbert, 2011, Resource orchestration to create competitive advantage. Breadth, depth and life cycle effects, *Journal of Management,* 37: in press.

9. M. S. Giarratana & S. Torrisi, 2010, Foreign entry and survival in a knowledge-intensive market: Emerging economy countries' international linkages, technological competences and firm experience, *Strategic Entrepreneurship Journal,* 4: 85–104; M. A. Hitt, L. Bierman, K. Uhlenbruck, & K. Shimizu, 2006, The importance of resources in the internationalization of professional service firms: The good, the bad, and the ugly, *Academy of Management Journal,* 49: 1137–1157.

10. S. Prashantham & C. Dhanaraj, 2010, The dynamic influence of social capital on the international growth of new ventures, *Journal of Management Studies,* 47: 967–994.

11. S. A. Fernhaber, P. P. McDougall-Covin, & D.A. Shepherd, 2009, International entrepreneurship: Leveraging internal and external knowledge sources, *Strategic Entrepreneurship Journal,* 3: 297–320; S. Fernhaber, B. A. Gilbert, & P. P. McDougall, 2008, International entrepreneurship and geographic location: An empirical examination of new venture internationalization, *Journal of International Business Studies,* 39: 267–290.

12. F. T. Rothaermel, S. Kotha, & H. K. Steensma, 2006, International market entry by U.S. Internet firms: An empirical analysis of country risk, national culture, and market size, *Journal of Management,* 32: 56–82.

13. T. W. Tong & J. J. Reuer, 2007, Real options in multinational corporations: Organizational challenges and risk implications, *Journal of International Business Studies,* 38: 215–230.

14. T. Yu & A. A. Cannella, 2007, Rivalry between multinational enterprises: An event history approach, *Academy of Management Journal,* 50: 665–686.

15. D. Luhnow & C. Terhune, 2003, Latin pop: A low-budget cola shakes up markets south of the border; Peru's Kola Real takes on Coke and Pepsi by cutting frills, targeting bodegas; how plastic leveled the field, *The Wall Street Journal,* October 27: Al.

16. J. Birchall, 2008, Pepsi in deal with Russia juice group, *Financial Times,* www. ft.com, March 20.

17. I. Brat, 2008, Overseas business boosts Caterpillar profit, *The Wall Street Journal,* www.wsj.com, April 19.

18. A. Delios, A. S. Gaur, & S. Makino, 2008, The timing of international expansion: Information, rivalry, and imitation among Japanese firms, *Journal of Management Studies,* 45: 169–195.

19. C.-H. Tseng, P. Tansuhaj, W. Hallagan, & J. McCullough, 2007, Effects of firm resources on growth in multinationality, *Journal of International Business Studies,* 38: 961–974.

20. C. Camison & A. Villar-Lopez, 2010, Effect of SMEs' international experience on foreign intensity and economic performance: The mediating role of internationally exploitable assets and competitive strategy, *Journal of Small Business Management,* 48: 116–151; R. D. Cremer & B. Ramaswamy, 2009, Engaging China: Strategies for the small internationalizing firm, *Journal of Business Strategy,* 30(6): 15–26.

21. A. Cuervo-Cazurra, M. M. Maloney, & S. Manrakhan, 2007, Causes of the difficulties in internationalization, *Journal of International Business Studies,* 38: 709–725.

22. P. Ghemawat, 2004, Global standardization vs. localization: A case study and model, in J. A. Quelch & R. Deshpande (eds.), *The Global Market: Developing a Strategy to Manage across Borders,* New York: Jossey-Bass, Chapter 8.

23. G. Hoffman, 1996, On foreign expansion, *Progressive Grocer,* September, 156.

24. Thales, Samtel form joint venture for avionics, 2008, *Thaindian News,* www. thaindian.com, May 8; D. Michaels, 2003, World business (a special report); Victory at sea: How did a French company capture several British naval contracts? Think "multidomestic," *The Wall Street Journal Europe,* September 26, R5.

25. Corporate profile, 2008, Daimler AG, www.daimler.com, May, 8; P. Wonacott & L. Hawkins Jr., 2003, A global journal report: Saying "beamer" in Chinese; Western luxury carmakers see sales boom in China as newly rich seek status, *The Wall Street Journal,* November 6, B1.

26. J. Birkenshaw, P. Braunerhjelm, U. Holm, & S. Terjesen, 2006, Why do some firms relocate their headquarters overseas? *Strategic Management Journal,* 27: 681–700.

27. S. J. Gould & A. F. Grein, 2009, Think globally, act glocally: A culture-centric comment on Leung, Bhagat, Buchan, Erez and Gibson (2005), *Journal of International Business Studies,* 40: 237–254.

28. 2010, IKEA, *Wikipedia,* en.wikipedia.org, October 2; C. Daniels, 2004, Create IKEA, make billions, take bus, *Fortune,* May 3, 44.

29. W. G. Sanders & A. Tuschke, 2007, The adoption of institutionally contested organizational practices: The emergence of stock option pay in Germany, *Academy of Management Journal,* 50: 33–56.

30. T. Chi & A. Seth, 2009, A dynamic model of the choice of mode for exploiting complementary capabilities, *Journal of International Business Studies,* 40: 365–387; K. Meyer, M. Wright, & S. Pruthi, 2009, Managing knowledge in foreign entry strategies: a resource-based analysis, *Strategic Management Journal,* 30: 557–554; X. Yin & M. Shanley, 2008, Industry determinants of the "merger versus alliance" decision, *Academy of Management Review,* 33: 473–491.

31. R. Salomon & B. Jin, 2010, Do leading or lagging firms learn more from exporting? *Strategic Management Journal,* 31: 1088–1113.

32. Electronic Arts, 2010, *Wikipedia,* en.wikipedia.org, May 8; C. Edward, 2004, Keeping you glued to the couch; In video games, top developer Electronic Arts zaps the competition, *BusinessWeek,* May 27, 58–59.

33. X. Luo, C.-N. Chung, & M. Sobczak, 2009, How do corporate governance model differences affect foreign direct investment in emerging economies? *Journal of International Business Studies,* 40: 444–467.

34. M. G. Colombo, L. Grilli, S. Murtinu, L. Pistello, & E. Piva, 2009, Effects of international R&D alliances on performance of high-tech start-ups: A longitudinal analysis, *Strategic Entrepreneurship Journal,* 3: 346–368.

35. H. Ren, B. Gray, & K. Kim, 2009, Performance of international joint ventures: What factors really make a difference and how? *Journal of Management,* 35: 805–832.

36. C. Lakshman & R. C. Parente, 2008, Supplier-focused knowledge management in the automobile industry and its implications for product performance, *Journal of Management Studies,* 45: 317–342.

37. Y. Luo, 2007, Are joint venture partners more opportunistic in a more volatile environment? *Strategic Management Journal,* 28: 39–60.

38. J.-P. Roy & C. Oliver, 2009, International joint venture partner selection: The role of the host country legal environment, *Journal of International Business Studies,* 40: 779–801; D. Li, L. Eden, M. A. Hitt, & R. D. Ireland, 2008, Friends, acquaintances, or strangers? Partner selection in R&D alliances, *Academy of Management Journal,* 51: 315–334.

39. C. Bouquet, L. Hebert, & A. Delios, 2004, Foreign expansion in service industries: Separability and human capital intensity, *Journal of Business Research,* 57: 35–46.

40. J. Li, J. Y. Yang, & D. R. Yue, 2007, Identity, community, and audience: How wholly owned foreign subsidiaries gain legitimacy in China, *Academy of Management Journal,* 50: 175–190.

41. J. F. Puck, D. Holtbrugge, & A. T. Mohr, 2009, Beyond entry mode choice: Explaining the conversion of joint ventures into wholly owned subsidiaries in the People's Republic of China, *Journal of International Business Studies,* 40: 388–404.

42. B. Aybar & A. Ficici, 2009, Cross-border acquisitions and firm value: An analysis of emerging-market multinationals, *Journal of International Business Studies,* 40: 1317–1338; K. Shimizu, M. A. Hitt, D. Vaidyanath, & V. Pisano, 2004, Theoretical foundations of cross-border mergers and acquisitions: A review of current research and recommendations for the future, *Journal of International Management,* 10: 307–353.

43. T. H. Reus & B. T. Lamont, 2009, The double-edged sword of cultural distance in international acquisitions, *Journal of International Business Studies,* 40: 1298–1316.

44. M. Y. Brannen & M. F. Peterson, 2009, Merging without alienating: Interventions promoting cross-cultural organizational integration and their limitations, *Journal of International Business Studies,* 40: 468–489; I. Bjorkman, G. K. Stahl, & E. Vaara, 2007, Cultural differences and capability transfer in cross-border acquisitions: The mediating roles of capability complementarity, absorptive capacity and social integration, *Journal of International Business Studies,* 38: 658–672.

45. I. Guler & M. F. Guillen, 2010, Home country networks and foreign expansion: Evidence from the venture capital industry, *Academy of Management Journal,* 53: 390–410; I. Filatotchev & J. Piesse, 2009, R&D, internationalization and growth of newly listed firms: European evidence, *Journal of International Business Studies,* 40: 1260–1276.

46. L. E. Lopez, S. K. Kundu, & L Ciravenga, 2009, Born global or born regional? Evidence from an exploratory study in the Costa Rican software industry, *Journal of International Business Studies,* 40: 1228–1238.

47. S. E. Feinberg & A. K Gupta, 2009, MNC subsidiaries and country risk: Internalization as a safeguard against weak external institutions, *Academy of Management Journal,* 52: 381–399.

48. E. Tatoglu, K. W. Glaister, & F. Erdal, 2003, Determinants of foreign ownership in Turkish manufacturing, *Eastern European Economics,* 41(2): 5–41.

49. J. Xia, K. Boal, & A. Delios, 2009, When experience meets national institutional environmental change: Foreign entry attempts of U.S. firms in the central and eastern region, *Strategic Management Journal,* 30: 1286–1309.

50. S. Estrin, 2009, The impact of institutional and human resource distance on international entry strategies, *Journal of Management Studies,* 46: 1171–1196; S. H. L. Slangen, 2006, National cultural distance and initial foreign acquisition performance: The moderating effect of integration, *Journal of World Business,* 41: 161–170.

51. W. Malone, 2004, Bringing the market inside, *Harvard Business Review,* 82(4): 107–114.

52. A. Ferner, P. Almond, I. Clark, T. Colling, & T. Edwards, 2004, The dynamics of central control and subsidiary anatomy in the management of human resources: Case study evidence from US MNCs in the UK, *Organization Studies,* 25: 363–392.

53. B. Ambos & B. B. Schlegelmilch, 2007, Innovation and control in the multinational firm: A comparison of political and contingency approaches, *Strategic Management Journal,* 28: 473–486.
54. J. Wolf & W. G. Egelhoff, 2002, A reexamination and extension of international strategy–structure theory, *Strategic Management Journal,* 23: 181–189.
55. A. Tempel & P. Walgenbach, 2007, Global standardization of organizational forms and management practices? What new institutionalism and business-systems approach can learn from each other, *Journal of Management Studies,* 44: 1–24.
56. G. Letto-Gillies, 2002, *Transnational corporations: Fragmentation amidst integration,* New York: Routledge.
57. S. Li & H. Scullion, 2006, Bridging the distance: Managing cross-border knowledge holders, *Asia Pacific Journal of Management,* 23: 71–92.

CHAPTER 9
Creating and Maintaining Alliances

KNOWLEDGE OBJECTIVES

Reading and studying this chapter should enable you to:

1. Define strategic alliances and explain the difference between equity and nonequity alliances.

2. Explain why firms develop strategic alliances.

3. Identify business-level strategic alliances and explain vertical and horizontal alliances.

4. Describe how strategic alliances are used to implement corporate-level strategies.

5. Explain why strategic alliances represent a common means of entering international markets.

6. Identify the major risks of strategic alliances. Explain how strategic alliances can be managed to increase their success.

© Shannon Fagan, Getty Images

FOCUSING ON STRATEGY

Foreign Firms Seek Joint Ventures to Enter China's Emerging Market While Chinese Firms Seek Joint Ventures to Expand Internationally

Traditional joint ventures in China have been quite compelling for foreign firms. The foreign partners from more developed countries would usually provide capital, knowledge, and access to international markets and high-technology capabilities. Alternatively, the Chinese partners provided access to cheap labor, local regulatory and market knowledge, and improved access to increasing demand by the emerging middle class for branded as well as other products. Furthermore, the Chinese government often provided land, tax breaks, and an attractive welcome to encourage foreign direct investment into China.

Although China protects many important industries such as financial services and automobile manufacturing through restrictive entry requirements, the future potential of the market as well as the availability of lower-cost production has created attractive market entry potential for companies.

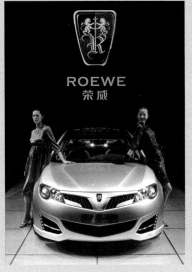

© Mark Ralston/AFP/Getty Images

For example, JP Morgan Chase formed a joint venture with a Chinese investment bank, First Capital Securities, which allows them to underwrite and sponsor deals in China's burgeoning securities market. First Capital is based in Shenzhen, and JP Morgan will hold 33 percent of the joint entity. Services provided by First Capital include asset management and mergers-and-acquisition advisory service, as well as service for IPOs and follow-on offerings. Goldman Sachs Group, USB AG, CLSA Asia-Specific Markets, and Morgan Stanley all are investment banks with joint ventures in China. Interestingly, Morgan Stanley put its investment-owned China International Corp. venture up for sale in 2009 in order to set up its own venture independent of a Chinese company. After Morgan Stanley formed its joint venture in 1995, the government put a 33 percent ownership ceiling on foreign owners of financial service firms. Credit Suisse AG and Deutsche Bank AG received approval to set up joint ventures in 2009, after the government had put in a two-year moratorium on new joint ventures to shield its domestic brokerage services from foreign competition. This shielding moratorium ended in December 2008.

The Chinese government is also increasing opportunities for the advancement of Chinese firms. For example, Nissan Motor Company, Daimler Benz, and Johnson Controls are seeking to set up cutting-edge electric-car technology manufacturing operations in China. Nissan is forming a joint venture with Dongfeng Motor Group to sell Nissan's Leaf electric cars in China. Also, Daimler AG and China's BYD have set up a 50-50 joint venture for developing an all-electric car for the Chinese market and for potential export abroad. BYD is one of China's leading battery producer and automakers, and the venture is scheduled to be headquartered in Shenzhen. However, the

Chinese government wants to "compel" foreign firms to transfer lithium-ion battery know-how and other technology to these joint ventures. This is a specific goal of the Chinese government to leapfrog into new technologies so as to become a leader in selling cars in the global market, and not just be a producer. Currently, China is the top automobile producer in the world, primarily for export, but also because of the expanding domestic demand with the burgeoning middle class in China. But they want to compete in global markets with their own branded products. As such, local Chinese firms have been pursuing partnerships domestically and internationally to improve their own competitive market share in world markets outside China.

Interestingly, although many joint ventures and partnerships in China have been successful, Chinese firms are not as hungry as they once were for capital; and many are implementing improved technology that they have learned to develop from international partners or from their own experience abroad. Moreover, demand for foreign branded products has fallen as local competitors' products have improved and the availability of cheap labor has fallen; as such, Chinese firms are less interested in providing access to foreign partners.

Also, many of the rules for foreign partners have led to difficulties. For instance, Peugeot (cars), Rémy Martin (spirits), Foster's (beer), Fletcher Challenge (steel), News Corporation (media), and a number of telecommunication firms have found their joint ventures to be problematic because of complex and contradictory rules, and difficulty in appropriating profits and controlling their investments. Even firms with 51 percent ownership, such as Danone, a large French food producer, are not able to control their ventures given the local rules in China. However, Wahaha, a local Chinese partner with Danone, has been able to wrestle control of the joint venture with Danone.

Sources: 2010, Corporate news: Daimler forms China electric-car venture, *The Wall Street Journal*, May 28, B2; J. Anderline & S. Daneshkhu, 2010, Danone cedes Chinese juice maker stake to buy-out firm for $260M, *Financial Times*, July 29, 1; D. Cameron, 2010, Corporate news: China is near deal with GE on jet, *The Wall Street Journal*, July 13, B3; D. Chen, Y. Paik, & S. Park, 2010, Host-country policies and MNE management control in IJVs: Evidence from China, *Journal of International Business Studies: Part Special Issue: Asia and Global Business*, 41(3): 526–537; E. Fang & Z. Shaoming, 2010, The effects of absorptive and joint learning on the instability of international joint ventures in emerging economies, *Journal of International Business Studies*, 41(5): 906–924; N. Gopalan, 2010, International finance: J. P. Morgan sets venture to tap into China's boom, *The Wall Street Journal*, June 10, C2; N. Shirouzu, 2010, China spooks automakers—companies fear rules will hurt intellectual property: Concerns about discrimination, *The Wall Street Journal*, September 17, A1; N. Shirouzu, 2010, Corporate news: Nissan charges ahead in China, *The Wall Street Journal*, September 21, B3; S. Wen & C. Cheng-Min, 2010, To teach or to compete? A strategic dilemma of knowledge owners in international alliances, *Asia Pacific Journal of Management*, 27(4): 697–726; D. Chen, S. Park, & W. Newburry, 2009, Parent contribution and organizational control in international joint ventures, *Strategic Management Journal*, 30(11): 1133–1156.

The popularity of Chinese markets is shown in *Focusing on Strategy*. Because of its size and subsequent sales potential as well as low-cost labor, firms from many parts of the world want to enter Chinese markets. *Focusing on Strategy* describes a recent joint venture by Nissan, an automaker, with Dongfeng Motor Group to sell electric cars in the Chinese market. It also illustrates how Chinese firms are accessing needed resources from foreign partners and how Chinese firms are teaming with other local firms as well as creating their own joint ventures abroad to learn and expand their product lines and gain market access. Combined, these actions emphasize the importance of strategic alliances to firms throughout the world, not only in China.

A **strategic alliance** is a relationship between firms in which the partners agree to cooperate in ways that provide benefits to each firm. A strategic alliance is a type of cooperative strategy. A **cooperative strategy** is an action plan a firm develops to form cooperative relationships with other firms. Although firms choose to cooperate with one another rather than compete when using a cooperative strategy, such as a strategic alliance, the purpose of doing so is the same in both instances: namely, to develop a competitive advantage.[1] Thus, a cooperative strategy adds to the repertoire of strategies firms use to build competitive advantages that can help them successfully compete in one or more markets.

strategic alliance

a relationship between firms in which the partners agree to cooperate in ways that provide benefits to each firm

cooperative strategy

an action plan a firm develops to form cooperative relationships with other firms

Two types of strategic alliances are equity alliances and nonequity alliances. In an **equity alliance,** each partner owns a percentage of the equity in a venture that the firms have jointly formed. If a separate business is created by this alliance, it is often referred to as a **joint venture**. A **nonequity alliance** is a contractual relationship between two or more firms in which each partner agrees to share some of its resources or capabilities.[2]

In previous chapters, we discussed business-level strategies, corporate-level (product diversification) strategies, and international strategies, which all concern actions the firm takes to compete in markets against other firms operating in the same markets. In this chapter, we explore the use of strategic alliances, the reasons for them, and their different types. We also examine alliances at the business and corporate levels along with international alliances. Finally, we explore the means of managing alliances, including balancing the risks of using such strategies. We begin with the reasons to develop strategic alliances.

Reasons for Developing Strategic Alliances

As suggested in *Focusing on Strategy,* strategic alliances are a highly popular strategy used by firms throughout the world. Strategic alliances represent a major trend in global business primarily because of the potential value they provide to partnering firms. They can help firms grow and likewise have a major effect on the performance of partner firms.[3] They are an important strategy for many reasons. We present some of these reasons in Table 9.1. Before examining Table 9.1, think of reasons you believe would cause firms to form alliances. You likely identified some of the reasons listed in the table and may have included a few others as well.

A major reason for firms to engage in strategic alliances is to allow them to enter restricted markets. China provides a prime example; the Chinese government requires foreign firms to form joint ventures with Chinese partners in order to enter many Chinese industries. For example, automobile firms and airlines form alliances with Chinese firms to enter and serve Chinese markets.[4] Alliances also can allow a firm to overcome trade barriers to enter a market. Thus a firm may form a joint venture in a country to produce and market products in order not to pay the major tariffs on them it would have to pay if the products were imported.

equity alliance

an alliance in which each partner owns a percentage of the equity in a venture that the firms have jointly formed

joint venture

a separate business that is created by an equity alliance

nonequity alliance

a contractual relationship between two or more firms in which each partner agrees to share some of its resources or capabilities

Table 9.1 Reasons for Strategic Alliances

- Gain access to a restricted market
- Develop new goods or services
- Facilitate new market entry
- Share significant R&D investments
- Share risks and buffer against uncertainty
- Develop market power
- Gain access to complementary resources
- Build economies of scale
- Meet competitive challenges
- Learn new skills and capabilities
- Outsource for lower costs and higher-quality output

R&D alliances to facilitate development of new goods and services have become increasingly common. R&D alliances help firms share the costs and risks associated with developing new products. The success of new products in the marketplace is low. Therefore, sharing the costs and risks allows individual firms either to invest less in R&D or to invest the same amount and increase the number of successes in the market (by introducing more new products, for example). Additionally, partner firms may develop better new-product ideas by cooperating to integrate resources from each to create new and different capabilities.[5]

As we noted previously, risks arise because success with new products is highly uncertain. Other forms of uncertainty exist as well. For example, entering new international markets presents uncertainty in the form of market demand, government actions, and competitor reactions. Therefore, firms may develop strategic alliances such as R&D alliances to overcome uncertainty and share the risks. Besides overcoming risk, such alliances also help international firms build their knowledge base.[6] Johnson Controls' actions illustrate this type of benefit.

Johnson Controls is a car parts producer and has focused recently on producing critical parts for the hybrid and the emerging electric car market. It is forming a joint venture with Hitachi, a Japanese firm, to produce lithium-ion batteries, as well as advanced power distribution systems. The focus will be on "next generation" batteries. Combining Hitachi's technological expertise in lithium-ion batteries with Johnson Controls' strong automaker client base and mass production infrastructure will benefit both firms. There are similar tie-ups between Toshiba Corporation and Mitsubishi Motors. Panasonic has a strong relationship with one of its independent subsidiaries, Sanyo Electric Company, which is forming an internal joint venture to focus on these next-stage, lithium-ion batteries as well.[7]

As suggested by the Johnson Controls example, companies may combine their resources and skills, and as such, alliances can provide access to complementary resources. **Complementary resources** are resources that each partner brings to the partnership that, when combined, allow for new resources or capabilities that neither firm could readily create alone. By integrating their complementary resources, partners can take actions that they could not take separately. So gaining access to complementary resources is a major reason for engaging in strategic alliances.[8] Johnson Controls expects that the complementary resources held by its partner, Hitachi, can help it improve battery technology in products it will produce to sell in global markets.

Firms can also use alliances to gain market power. For example, China Air Lines, Taiwan's largest airline by revenue, signed an agreement with SkyTeam Global Alliance anchored by Delta Airlines and Air France–KLM. SkyTeam's approach is to expand into Asia, in particular South Asia and India, to increase its traffic in the region. SkyTeam is one of three major global airline alliances, the others being the Star Alliance with United and Lufthansa as anchors, and One World, with American and British Airways as key partners. Each of these airline alliances maintains code-sharing arrangements for flights and shares maintenance facilities among member carriers. With the addition of China Air, for instance, SkyTeam will have 13 airlines among its partners expanding their potential market power in Asia.[9]

At times, firms form alliances to meet competitive challenges. In fact, they may need to gain access to partners' resources to compete effectively. For example, Sematech was formed in Austin, Texas, during the 1980s by a group of U.S. semiconductor firms with the blessing of the U.S. government. It was developed to conduct joint R&D to meet the competitive challenges of foreign semiconductor

complementary resources
resources that each partner brings to the partnership that, when combined, allow for new resources or capabilities that neither firm could readily create alone

firms, particularly Japanese businesses at the time. The consortium was so successful that Sematech has a variety of different purposes today, although its general focus remains on improving knowledge in the semiconductor industry.

Of critical importance is the amount of knowledge a firm holds. In fact, some argue that firms holding greater stocks of knowledge often have a competitive advantage. For this reason, many alliances are formed to gain access to a partner's valuable knowledge. So a primary reason for developing alliances is to learn from partners, which can contribute to higher performance by the firm.[10] In some cases, firms may attempt to learn from partners in order to explore new areas (such as in the alliance example between Johnson Controls and Hitachi). In other cases, firms may want to learn from partners in order to know how to better use their current capabilities. For example, large multinational corporations often enter emerging markets to exploit their current technological knowledge. To do so, they must learn the local culture and marketplace. They must also learn how to deal with the foreign government and distributors. This knowledge can be obtained from local partners, as illustrated by firms entering China in *Focusing on Strategy.*

A final reason why firms develop alliances is to outsource an important function or activity of their business. *Outsourcing* (defined in Chapter 4) involves acquiring a capability from an external supplier that contributes to creating value for customers. As we explained in Chapter 4, outsourcing is a popular trend among U.S. firms. Even though much outsourcing occurs in manufacturing, outsourcing of IT, human resources, and other internal staff functions has become more frequent as well.

Outsourcing is commonly used to reduce costs. However, firms also outsource to gain access to special skills for higher-quality output. For example, many pharmaceutical firms outsource R&D to improve the effectiveness of the research operations.[11] This is also happening in manufacturing firms. For example, Siemens AG is Germany's largest manufacturer and R&D organization. Although Siemens has a vast R&D organization with over 30,000 employees globally, it collaborates with hundreds of external innovation partners. These partners include universities, suppliers, customers, and start-ups, as well as competitors. For instance, key partners are universities and start-ups which have new technology, breakthrough ideas, and/or improved theoretical frameworks for producing new products. Customers often provide access to new markets whereas suppliers provide production or technology knowledge that reduces costs. Competitors often provide complementary knowledge, but often involve competitive threats and thus need to be managed with particular attention.[12]

Because international outsourcing is believed to be responsible for exporting jobs to other countries, it is controversial. A significant amount of outsourcing has occurred by firms seeking to reduce their expenditures in IT and services. Three large firms in India have made a big business of receiving this high-technology outsourcing: Infosys Technologies, Tata Consultancy Services (TCS), and Wipro. Approximately 10 percent of the global technology service is now outsourced to foreign service providers, and Indian companies hold about 70 percent of the market share in this large and growing segment. Outsourcing often occurs as companies seek to cut costs. However, from a strategic management perspective, outsourcing has the potential to help firms successfully implement their strategies and

© Jim West/Photo Library

The alliance between Johnson Controls and Hitachi focused on the development of lithium-ion batteries and advanced power distribution systems offers a number of benefits. Each firm benefits from the collective complementary resources gained through their partnership and gains important knowledge applicable to their overall goals.

to earn returns for shareholders as a result. However, outsourcing can slow if large firms get too much market power relative to those clients who need outsourcing services.[13] You will read more about outsourcing in this chapter's Mini-Case.

In the global electronics industry, Intel, Dell, HP, Sony, and IBM all outsource production and design of products to global networks of contract manufacturers, especially in Pacific Rim countries, including China, Taiwan, Malaysia, and others. These vendors are being classified in more fine-grain terms: offshore, near-shore, captive, and onshore. Offshore are located abroad in distant places like India, Taiwan, and China. Others, in countries like Mexico and Chile, are quickly being preferred for their time zone advantage and English capabilities and are referred to as near-shore vendors. They have advantages because of shorter travel times and cultural similarities. Captive outsourcing is often associated with company-owned operations abroad where process activities are performed. Large management consulting companies, for example, own operations in India that provide centralized support for market research and data analysis to all their offices around the globe. Interestingly, as outsourcing vendors grow, they are developing onshore operations to serve their clients and improve their level of service as well as cultural and language alignment. Infosys, an offshore provider headquartered in India, now has offices in the United States. Firms form alliances for use at different levels in their hierarchy of strategies. First, we'll explore business-level alliances.

Business-Level Strategic Alliances

Two types of business-level strategic alliances are vertical alliances and horizontal alliances. Next, we explore how a firm can use either type of business-level alliance to help create or maintain a competitive advantage.

Vertical Strategic Alliances

A **vertical strategic alliance** is an alliance that involves cooperative partnerships across the value chain. (The value chain was discussed in Chapter 4.) A relationship between buyers and suppliers is a common type of vertical alliance. Some firms use vertical alliances to produce their products. Nike uses quite a few vertical alliances to produce many of its athletic shoes.

Although contracts are usually written to form them, vertical alliances are most effective when partners trust each other.[14] Trust enables partners to invest less time and effort to ensure that a contract's terms are fulfilled. Trust also helps partners learn from each other in ways that benefit both firms. In fact, when developed and sustained over long periods of time, trust even facilitates the transfer of technological knowledge from buyers to suppliers; the supplier is more likely to help improve the performance of the buyer, and the alliance is more likely to be successful.[15]

Many firms are finding it necessary to manage their supply chain through strategic alliances and relationships rather than use an arm's-length pricing strategy focused on purchasing inputs as cheaply as possible. For example, Nike sought to manage its relationships with contract manufacturers for its shoes by having different types of suppliers. Tier 1 suppliers are firms with a stronger relationship to the main contracting company (Nike), more like a strategic alliance than a pure contractual relationship. However, Tier 2 manufacturers may be associated with pricing and may be managed by Tier 1 suppliers or more closely related manufacturers.[16] This more relationship-oriented approach has

vertical strategic alliance
an alliance that involves cooperative partnerships across the value chain

required that supply-chain managers develop a whole new set of skills in alliance management.[17]

Horizontal Strategic Alliances

A **horizontal strategic alliance** is an alliance that involves cooperative partnerships in which firms at the same stage of the value chain share resources and capabilities. Horizontal alliances are often intended to enhance the capabilities of the partners to compete in their markets. Firms sometimes develop horizontal alliances to respond to competitors' actions or to reduce the competition they face.[18] *Understanding Strategy: Learning from Failure* illustrates several horizontal alliances.

Because of dynamic and highly competitive markets, firms often face substantial uncertainty. To buffer against this uncertainty, they frequently form alliances to share the risks (as noted earlier in the chapter). High uncertainty has become increasingly common in many markets, not just markets that you would expect to be highly uncertain, such as high-technology markets. For example, markets for banks have become highly competitive as they experience significant change. One response has been to acquire other banks to increase market power. However, compared to acquisitions, alliances can accomplish similar objectives, but with a smaller investment of a bank's financial capital. Of course, care must be taken in horizontal alliances to avoid explicit or tacit collusion. Rio Tinto and BHP Billiton (both companies are natural resource producers with a principal focus in the mining sector) had planned a joint venture to produce iron ore in Western Australia. Rio Tinto is headquartered in Britain but with many assets in Australia as well. BHP Billiton is headquartered in Australia, but also listed on the London exchange. Even though this joint venture may have created significant synergies between the two companies and reduced iron ore production costs, the regulators in a number of countries suggested that the partnership would create too much market power for one entity. Accordingly, these firms abandoned their iron ore production joint venture proposal.[19]

Although explicit collusion is illegal, tacit collusion is more difficult to identify.[20] *Tacit collusion* occurs when firms signal intentions to one another through their actions. The market signaling observed when firms tacitly collude is more likely to occur in concentrated industries with only a few large competitors. For example, Kellogg, General Mills, Post (Kraft sold this brand to Ralcorp in 2007), and Quaker have almost 80 percent of the ready-to-eat cereal market.[21] An example of tacit collusion in this industry would be if most or all of these four competitors took no action to reduce the price of their products when the demand for them declined.[22] A similar example would be too much cooperation between Yahoo! and Google in the example explained in *Understanding Strategy*; that is, a possible alliance between Yahoo! and Google was examined by both companies, but it would have given the joint company too much market power. Ultimately, Yahoo! settled on an alliance with Microsoft which resulted in using Microsoft's Bing search engine on Yahoo!'s Web site.

Vertical alliances often have the highest probability of producing positive returns, while horizontal alliances usually are the most difficult to manage and sustain. In particular, vertical alliances in which partners have complementary capabilities and the relationship between the partners is strong are likely to be successful. Horizontal alliances are difficult because often the partners are also competitors. Firms in these alliances must guard against opportunistic actions (being unfairly taken advantage of) by their partners because of the potentially serious implications those actions might have for the firms' ability to remain competitive. Also, because of the differences between competitors, horizontal alliances are ripe for conflict.

horizontal strategic alliance

an alliance that involves cooperative partnerships in which firms at the same stage of the value chain share resources and capabilities

Horizontal Alliances in Search Engines and Wind Power

In February 2010, regulators cleared an alliance between Microsoft and Yahoo!. The intent of the alliance was to use Microsoft's Bing search engine, which is in competition with Google's dominant search engine, as the search engine on Yahoo!'s Web site. This is an interesting alliance because Yahoo! has had its own search engine for a long time, although it has been losing market share to Google. Interestingly, advertisers have been in favor of the Microsoft-Yahoo! agreement because they want a strong alternative to Google, and not a lot of smaller players each with its own accounts and technologies. It will be interesting to see if Microsoft, combined with Yahoo!, can challenge Google's dominant 65 percent market share in Internet searches.

It is also interesting to note that Yahoo! and Google are trying to form a partnership in Japan on search engines. Paradoxically, some see the Japanese alliance as undermining Microsoft's renewed efforts to challenge Google in the search arena. However, Rakuten has filed a petition with the Japan Fair Trade Commission suggesting that this partnership represents unfair competition. Rakuten is a Japanese online shopping-mall operator comparable to Amazon in the U.S. As one can see, these horizontal alliances change depending upon the competitive conditions in different countries.

In another example, GE has formed a joint venture with a Chinese power equipment company to gain market share in the global wind turbine business. GE's electronic power equipment business is joining forces with Harbin Electric Machinery Company to produce GE-designed onshore and offshore wind turbines. Interestingly, although the venture

Despite its technological prowess and scale, GE is facing considerable competition in the wind turbine market from local producers, especially in China. To remain competitive in China in particular, GE has formed a joint venture, in which it has a minority stake, with China-based Harbin Electric Machinery Company to produce both onshore and offshore wind turbines.

will be dominated by GE due to its technological prowess, GE is taking a minority 49 percent ownership stake, due to government regulations. The venture could help GE maintain its position as one of the top global suppliers. In recent years, GE's prospects for selling more wind turbines have dimmed as local producers have become more competitive. For example, Chinese wind turbine producers, Sinovel Wind, Goldwind, and Dongfang Electric, have moved into the top ten producers globally.

As these examples show, horizontal alliances are often used when competition is strong and one firm does not have all of the capabilities needed to produce the next advance to keep it competitive. Furthermore, firms observe rivals who have already pursued strategic alliances and believe it important to enter into a cooperative agreement in order to maintain a stronger level of competitiveness with those rivals. When a great deal of uncertainty characterizes the industry and it is necessary to maintain competitive strength, rivals at the same level of the value chain often cooperate to make progress and competitive advances. These cooperative agreements often lead to improved performance and create value for the potential customers of the products.

Sources: W. Cooper, 2010, Yahoo finalizes team to lead agency transition to Bing search platform, *New Media Age*, October 21, 3; P. Glader, 2010, Corporate news: GE in China wind-power venture—Companies will make and sell turbines to booming markets as GE fights to boost Chinese revenue, *The Wall Street Journal*, September 28, B3; B. Kindle & S. Morrison, 2010, Regulators clear Microsoft-Yahoo alliance, *The Wall Street Journal*, February 19, B5; K. Li, 2010, AOL and Google expand advertising deal, *Financial Times*, September 3, 15; M Shields, 2010, Bing, boom or bust?, *Mediaweek*, August 30, 5; 2009, Business: Bingoo!: A deal between Microsoft and Yahoo!, *Economist*, August 1, 57; S. Forbes, 2009, Who needs antitrust? We don't, *Forbes*, www.forbes.com, August 24.

© Dennis Cox / Alamy

© kimeveruss, iStock

Even though business-level partnerships are important, corporate-level alliances also can have substantial effects on firm performance. We examine these types of alliances next.

Corporate-Level Strategic Alliances

Corporate-level strategic alliances usually focus on the firm's product line and are designed to enhance firm growth. Corporate-level alliances are particularly attractive because they often have the same purpose as acquisitions but are much less costly.[23] Corporate-level strategic alliances include those for diversification, for synergy, and for franchising.

Diversification by Alliance

R&D strategic alliances may be formed with the intent to develop new products that serve markets distinct from those that the partners currently serve. Partners operating in different industries may be able to integrate unique knowledge stocks to create products that serve new markets and customers. In this way, the new products add to each partner's current product line. In fact, developing new products for markets different from those served may be difficult for firms without help from partners who have the additional knowledge needed. Diversification alliances can be especially valuable if the new products developed are related to the current products in some way such that synergy can be created.

However, alliances can also be used to refocus the firm and reduce its level of diversification, changing its direction into new businesses. Using joint ventures to create new businesses in combination with other firms can lead to organization restructuring and renewal.[24] For example, there is a clear consensus that many large pharmaceutical firms' R&D operations need restructuring. In particular, more specialization is needed to create new products. One of the solutions proposed is that through strategic alliances with venture capital, private equity, and even hedge funds, more opportunity for early-stage drug development specialization might be created. These financial service firms would have incentives to increase the specialization and improve investment for big pharmaceutical firms as well as other life science firms, such as Monsanto.[25]

Synergy by Alliance

Strategic alliances at the corporate level between firms can be used to create synergy. Synergy is created when partners share resources or integrate complementary capabilities to build economies of scope.[26] In fact, a synergistic strategic alliance is similar to a complementary business-level alliance in that both types of alliances are intended to synergistically involve partners with new businesses. As noted in *Understanding Strategy,* General Electric (GE) has a joint venture with Harbin to create wind turbines. Interestingly, this is not the only joint venture GE has with Harbin. The two companies previously established a partnership in 2003 to produce large gas turbines in China. GE pursues minority joint ventures across many of its businesses similar to the joint venture with Harbin. These joint ventures are found in avionics, rail locomotives, and "clean coal" technology. GE uses its experiences in many of its joint ventures to create synergistic relationships with other firms to produce joint products and seek complementary relationships.[27]

Franchising

Franchising is a well-established and successful type of corporate-level strategic alliance. As defined in Chapter 8, *franchising* is the licensing of a good or service and business model to partners for specified fees (usually a signing fee and a percentage of the franchisee's revenues or profits). Franchising allows a firm to expand a successful venture and earn additional returns without taking large financial risks. Franchising has the added advantage of allowing the franchisor to maintain control of its product and business model. Usually, the franchisor establishes tight controls on the actions a franchisee can take with its product and business name.

Many well-known firms franchise. McDonald's, Hilton International, and 7-Eleven all have franchisees operating some of the businesses carrying their name and products. For example Choice Hotels International franchises hotels under the following brands: Comfort Inn, Comfort Suites, Quality Inn, Sleep Inn, Clarion, Cambria Suites, MainStay Suites, Suburban Extended Stay Hotel, Econo Lodge, and Rodeway Inn. It has franchises for more than 6000 hotels representing more than 490,000 rooms in the United States and in 35 countries and territories.[28]

For franchising to be highly effective, the partners must cooperate. The franchisor must develop and transfer successful programs and means of managing the operation to the franchisee. The franchisee must have the knowledge and capabilities necessary to compete in the local market. And franchisees must provide feedback to the franchisor about activities that work and those that do not. Franchisees should also inform the franchisor about the important characteristics of competitors and market conditions in their local markets. Franchising can also enable a franchisor to gain a first-mover advantage without some of the risks involved in being a first mover.[29]

Sony develops highly related new products using alliances. One of Sony's most important alliances is with Ericsson, a European electronics and mobile phone producer. Because both firms were not able to do well in the mobile phone hardware market alone, they joined forces in a joint venture. Although they have not done well, especially in smartphone products such as the RIM's BlackBerry and Apple's iPhone, they plan on developing a new generation smartphone for the Chinese market. Along with this plan, they are seeking to enter a partnership with China Telecomm Corp., China's third-largest mobile phone service. The new smartphone will build on Sony Ericsson's 9.3 percent of the market share in mobile phone products.[30] Interestingly, Sony's alliance with Ericsson is a cross-border alliance, the next topic of discussion.

International Strategic Alliances

Cross-border strategic alliances have become the most prominent means of entering foreign markets. One reason is that some countries require that firms form joint ventures with local firms in order to enter their markets. This is the case for many industries in China, as explained in *Focusing on Strategy*. Additionally, foreign firms need knowledge and perhaps other resources to understand and compete effectively in the newly entered markets. As noted earlier, even if the Chinese government did not require joint ventures, foreign firms would do well to form them anyway. They can use the alliances to learn about the different culture and characteristics of the market, and to develop relationships with distributors and important government units. As noted above, this has been the strategy used by GE in China. Also, outsourcing to businesses in foreign countries with lower labor costs increases the number of cross-border strategic alliances. Therefore, as noted in Chapter 8, entering foreign markets through cooperative strategies is an attractive option for many firms.[31]

All strategic alliances carry risks. However, the use of international strategic alliances, a popular strategy for entering markets or gaining access to special skills and resources, carries some additional risks and potential costs. In the Danone and Wahaha joint venture noted in *Focusing on Strategy,* the differing strategic intents and cultures of the two companies' executives created an early barrier to an effective alliance. Different cultures and a lack of trust can hinder the transfer of knowledge or sharing of other resources necessary to make an alliance successful. Top executives warn against making assumptions when moving into new international markets. A firm's products often must be adapted to the local market. These adaptations require close cooperation of local partners. Firms may have to adapt their products and use different distribution channels as they cross into new international markets. For example, India does not allow foreign retailers to sell directly to consumers. Accordingly, Walmart has chosen to enter the market through a wholesaling operation in a joint venture with India's Bharti Enterprises. Walmart opened its first cash-and-carry wholesale joint venture store in 2008, and followed with more stores in 2009. Walmart intends to further develop "back office operations" with a significant amount of investment to help modernize India's retail industry and supply chains. However, Walmart has had difficulty getting trademarks approved for their private label branded products, "Great Value"; one analyst noted, "Bharti-Walmart's trademark applications were made public late last year [2009] and most of its applications are being opposed."[32] Part of the opposition may be indirect protests from mom-and-pop store owners and the intermediaries that supply them to changes that Walmart is proposing to increase efficiencies into the Indian distribution system.

Managing Risks in Strategic Alliances

Each type of strategic alliance (business-level, corporate-level, and cross-border) has its own risks and potentially generic risks as well. Many strategic alliances fail, even some that were formerly successful, as in the case of Disney and Pixar. Estimates of alliance failure range from 50 percent to 70 percent. The failure of alliances is an important issue because often value creation and up to a third of revenues for many companies come through alliances, which can account for up to 25 percent of annual growth in revenues.[33]

One major issue is the development of trust. Given the substantial conflict in the Danone and Wahaha alliance, the risks related to lack of trust are evident. When partners don't trust each other, they are less likely to share resources, particularly the most valuable ones. Without trust, partners also must invest more time and energy (resulting in extra costs) to guard against possible opportunistic behavior by the other firm. As a result, alliances without trust between partners are unlikely to meet their goals.

Of course, all alliances suffer from the potential differences in corporate and national cultures. These differences reflect emphases on separate values and may lead to communication problems between partners as well as an inability to understand each other's intentions. Additionally, because it is impossible to know all of a firm's capabilities before alliances are formed, participants in alliances often discover that the partner's competencies are not as strong or complementary as assumed.

In the failed alliance of Disney and Pixar, the motivation for Pixar to share its technical and creative expertise seemed to lessen as its need for Disney's sheer market power declined as the power of the Pixar brand itself grew. In perhaps the final comment on who needed who more, Disney eventually did acquire Pixar.

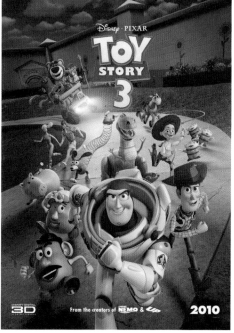

© Buena Vista Pictures/courtesy Everett Collection

Firms also may be unwilling to share important resources as assumed when the alliance was formed.[34] For example, Pixar's market power grew considerably during the time of its alliance with Disney because of the substantial success of their jointly produced animated films, so Pixar likely became unwilling to share its creative talent with Disney, at least under the old arrangement. When the alliance ended, Disney may have needed Pixar more than Pixar needed Disney, as evidenced by Disney's later acquisition of Pixar.[35]

Effectively managing alliances can reduce some of their risks. But it isn't easy to manage the risks of alliances, as evidenced by the demise of successful alliances such as those between Disney and Pixar and Danone and Wahaha. Some firms use detailed contracts to try to guard against opportunistic behavior by a partner. A detailed contract can help, but it isn't possible to identify and then specify in a contract all partner actions that are acceptable as alliance partners.[36] Thus, problems with overseas alliance partners can have a substantial negative effect on a firm's performance and can lead to a loss of control, as the Danone and Wahaha joint venture illustrates.

Indeed, the best action that most firms can take is to attempt to develop a trusting relationship. Trust is the best preventive medicine against opportunistic behavior. In addition, trust promotes the sharing of resources and even the willingness to cooperate with and help alliance partners. We emphasize the importance of trust in our discussion of managing alliances.

Managing Strategic Alliances

Given the importance of strategic alliances and their potential effects on firm performance, businesses have started to emphasize the management of alliances as a way to develop a competitive advantage and create value for their shareholders.[37] As a result, firms are even creating units with the responsibility of managing their multiple strategic alliances.[38] The actions required to successfully manage alliances and their outcomes are shown in Figure 9.1.

Selecting partners is the first step in managing alliances to make them successful. If an incompatible partner is selected, the alliance is likely to fail. Furthermore, the firm should understand its partner well enough to ensure that it has the resources desired. An important part of the analysis and selection of a partner is to understand the context in which the partner operates, its competitive landscape, and the institutional forces (such as banks and government policies) with which it must deal (especially for international alliances).[39]

After selecting the partner and starting the alliance, each partner must access the resources desired from the other partner and learn the knowledge needed to successfully participate in the alliance. If either or both partners fail to achieve their goals, the alliance will fail. To increase the probability of alliance success, then, both partners must provide access to resources and be willing to help the other partner learn. The willingness to help partners may require extra effort until trust between the firms grows. Firms should attempt to build trust with the intent of establishing social capital in the alliance.[40] Trust is the basis for social capital, which in turn leads to cooperation between partners. Social capital implies that firms will help their partners gain value from an alliance. Of course, the partner is expected to reciprocate. Because of the difficulty in building trust and social capital, firms often form alliances with former partners with whom social capital already exists.

One measure of an alliance's success, in addition to its longevity, is the extent to which knowledge is transferred between partners and integrated into the

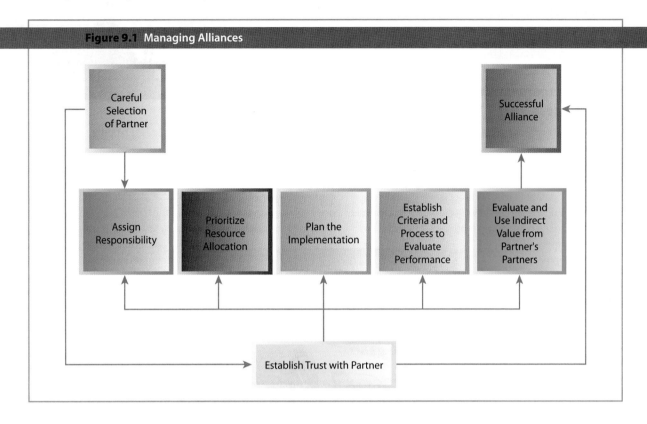

Figure 9.1 Managing Alliances

alliance operations. Integrating separate knowledge sets is important because this helps produce synergy and innovation, as illustrated in *Understanding Strategy: Learning from Failure* on GE's venture with Harbin. Its previous minority joint ventures across its businesses in avionics, rail locomotives, and "clean coal" technology, allowed it to have the courage to undertake the joint venture with Harbin in wind-power turbines. Harbin could also see that there were previous successes in China with other GE alliance partners. Thus, alliance managers should invest time and effort to ensure that both partners learn (add knowledge) from the alliance and that their two complementary knowledge stocks are integrated to create value in the alliance. Such activities will lead to improved reputation for any future alliances one might want to undertake.

According to some recent research, firms would do well to pay careful attention to equity investments in the alliances. The failure rate is high in alliances in which the foreign investors have a low equity investment or the equity investment is changed frequently. However, the success rate is higher when the foreign investor makes a large equity investment.[41] Obviously, when the equity is high, the investor has an incentive to ensure that the alliance succeeds. As such, more effort also is invested to make the alliance work. Additionally, foreign investors are likely to have greater technological and management expertise. Therefore, a higher equity stake encourages them to use more of their expertise to make the alliance successful.

Alliance success also is more likely when alliances are managed to identify and take advantage of opportunities rather than to minimize costs. Alliances formed on the basis of detailed formal contracts with extensive monitoring mechanisms are more likely to fail. Rather, firms should build trust in order to take maximum advantage of opportunities generated by forming the alliance. Such outcomes require careful and dedicated management to ensure cooperative efforts in strategic alliances.[42]

Alliance Management that Leads to Success

General Motors (GM) recently reorganized (2009) and emerged from bankruptcy court thinking that it was large enough to achieve economies of scale and develop most technologies on its own. Daniel Akerson took over as Chief Executive after the quick succession of both Rick Wagoner and Edward E. Whitacre. With the new Chief Executive in place, GM is shifting its focus to increase the number of partnerships it has with hopes of cutting costs and sharing the development burden of creating new technologies. It started a $100 million venture-capital fund to develop technologies with other small companies such as an Indiana electronic car company and a Michigan-based battery start-up. Although GM has used partnerships in the past such as building transmissions with Ford and trucks with Chrysler and BMW, this shift to focusing on partnerships is an important strategic move for the future. Making sure that it follows sound principles in this strategic shift is paramount to success.

Strategic alliances with small firms focused on key areas such as electric cars and battery technology is an increasingly important part of the new General Motor's strategy of spreading the costs and challenges of developing next generation vehicles.

For example, large airline alliances were often managed in a cumbersome way because there was no clear strategic center as in large vertical alliances such as Toyota's relationship with its many suppliers. In most airline alliances there are two anchor carriers, such as British Airways and American (Oneworld), KLM and Northwest (SkyTeam), and United and Lufthansa (Star Alliance). The SkyTeam airline alliance, for instance (now headed by Air France and Delta through the acquisition of KLM by Air France and Northwest by Delta), in the beginning was problematic because of poor governance and management structures. As time moved along, KLM and Northwest learned how to manage multiple alliances in a much more successful way. At the corporate level, each firm developed cross-board positions to facilitate high level contacts on each other's board of directors. Furthermore, at the next level down, there were teams of alliance managers in both firms, and these alliance managers formed steering committees composed of key partners. Furthermore, deeper in the

organization, there were working groups from both organizations as well as the other partners. These working groups focused on passengers, flight networks and code-sharing between airlines, fleet management and operational aspects, cargo management, and financial arrangements including profit sharing agreements between the firms. This arrangement led to improved goal attainment by increasing revenues and reducing operational costs. In particular, the financial agreements with 50-50 profit sharing were critical to establishing proactive coordination between the airlines. They needed to establish important decision-making styles, particularly focused on consensus. Making sure that the governing bodies met and accomplished their goals was facilitated by better communication structure, improved cultural arrangements, and a longer term (10 year) contract. Additionally, social events facilitated better personal relationships. Improved union representation at the board levels and inside the company working groups also helped smooth problems out in the cooperative agreements.

Another example involves two pharmaceutical firms, Solvay Pharmaceuticals and Quintiles. Solvay is a top-40 pharmaceutical company headquartered in Brussels with 10,000 employees. Although they had been internally focused to bring new drugs to market, they felt they could be more successful by outsourcing clinical trials research to a supplier. They chose Quintiles, a North Carolina-based firm employing 23,000 people in more than 50 countries. In creating the partnership agreement, Solvay consolidated a significant number of outsourced projects under Quintiles and, in return, Quintiles reduced their normal pricing for such research. In 2006, they decided to upgrade their partnership to a true strategic alliance. They formed a seven person joint steering committee to oversee the creation of the governance approaches. There were two alliance managers, one from each company, who participated in the seven person joint steering committee. The steering committee

© AP Photo/Paul Sancya

© Greg Epperson, iStock

asked important questions: How can we create shareholder value for both companies? How can we create differentiation in the marketplace? What issues and current problem areas should we address? Once these strategic issues were formulated, they developed objectives in five strategic themes: (1) Living the alliance to ensure that the right culture, trust, and communication were in place; (2) Creating collaboration based on transparency in the use of resources and services; (3) Doing things right to leverage the process of innovation; (4) Managing growth and investment decisions to accelerate the flow of compounds into the clinical development phase; and (5) Creating value for both organizations by jointly driving all activities in the alliance.

As one can see, it is clear that establishing goals, setting up appropriate management and governance structures and

incentives, and seeking to have joint management responsibility and ownership of all activities are critical to establish a successful partnership.

Sources: A. deMan, N. Roijakkers, & H. de Graauw, 2010, Managing dynamics through robust alliance governance structures: The case of KLM and Northwest Airlines, *European Management Journal*, 28(3): 171–181; R. Kaplin, D. Norton, & B. Rugelsjoen, 2010, Managing alliances with a balanced scorecard, *Harvard Business Review*, 88(1/2): 114–120; S. Terlep, 2010, In shift, GM now pursues partners, *The Wall Street Journal*, October 4, B1; U. Wassmer, P. Dussauge, & N. Planellas, 2010, How to manage alliances better than one at a time, *MIT Sloan Management Review*, 51(3): 77–78; K. Weber & B. Sparks, 2010, Service failure and recovery in a strategic airline alliance context: Interplay of locus of service failure and social identity, *Journal of Travel & Tourism Marketing*, 27(6): 547–564; 2009, SkyTeam moves to the next level, *Airline Business*, August 8, 8; C. Chetwynd, 2009, Airline alliances, *Buying Business Travel*, 41: 64–67; M. Schreiner, P. Kale, & D. Corsten, 2009, What really is alliance management capability and how does it impact alliance outcomes and success?, *Strategic Management Journal*, 30(13): 1395–1419.

In addition to the actions suggested previously, the following steps are recommended as guidelines for effectively managing strategic alliances:

1. Even if the firm has a unit with the overall responsibility of managing its network of alliances, a manager or sponsor should be named for each alliance (and a similar person should be named by the partner). These managers keep each other informed of major alliance activities, resource allocations, and outcomes.
2. The organization should analyze the alliance's priority within its resource allocations and ensure the commitment needed for each alliance to succeed.
3. A clear plan for implementing the alliance should be created and activated after the partners have agreed to the alliance.
4. The means for analyzing the performance of the alliance and distribution of performance outcomes to the partners should be clearly established. Important stakeholders' interests need to be considered when establishing the performance criteria.
5. In the evaluation of an alliance's value, the partners' partners in other alliances should be considered. The indirect network of partners from other alliances may be of value for future alliances or provide indirect value through the benefits derived by the firm's partner.[43]

Understanding Strategy: Learning from Success provides examples illustrating how these principles can help firms to better manage their cooperative strategies.

SUMMARY

The purpose of this chapter is to explain how a firm can develop and manage strategic alliances to develop or maintain a competitive advantage. In doing so, we examined the following topics:

● A strategic alliance is a relationship between firms in which the partners agree to cooperate in ways that

provide benefits to each of them. In an equity alliance, each partner owns a specified percentage of the equity in a separate venture. These ventures are often called joint ventures. In a nonequity alliance, a contractual relationship is established between two or more firms that allows them to share resources or capabilities.

● Firms form alliances for many reasons. Alliances can be helpful for entering new markets, especially those that are restricted (e.g., by governments). Alliances can be useful for sharing the risks of entering markets or in developing new products. In some cases, alliances help firms expand their economies of scale and market power. Oftentimes, strategic alliances are helpful in meeting competitive challenges, especially when the firms involved gain access to complementary resources or learn new capabilities. Finally, strategic alliances have played a major role in the recent outsourcing trend.

● Strategic alliances can be established at the business level. They may be vertical alliances across separate activities in the value chain or horizontal alliances between competitors.

● Corporate-level strategic alliances include alliances for diversification and/or those designed to create synergy. Additionally, franchising is a form of strategic alliance, and international strategic alliances have become common for entering new foreign markets.

● While strategic alliances can provide several benefits to the partners, they also present some important risks. A major risk is the potential for opportunism by one of the partners. There is a high alliance failure rate often because of differences in corporate or national culture and due to information asymmetries. Differences in culture may produce conflicts, and information asymmetries can lead to inaccurate assumptions about resources and capabilities held by partners.

● To increase the probability of success, strategic alliances need to be managed. First, firms should take great care in selecting compatible partners that have the needed resources. Examining the amount of equity used in forming an alliance is also important. After the alliance is formed, the partners should invest in establishing trust, which will ensure the transfer of resources and learning. They should also assign responsibilities within the firm, develop priorities for allocating resources, plan for the alliance's implementation, and develop means for evaluating its performance and distributing performance outcomes back to partners.

KEY TERMS

Complementary resources, 194	Horizontal strategic alliance, 196	Strategic alliance, 192
Cooperative strategy, 192	Joint venture, 193	Vertical strategic alliance, 196
Equity alliance, 193	Nonequity alliance, 193	

DISCUSSION QUESTIONS

1. What is a strategic alliance, and what are the differences between equity and nonequity alliances?
2. Why do firms form alliances? Explain.
3. What are vertical and horizontal business-level alliances?
4. What are corporate-level strategic alliances?
5. Why do firms commonly use strategic alliances to enter international markets?

6. What are the major risks involved in forming strategic alliances?
7. What can firms do to manage strategic alliances in ways that increase their probability of success?
8. What is the best way to end a strategic alliance or joint venture?

Introduction

Before entering a strategic alliance, a firm must carefully analyze the supporting logic and rationale. It is a good time to consider external consultants, even though the initial assessment process can be done internally. This chapter's tool—the Alliance Decision Evaluation Grid—can be a helpful way to evaluate whether the alliance makes sense.

Alliance Decision Evaluation Grid

Rationale	A. Relative Importance [1 (low) to 5 (high)]	B. Support for Alliance [1 (low) to 5 (high)]	Calculated Attractiveness [A × B]
Gain access to a restricted market			
Develop new goods or services			
Facilitate new market entry			
Share significant R&D investments			
Share risks and buffer against uncertainty			
Develop market power			
Gain access to complementary resources			
Build economies of scale			
Meet competitive challenges			
Learn new skills and capabilities			
Outsource for lower costs and higher-quality output			

Is Outsourcing Good or Bad for Firms?

Outsourcing by U.S. firms has increased significantly in recent years as a way to lower costs and improve their focus on their capabilities. However, firms are now outsourcing professional jobs done by white-collar workers (engineering and software development jobs); most previous outsourcing involved blue-collar manufacturing jobs. Because it is affecting a large number of all types of jobs, outsourcing has become a political issue. However, some argue that outsourcing, such as in the automobile industry, will lead to production and sales in foreign countries with growing demand, such as China. In fact, as we noted in *Focusing on Strategy* at the beginning of the chapter, China is the top automobile producer in the world, primarily for export through outsourcing, but also because of the expanding domestic demand. More broadly, some argue that trade with foreign countries such as China has fostered moves away from past political repression toward more economic freedom. Thus, as discussed next, most of the focus of outsourcing is to improve efficiency and effectiveness, but political ramifications must also be considered.

Even though outsourcing to low-cost manufacturers has been common for some time, software development, programming, and even high-technology professional activities such as interpreting medical X-rays are more recent examples of work activities being outsourced. For example, AstraZeneca, a large U.K. pharmaceutical firm, has contracted much of its drug production and even some of its R&D to manufacturers in China and India, which will come online in the coming decade. One executive indicated that "manufacturing is not a core activity for the company" and "that there are a lot of organizations that are better at manufacturing." However, he also pointed out that "it will never make sense for a major pharmaceutical company to outsource 100 percent of its manufacturing requirements." In fact, the decision will be based on keeping knowledge of important products and processes in-house to protect intellectual property, as well as basic supply (sourcing and transportation), financial, regulatory, and restructuring

considerations. However, another analyst noted: "Emerging markets are being seen as a prominent driver of top-line growth by the pharma majors. It is in this environment that R&D activities too are becoming increasingly global."

Outsourcing professional activities means that higher-paying jobs are going overseas and may become a political liability for organizations doing such outsourcing. Yet businesses argue that outsourcing is necessary to remain competitive in global markets. In fact, managers suggest that outsourcing important activities not only saves money (by reducing costs) but also increases quality in some cases because those doing the outsourced work are specialists. Still, drawbacks are a factor. Outsourcing firms lose the capability to perform the activity when they outsource it, meaning that it will be difficult and costly to redevelop that capability at a later date, if desired. Additionally, even though outsourcing provides flexibility that is important in a dynamic competitive landscape, firms must be careful not to outsource key areas. Managers must also ensure that the firm does not lose a core competence or an activity important for supporting a core competence because of their outsourcing decisions. Additionally, outsourcing may involve risks to reputation and even legal liability problems if work is done poorly. For example, Delta and United Airlines brought back their outsourced customer service operations to North America when they started to experience a lower rate of satisfaction from more sophisticated conversations with customers. Often, voice-based processes that are combined with knowledge-based activities are not good candidates for outsourcing to offshore or even near-shore vendors. Onshore vendors may be more suitable to mitigate such risks.

The outsourcing trend has reached Japan and Europe. However, the cost of outsourcing in Europe is more expensive. For example, in Denmark, although firms have more flexibility to decide to outsource than most European companies, workers can receive up to 90 percent of their wages for six months as severance paid by the company before they receive any unemployment payments from the government insurance program. By law, they also receive up to six weeks of retraining to facilitate movement into new jobs. However, the reverse trend toward outsourcing to higher-level capabilities is evident. For example, many U.S. financial service firms expect to receive significant levels of outsourcing by sovereign wealth funds (national governments that often have funds due to trade surpluses, such as Saudi Arabia) to provide expertise in portfolio management.

Many arguments are made on both sides about the costs and benefits of outsourcing. Firms must decide whether outsourcing is positively linked to performance, what to outsource, and to whom to outsource. They may have to fend off politicians who provide incentives not to outsource. In addition, legislation may be introduced that calls for a tax to be levied on imported goods or services that have been developed through outsourcing. The problems managers face related to outsourcing are complex, and the solutions may not be simple.

Sources: A. Bhagwat, 2010, Trends in pharmaceutical R&D outsourcing, *Pharma*, July, 32–33; L. Cusmano, M. Mancusi, & A. Morrison, 2010, Globalization of production and innovation: How outsourcing is reshaping an advanced manufacturing area, *Regional Studies*, 44(3): 235–252; H. Glimstedt, D. Bratt, & M. Karlsson, 2010, The decision to make or buy a critical technology: Semi-conductors at Ericsson, 1980–2010, *Industrial and Corporate Change*, 19(2): 431–464; H. Gospel & M. Sako, 2010, The unbundling of corporate functions: The evolution of shared services and outsourcing in human resource management, *Industrial and Corporate Change*, 19(5): 1367–1396; K. W. Platts & N. Song, 2010, Overseas sourcing decisions—total cost of sourcing from China, *Supply Chain Management*, 15(4): 320–331; M. Reitzig & S. Wagner, 2010, The hidden cost of outsourcing: Evidence from patent data, *Strategic Management Journal*, 31(11): 1183–1201; C. Sanchez, 2010, The benefits and risks of knowledge process outsourcing, *Ivey Business Journal*, www.iveybusinessjournal.com, May/June; A. Drakulich & P. Van Arnum, 2009, Evaluating the pieces of the pharma supply chain, *Pharmaceutical Technology*, December, 80–86; C. Raiborne, J. Butler, & M. Massoud, 2009, Outsourcing support functions: Identifying and managing the good, the bad and the ugly, *Business Horizons*, 52(4): 347–356.

Questions

1. From the perspective of strategic management, what are the costs and benefits of outsourcing?
2. As a manager, what type of information would you gather and what analyses would you conduct to decide whether to outsource an activity?
3. How do you predict that outsourcing from U.S., Japanese, and European firms to China, Taiwan, and India will affect the economies and firms in the three sourcing countries?

EXPERIENTIAL EXERCISES

Exercise One: Alliances in the Airline Industry

In Groups

Each group will be assigned one of the following airline alliances. Use the alliance Web site and other information sources to answer the following questions:

1. What kind of alliance is used? Equity or nonequity? Horizontal or vertical?
2. When was the alliance formed, and which airlines are members of the alliance?
3. How do airlines cooperate within this alliance (e.g., what kinds of resources are shared), and what are the specific benefits to the airlines and customers?
4. Refer to Table 9.1 in the chapter. Which of the reasons for strategic alliances are most applicable to this alliance?

5. What are the main risks associated with being a member of this alliance?

Whole Class

Each group should present its answers to the preceding questions, and the class should discuss the similarities and differences among the three alliances. To what extent do these alliances help airlines overcome the current challenges facing them?

Airline Alliances

oneworld: www.oneworld.com

SkyTeam: http://skyteam.com

Star Alliance: www.staralliance.com

© vndrpttn, iStock

Exercise Two: Franchising in the Hotel Industry

Choice Hotels International was used in the chapter as an example of a firm using the franchising corporate-level strategic alliance. For the first part of this exercise, update the information provided in the chapter—for example, the number of brands (e.g., Comfort Inn, Clarion Inn), the total number of hotels franchised, and the number of foreign countries in which franchises are located. For the second part of the exercise, go to the company Web site (www.choicehotels.com) and other sources to determine whether the franchising arrangement has any of the following requirements or characteristics (suggested in the chapter) to ensure effectiveness:

- There is close cooperation between the partners.
- The development and transfer of successful programs takes place, and the franchisor has a means of managing the operation.
- Franchisee possesses knowledge and capabilities necessary to compete in the local market.
- Franchisees provide feedback to the franchisor about activities that work and those that do not.
- Franchisees inform the franchisor about the important characteristics of competitors and market conditions in their local markets.

ENDNOTES

1. O. Schilke & A. Goerzen, 2010, Alliance management capability: An investigation of the construct and its measurement, *Journal of Management*, 36: 1192–1219.
2. C. C. Phelps, 2010, A longitudinal study of the influence of alliance network structure and composition on firm exploratory innovation, *Academy of Management Journal*, 53: 890–913.
3. R. Jiang, Q. Tao, & M. Santoro, 2010, Alliance portfolio diversity and firm performance, *Strategic Management Journal*, 31(10): 1136–1144.
4. D. Cameron, 2010, Corporate news: China is near deal with GE on jet, *The Wall Street Journal*, July 13, B2.
5. H. Hoang & F. Rothaermel, 2010, Leveraging internal and external experience: Exploration, exploitation and R&D project performance, *Strategic Management Journal*, 31(7): 734–756.
6. J. Zhang & C. Baden-Fuller, 2010, The influence of technological knowledge base and organizational structure on technology collaboration, *Journal of Management Studies*, 47(4): 679–704.
7. J. Osawa, 2010, Corporate news: Johnson, Hitachi in battery tie-up, *The Wall Street Journal*, October 19, B2.
8. Y.-S. Hwang & S. H. Park, 2007, The organizational life cycle as a determinant of strategic alliance tactics: Research propositions, *International Journal of Management*, 24(3): 427–435; M. A. Hitt, M. T. Dacin, E. Levitas, J.-L. Arregle, & A. Borza, 2000, Partner selection in emerging and developed market contexts: Resource-based and organizational learning perspectives, *Academy of Management Journal*, 43: 449–467.
9. P. Mozur and B. Koster, 2010, Update: China Airlines to join SkyTeam; Alliance aims to grow, *The Wall Street Journal*, www.wsj.com, September 14.
10. D. Duso, E. Pennings, & J. Seldeslachts, 2010, Learning dynamics in research alliances: A panel data analysis, *Research Policy*, 39(6): 776–789; C. Lakshman & R. C. Parente, 2008, Supplier-focused knowledge management in the automobile industry and its implications for product performance, *Journal of Management Studies*, 45: 317–342.
11. R. Boehner, 2009, Make innovation an off-shore thing, *Manufacturing Chemist*, September, 92; J. Howells, D. Goiardi, & K. Malik, 2008, The growth and management of R&D outsourcing: Evidence from U.K. Pharmaceuticals, *R&D Management*, 38(2): 205–219.
12. Z. Cui, C. H. Loch, B. Grossmann, & R. He, 2009, Outsourcing innovation, *Research Technology Management*, 52(6): 54–63.
13. A. Hecker & T. Kretschmer, 2010, Outsourcing decisions: The effect of scale economies and market structure, *Strategic Organization*, 8(2): 155–175.
14. C.-L. Liu, P. N. Ghauri, & R. R. Sinkovics, 2010, Understanding the impact of relational capital and organizational learning on alliance outcomes, *Journal of World Business*, 45(3): 237–247; R. Gulati & M. Sytch, 2008, Does familiarity breed trust? Revisiting the antecedents of trust, *Managerial and Decision Economics*, 29: 165–190.
15. J. Yang, J. Wang, C. W. Y. Wong, & J.-H. Lin, 2008, Relational stability and alliance performance in supply chain, *Omega*, 36(4): 600–608.
16. R. Locke & M. Romis, 2007, Improving work conditions in a global supply-chain, *MIT Sloan Management Review*, 48(2): 54–62.
17. Schilke & Goerzen, Alliance management capability; L. C. Giunipero, R. B. Handfield, & D. L. Johansen, 2008, Beyond buying: Supply-chain managers used to have one main job: Purchasing stuff cheaply; They need a whole new skill set now, *The Wall Street Journal*, March 10, R8.
18. T. Tong & J. Reuer, 2010, Competitive consequences of interfirm collaboration: How joint ventures shape industry profitability, *Journal of International Business Studies*, 41(6): 1056–1073.
19. D. Fickling, 2010, Corporate news: Rio Tinto BHP scrap venture—Mining giants planned $116 Billion iron-ore alliance terminated due to opposition from regulators, *The Wall Street Journal*, October 18, B3.
20. J. B. Barney, 2007, *Gaining and Sustaining a Competitive Advantage*, 3rd ed., Upper Saddle River, NJ: Prentice Hall.
21. B. Chidmi & R. A. Lopez, 2007, Brand-supermarket demand for breakfast cereals and retail competition, *American Journal of Agricultural Economics*, 89: 324–337; L. C. Strauss, 2006, They're grrrreat! *Barron's*, January 2, 19.
22. Barney, *Gaining and Sustaining a Competitive Advantage*, 276.
23. L. Sanchez-Peinado & M. Menguzzato-Boulard, 2009, Antecedents of entry mode choice when diversifying, *Industrial Marketing Management*, 38(8): 971–983; J. S. Harrison, M. A. Hitt, R. E. Hoskisson, & R. D. Ireland, 2001, Resource complementarity in business combinations: Extending the logic to organizational alliances, *Journal of Management*, 27: 679–699.
24. E. Garnsey, G. Lorenzoni, & S. Ferriani, 2008, Speciation through entrepreneurial spin-off: The Acorn-Arm story, *Research Policy*, 37: 210–224.
25. J. Greene, D. Purcell, B. Edelman, D. Giordano, R. Ruback, D. Milas, & G. Giovannetti, 2010, The role of private equity in life sciences, *Journal of Applied Corporate Finance*, 22(2): 8–35.
26. S. Vivek, R. G. Richey, & V. Dalela, 2009, A longitudinal examination of partnership governance in offshoring: A moving target, *Journal of World Business*, 44(1): 16–30.
27. P. Glader, 2010, Corporate news: GE in China wind-power venture—Companies will make and sell turbines to booming markets as GE fights to boost Chinese revenue, *The Wall Street Journal*, September 28, B3.
28. J. Q. Freed, 2010, Choice Hotels tweaks brand growth strategies, *Hotel & Motel Management*, June, 4, 49.
29. S. C. Michael, 2003, First mover advantage through franchising, *Journal of Business Venturing*, 18: 61–80.
30. L. Chao, 2010, Sony Ericsson says China is embracing Smartphones, *The Wall Street Journal*, September 1, B7.

31. T. Vapola, M. Paukku, & M. Gabrielsson, 2010, Portfolio management of strategic alliances: An international business perspective, *International Business Review*, 19(3): 247–260; A. C. Inkpen, 2008, Knowledge transfer and international joint ventures: The case of NUMMI and General Motors, *Strategic Management Journal*, 29: 447–453.

32. R. Bailay, 2010, Bharti-Walmart flagship brand faces opposition, *Mint*, www.livemint.com, January 13.

33. P. Kale & H. Singh, 2009, Managing strategic alliances: What do we know now, and where do we go from here?, *Academy of Management Perspectives*, 23(3): 45–62.

34. G. Deitz, M. Tokman, R. G. Richey, & R. Morgan, 2010, Joint venture stability and cooperation: Direct, indirect and contingent effects of resource complementarity and trust, *Industrial Marketing Management*, 39(5): 862–873.

35. R. Grover, 2007, How Bob Iger unchained Disney, *BusinessWeek*, February 5, 74–79.

36. B. Nielsen, 2010, Strategic fit, contractual, and procedural governance in alliances, *Journal of Business Research*, 63(7): 682–689; J. J. Reuer & A. Arino, 2007, Strategic alliance contracts: Dimensions and determinants of contractual complexity, *Strategic Management Journal*, 28: 313–330.

37. A. Kos, 2010, An explanatory model for the decision to enter emerging markets: A shareholder perspective, *International Journal of Management*, 27(2): 320–325.

38. P. Kale & H. Singh, 2009, Managing strategic alliances; J. H. Dyer, P. Kale, & H. Singh, 2001, How to make strategic alliances work, *MIT Sloan Management Review*, 42(4): 37–43.

39. H. Hoang & F. Rothaermel, 2010, Leveraging internal and external experience: Exploration, exploitation, and R&D project performance, *Strategic Management Journal*, 31(7): 734–758; M. A. Hitt, D. Ahlstrom, M. T. Dacin, E. Levitas, & L. Svobodina, 2004, The institutional effects on strategic alliance partner selection in transition economies: China versus Russia, *Organization Science*, 15: 173–185.

40. M. H. Hansen, R. E. Hoskisson, & J. B. Barney, 2008, Competitive advantage in alliance governance: Resolving the opportunism minimization-gain maximization paradox, *Managerial and Decision Economics*, 29(2/3): 191–208.

41. C. Chung & P. Beamish, 2010, The trap of continual ownership change in international equity joint ventures, *Organization Science*, 21(5): 995–1015; C. Dhanaraj & P. W. Beamish, 2004, Effect of equity ownership on the survival of international joint ventures, *Strategic Management Journal*, 25: 295–305.

42. D. Faems, M. Janssens, A. Madhok, & B. Van Looy, 2008, Toward an integrative perspective on alliance governance: Connecting contract design, trust dynamics, and contract application, *Academy of Management Journal*, 51(6): 1053–1078; J. H. Dyer & C. Wujin, 2003, The role of trustworthiness in reducing transaction costs and improving performance: Empirical evidence from the United States, Japan and Korea, *Organization Science*, 9: 285–305.

43. U. Wassmer, P. Dussauge, & M. Planellas, 2010, How to manage alliances better than one at a time, *MIT Sloan Management Review*, 51(3): 77–84; K. E. Klein, 2004, Fine-tune that alliance, *BusinessWeek Online*, www.businessweek.com, February 10.

CHAPTER 10

Innovating through Strategic Entrepreneurship

KNOWLEDGE OBJECTIVES

Reading and studying this chapter should enable you to:

1. Define innovation, entrepreneurship, and entrepreneurs.

2. Describe entrepreneurial opportunities and entrepreneurial capabilities.

3. Understand strategic entrepreneurship and explain how organizations use it.

4. Describe how firms internally develop innovations.

5. Explain how firms use cooperative strategies to develop innovations.

6. Discuss acquisitions as a means of innovation.

7. Summarize the use of strategic entrepreneurship as a means of innovation and market entry.

© Shannon Fagan, Getty Images

FOCUSING ON STRATEGY

Entrepreneurship and Innovation: Flourishing in India

> If "outsourcing" was the buzz word of the 90s, there is very little one hears about the India story today without the mention of entrepreneurship or innovation.
>
> *Pranay Gupta, Joint CEO, Center for Innovation, Incubation, and Entrepreneurship*

The products: novel treatments for migraine headaches and for psoriasis, a serious skin condition. The question: what do these treatments have in common? The answer: both were developed by Indian scientists working in a country that is increasingly oriented to innovation and entrepreneurship. Many other innovative products are being designed and produced in India today as well, which some consider to be "…one of the world's burgeoning centers of new entrepreneurship." In fact, after a recent visit to India, an innovation expert said that the innovation energy in the country is tremendous and that India appears to be a "nation of entrepreneurs."

India's expanding innovation capabilities took root in the early 1980s when a group of software engineers formed Infosys. An innovative firm to which companies across the globe outsourced work, Infosys is credited with contributing to the "flattening of the world" as it provided technology services to overseas clients, initially using India's widely available but low-cost human capital as the foundation for its success.

The relationship between India and innovation and entrepreneurship demonstrates that innovation talent and capabilities are spread across the globe instead of being concentrated in North American and European countries and companies. Because of this, firms are seeking to "globalize" their innovation efforts by establishing innovation centers in a number of regions and countries. In addition to the availability of talent though, the sheer size of emerging economy markets is another reason companies want to be able to innovate in these economies.

© AP Photo/Aijaz Rahi

GE is an example of a company that is committed to establishing the ability to innovate in India. To facilitate these efforts, the firm built the John F. Welch Technology Center in Bangalore, India. Employing over 3,500 scientists, patents on aircraft engines, locomotives, and medical devices are flowing from this center. These patents are foundational to the firm's efforts to innovate across multiple product categories that will be produced and sold in many parts of the world.

The MAC 400 is an example of a product that GE Healthcare has developed in India, using some of the patents developed at the technology center to do so. A portable electrocardiogram machine, the MAC 400 "…can take 100 EKGs on a single battery charge and weighs less than three pounds." This product is highly appropriate for those in rural areas where electricity may not be available and for use with patients who may lack the ability to travel to urban areas for diagnoses and treatments.

Firms such as Gillette are also using their R&D capabilities in other parts of the world to develop innovative products that are intended to serve the needs of customers in emerging markets. Introduced in India in late 2010, the Gillette Guard is an example of such a product. With a single blade and a light plastic handle, this razor is selling in India for 15 rupees, or about 34 cents. Designed around what customers can afford to pay rather than around what the firm's technological capabilities make possible, the Gillette Guard is targeted to 400 million men in India who are double-blade users. Gillette believes that its single blade razor provides a shave that is equal to, if not superior to, what is provided by many of the currently available double-blade razors.

Although embryonic in development, it appears that the innovation occurring in India is positively affecting the nation's efforts to improve the overall strength of its economy. Simultaneously, developing innovative products to serve customers' needs in emerging economies such as India is an avenue of growth for companies engaged in global competition.

Sources: S. Anthony, 2010, Innovation notes from India, *Harvard Business Review Blogs*, www.blogs.hbr.org, August 12; S. R. Das, 2010, Frugal innovation: India plans to distribute low-cost handheld computers to students, *Scientific American*, www.scientificamerican.com, September 28; P. Gupta, 2010, The rise of incubation in India, 2010, *The Wall Street Journal Online*, www.wsj.com, April 7; R. Salkowitz, 2010, What's next for India's tech entrepreneurs?, *Bloomberg Businessweek*, www.businessweek.com, August 25; G. Bagla & A. Goel, 2009, Innovation from India: The next big wave, *Bloomberg Businessweek*, www.businessweek.com, February 11.

In this chapter, we explain how firms use innovation as a means for entering new markets, creating entirely new markets, or more successfully serving markets in which they currently compete. Discussed in *Focusing on Strategy*, the Gillette Guard is an example of a product innovation that is intended to better serve the needs of customers in a market where the firm already competes. As an innovation, GE's MAC 400 has created what is essentially a new market in that the product moves EKG testing from a "...cardiologist's domain to that of a general physician anywhere in the country."[1]

Today, a firm's ability to innovate across time couldn't be more important in that "continuous innovation is the engine that drives highly successful companies such as Apple, General Electric, Google, Honda, HP, Microsoft, P&G, Sony, Tata group, and many others."[2] From an operational perspective, when innovating, companies develop unique and successful solutions to problems facing their target customers and/or potential customers.[3] Customers who are able to continuously buy innovative goods or services from a company that create value for them become loyal to that firm;[4] in turn, customer loyalty makes it more difficult for competitors to successfully compete against the innovative company.

As we explain in *Focusing on Strategy*, innovation is critical to the ongoing success of firms such as GE and Gillette. This is not surprising in that innovation is thought to be critical to the success of most if not all companies.[5] In fact, results from a number of studies suggest a positive link between innovation and firm performance.[6] These findings corroborate the experiences of many of the companies we mention in this chapter.

As is true for GE and Gillette, many organizations, especially larger ones, use three methods to innovate: internal development, cooperative relationships, and acquisitions. We consider these three means for developing innovation in this chapter. As a foundation for doing this, we first define innovation and then describe innovation's relationships with entrepreneurship and entrepreneurs. We also introduce the characteristics and behaviors of entrepreneurs and explain the concept of strategic entrepreneurship (essentially, strategic entrepreneurship is a set of practices through which firms use a strategic perspective to pursue entrepreneurial opportunities). The chapter then describes the three ways firms innovate, often relying on strategic entrepreneurship to do so. After discussing internal innovation, we examine innovation through cooperative relationships and then through acquisitions. We close the chapter with a summary analysis of how firms can create value by successfully using strategic entrepreneurship.

Our focus in this chapter is on innovation and entrepreneurship in existing organizations. This phenomenon is called **corporate entrepreneurship,** which is an organization-wide reliance on entrepreneurship and innovation as the link to solid financial performance.[7] Thus, our concern is with entrepreneurship and the innovation it spawns within established firms rather than how entrepreneurship is the

corporate entrepreneurship

an organization-wide reliance on entrepreneurship and innovation as the link to solid financial performance bedrock for starting new ventures. Courses in entrepreneurship describe how innovation often is the foundation on which new entrepreneurial ventures are built.

Before beginning our discussions of these topics, you should know that uncertainty surrounds innovation. Uncertainty exists when the probability of a certain outcome being achieved is unknown.[8] Even when firms do everything the way it should be done, they have no guarantees that what they are doing will lead to successful innovations. Firms must accept uncertainty and the possibility of failure when innovating. Uncertainty does not diminish the value of innovation at all, although firms can't expect every innovative effort to succeed.

Of course, many actions that firms take are uncertain in terms of their outcomes. Uncertainty is reduced, however, when the firm successfully follows the steps in the strategic management process. We add to the basic strategic management model in this chapter by describing when certain approaches to innovation are better than others.

Innovation, Entrepreneurship, and Entrepreneurs

Innovation

What image comes to mind when you think of *innovation*? Are you thinking of a new good or service that a company is offering or might offer? If so, your thoughts are on target: **Innovation** is the development of something new—a new good, a new type of service, or a new way of presenting a good or service to a market. From the perspective of a consumer of an innovation, innovation is all about an opportunity to choose something that is new.[9]

Newness sometimes finds a firm creating a new market niche (e.g., Subway's creation of the "health-conscious" niche in the fast-food industry) or even redefining an industry as Apple did in the tablet computer industry with the iPad. However, innovation success, such as Apple is having with the iPad, influences competitors to innovate as well to develop similar goods or services but with different and hopefully greater functionality for users. For example, Research in Motion (RIM), the maker of the BlackBerry, launched its Play-Book in late 2010. Smaller and lighter than the iPad, RIM claims that its product "...boasts several features the iPad lacks, including front- and rear-facing cameras for teleconferencing and the ability to play online videos made with Adobe's Flash technology."[10] In other instances, firms rely on continuous innovation to build market share in existing markets or to enter new markets. This is the case for Gillette as it introduces new razors and new versions of current razors to satisfy customers' needs and to generate loyalty among those customers.[11] Recently, Gillette introduced its Fusion ProGlide razor, saying that it is the most technologically sophisticated razor the firm has produced and offered to customers.[12]

As customers, new goods and services are visible to us. However, process and administrative innovations are also important to firms' innovation efforts; typically though, as customers, we are not aware of these innovations. **Process innovations** are new means of producing, selling, and supporting goods and services.[13]

Apple's iPad has inspired no shortage of competitors (including RIM's PlayBook and numerous tablets running Google's Andriod operating system) eager to battle it out in a form and feature war. Of course, Apple isn't standing still either and in March 2011 launched the iPad 2, which added new features such as front- and rear-facing cameras.

© All Canada Photos / SuperStock

innovation

the development of something new—a new good, a new type of service, or a new way of presenting a good or service to a market

process innovations

new means of producing, selling, and supporting goods and services

Dell's famous direct-sales model is an example of a process innovation. Before Dell, personal computers (PCs) were sold through store-front retailers. Seeing an opportunity, Michael Dell developed a new process to sell PCs, which was to sell directly to customers rather than indirectly through retailers. Across time, virtually all PC manufacturers (including HP, Acer, and Lenovo) learned how to imitate Dell's process innovation.

During his time at the helm of GM, Alfred P. Sloan, Jr., "invented the very idea of the modern American corporation."[14] An **administrative innovation** is a new way of organizing or handling the organizational tasks firms use to complete their work.[15]

Sloan's administrative innovation was to break GM into smaller divisions that could operate autonomously as long as they met their financial goals. Initially, the divisions focused on different products (Chevrolet, Buick, Pontiac, Oldsmobile, and Cadillac) that were intended to meet customers' different needs (family transportation, sporty performance, luxury, and so forth). Sloan believed that his innovative organizational structure would enable employees to work more independently in each division. Division independence from the direct control of the firm's upper-level managers, he thought, would cause employees in those divisions to be more creative and innovative and that the firm's performance would be enhanced as a result. Making it possible for employees to use their abilities proved to be an important outcome from Sloan's administrative innovation in that at the end of the day, many believe that innovations come from a firm's employees, who after all are "…the people who daily fight the company's battles, who serve the customers, explore new markets and fend off the competition."[16] In this sense, Sloan's administrative innovation allowed GM to get the best from its people.[17]

It is important to understand that the purpose of innovation is to increase the firm's performance. In this regard, innovating simply for the sake of innovating is not a sustainable path for companies to follow. Although sales can be somewhat cyclical in nature, firms producing innovative flat-screen televisions based on different technologies such as LCD, DLP, and plasma gas, as well as companies making components for flat screens, appeared to be increasing their performance in late 2010. This was the case for LG Electronics for example, as its sales volume and profitability both improved from 2009 to 2010.[18] As noted, innovations are always critical to performance improvements for firms producing these products. 3D TV is another innovation that is predicted to soon be available to flat-screen customers.[19]

When studying innovation, we also want to understand that firms are simultaneously challenged to operate efficiently while producing and selling the goods and services they offer currently and to focus on developing innovations. Finding the "right" balance between operational efficiency and innovation is difficult. As we discuss in *Understanding Strategy: Learning from Failure*, some believe that in recent years, the relationship between efficiency and innovation became out of balance at 3M, a company long known for its innovations. However, recent actions and their results suggest that a balance between efficiency and innovation that is "right" for 3M has been restored.

What helps firms such as 3M in their efforts to continuously innovate? As we discuss next, entrepreneurship and the entrepreneurs who are its foundation play important roles in a firm's ability to innovate.

Entrepreneurship

Joseph Schumpeter, the famous economist, saw **entrepreneurship** as a process of "creative destruction" through which existing products, methods of production, or ways of administering or managing the firm are destroyed and replaced with

administrative innovation

a new way of organizing or handling the organizational tasks firms use to complete their work

entrepreneurship

a process of "creative destruction" through which existing products, methods of production, or ways of administering or managing the firm are destroyed and replaced with new ones

Refocusing on Innovation at 3M

3M has long been known as an innovative company. There are many reasons for this, including the fact that it produces over 55,000 products that are components of multiple thousands of products other companies produce. The firm's ability to introduce over 1,000 new products during 2009 alone, a year that was characterized by recessionary conditions throughout the world, is another indicator of its innovative abilities as is the fact that researchers are encouraged to spend up to 15 percent of their time to pursue their own innovative ideas. Some of 3M's most famous products, including Scotch Tape and Post-it Notes, resulted from researchers' efforts while working on their own projects. Third-quarter 2010 results showed that, compared to the third-quarter of 2009, the firm's sales increased 11 percent and its margins increased 23 percent, suggesting the likelihood that 3M's innovations are leading to performance improvements. According to CEO George W. Buckley, "New products are fueling market share gains and filling adjacent spaces everywhere, but particularly in emerging markets, the fastest-growing area of our company."

Even 3M, a company known for its product innovations, can struggle to find balance. All firms experience difficulty in maintaining efficiencies while at the same time promoting the freedom necessary to support the investigation of new product or service innovations.

These results suggest a resurgence of 3M's commitment to innovation as well as the positive outcomes the innovation generates. The resurgence came about as a result of previous CEO James McNerney's emphasis on efficiency. During his tenure (2001–2005), McNerney (a GE alumnus) "…streamlined operations, laid off 8,000 people, and imported Six Sigma management techniques, popularized by GE, to analyze processes, curb waste, and reduce defects." In ways, these actions were necessary in that 3M had become sluggish and perhaps a bit bloated while emphasizing innovation and paying relatively little attention to efficiency.

It isn't that efficiency shouldn't have been given more attention as a means of bringing balance between efficiency and innovation at 3M. However, it turned out that concentrating on efficiency improvements came at a price to the firm's innovativeness. Evidence suggests that following Six Sigma practices "choked" researchers working in the labs, which were the sources of the firm's innovation. In the words of a researcher: "It's really tough to schedule innovation." Historically, 3M's goal was to generate 30 percent of revenue from new products that were introduced in the previous five years. Following Six Sigma practices and other measures McNerney put in place caused this percentage to drop to 21 percent; in turn, this drop led to declines in the firm's overall performance.

Believing that 3M is "…an engineer's and scientist's Toys 'R' US," new CEO Buckley's leadership is finding the firm again emphasizing innovation, to some degree at the expense of efficiency. (While Six Sigma practices remain in force in 3M's operations, it is gone from the labs.) Seemingly, Buckley is finding the balance between efficiency and innovation that is "right" for 3M. He is a tireless champion of the importance of the labs and continues allocating well over $1 billion annually to R&D. In terms of the "30 percent rule," the results of these efforts are impressive in that 3M is again generating 30 percent of its revenue from products introduced over the past five years. To support the goal of continuous innovation, 3M now employs 6,500 (out of 75,000 total employees) in its R&D functions.

Sources: M. Gunther, 2010, 3M's innovation revival, *CNNMoney.com*, www.cnnmoney.com, September 24; D. Mattioli & K. Maher, 2010, At 3M, innovation comes in tweaks and snips, *The Wall Street Journal Online*, www.wsj.com, March 1; 2010, 3M profits as post-it notes turns 30 years, *Securing Innovation*, www.securinginnovation.com, April 27, 2010, 3M facts, 3M Home page, www.3m.com, October 25; 2010, 3M achieves record sales of $6.9 billion on 11 percent organic volume growth, 3M Home page, www.3m.com, October 28.

© kimeveruss, iStock

© AP Photo/Matt Rourke

Intel identified an entrepreneurial opportunity in what appeared to be a breakdown in the observation of Gordon E. Moore, co-founder of the company, known as Moore's Law. While microcircuits became ever smaller and more powerful, they also generated more heat. The solution to this problem was the design of entirely new type of transistor.

new ones.[20] Firms encouraging entrepreneurship are willing to take risks as well as to be creative while using innovation as a key means of trying to outperform competitors.[21] Peter Drucker provided a classic description that directly describes the relationship between innovation and entrepreneurship: "Innovation is the specific form of entrepreneurship, whether in an existing business, a public service institution, or a new venture started by a lone individual."[22]

The specific focus of entrepreneurship is on identifying and then exploiting profitable entrepreneurial opportunities. **Entrepreneurial opportunities** are circumstances suggesting that new goods or services can be sold at a price exceeding the costs incurred to create, make, sell, and support them.[23] Sometimes opportunities are borne out of cold, hard realities. For example, Moore's Law suggests that the number of transistors (the microscopic, silicon-based switches that process the digital world's ones and zeros) on a chip roughly doubles every two years. This doubling creates more features, increased performance, and reduced cost per transistor. But in the 1990s, it became obvious that the limitations of existing technologies would rather quickly prevent continuing repetition of Moore's Law. Essentially, the problem facing chip manufacturers such as Intel was that as microcircuits continue to shrink while becoming more powerful, they run hotter and hotter, making it impossible to satisfactorily provide cooling. Intel's decision makers concluded that a different type of transistor had to be developed if the PC industry was to continue growing (and Intel along with it). As we discuss next, entrepreneurs are people in organizations who identify entrepreneurial opportunities and then convert those opportunities into successful innovations.

Entrepreneurs

Entrepreneurs are people who recognize entrepreneurial opportunities and then take risks to develop an innovation to pursue them. Entrepreneurs are found throughout an organization. This fact explains why some innovations are new products while other innovations are new processes or new administrative or managerial activities.

A number of characteristics describe entrepreneurs. For example, entrepreneurs are optimistic,[24] highly motivated, courageous, and willing to take greater financial responsibility for their projects and accept uncertain outcomes.[25] By responding to the issues in Table 10.1, you will have some perspective about the degree to which characteristics such as these describe you.

The characteristics of an entrepreneur certainly describe Thomas J. Watson, Jr. As the CEO of IBM, Watson was an innovator who bet his firm's future when he decided in 1964 to replace all of the firm's existing computer lines with a radically different type of machine called the System/360. Before the introduction of this innovative product line, firms required different software programs for every computer model. In contrast, the System/360 was a family of computers that allowed programs written for one computer to work on another computer in the family. Questioned at the time about his decision to push IBM in this direction, Watson is now thought of as a courageous and brilliant innovator. Entrepreneurs such as Watson make unique connections among seemingly unconnected events

Table 10.1 Characteristics of Entrepreneurs—Where Do I Stand?

Entrepreneurs are known to have certain characteristics. For each characteristic, rate yourself on a scale of 1–4 with the following scale values:

1 This characteristic does not describe me.
2 This characteristic slightly describes me.
3 This characteristic accurately describes me.
4 This characteristic strongly describes me.

Characteristic	Rating
Highly motivated	_____
Very optimistic	_____
Very willing to take responsibility for the outcomes of projects	_____
Consistently view uncertainty as an opportunity	_____
Highly tolerant of ambiguous situations	_____
Highly committed to the importance of innovation	_____
Very willing to tackle tasks, even with insufficient resources	_____

The higher your score, the greater the probability that you have many of the characteristics of entrepreneurs.

and see possibilities others haven't noticed.[26] Of course, these possibilities are actually entrepreneurial opportunities.

After identifying entrepreneurial opportunities, entrepreneurs turn their attention to developing capabilities that will be the basis of the competitive advantages required to make a profit from pursuing the opportunities.[27] Identifying entrepreneurial opportunities is necessary, but insufficient as a single action leading to innovation and subsequently to corporate success. As we learned in Chapter 4, to successfully exploit opportunities, firms must develop capabilities that are valuable, rare, difficult to imitate, and nonsubstitutable. Capabilities satisfying these four criteria are competitive advantages and are the basis on which entrepreneurial opportunities can be successfully pursued.

Therefore, to innovate and to use innovation as a path to enhancements in the firm's performance, opportunities must be identified and decisions must be made about how to take advantage of them. As you may have already concluded, identifying opportunities is primarily an entrepreneurial process while developing the capabilities needed to exploit them is primarily a strategic process. When innovations are successfully exploited, they contribute to maintaining or creating competitive advantages.

Strategic entrepreneurship is the comprehensive process of taking entrepreneurial actions using a strategic perspective by combining entrepreneurial and strategic management processes to enhance the firm's ability to innovate, enter or create new markets, and improve its performance. Strategic entrepreneurship allows the firm to first identify and then exploit entrepreneurial opportunities. Strategic entrepreneurship also helps the firm balance its need to find and exploit tomorrow's innovations (in the form of new products, new processes, and new administrative actions) while exploiting its current marketplace successes. In this respect, strategic entrepreneurship helps the firm find the "right" balance between innovation and efficiency.

strategic entrepreneurship
the comprehensive process of taking entrepreneurial actions using a strategic perspective by combining entrepreneurial and strategic management processes to enhance the firm's ability to innovate, enter or create new markets, and improve its performance

Table 10.2 Three Ways to Innovate
Internal Innovation   • Using a firm's own resources and capabilities to innovate   *Cooperating to Innovate*   • Two or more firms forming an agreement to join some of their resources and capabilities to innovate   *Acquiring Innovation*   • Buying ownership of another firm's innovations and innovation capabilities

As we said earlier, firms can use strategic entrepreneurship to innovate in three ways. Next, we examine these methods, summarized in Table 10.2.

Three Ways to Innovate

Internal Innovation

A firm uses its own resources and capabilities when engaging in *internal innovation.* Of the organizational functions around which resources and capabilities are developed, R&D is most critical for developing innovations internally. Indeed, in most industries, the battle to innovate and use innovation to enter or create new markets begins in R&D labs. Industries that are highly dependent on innovations for continuing success, such as pharmaceuticals, devote large amounts of their total sales to R&D. In 2009, for example, the pharmaceutical industry allocated nearly 19 percent of sales to R&D. In contrast, the historical percentage of sales allocated to R&D in the aerospace and auto industries averages below 5 percent and below 4 percent per year respectively in these industries. Worrisome for firms throughout the global economy though is the trend during the recent economic crisis to reduce allocations to R&D. History shows that certainly over time, fewer R&D dollars lead to reductions in firms' ability to innovate and subsequently, to declines in performance.[28]

Often firms in high-technology industries grapple with two conflicting pressures: the need to boost profit margins and the need to invest in new technologies to fuel future growth. During the recent difficult economic environment, this pressure has become even more salient. Recently, for instance, HP and IBM, two of the largest information technology firms by revenues, increased their overall research and development budget by 1 percent. At the same time, IBM placed fewer but larger bets on its research projects. Similarly, HP Labs, HP's basic research arm, decided to move from funding 150 smaller projects to focusing on 20 to 30 more significant projects in order to sharpen its research focus.[29]

The internal innovation process can also change low-tech firms such as those found in the food industry. The R&D expenditure relative to sales in the food-processing sector is estimated to be about 0.3 percent compared with a 2.1 percent average in the manufacturing sector as a whole. Although many firms such as P&G have been successful at creating new products through internal innovation, this process is accelerating through additional biotechnology discoveries in basic agricultural firms. The firms that have experimented with biotechnology have significantly increased the rate of R&D expenditure per dollar of sales, yielding significant increases in new product developments.[30] For example, the way farmers use sophisticated computer systems and global positioning satellites can help modify the amount of fertilizer, seeds, and water applied in a single field and raise efficiencies from 7 to 15 percent. Additionally, the genomic revolution is influencing the rate of scientific discovery for food producers as well. Seed producers are identifying gene traits for various crops faster and more inexpensively. As such, they can help specify certain crops, such as corn and sugar, to be raised as fuel or food and thereby improve agricultural productivity and the food supply, which is important when basic foods, such as rice, are scarcer than in the past.[31]

Some innovations are incremental, while others are radical. For the most part, incremental innovations "...sustain things that already exist—they make things better, they make business models stronger;" in contrast, radical innovations "...disrupt what is there—they create markets that didn't exist or they transform markets that do exist by doing things fundamentally differently."[32]

P&G's new toothpastes are primarily *incremental innovations*, meaning that each one builds on the firm's existing knowledge about toothpaste to extend the breadth and depth of its offerings. Product line extensions such as those we see in laundry detergents (e.g., liquid Tide as an extension of Tide powder) are another example of incremental innovations. On the other hand, the handheld cellular phone was a radical innovation relative to landline phones. Once a radical innovation is established, incremental innovations are then possible. Radical innovations usually involve technology breakthroughs and the discovery of new knowledge such as the move to integrated circuits from single transistors in the electronics industry.

Both incremental and radical innovations have the potential to create value. However, radical innovations may lead to more substantial improvements in a firm's performance. Nonetheless, it is important to understand that incremental innovations can be particularly profitable. (P&G's introduction of Crest Whitestrips is an example of a successful incremental innovation.) In general, though, the firm can use its current capabilities to successfully exploit incremental innovations and maintain its competitive advantages. In contrast, new capabilities are usually required to gain full value from radical innovations, thereby creating new competitive advantages.

Firms accept risks when innovating through internal means. The most prominent risk is that internal innovations tend to take a great deal of time to develop in order to realize commercial success. This issue can be serious when rapid innovation is important to a firm's success. In the words of the chairperson and CEO of Charles River Laboratories International: "Everything in this business is about speed to market."[33]

In the final analysis, firms learn a great deal from their efforts to innovate internally, especially when radical innovations are developed. However, firms also learn from internally created innovations that fail. Microsoft, Google, Virgin Industries, and Apple are thought to be firms that gain valuable insights from product failures. The design of Apple's Macintosh PC, for example, was influenced by the failure of Lisa, an earlier Apple PC that failed.[34] Learning from failure demands leadership from individuals with strong commitments to innovation's importance and who let it be known throughout the company that understanding the reason for a failure brings the firm one step closer to the success it seeks.[35]

Innovating by Cooperating

As we previously noted, firms pursuing internal innovations use their own resources and capabilities to innovate. When an organization partners with one or more other firms to combine two sets of resources and capabilities as the source of innovation, it is labeled *innovating by cooperating*. Strategic alliances and joint ventures are common organizational forms partner firms use to cooperatively develop innovations. One reason firms decide to cooperate on innovation is that it is becoming increasingly rare for a single company to have all the resources and capabilities needed to successfully innovate in today's dynamic marketplaces.

From a strategic entrepreneurship perspective, a partnership formed to innovate can involve one partner bringing to the cooperative relationship its capability to identify entrepreneurial opportunities while the other partner brings its capability to exploit opportunities and create competitive advantages. Strategic entrepreneurship is often practiced in relationships between large pharmaceutical companies and more entrepreneurial biotechnology companies. In these instances, the smaller biotechnology company provides its capability to identify entrepreneurial opportunities and develop innovative products in light of them. The larger organization in the partnership commonly has the skills (often called complementary assets[36]) needed to exploit those innovations (i.e., manufacturing, marketing, and distribution) and to form competitive advantages in the marketplace.

An agreement between Novartis AG and Synthetic Genomics Vaccines demonstrates this type of partnership. Small in size but rich in technological capabilities, Synthetic Genomics Vaccines has developed new technologies with the potential to speed up identifying and then producing seasonal and pandemic flu vaccines. The two firms are combining their resources and technologies with the purpose of developing "...a bank of synthetically constructed seed viruses ready to go into production as soon as the World Health Organization identifies the flu strains." If successful, the partners believe they will be able to reduce the time needed to produce flu vaccines from five to six months to three to four months. A shorter production cycle (and a shorter cycle to identify effective vaccines) might yield a competitive advantage in that through the partnership, the firms would be able to introduce new flu vaccines more rapidly to the market. Novartis' primary contribution to this partnership is its "complementary assets" in the form of its marketing and distribution size and capabilities while Synthetic Genomics Vaccines' primary contribution is its technologies and technological skills.[37]

Cooperating to innovate is not without risk, however. One firm might "steal" its partner's knowledge with the intention of improving its own competitive ability. A second risk is that before the work of a partnership actually commences, the partners may feel uncertainty about the true level of skills each possesses. Because of these types of risks, a firm needs to be careful in choosing a partner before trying to cooperate to innovate.

On a more positive note, partnering with others shares the risks, which can be substantial, so that one firm does not have to shoulder all of the risk and uncertainty associated with innovation attempts. Additionally, partners can share the cost of successfully introducing an innovative good or service to the marketplace.

Innovating Through Acquisitions

A firm that acquires a fully developed product from another entity or acquires an innovation capability by buying another company is *innovating through acquisitions*.[38] A firm may pursue innovation this way for several reasons: to add a complementary product to its existing line, to gain immediate access to different markets or market segments, to substitute an acquired firm's superior technology for its own less effective technology, to add talented scientists and innovative personnel to the firm's labor pool, and to achieve firm growth. Clearly, acquiring innovations allows much faster growth compared to internal development and cooperative arrangements.

The majority of large companies use the three types of innovation we are describing in this chapter. As discussed in the Mini-Case, this is true for Google; and, this is the case for 3M (the focus of *Understanding Strategy: Learning from Failure*) as well. In fact, 3M frequently acquires innovation. In October of 2010 alone, 3M acquired Arizant and Attenti Holdings S.A. Arizant is a leading manufacturer of patient warming solutions that are designed to prevent hypothermia in surgical settings. Patient warming capabilities are integral to 3M's infection protection product offerings.[39] By acquiring Attenti, 3M gains access to that firm's remote people monitoring technologies. These technologies are used for several monitoring purposes such as people on probation and to assist in checking the safety of patients in elder care facilities. Monitoring for these purposes is a high growth area to which 3M is committed as part of its track and trace business.[40]

As with the other two means of innovating, acquiring innovations isn't risk free. A key risk is that acquiring innovation may reduce a firm's ability to innovate internally. Indeed, a failure to support R&D as the base for internal innovations can cause bright and talented people to leave a firm. Research evidence indicates that firms acquiring innovations introduce fewer new products into the marketplace, highlighting the dangers of relying heavily on acquisitions as a means of innovating. Additional research suggests that firms pursuing innovation through acquisition need to maintain internal expenditures for R&D in order to continue to create value through such acquisitions.[41]

This evidence about the results firms achieve when acquiring innovation suggests that following certain practices may increase the probability of success when using this approach to innovation. In the *Understanding Strategy: Learning from Success* we discuss actions firms can take to increase the likelihood of being successful when acquiring innovation.

Across time and events, the most successful firms learn how to innovate internally, through cooperative relationships, and by acquiring other companies. However, as indicated in *Understanding Strategy,* the firm must balance its use of the three innovation methods in ways that create maximum additional value for customers as well as enhance the wealth of its shareholders. In the final section, we discuss how firms can create this balance by identifying and exploiting entrepreneurial opportunities.

Innovation and Strategic Entrepreneurship

As already discussed, strategic entrepreneurship involves identifying an opportunity and creating innovation to pursue that opportunity to create value for customers and wealth for shareholders. *Fast Company* writers also suggested strategic entrepreneurship's importance when presenting its list of "the world's most innovative companies" in 2010.[42] To be on this list, firms must be able to use entrepreneurial capabilities to identify entrepreneurial opportunities and to develop innovations in light of them *as well as* to use strategic capabilities to exploit the innovations and opportunities and build competitive advantages.

One of the important skills companies such as those included on *Fast Company's* "Most Innovative" list in 2010 is the ability to choose among the alternatives for pursuing an entrepreneurial opportunity: internal innovation, cooperative innovation, and innovation from acquisitions.[43] A central issue in determining whether a firm should pursue an internal venture focuses on its internal skills and abilities. If the firm has a strong set of skills and capabilities to innovate, the targeted innovation should largely remain internal. Firms that have developed strong, intangible capabilities in a specific domain are often in an

Actions Contributing to Success When Acquiring Innovation

There are many well-known products that were launched by smaller firms that were in turn acquired by larger companies to gain access to those firms' product innovation and/or technology-based skills. Here are some examples of this phenomenon: (1) PowerPoint—a product of Forethought, a company that Microsoft bought in 2007; (2) Android—Google's Android OS was established by Android, a company Google acquired in 2005; and (3) Blogger—this is Google's free tool for creating blogs. Google acquired Pyra Labs, the developer of this capability, in 2003. The success of these three acquisitions of product innovations is encouraging. But, other attempts to acquire innovation have failed. For example, News Corp. paid $580 million to acquire MySpace. To date however, the firm has not found a way for the innovative MySpace to compete effectively against the likes of Facebook and Twitter. What accounts for the difference between a successful acquisition of innovation and an unsuccessful one? We identify some of these factors next.

The firm acquiring an innovation or a set of innovation skills should have a clear understanding of how what is being acquired supports its existing innovations and innovation skills and strategy. In this respect, the proposed acquisition should be carefully studied to verify that the innovation can indeed be successfully integrated with the firm's existing innovations and innovation skills as the foundation for improving the quality of existing innovations or as a foundation for enabling the firm to use newly integrated innovation skills to develop innovations that will allow it to enter what are new markets for it or perhaps even create entirely new markets. Additionally, the acquired innovation should support the firm's strategy. The value of this perspective is emphasized at Saudi Basic Industries Corp (SABIC) where the firm's leader says, "We can look at acquisitions if they fit our overall strategy."

Recognizing that time may be required to effectively integrate acquired innovations is another important factor to

successful acquisitions of innovation. For example, acquiring a firm whose products are based on different technological platforms may pose significant integration challenges. Microsoft's acquisition of Hotmail is an example of this issue. When Hotmail was acquired, Microsoft's platform was based on Windows while Hotmail's platform was based on UNIX. Accordingly, "it took a few years to integrate those functionalities seamlessly."

It is tempting to believe that a single method should be used to integrate innovation-oriented acquisitions. However, uniformity with respect to integration is not the best approach to adopt in that different acquisitions demand different methods of integration. In some instances, blending the acquired firm's operations with those of the acquiring company immediately is best; in other instances, keeping the operations separate until the synergy that can result from integration is discovered is best.

A final condition influencing the success of acquisitions of innovation is a commitment to explicitly incorporate this approach to innovation with the other two approaches of internal innovation and innovation through cooperative relationships. In this sense, firms must recognize the tradeoffs being made as a result of how they choose to pursue innovation. Allocating resources to one innovation approach typically reduces the resources available to pursue innovation through the other approaches. Thus, the most successful firms jointly consider the three approaches to innovation and carefully integrate their choices to maximize their overall innovation-oriented success.

© PRNewsFoto/NVIDIA/AP Photo

Google's acquisition of the Android OS in 2005 has provided the company with a versatile platform which has become the foundation of its mobile computing experience, from smart phones, tablet computers, to an apps marketplace second only to Apple's.

Sources: T. Greenberg, 2010, Save the entrepreneur—big business keeps buying startups, and killing 'em, *Huffington Post*, www.huffingtonpost.com, June 3; J. Phillips, 2010, Four innovation perspectives you need to understand, *Innovate on Purpose*, http://innovateonpurpose.blogspot.com, July 7; 2010, Drug makers are seeking biotechnology acquisitions to bolster their product pipelines as biologics become a hot area of research, *ICIS*, www.icis.com, February 12; Royal Pingdom, 2010, Innovation by acquisition, http://royal.pingdom.com, March 10; P. Viswanathan, 2009, SABIC looks to acquisitions to access tech, markets, *ICIS*, www.icis.com, December 10.

© Greg Epperson, iStock

excellent position to leverage these capabilities through a new internal venture when a related opportunity is perceived.

If a firm's executives perceive a significant entrepreneurial opportunity that is also important strategically but circumstances suggest that the firm does not currently have the skills and capabilities to take advantage of the opportunity, one of the external options (cooperation or acquisition) should be considered.[44] We suggest that a cooperative venture is the appropriate choice to facilitate rapid development of the skills needed to take advantage of an opportunity, especially in the face of significant uncertainty about whether the technology is available or whether the market will accept the potential good or service. The uncertainty of success suggests that it would be wise to share this risk with partners who have complementary skills; combining those skills with other partners' provides sufficient incentive to take advantage of the opportunity. As discussed above, these conditions describe the reasons for and nature of the cooperative relationship Novartis and Synthetic Genomics Vaccines formed to quickly identify new flu vaccines and then rapidly introduce the products to the marketplace.

If, on the other hand, the opportunity is less uncertain and additional speed is required, an acquisition approach might be more successful. Acquisitions attempt to create value by uniting the complementary innovative resources or capabilities of the acquiring firm and the acquired firm in order to create whole capabilities that did not exist previously. Companies seeking to enhance their technical capabilities with speed and efficiency often target innovative firms with expertise in the area of the perceived entrepreneurial opportunity and complementary R&D capabilities necessary for the acquiring firm to succeed.

Combining entrepreneurial and strategic processes to successfully innovate is a relatively new concept. But companies that can do so outperform those that cannot. In increasingly competitive markets, the highest returns accrue to companies that can quickly identify entrepreneurial opportunities, innovate, and then use novel capabilities to exploit innovations and develop them into commercial successes.

SUMMARY

The primary purpose of this chapter is to explain how a firm's entrepreneurs use three innovation approaches to enter existing markets, better serve markets in which they currently compete, or create entirely new markets. To discuss these issues, we examined the following topics:

- **Innovation** is concerned with creating newness—that is, with bringing something new into use. New goods (e.g., a medicine that significantly improves a patient's chance of recovering from an illness) and services (e.g., the ability to purchase low-cost tickets for travel and entertainment from Internet vendors) are commonly used to satisfy consumers' needs. However, for firms, **process innovations** (wherein firms discover new means of producing, selling, and

supporting goods and services) and **administrative innovations** (which are new ways of organizing or handling the tasks firms use to complete their work) are also important. Effective innovation helps firms create value for customers and wealth for shareholders. Innovation helps firms differentiate their goods and services from competitors' offerings and facilitates organizational efforts to rapidly introduce products to the marketplace.

- As a process of creative destruction, **entrepreneurship** is an organizational process through which firms innovate. Entrepreneurial firms are willing to take risks and strive to innovate to quickly introduce goods or services to the marketplace.

- **Entrepreneurs** are people who recognize entrepreneurial opportunities and are willing to take risks to develop an innovation to pursue them. Entrepreneurs have certain characteristics, including being highly motivated, being able to tolerate uncertainty, and being willing to take greater financial responsibility for the outcomes attained through their innovation-focused efforts.

- **Entrepreneurial opportunities** are circumstances suggesting that a new good or service can be sold at a price that exceeds the cost of developing, producing, selling, and servicing it. The most effective firms rely on strategic entrepreneurship to innovate. **Strategic entrepreneurship** is the comprehensive process of taking entrepreneurial actions with a strategic perspective. Strategic entrepreneurship is becoming increasingly important for firms trying to innovate and to use innovation as a means of entering new markets, better serving existing markets, or creating new markets.

- Firms use one or more of three means to innovate (increasingly, firms use all three means). Internal innovation takes place when the firm uses its own resources and capabilities to innovate. Each firm develops an innovation process that is unique to it. Because most firms lack all resources and capabilities required for consistently effective innovation, they also form cooperative relationships such as strategic alliances and joint ventures to innovate. Finally, firms may acquire specific innovations as well as another firm's innovative capabilities. Each means of innovation has benefits and risks. The most effective firm learns how *and* when to use each means of innovation.

- If a firm finds an entrepreneurial opportunity that fits its skills and abilities, it probably should use an internal innovation process to pursue such an opportunity. Alternatively, if a firm's skills do not currently fit the opportunity, it probably should use one of the external approaches (cooperatively develop the skills or acquire the skills) to pursue the opportunity. The cooperative option is more likely to be successful in situations involving significant uncertainty about the technology or market because it allows risk sharing. The acquisition approach might be better when the opportunity is more certain because speed to market becomes more important in developing the necessary skills.

KEY TERMS

Administrative innovation, 216
Corporate entrepreneurship, 214
Entrepreneurial opportunities, 218

Entrepreneurs, 218
Entrepreneurship, 216
Innovation, 215

Process innovations, 215
Strategic entrepreneurship, 219

DISCUSSION QUESTIONS

1. What is innovation and what is entrepreneurship? Who are entrepreneurs? What is the relationship between entrepreneurship and entrepreneurs?
2. What are entrepreneurial opportunities and entrepreneurial capabilities? Why must a firm have entrepreneurial capabilities as well as entrepreneurial opportunities to use innovation as a means of entering new markets?
3. What is strategic entrepreneurship? Why do firms use strategic entrepreneurship when innovating?
4. How do firms develop innovations internally?

5. How are cooperative strategies used to develop innovations?
6. How do firms use acquisitions as a way to innovate?
7. How is strategic entrepreneurship important to firms committed to innovation and to the use of innovation as a way to enter markets that are new to them? Under what circumstances would you use each of the three approaches (internal innovation, cooperative relationships, and acquisition) to pursue an entrepreneurial opportunity?

STRATEGY TOOLBOX

Introduction

CEOs need to have some of the key skills associated with entrepreneurship, such as being willing to change and being able to articulate the long-term vision. That being said, pure entrepreneurs are somewhat of a different breed, as they often find the confines of corporate hierarchies constraining. The last tool of this book—the Entrepreneurial Mind-Set Checklist—is a way to quickly assess whether you would be better suited as a corporate CEO or an entrepreneur. Answering "yes" to questions 1, 5, 6, 8, and 10 and answering "no" to questions 2, 3, 4, 7, and 9 indicates that you would be well suited to be an entrepreneur.

The Entrepreneurial Mind-Set Checklist

1	Do I generally enjoy taking chances?	Yes/No
2	Am I more comfortable with an established infrastructure?	Yes/No
3	Do I generally accept situations rather than try to change them?	Yes/No
4	Do I think I would prefer a guaranteed base pay over commission?	Yes/No
5	Am I comfortable in situations of high ambiguity?	Yes/No
6	Am I creative?	Yes/No
7	Do I generally rely on others' opinions to guide my actions?	Yes/No
8	Have I ever brainstormed carefully about an unmet business need?	Yes/No
9	Do I generally have problems articulating my ideas to others?	Yes/No
10	Do I occasionally have difficulty fitting in when others seem comfortable?	Yes/No

MINI-CASE

Google's Capabilities and Approaches for Successful Innovation

Google's innovative search technologies connect millions of people around the world with information every day.

About Google Inc.

In this chapter, we discussed different approaches firms take to continuously develop valuable innovations. As you have seen, firms successfully innovate when they effectively integrate entrepreneurial actions and strategic actions. Google is an excellent example of a company that has strong innovative capabilities and uses all three approaches to innovation we examined in this chapter.

First, Google has an internal innovation system that can be characterized as the "Patient Strategy," or incremental gradualism. In other words, Google has developed an operating system that is scalable, meaning that when a new application is present, the flexibility built into the system allows Google to simply download the application. Once in the system, the application can address the large, varied content database. Google has also made huge investments in data movement and database management tools that accelerate the product development life cycle.

Its data versions evolve over time and can be improved and customized based on continual customer feedback.

Overall, these internal innovation capabilities allow the firm to continuously develop new products such as Google TV. Billed as an "open platform that adds the power of the Web to the television viewing experience," Google TV allows users to expand their search capabilities to access content from multiple sources including the Web, TV providers, their personal content libraries, and mobile applications. Autonomous driving technology is another recent internal innovation. Saying, "Your car should drive itself; it just makes sense," Eric Schmidt, Google's CEO, recently announced that the firm is test marketing its technology that drives cars. Initially however, there are questions about the financial viability of this internally developed innovation.

Second, Google's basic software and operating capability allow cooperative relationships with third-party creators. Such relationships created services such as Gmail, Google Maps, Google AdWords, and Outsense (an advertising placement system). For instance, *Zillo.com,* by displaying elements on Google Maps for customers, provides high-quality data on real estate properties for sale, which benefits the third-party provider as well as Google. Similar combinations are available from *housingmaps.com,* a service that combines data from Craig's List and Google Maps for those seeking apartments for rent or houses for sale plotted on a map of a local area. Comparable software applications, available for advertisers as well as content providers, allow Google's system to create working relationships with consumers, innovators, advertisers, and content providers in an "innovation ecosystem" that facilitates cooperation among all parties.

Newly developed partnerships with Dish Network and Sony Corporation also demonstrate how Google uses strategic alliances to innovate. (Recall from *Learning from Failure* in Chapter 9 that Yahoo! and Google are evaluating the possibility of forming a partnership that would find them working together in Japan. This is yet another potential relationship with which Google may become involved.) The relationship with Dish is one through which Google TV is being seamlessly integrated with Dish's content to provide users with multichannel television and rich Web media content. Through the second partnership, Sony Internet TV is becoming the world's first TV to incorporate the Google TV platform, which makes it possible for users "…to search and access content from their TVs and across the Internet."

Third, when Google executives realize they do not have critical capabilities or information management tools needed, they seek to obtain them via acquisitions such as Picasa for photo management, YouTube for online videos, DoubleClick for Web ads, Keyhole for satellite photos (now Google Earth), and Urchin for Web analytics (now Google Analytics). At the end of the first three quarters of 2010, Google had already completed 23 acquisitions, a total that exceeded the combined number of acquisitions Google made during the three previous years combined. This level of activity in 2010 suggests that Google was identifying technologies and capabilities in other firms that it believed had the potential to support its ongoing efforts to continuously innovate.

Google's culture supports its efforts to innovate. For example, the firm's engineers are allowed to focus 20 percent of their time on new ventures they would like to see developed further. Managerial personnel too are encouraged to spend some of their time on innovation. Thus at Google, innovation is literally built into job descriptions for all working in the firm. "Managers spend 70 percent of their time on core business, 20 percent on related but different projects, and 10 percent on anything else. Technical employees spend 80 percent of their time on core business and 20 percent on projects of their own choosing."

In summary, Google has built an internal culture focused on innovation and has developed the infrastructure (such as the ability for employees to devote some of their time to innovation-related activities and projects) that is necessary to support this culture. Additionally, the company has built a structure so that it can cooperate with customers and strategic partners, advertisers, and content providers to facilitate innovation. Finally, as mentioned previously, when Google does not have an application that it needs or foresees as a new development opportunity, it partners with others or acquires a firm that has the capabilities to develop a new product or service. Collectively, all of these efforts make Google a "true innovation machine."

Sources: 2010, Google acquisition activity in 2010 matches last three years combined, CB Insights, www.cbinsights.com, October 15; 2010, Google and Dish Network collaborate to develop integrated multichannel TV and Web platform, Google press center, www.google.com, May 20; 2010, Google closes On2 Technologies acquisition, Google investor relations, www.google.com, February 19; 2010, Google launches Google TV, ITVT, www.itvt.com, May 24; 2010, Sony and Google establish strategic alliance to deliver compelling new cloud-based products and services with the Android platform, Sony news, www.sony.com, May 20; C. C. Miller & B. Stelter, 2010, Google TV announces its programming partners, but the top networks are absent, *The New York Times Online,* www.nytimes.com, October 4; S. Weintraub, 2010, Would you let Google drive your car? *Fortune.com,* www.tech.fortune.cnn.com, October 9.

Questions

1. Based on the materials you read in this chapter, what is your evaluation of Google's efforts to continuously innovate? Does the firm appear to be effectively using the three types of innovation? Why or why not? Which of these approaches to innovation do you believe will be the most important to Google over the next 10 years and why?

2. Firms use strategic entrepreneurship to integrate entrepreneurial and strategic processes as a foundation for successful innovations. Find evidence in the Mini-Case that Google is in fact using strategic entrepreneurship as it uses the three approaches to innovation.

3. Use the Internet and other sources of information available to you to identify some of Google's most recent innovations. How many of these are related to search capabilities Google has made available to users? Do any of the recent innovations move Google in directions other than search capabilities and functionalities? Which of the innovations you identified have the greatest probability of leading to improvements in the firm's performance? Why?

EXPERIENTIAL EXERCISES

Exercise One: Innovating in the World's Most Innovative Companies

This chapter mentioned *Fast Company's* 2010 list of "Fast 50: The World's Most Innovative Companies." As you will see, this group includes companies of different sizes that compete in a wide range of industries and are based in different regions of the world.

Form teams of two or three people each to complete this exercise. Each team should choose one of the firms listed below and answer the following questions for it. (Use the Internet and other sources [e.g., each firm's Home page] to obtain the information and data you will need to answer these questions.)

1. What approaches were used to develop innovations in your firm (i.e., internal development, cooperative relationships, or acquisitions)? If other approaches were used to generate innovations, explain them.

2. Are the firm's innovations incremental, radical, or both?
3. What role do entrepreneurs play in the innovation process in the firm?

Top 15 of the World's 50 "Most Innovative Companies" for 2010

1. Facebook
2. Amazon
3. Apple
4. Google
5. Huawei
6. First Solar
7. PG&E
8. Novartis
9. Walmart
10. Hewlett-Packard
11. Hulu
12. Netflix
13. Nike
14. Intel
15. Spotify

Source: S. Schomer, 2010, Fast 50: The World's Most Innovative Companies, *Fast Company*, March.

Exercise Two: Characteristics of Entrepreneurs

Choose an entrepreneur from the following list or one assigned by your instructor and use the Internet or other sources to investigate her/his characteristics. Then, using Table 10.1, rate the entrepreneur according to the characteristics given in the table. Did the entrepreneur have any characteristics that you thought contributed to success that are not in the table? Explain why you think those characteristics were important to success.

1. Richard Branson — Virgin Industries
2. Michael Dell — Dell Inc.
3. Walt Disney — The Walt Disney Company
4. Debbi Fields — Mrs. Fields' Cookies
5. Bill Hewlett and David Packard — HP
6. Robert Johnson — BET
7. Ingvar Kamprad — IKEA
8. Herb Kelleher — Southwest Airlines
9. Rupert Murdock — News Corp.
10. Donald Trump — Trump Organization, Trump Entertainment Resorts

© vndrpttn, iStock

ENDNOTES

1. 2010, Reverse innovation: GE makes India a lab for global markets, *India Knowledge@Wharton*, www.knowledge.wharton.upenn.edu, May 20.

2. F. T. Rothaermel & A. M. Hess, 2010, Innovation strategies combined, *MIT Sloan Management Review*, Spring, 13–15.

3. K. E. Klein, 2010, Marketing a copycat product, *Bloomberg Businessweek Online*, www.businessweek.com, October 22.

4. D. Mattioli, 2010, Focusing inward at FreshDirect, *The Wall Street Journal Online*, www.wsj.com, October 27.

5. L. A. Bettencourt, 2010, Four innovation questions, *Bloomberg Businessweek Online*, www.businessweek.com, September 30.

6. M. Terziovski, 2010, Innovation practice and its performance implications in small and medium enterprises (SMEs) in the manufacturing sector: A resource-based view, *Strategic Management Journal*, 31: 892–902; B. A. Gilbert, P. P. McDougall, & D. B. Audretsch, 2008, Clusters, knowledge spillovers, and new venture performance: An empirical examination, *Journal of Business Venturing*, 23: 405–422; Y. Zhang, H. Li, M. A. Hitt, & G. Cui, 2007, R&D intensity and international joint venture performance in an emerging market: Moderating affects of market focus and ownership structure, *Journal of International Business Studies*, 38: 944–960.

7. R. D. Ireland, J. G. Covin, & D. F. Kuratko, 2009, Conceptualizing corporate entrepreneurship strategy, *Entrepreneurship Theory and Practice*, 33: 19–46.

8. F. H. Knight, 1921, *Risk, Uncertainty, and Profit,* Houghton Mifflin (reprint ed.). Chicago: University of Chicago Press

9. D. J. Teece, 2010, Business models, business strategy and innovation, *Long Range Planning*, 43: 172–194.

10. H. Miller, 2010, RIM's PlayBook runs onto a crowded field, *Bloomberg Businessweek*, October 4–October 10, 41.

11. E. Bryon, 2010, Razor burn: A flood of fancy shavers leaves some men feeling nicked, *The Wall Street Journal Online*, www.wsj.com, July 12.

12. 2010, Shaving, razors, & men's style, Gillette homepage, www.gillette.com, October 15.

13. C. B. Bingham, K. N. Eisenhardt, & N. R. Furr, 2007, What makes a process a capability? Heuristics, strategy, and effective capture of opportunities, *Strategic Entrepreneurship Journal*, 1: 11–32.

14. D. Welch, 2004, Reinventing the company, *Business Week,* March 22: 24.

15. L.-Y. Wu, 2010, Which companies should implement management innovation? A commentary essay, *Journal of Business Research*, 63: 321–323; A. M. Kleinbaum & M. L. Tushman, 2007, Building bridges: The social structure of interdependent innovation, *Strategic Entrepreneurship Journal*, 1: 103–122.

16. J. C. Spender & B. Strong, 2010, Who has innovative ideas? Employees, *The Wall Street Journal Online*, www.wsj.com, August 23.

17. T. H. Davenport, J. Harris, & J. Shapiro, 2010, Competing on talent analytics, *Harvard Business Review*, 88(10): 53–58.

18. 2010, LG announces third-quarter 2010 financial results, LG Electronics homepage, www.lg.com, October 28.

19. E. Wistrom, 2010, New television technology, *Bright Hub*, www.brighthub.com, October 24.

20. J. Schumpeter, 1934, *The Theory of Economic Development,* Cambridge, MA: Harvard University Press.

21. S. Gifford, 2010, Risk and uncertainty, in *Handbook of Entrepreneurship Research*, Vol. 5, No. 3, 303–318; K. D. Miller, 2007, Risk and rationality in entrepreneurial processes, *Strategic Entrepreneurship Journal*, 1: 57–74.

22. P. F. Drucker, 1998, The discipline of innovation, *Harvard Business Review*, 76(6): 149–157.

23. J. C. Short, C. L. Shook, D. J. Ketchen, Jr., & R. D. Ireland, 2010, The concept of "opportunity" in entrepreneurship research: Past accomplishments and future challenges, *Journal of Management*, 36: 40–65; D. A. Shepherd, J. S. McMullen, & P. D. Jennings, 2007, The formation of opportunity beliefs: Overcoming ignorance and reducing doubt, *Strategic Entrepreneurship Journal*, 1: 75–96.

24. G. Dushnitsky, 2010, Entrepreneurial optimism in the market for techno-logical inventions, *Organization Science*, 21: 150–167.

25. J. A. Elston & D. B. Audretsch, 2010, Risk attitudes, wealth and sources of entrepreneurial start-up capital, *Journal of Economic Behavior & Organization*, 76: 82–89; M. Minniti & M. Levesque, 2010, Entrepreneurial types and economic growth, *Journal of Business Venturing*, 25: 305–314.

26. I. P. Vaghely & P.-A. Julien, 2010, Are opportunities recognized or constructed? An information perspective on entrepreneurial opportunity identification, *Journal of Business Venturing*, 25: 73–86.

27. A. S. Habiby & D. M. Coyle, Jr., 2010, The high-intensity entrepreneur, *Harvard Business Review*, 88(9): 75–78; H. L. Sirkin, J. P. Andrew, & J. Butnam, 2007, *Payback: Reaping the Rewards of Innovation*, Cambridge, MA: Harvard Business School Press.

28. P. Coy, 2010, The other U.S. energy crisis: Lack of R&D, *Bloomberg Businessweek Online*, www.businessweek.com, June 17.

29. K. Allison & R. Waters, 2008, High-tech companies focus their R&D spending, *Financial Times*, www.ft.com, March 16.

30. J. K. Sankaran & B. S. Mouly, 2008, Managing innovation in an emerging sector: The case of marine-based nutraceuticals, *R&D Management*, 37: 329–344.

31. S. Hamm & J. Karey, 2008, Solutions from a hunger crisis; The global food shortage could lead to lower trade barriers and innovation that may raise farm productivity, *Business Week*, May 12, 26.

32. N. Clayton, 2010, Blueprint for fostering innovation, *The Wall Street Journal Online*, www.wsj.com, April 12.

33. A. Barrett, C. Palmeri, & S. A. Forest, 2004, The 100 best small companies, *Business Week,* June 7: 86–90.

34. R. Bel, 2010, Leadership and innovation: Learning from the best, *Global Business and Organizational Excellence*, 29(2): 47–60.

35. G. M. Maddock & R. L. Viton, 2010, The CEO's innovation nightmare, *Bloomberg Businessweek Online*, www.businessweek.com, September 13.

36. D. J. Teece, 1986, Profiting from technological innovation, *Research Policy*, 15: 285–305.

37. G. Mijuk, 2010, Novartis in pact to speed up vaccine production, *The Wall Street Journal Online*, www.wsj.com, October 8.

38. B. Bowonder, A. Dambal, S. Kumar, & A. Shirodkar, 2010, Innovation strategies for creating competitive advantage, *Research-Technology Management*, 53(3): 19–32; T. Laamanen & T. Keil, 2008, Performance of serial acquirers: Toward an acquisition program perspective, *Strategic Management Journal*, 29: 663–672.

39. 2010, 3M completes acquisition of Arizant, Inc., 3M Press Room, www.3m.com, October 13.

40. 2010, 3M completes acquisition of Attenti Holdings S.A., 3M Press Room, www.3m.com, October 20.

41. K.-H. Tsai & J.-C. Wang, 2008, External technology acquisition and firm performance: A longitudinal study, *Journal of Business Venturing*, 23: 91–112.

42. S. Schomer, 2010, Fast 50: The world's most innovative companies, *Fast Company*, www.fastcompany.com, March.

43. C. E. Hull & J. G. Covin, 2010, Learning capability, technological parity, and innovation mode use, *Journal of Product Innovation Management*, 27: 97–114.

44. S. A. Hill & J. Birkinshaw, 2008, Strategy-organization configurations in corporate venture units: Impact on performance and survival, *Journal of Business Venturing*, 23: 423–444.

A

acquisition a transaction in which a firm buys a controlling interest in another firm with the intention of either making it a subsidiary business or combining it with its current business or businesses

acquisition strategy an action plan that the firm develops to successfully acquire other companies

administrative innovation a new way of organizing or handling the organizational tasks firms use to complete their work

B

balanced scorecard provides a framework for evaluating the simultaneous use of financial and strategic controls

benchmarking the process of identifying the best practices of competitors and other high-performing firms, analyzing them, and comparing them with the organization's own practices

business-level strategy an action plan the firm develops to describe how it will compete in its chosen industry or market segment

C

capabilities result when the firm integrates several different resources in a way that allows it to effectively and efficiently complete a task or a series of related tasks

competitive advantage exists when the firm's core competencies or its distinctive competencies allow it to create value for customers exceeding the value competitors create for them

competitive M-form an organizational structure in which there is complete independence between the firm's divisions

competitive rivalry the set of actions and reactions between competitors as they compete for an advantageous market position

complementary resources resources that each partner brings to the partnership that, when combined, allow for new resources or capabilities that neither firm could readily create alone

complementors the network of companies that sell goods or services that are complementary to another firm's good or service

cooperative M-form an organizational structure in which horizontal integration is used so that divisions can share resources and activities

cooperative strategy an action plan a firm develops to form cooperative relationships with other firms

core competencies capabilities the firm emphasizes and performs especially well while pursuing its vision

corporate entrepreneurship an organization-wide reliance on entrepreneurship and innovation as the link to solid financial performance

corporate relatedness achieved when corporate-level core competencies are successfully transferred into some of the firm's businesses

corporate-level core competencies complex sets of resources and capabilities that link different businesses, primarily through managerial and technological knowledge, experience, and expertise

cost leadership strategy an action plan the firm develops to produce goods or services at the lowest cost

country-specific or location advantages advantages that are concerned with the desirability of producing in the home country versus locating production and distribution assets in the host country

D

demographic trends changes in population size, age structure, geographic distribution, ethnic mix, and income distribution

differentiation strategy an action plan the firm develops to produce goods or services that customers perceive as being unique in ways that are important to them

distinctive competencies core competencies that differ from those held by competitors

divestiture a transaction in which businesses are sold to other firms or spun off as independent enterprises

due diligence the rational process by which acquiring firms evaluate target firms

E

economic trends the direction of the economy in which a firm competes or may choose to compete

economies of scale the improvements in efficiency from incremental increases in the size of a firm's operations

economies of scope cost savings the firm accrues when it successfully shares some of its resources and activities between its businesses or transfers corporate-level core competencies into its businesses

entrepreneurial culture encourages employees to identify and exploit new opportunities

entrepreneurial opportunities circumstances suggesting that new goods or services can be sold at a price exceeding the costs incurred to create, make, sell, and support them

entrepreneurs people who recognize entrepreneurial opportunities and then take risks to develop an innovation to pursue them

entrepreneurship a process of "creative destruction" through which existing products, methods of production, or ways of administering or managing the firm are destroyed and replaced with new ones

equity alliance an alliance in which each partner owns a percentage of the equity in a venture that the firms have jointly formed

exporting the process of sending goods and services from one country to another for distribution, sale, and service

external environment a set of conditions outside the firm that affect the firm's performance

F

financial controls focus on shorter-term financial outcomes

financial economies cost savings or higher returns generated when the firm effectively allocates its financial resources based on investments inside or outside the firm

focus strategy an action plan the firm develops to produce goods or services to serve the needs of a specific market segment

focused cost leadership strategy an action plan the firm develops to produce goods or services for a narrow market segment at the lowest cost

focused differentiation strategy an action plan the firm develops to produce goods or services that a narrow group of customers perceive as being unique in ways that are important to them

foreign direct investment a process through which a firm directly invests (beyond exporting and licensing) in a market outside its home country

franchising the licensing of a good or service and business model to partners for specified fees (usually a signing fee and a percentage of the franchisee's revenues or profits)

functional structure an organizational structure consisting of a CEO and a small corporate staff

G

general environment the trends in the broader society that influence an industry and the firms in it

geographic-area divisional structure a decentralized organizational structure that enables each division to focus on a geographic area, region, or country

global matrix structure an organizational structure in which both functional and product expertise are integrated into teams so the teams will be able to respond quickly to requirements in the global marketplace

global mind-set a cognitive model that motivates a manager to search for opportunities in foreign markets; to develop strategies that exploit those opportunities; and to coordinate units, tasks, and people in multiple geographic locations throughout the world

global strategy an action plan that the firm develops to produce and sell standardized products in different markets

global trends changes in relevant emerging and developed country global markets, important international political events, and critical changes in cultural and institutional characteristics of global markets

greenfield venture a venture in which a firm buys or leases land, constructs a new facility and hires or transfers managers and employees, and then independently launches a new operation (commonly called a *wholly owned subsidiary*) without involvement of a partner

H

horizontal acquisition the purchase of a competitor competing in the same market or markets as the acquiring firm

horizontal strategic alliance an alliance that involves cooperative partnerships in which firms at the same stage of the value chain share resources and capabilities

human capital includes the knowledge and skills of those working for the firm

I

industry a group of firms producing similar products

innovation the development of something new—a new good, a new type of service, or a new way of presenting a good or service to a market

intangible resources assets that contribute to creating value for customers but are not physically identifiable

integrated cost leadership/differentiation strategy an action plan the firm develops to produce goods or services, with a strong emphasis on both differentiation and low cost

internal coordination or administrative advantages advantages that make it desirable for a firm to produce the good or service rather than contract with another firm to produce or distribute it

internal organization the set of conditions (such as strengths, resources, capabilities, and so forth) inside the firm that affect the choice and use of strategies

J

joint venture a separate business that is created by an equity alliance

L

leveraged buyout (LBO) a restructuring strategy in which a party buys all or part of a firm's assets in order to take the firm or a part of the firm private

liability of foreignness the costs and risks of doing business outside a firm's domestic market

licensing the process of entering an international market by leasing the right to use the firm's intellectual property—technology, work methods, patents, copyrights, brand names, or trademarks—to a firm doing business in the targeted international market

M

market power power that exists when the firm sells its products above competitive prices or when its costs are lower than those of its primary competitors

merger a transaction in which firms agree to combine their operations on a relatively equal basis

mission defines the firm's core intent and the business or businesses in which it intends to compete

multidivisional (M-form) structure an organizational structure in which the firm is organized to generate economies of scope or financial economies

multidomestic strategy an action plan that the firm develops to produce and sell unique products in different markets

multiproduct strategy an action plan the firm uses to compete in different product markets

N

nonequity alliance a contractual relationship between two or more firms in which each partner agrees to share some of its resources or capabilities

O

operational relatedness achieved when the firm's businesses successfully share resources and activities to make and sell their products

opportunities conditions in the firm's external environment that may help the firm reach its vision

organizational culture the set of values and beliefs that are shared throughout the firm

organizational structure specifies the firm's formal reporting relationships, procedures, controls, and authority and decision-making processes

outsourcing acquiring a capability from an external supplier that contributes to the focal firm's ability to create value for customers

P

physical environment trends changes in the physical environment and in the business practices that are intended to sustain it

political/legal trends the changes in organizations and interest groups that compete for a voice in developing and implementing the body of laws and regulations that guide interactions among firms and nations

premium occurs when firms pay more than the current market value to acquire another firm

primary activities inbound logistics (such as sources of parts), operations (such as manufacturing if dealing with a physical product), sales and distribution of products, and after-sales service

process innovations new means of producing, selling, and supporting goods and services

R

related-party transactions paying a person who has a relationship with the firm extra money for reasons other than his or her normal activities on the firm's behalf

resources the tangible and intangible assets held by the firm

S

simple structure an organizational structure in which the owner/manager makes all of the major decisions and oversees all of the staff's activities

social capital includes all internal and external relationships that help the firm provide value to customers and ultimately to its other stakeholders

sociocultural trends changes in a society's attitudes and cultural values

stakeholders individuals and groups who have an interest in a firm's performance and the ability to influence its actions

strategic alliance a relationship between firms in which the partners agree to cooperate in ways that provide benefits to each firm

strategic business unit (SBU) a semi-autonomous unit of a diversified firm with a collection of related businesses

strategic business unit (SBU) M-form an organizational structure in which corporate headquarters personnel try to transfer corporate-level core competencies into the firm's businesses

strategic controls focus on the content of strategic actions rather than on their outcomes

strategic entrepreneurship the comprehensive process of taking entrepreneurial actions using a strategic perspective by combining entrepreneurial and strategic management processes to enhance the firm's ability to innovate, enter or create new markets, and improve its performance

strategic intent the firm's motivation to leverage its resources and capabilities to reach its vision

strategic leaders the individuals practicing strategic leadership

strategic leadership developing a vision for the firm, designing strategic actions to achieve this vision, and empowering others to carry out those strategic actions

strategic management the ongoing process companies use to form a *vision, analyze* their external environment and their internal organization, and select one or more *strategies* to use to create value for customers and other stakeholders, especially shareholders

strategy an action plan designed to move an organization toward achievement of its vision

strategy implementation the set of actions firms take to use a strategy after it has been selected

strengths resources and capabilities that allow the firm to complete important tasks

substitute products goods or services that perform functions similar to functions of an existing product

support activities provide support to the primary activities so that they can be completed effectively

switching costs the one-time costs customers incur when they decide to buy a product from a different supplier

T

takeover a specialized type of acquisition in which the target firm does not solicit the acquiring firm's offer

tangible resources valuable assets that can be seen or quantified, such as manufacturing equipment and financial capital

technological trends changes related to creating new knowledge and translating that knowledge into new products, processes, and materials

threats conditions in the firm's external environment that may prevent the firm from reaching its vision

top management team the group of managers charged with the responsibility of developing and implementing the firm's strategies

transnational strategy an action plan that the firm develops to produce and sell somewhat unique, yet somewhat standardized, products in different markets

V

value the satisfaction a product (a good or service) creates for customers; value is measured by the price customers are willing to pay to buy a product

value chain the structure of activities the firm uses to implement its business-level strategy

vertical acquisition the purchase of a supplier or distributor of one or more of a firm's goods or services

vertical strategic alliance an alliance that involves cooperative partnerships across the value chain

vision contains at least two components—a mission that describes the firm's DNA and the "picture" of the firm as it hopes to exist in a future time period

W

weaknesses resource and capability deficiencies that make it difficult for the firm to complete important tasks

worldwide divisional structure a centralized organizational structure in which each product group is housed in a globally focused worldwide division or worldwide profit center

NAME INDEX

A

Abkowitz, A., 147
Adams, R. B., 43n34
Adner, R., 93n28
Agarwal, A., 120n9
Ahlstrom, D., 210n39
Akerson, Daniel, 204
Albalate, D., 69n9
Allison, K., 230n29
Allred, B. B., 121n37
Almond, P., 188n52
Al-Shammari, H., 26n
Ambos, B., 188n53
Amit, R., 120n11
Amst, C, 147
Anderline, J., 192
Andersen, T. J., 121n38
Anderson, C., 42n
Anderson, M. H., 69n1
Andrew, J. P., 230n27
Anthony, S., 43n31, 214
Antia, K. D., 187n1
Arikan, A. T., 93n15
Arino, A., 210n36
Arino, M. A., 23n45
Arregle, J.-L., 210n8
Ashton, J. E., 164n3
Audretsch, D. B., 230n6, 230n25
Aulakh, P. S., 70n15
Autry, C. W., 120n10
Avadikyan, A., 93n16
Avery, G. C., 23n3
Aybar, B., 164n2, 188n42

B

Baden-Fuller, C., 210n6
Baer, J., 164n4
Bagla, G., 214
Bailay, R., 210n32
Balasubramanian, S., 70n36, 70n41
Banwet, D. K., 93n34
Bararata, Larry, 3
Barbaro, M., 120n2
Barboza, D., 167
Bardolet, D., 145n24
Bardsley, D., 23n13

Barney, J., 93n25, 210n20, 210n22, 210n40
Baron, R. A., 43n30
Barr, P., 69n1
Barreto, I., 93n22
Barrett, A., 230n33
Bartz, Carol, 32
Basu, K., 23n27
Baumgartner, F. R., 69n8
Bayus, B., 70n36, 70n41
Beamish, P., 210n41
Becker, N., 35n
Beechler, S., 187n4
Beer, M., 120n3
Beisheim, O., 145n9
Bel, G., 69n9
Bel, R., 230n34
Belenzon, S., 145n9
Benavides-Velasco, C. A., 93n24
Benedetti-Valentini, F., 163
Benmosche, Robert, 157
Bennis, W., 23n40
Berchicci, L., 70n17
Bercovitz, J., 120n17
Bergen, M., 145n8
Bergh, D. D., 145n21
Bergsman, S., 52n
Berkovitz, T., 145n9
Bernard, S., 63n
Berner, R., 23n26
Berry, J. M., 69n8
Bettencourt, L. A., 230n5
Bhagwat, A., 209
Bhambri, A., 43n14
Bhanoo, S. N., 97n
Bierman, L., 164n38, 187n9
Bingham, C. B., 230n13
Birchall, J., 105n, 188n16
Birkinshaw, J., 145n7, 188n26, 230n44
Bjorkman, I., 188n44
Black, J. S., 93n29
Blitstein, R., 127
Blyler, M., 164n31
Boal, K., 188n49
Bodolica, V., 164n43
Boehner, R., 210n11

Bogjin, K., 44n39
Bontis, N., 43n19
Borza, A., 210n8
Boulding, W., 93n17
Bouquet, C., 188n39
Bowen, H. P., 145n1
Bowen, M. G., 23n41
Bower, J. L., 43n18, 145n35
Bowonder, B., 230n38
Boyacigiller, N. A., 187n4
Boyd, B., 26n
Boyd, J., 41–42, 70n35
Brady, D., 23n26
Brancatelli, J., 124
Brandenburger, A., 70n42
Brandes, P., 145n1
Brannen, M. Y., 164n30, 188n44
Brat, I., 188n17
Bratt, D., 209
Braunerhjelm, P., 188n26
Breen, B., 43n22
Breen, Ed, 33
Bresman, H., 145n7
Bresser, R., 70n35
Breton-Miller, I. L., 145n29
Bretting, S., 23n1
Brief, A. P., 70n17, 164n23
Brouthers, K. D., 164n46
Brown, D. A., 44n41
Brown, J. R., 120n9
Brown, M. E., 120n5
Brown, S., 43n23
Browning, D., 70n18
Bruehl, R., 93n20
Bryon, E., 230n11
Bucholtz, A. K., 164n37
Buckley, George W., 217
Bunkley, N., 84n
Burke, A., 23n28
Burns, M. L., 44n39
Burows, P., 68n
Burrows, P., 43n3
Busenitz, L. W., 164n52
Bustilo, M., 97n
Butler, J., 209
Butnam, J., 230n27
Byron, E., 69n7

C

Caliskan, Z., 69n3
Cameron, D., 192, 210n4
Camison, C., 188n20
Campa, J. M., 164n1
Campbell, J. L., 23n30
Camuffo, A., 70n25
Cang, A., 167
Cannella, A., 43n8, 43n13, 70n39, 120n24, 188n14
Capron, L., 70n40, 145n21, 164n24, 164n35
Cardinal, L. B., 93n7
Carey, S., 23n24, 120
Carlson, D. S., 23n46
Carpenter, M. A., 164n11
Carr, A., 105n
Casselman, B., 152
Cendrowski, S., 110n
Certo, S. T., 164n23
Cespedes, J., 145n11
Chakrabarti, R., 164n25
Challagalla, G., 120n20
Chambers, John, 26
Champ, J., 43n25
Chao, L., 210n30
Chatain, O., 70n40
Chatterjee, R., 42n
Chen, D., 192
Chen, M. J., 70n28
Chen, S.-F., 164n16
Chen, W., 120n26
Cheng, J., 11n
Cheng, R., 43n20
Cheng-Min, C., 192
Chetwynd, C., 205
Chi, T., 188n30
Chidmi, B., 210n21
Chinta, R., 145n10
Chipman, K., 127
Chittoor, R., 70n15
Choa, L., 167
Chonko, L. B., 23n46
Christensen, H. K., 93n25
Chung, C., 210n41
Chung, C.-N., 188n33
Cimilluca, D., 157
Ciravenga, L., 188n46

© Jacob Wackerhausen, iStock

I-1

Innovation. *See also* Research
and development
at 3M, 217, 218
actions contributing to
success when acquiring,
224
administrative, 215–216,
225
of competitors, 104
cooperative, 223
defined, 215, 225
exercises on, 229
at General Mills, 35, 36
at Gillette, 5, 213–214
Google's capabilities and
approaches, 227–228
in high-technology
industries, 36, 220
incremental, 221
in India, 213–214
internal, 220–221, 227–228
organic growth through, 151
in pharmaceutical industry,
147–148
in processes, 215–216, 225
in products, 73, 81, 82,
106, 110, 215
radical, 221
refocusing on at 3M, 217
strategic entrepreneurship
and, 223–225
in technology, 106, 131
through acquisitions,
222–223
Intangible resources, 5, 33–34,
75–77, 89, 92, 131
Integrated cost leadership/
differentiation strategy,
112, 114–115, 116
Integrating firms operations,
156, 161
Integrity, 36–37, 40
Intellectual property, 33, 208
Interest rates, 50
Internal analysis, conducting,
75
Internal business processes, 39
Internal capital market
allocation, 132–133
Internal coordination
or administrative
advantages, 180
Internal innovation
description of, 220–221
systems of Google, 227–228
Internal organization/
environment
defined, 5, 19
exercise on, 22
resource-based view model
analysis, using, 15
Internal social capital, 34

Internal stakeholders, 15
International acquisition, 179
International businesses,
Olympic Games as
growth opportunity,
185–186
International expansion
balances risks, 170
International market entry
modes. *See* Market entry
modes, international
International modes of entry
and decision factors, 177
International Olympic
Committee (IOC),
185–186
International outsourcing. *See*
Outsourcing
International strategic alliances,
178, 200–201, 206. *See
also* Joint ventures
International strategies.
See also Cross-
border acquisitions;
Globalization
Apple's entry into China,
168–169
emerging-market
multinationals, 187
factors affecting entry mode
selection, 179–180
at Hershey, 115
implementing, 180–183
market entry modes. *See*
Market entry modes,
international
market entry mode
selection, factors
affecting, 179–180
motives for, 169–171, 183
overview of, 168–169
at Starbucks, 8
types of, 171–173, 183
at Walmart, 97
International transactions,
168, 180
Internet-based distribution
channel, 55
Internet technology, 53,
86–87, 168
Inventory management, 9, 10
Investment bankers, 158
Investments in technology and
globalization, 168, 178,
184, 192
Investors, 86. *See also*
Shareholders
Invisible competitors, 142
Italy
banking industry, 163
historical use of social
capital, 169–170

J
Japan
alliances in, 198
automobile market in, 170
human capital shortage, 53
managerial work values
affected by national
cultures, 51
Nissan's management team,
30
outsourcing trend in, 208
sociocultural trends in, 51
Japan Fair Trade Commission,
198
John F. Welch Technology
Center (Bangalore, India),
213
Joint ventures
China's entry restrictions
and, 191–192
defined, 193
market entry modes,
international, 178, 184
market power concerns,
197
strategic alliance vs., 193,
205
Justice Department, US, 13,
51
Just-in-time production, 84

K
Knowledge
alliances gain access to
partner's, 195, 202
of customers, 85
importance of at GE, 131,
203
integrating with alliance
partners, 203
of workforce, 33, 39

L
Labor laws, 51
Language challenges in
international markets,
172–173
Latin American bank
subsidiaries in Miami,
Florida, 106
LBO (Leveraged buyout), 160,
161
Leadership. *See* Strategic
leadership
Lean manufacturing system,
84
Learning and growth
culture of, 39
opportunities in
international markets,
171
Legal trends, 50–51

Leveraged buyout (LBO), 160,
161
Liability of foreignness, 168
Licensing requirements, 57,
176–177, 184
Logistics
capabilities of General
Mills, 35
challenges, 175–176
inbound, 85
services, 126
Los Glaciares National Park,
Argentina, 129
Low-end products, 57
Low levels of diversification,
125–127

M
Management
acquisitions, overly focused
on, 158
motives to diversify in
multiproduct strategies,
134, 141, 158
strategic. *See* Strategic
management
succession plan, 30–31, 39
team, 29–30, 39
Management agreements/
contracts, 178, 184
Managerial work values,
affected by national
cultures, 51
Manufacturing
controls, 81
processes, 101
Market analysis capability, 81
Market dependence, 62, 64
Market entry modes,
international
China's restrictive
requirements, 191–192
entry modes, 175–178
greenfield ventures, 175,
178–179, 184
international acquisition,
179
international strategic
alliances, 178
joint ventures, 178, 184
selection factors affecting,
179–180
Market power, 150, 152, 197
Markets, expansion or
development of, 170
Market segments, 109
Merger repair, 160
Mergers and acquisitions
(M&As). *See also*
Acquisitions
acquisition, defined, 148,
160